The True Confessions of an
Albino Terrorist

By Breyten Breytenbach

In Africa even the flies are happy
A Season in Paradise
Mouroir: Mirrornotes of a Novel

The True Confessions
of an
Albino Terrorist

BREYTEN
BREYTENBACH

McGraw-Hill Book Company
New York St. Louis San Francisco Bogotá
Guatemala Hamburg Lisbon Madrid Mexico
Montreal Panama Paris San Juan São Paulo Tokyo

Reprinted by arrangement with Farrar, Straus & Giroux, Inc.

First McGraw-Hill Paperback edition, 1986

1 2 3 4 5 6 7 8 9 A G A G 8 7 6

ISBN 0-07-007674-X

LIBRARY OF CONGRESS CATALOGING IN PUBLICATION DATA

Breytenbach, Breyten.
   The true confessions of an albino terrorist.
   Reprint. Originally published: New York: Farrar,
Straus, Giroux, c1984.
   1. Breytenbach, Breyten—Biography—Imprisonment.
2. Authors, Afrikaans—20th century—Biography.
3. Political prisoners—South Africa—Biography.
4. South Africa—Race relations. I. Title.
[PT6592.12.R4Z475   1986]   839.3'615 [B]   85-24142
ISBN 0-07-007674-X (pbk.)

SONG OF THE ORIGIN OF THE FOUR NATURES

Others do not know my nature.
As I know not the nature of others,
The nature of things as that of men,
Just like universal nature.
This universal nature is like my partial one.
If I were to know my nature well,
I should be knowing universal nature.

Quoted in *Tai-ji Quan* by Jean Gortais

Contents

Part One

THE MOUTH OF VOICES AND OF EARTH

being the veritable account in words and in breaks of how a foolish fellow got caught in the antechamber of No Man's Land; describing the interesting events, including a first trial where various actors and clowns perform, flowing from the arrest; continuing by sketching the story which took our protagonist to the land of sadness and of spiritual mirages in the first place; in which the reader is introduced to Skapie Huntingdon and his henchmen, to a judge and lawyers and informers and heroes; containing reflections provoked by guilt; as also a flowering sunset; consisting of fourteen sections of which five are inserts:

The name you will see under this document is Breyten Breytenbach. That is my name. It's not the only one; after all, what is a name? I used to be called Dick; sometimes I was called Antoine; some knew me as Hervé; others as Jan Blom; at one point I was called Christian Jean-Marc Galaska; then I was the Professor; later I was Mr Bird: all these different names with different meanings being the labels attached to different people. Because, Mr Investigator, if there is one thing that has become amply clear to me over the years, it is exactly that there is no one person that can be named and in the process of naming be fixed for all eternity.

What did your face look like before you were born? What did *you* look like before you or your father or your mother were born? Where were you then? In fact, where do you come from? And will it be possible one day to know where you come from, and therefore where you are, and therefore where you're heading, and therefore what you are, in which case you should be able to attach a name to it? Isn't that the whole process of our being, this looking for a name?

And then, this same process is an open-ended one; I can hear the echoes. As it continues – this jumble-talk, this trial – I can go on searching, and I can hear the reverberation of my own voice. I'm sitting here – I have this little instrument in my hand; I have the earphones on my head and I speak to you and I listen to the voice coming back. And I learn from these words the reality as it is being presented at the moment of emitting the sounds. That is perhaps as close as I can come to what the identity is considered to be. That is as close as I come to the truth. Here I am. Here the truth is also.

I hope, Mr Investigator, that that is what you expect of me. Because, you know, you could force me to deny whatever I say immediately after having said it; and you could probably force me to start all over again. I can tell you in advance that if I were to do that it would come out differently; it would be different; I'd no longer be there; I'd be somebody else – as sincere, as keen to help, as obsessed by the necessity to confess.

But let us push him back into the darkness of non-existence and let us go forward with what we have in hand at the moment. May I be your humble servant, Mr Investigator? Listen to me. I shall confess.

1

Here I Was

It's dark outside. Against the slanted window set into the roof there is this very soft rustling of rain coming down. I can look at it and I can see the wet tracks on the dusty surface. Across a dark space beyond the building there are windows alight and if one looks long enough you can see people moving behind the curtains, intent upon their nightly tasks and fancies, each living in his own little cocoon of fantasy and desire and ritual and habit.

When they finally identified me that other night, more than seven years ago now, it was dark too, though it was not winter then, at least it was not winter in Europe and it's never really winter in Africa, not on the Highveld. It was in August 1975. I had arrived earlier that evening at Jan Smuts Airport on my way back to France. I had known even as I arrived that I was blown, that they knew about me and rather in the fashion of a small child closing its eyes hoping that in so doing the hideousness will go away, I'd hoped against hope that I'd be able to slip through the net which had been closing around me for some time.

As I booked in at the departure counter I noticed a man, young, rather well dressed, looking at me. He then turned around, walked to the telephone, picked it up, talked to someone. You know how it is when you get that tingling feeling down your back. In later years I'd get to recognize that sensation and respect it far more clearly, in the same way as one develops in due time a heightened sense of smell: being able to sniff out these policemen from quite a long way away.

I booked in. I reserved a seat by the window. I spoke to the counter girl in Italian, which I was rather proud of, and then I moved through customs and the customs official looked at my passport, stared at me for a few seconds, did something else with his hands below the counter where I couldn't see, flipped my passport back at me, and I continued. In the departure hall I became intensely aware of several men sitting there, moving around, watching me. One is never so obvious as when you're trying to integrate with your surroundings. In fact, I became so paranoid that I went downstairs to the gents' toilets with one of them dogging my footsteps, and there, unzipping my pants, hunching my shoulders, I managed to swallow a few lines of paper with names on it. Not everything, unfortunately, could be disposed of in that way. If only I had been more rational I might have been able to get rid of more incriminating evidence. I then went back upstairs and suddenly over the intercom system an announcement came asking for Monsieur Galaska to present himself at counter so and so. I didn't budge.

The soothing voice with the airport accent called again. I realized that there was no way out: I couldn't go back the way I'd come in – that would have meant going through customs again – and there was no other exit. I therefore went up to the counter where a girl from South African Airways was talking to various passengers and before I could even address her a gentleman at my elbow put his hand on my shoulder and said, 'Are you Mr Galaska?' I said, 'Yes.' He said, 'Would you mind following me please?' and he led me off into a little office giving on to this departure hall. He then asked me for my passport, my ticket – which I gave to him – and with these he disappeared, leaving me in the care of a young man loitering behind a big table.

Just so one is delivered into the hands of one's enemies . . . Well, it was obvious that the game was up. My plane hadn't departed yet. I enquired after the reason for my hold up and was told by the young man that he didn't know any more than I did, but surely it was just a matter of checking my identity and that everything should be all right in a few minutes when I would be allowed to proceed. In any event, he said, I needn't worry about my luggage or anything like that – they'll take care of those little mundane matters. At one stage during this interval a young Black girl came in, very distraught: she was due to have left on the same flight and she now suddenly found that she had lost her passport somewhere in the departure hall and was therefore prevented from going. A big search was started and the passport wasn't found. Time passed. The young man asked me if I'd like to smoke. I said I'd rather have one of my own cigarettes and took out a packet of Gauloises and my body was cold. The door then opened and in walked the man who had originally asked me to follow him, now accompanied by two others, one of whom was very familiar to me indeed. Colonel, I believe he had the rank of colonel, Jan Snaaks. With him a man younger than he was, medium height, very athletically built, very sharp blue eyes, the obligatory civil service moustache; and in a very friendly, even quite polite way, they started asking me questions. They meticulously searched my hand luggage which I had with me. They then asked me to strip and went through all my clothing and came up among other things with a strip of paper which I had unfortunately not destroyed, upon which was marked, 'La révolution est un art d'exécution'—which, I think, one can translate as 'Revolution is a practice.' As in a hallucination I saw on the table the small personal belongings, inconsequential as these things always are, being an element or an indication of the stranger's identity, of the foreigner, the I.

I was subsequently asked to write briefly my *curriculum vitae*. One did so. I remember that it was with a feeling somewhat akin to having a high. It came right off the top of my head. I had to invent on the spur of the moment thirty years of life, starting with where I was born, which I knew from the passport; going on to primary school, to secondary school, to my studies after school, to the work I did; including references to friends, to the area in which I lived, to the bank where I was supposed to work; and I remember that I had parading in front of my mind's eye the faces of my mates and I included them in this picture that I was asked to draw up. In fact, I borrowed heavily from what I remembered, knew or surmised

of their young years in France. One stole from life in
a derisory attempt to stave off death. I think that my
interrogator was quite impressed by my effort. Much
later he would tell me that he remained convinced
that I'd been given this cover and that I'd memorized
it carefully. He did not deem it possible to invent a
life at the drop of a hat. But you would understand
that, Mr Investigator. *You* know that we're always
inventing our lives. *You* know that what I'm confessing
now is also the instantaneous invention of what might
have happened.

   'You are a Russian agent!' Snaaks snarled, his eyes
close to his nose. He has the strawberry nose of a
toper. What could I answer? The man was so desperately and bravely living for the *big* catch.

   It became obvious that they weren't going to let
me go. I asked for permission to make contact with
my Ambassador and this was refused. Sarcastically.
As the night wore on it more and more happened that
the various officers—I cannot call them gentlemen—
spoke to one another in Afrikaans within my hearing,
watching for the reaction that it might have on me. I
remember Blue Eyes saying to Snaaks, 'Look, his knees
are trembling, he must be scared shitless'; and I tried
to control my knees. At a later stage Snaaks would
look very keenly at me several times. Again he left
this holding area. Apparently went to phone. Came
back. Asked me to take hold of the pipe which he'd
found in my luggage. And then pointed to the little
wart smack between my eyes and said in Afrikaans,
'Come on, Breyten, the game's up, we know who you
are. Do you want us to go and fetch one of your
brothers and confront you with him?' And knowing
that he could do so I said in Afrikaans too, 'No, it

won't be necessary.' I learned later that I had had rather bad luck—as I was preparing to leave from Jan Smuts Airport the plane bearing John Vorster, then Prime Minister of South Africa, and his entourage, on return from a visit to South America, landed. One of my brothers happened to be in the party accompanying Big Chief Sitting Bull and of course there was a large number of security officials both arriving with him and awaiting him at the airport, so that the place was literally crawling with lice. (And flushed with excitement they were, having just cemented ties with staunch fellow democrats like Stroessner and Pinochet.)

Snaaks and Blue Eyes were BOSS agents.* Not only did Snaaks insist, foaming at the mouth, that I'm a KGB man, but that I'm one of an ultra-secret section of killers led by a certain Colonel Unpronounceable. In the following days, as the interrogation unfolded, 'Uncle Jan' Snaaks would drop away—Blue Eyes would be BOSS's man with the Security Police proper—and I, after having been successively (unsuccessfully) a French, British and Israeli agent, would end up being accused of working for the CIA. How Blue Eyes stumbled over my glorious career in the CIA I shall describe later . . .

After this undramatic revelation of my true identity I was allowed to take hold of my hand luggage, pocket my half-empty packet of Gauloises, and told

*BOSS—the Bureau for State Security; after the so-called 'Information Scandal', the demise of General van den Berg, and the coming to national power of P. W. Botha (by means of a camouflaged *coup d'état* in fact), BOSS became the DNS—Department of National Security.

to follow a young man who had turned up in the meantime. This young man escorted me to a car, one of the very typical broad, comfortable security vehicles, parked in an underground parking lot. Another man came up out of the dark dressed incongruously in a battle jacket, and took the wheel. I was told to sit in the back next to the young man in his little navy-blue blazer. He was tough, with a modish haircut. He sat in his corner and never let me stray from his eyesight. The he-man in front drove at a comfortable pace from Johannesburg, at least from the airport, to Pretoria, all the while shooting questions at me, wanting to know why, why, why do you people *do* this? *What* is it that motivates you? He said, 'I'm not interested in the small facts, the petty crimes, the little political actions. I want to know what *causes* you to do something like this? *What* is the ideology line behind it? I want you to tell me all about socialism, I want you to tell me about Marxism, I want you to get to the gist of the matter.' He sounded very much like the university professor he probably was in real life, which he probably still is. Because, Mr Investigator, I don't know if I need tell you this; surely you must know that so many of the agents working for BOSS are very respectable, well-to-do bourgeois professionals holding down positions at university, or at law firms, or as insurance agents or whatever. Some of them are even, quite improbably, disguised as policemen. BOSS/ DNS constitute a *political* force *in* the country, both as a decision-making organ and a controlling agent. They are in fact deeply involved in internal mind-control. The demarcation of territories isn't very clear, and there's much strife and jealousy among the various intelligence groups. The SP (Security Police or Special

Branch) have their own agents abroad – witness the Williamson incident.*

Koos Bruin, smooth and rather likable BOSS operator, once told me of how he was involved, as a student representative, in organizing a staff/student protest meeting on the campus of Witwatersrand University. The lady professor chairing the meeting expressed to him, her confidant, concern because she knew for a fact that there must be three 'government spies' present. He had to laugh in his sleeve, he told me, as he was one of the *seven* undercover agents in the hall that day.

Maybe it was all a farce. Maybe the spooks and the controllers only feigned surprise at coming across a mask called Breytenbach under a mask named Galaska. Their being at the airport had nothing to do with the arrival of Sitting Bull. And they were loath to turn me over to the SP. Blue Eyes later explained to me that they would have preferred to whisk me off to 'The Farm' without anyone (ever) knowing. ('The Farm', as far as I could make out, is indeed a farm where the BOSS/DNS people prepare their 'dirty tricks' in all impunity, and where they can work over their suspects in absolute secrecy – without the intervention of the Prisons Department or the Department of Justice.) Had it not been for crossed lines and inter-

---

*Craig Williamson, an officer in the Special Branch (as opposed to BOSS) infiltrated opposition forces – starting with the National Union of South African Students when he was still a student, and eventually the International University Exchange Fund based in Geneva, from where he reported on the Liberation Movement and Anti-Apartheid groups. When finally unmasked in the late 1970s, General Johan Coetzee (his 'handler' later to be head of the SP) went to Switzerland to retrieve his agent.

agency rivalry I might never have been here to whisper to you, dear Investigator. Blue Eyes—he's still there—fancies himself as a psychologist, an experimenter, a washer of brains.

It was unreal: going for a quiet spin to Pretoria in a big limousine with a phosphorescent-green dashboard —being chauffeured by a ranting political scientist who believes himself to be in the Bush, facing clever ideologues.

We arrived in Pretoria. My two accompaniers, if that's the right word, handed me over into the care of two gentlemen from the Security Police proper. I was introduced into the masher. I was delivered at the Compol Buildings which served as the headquarters of the political police in that area. It's an old building, claimed to have been built during the time of Paul Kruger. The walls are very thick. In the daytime, because over the next month I got to know the building rather well, in daytime there will be quite a lot of people moving through the corridors, mumbling away behind doors. At the back they had a cell where I was to spend a lot of time; it had a barred window giving onto the street level outside. Upstairs they had a police museum. In due time I believe my passport, my beautifully crafted false passport, would figure there amongst the exhibits honouring the grand exploits of the South African Police, probably tucked in between a bloodied axe and a few sticks of dynamite.

But that night the place was quiet; not even the blind lift attendant whom I would get to know later on and who knew his way around the building so well—what a horrible thing it must be to spend one's blindness in a place like that—not even he was there then. As far as I could hear and see we were the only ones present in the caverns of the night. They took me into an office, cold, giving off the smell and the presence and the colour of brownness: the kind of chocolate station waiting room brownness; and stale, dusty, impersonal walls having witnessed many breakdowns. Walls which in the way of all wlls will never say anything about it. On one such wall behind one of the tables there hung a framed picture of C. R. Swarts who had been, a long time before, the Minister of Justice. I don't know whether this was out of particular loyalty to whatever he stood for or whether time hadn't moved since the period of his tenure as minister.

My hosts weren't violent in any way. Why should they be? I was dead. All they had to do was to process the dead, to pick over the bones. They weren't particularly interested. Again I had to go through the procedure of stripping and then I was counted: that is, all my possessions were itemized and these were then carefully noted in red ink on a large sheet of paper. Night was ticking away like an unsatiable beast.

Mr Investigator, as we arrive at the end of this first talk, permit me to give you a brief extract of what I consisted of as written down on this sheet of paper. I have it here in my hand. The paper's called P21: i.e., it is a lined single sheet of folio paper. I translate:

    1 bed ticket
    1 SAA ticket No. 710902 dated 6/8/75
    1 red handbag with the following items therein:
        3 ballpoint pens: 2 green, 1 silver
        3 keys
        Scissors and keyholder
        1 book *A Universal History of Infamy*

1 blue notebook
14 envelopes and Hotel Elizabeth writing
    paper
1 Hotel Elizabeth receipt No. 39110 for
    R41.25
1 500 lire note, Italian
1 silver coin, 100 lire
3 glass bangles
1 necklace of beads, yellow, black and white
1 French matchbox
1 blue toothbrush
1 tube of toothpaste
Receipt No. 3570, some sum (I can't make out
    the writing there), Berg resort
1 Banca Nazionale del Lavoro statement
1 Alitalia boarding pass
1 Alitalia passenger ticket and baggage check
1 piece of paper with '*L'art de la révolution*'
    etc. written on it
1 strip of paper with Bergville code 03647/
    1801 written on it
1 Jøhannesburg street map
1 shorthand notebook
1 piece of paper with 433236 written on it
1 bottle of brandy Oudemeester
1 paper bag with the following therein:
A packet of protea seeds
1 gramophone record
1 small clay flute
1 light brown envelope marked 'Dollars $370',
    with the following notes in it:
five $10 = $50
eleven $20 = $220
one $100 = $100

seventeen notes altogether $370

(On the back is written, according to the writing
 of the police scribe):
 'W 430730' (scratched out)
 'W 930430/km 877314'

1 tie black with blue dots

1 pair of glasses

1 glass bangle

1 match folder 'Berg Holiday Resort Bergville'
 written on it

1 box of matches, Lion matches

1 brown portfolio with the following contents:
 R15 (fifteen Rands) in notes equalling R15
 R4.70 (four Rands seventy cents in silver
  equalling R4.70)
 15½ (fifteen and a half cents copper equalling
  15½ cents) the total being R19.85½ cents
 7 silver French coins
 1 $50 note equalling $50
 4 dix francs notes equalling F10
 3 cent francs notes (F100)
  (I can't imagine how they got those totals.)
 4 Banca d'Italia Lire Mille
 1 Banca d'Italia Lire Cinque Milla
 2 Volkskas cash receipts for R69.93 (a little bit
  further on they've written $100)

1 Barclays Bank receipt for R70.14 (again it's
 written $100)*

And 6 *metro-autobus* tickets

---

*The Japanese tourist, complaining on the third day about the
jumping exchange rate, is told by the cashier it is due to 'Fluctuations'. 'Fluctuations?' the Japanese splutters. 'Well, fluck the
Eulopeans too!'

1 pipe
1 tobacco pouch
And finally one inoculation certificate in the
     name of C. Galaska, 672774.

There you see me, Mr Investigator, in all my naked glory, with all my possessions around me, as I stand that first evening. *Ecce homo*.

I was quite rich, wasn't I? There was something for them to work on, something to keep them busy. What a beautiful collection of clues! But of course, that was not what they were interested in. Maybe that's not even what would interest *you*. (Am I reading the signals correctly?) They would much rather want to know the whole history and all the schemes and all the dreams that I was carrying around with me. You see, I was a travelling salesman in dreams and illusions.

And even more than that—they must have been dying to use me to get hold of all manner of other people, to sniff out the dark secrets threatening the State, to bring to light all the evil conspiracies; particularly to prove that this was only one more manifestation of the worldwide onslaught against this small, embattled nation of pure and upright, Godfearing, chosen ones.

So, perhaps, once and for all, I should tell you about those dreams, about where I came from and where I thought I was heading.

INSERT

Where did I know Colonel Jan Snaaks from and where does the pipe and the tobacco pouch fit into the story?

You remember, Mr Investigator, I am sure, that I tried to describe how, when we visited No Man's Land in 1973 and spent one season in that paradise, I was followed all over the country by certain security agents, and how towards the end of our stay, one night in Paarl, thanks to the intervention of one of my brothers who is certainly a close friend and colleague of these people, I was confronted by two grey eminences chomping at the bit, and this was exactly then Jan Snaaks and another big, bulky fellow called 'Kleintjie' (the little one) Heiden, I believe, with the head of a dog and a long history as hunter of political dissidents. (In a totalitarian state the political police operate quite openly, *à visage découvert*, although they always have their underground activities also of course. The point is: to fulfil their function of intimidating and terrorizing the population they also have to be visible to some extent. They can be affable people to meet, real Afrikaner gentlemen, good drinking companions, opening doors for ladies. What distinguishes them will be the way they look at one, something around the eyes, and the brutal power they exude.) During the ensuing evening they tried to impress upon me the extent of their knowledge of my activities and contacts, and tried frightening me into giving them information. That was my first mask to mask confrontation with the Greyshit, the BOSS people, and as my luck would have it, it had to be the same Jan Snaaks at the airport that specific night. Was it coincidence? Wasn't he on my tracks the whole time of my passage in South Africa? Since I was known to be a pipe smoker I deliberately took no pipe or tobacco with me into the country, but started smoking cigarettes – hence the packet of Gauloises. Then, whilst passing through Cape

Town, I remember going to Greenmarket Square where, years before, many, many years ago when I lived and dreamed around the corner, in Long Street, I used to buy my supply of tobacco. One could have it mixed on the spot to one's taste and I couldn't resist the temptation of walking in there again, into old times' youth, sniffing the beautiful aroma of freshly prepared tobacco. (I was on the run then: perhaps I was looking for some form of innocence.) Having bought some tobacco I obviously also had to acquire a pipe. I thought I'd be clever, I thought I'd leave it in my suitcase to smoke it only in the secret of my hotel room. And of course they dug it up at the airport and they had me hold it and they recognized my way of fondling the pipe as someone else might have recognized my way of handling a pen or my way of stuttering into a tape recorder. These are the indelible finger prints of the fugacious identity. There is no 'I', there is no name, there is no identity. But there are unchanging manifestations, habits, a hulk, a carcass, recognizable. There is a sore thumb. The cause has disappeared, the symptoms remain.

What fastidious workers they are, how obsessed they must be! Look how they dig into one's past, how they project one's future, how they alter one's present. I have no private lives: it's all in their hands; they know the I better than I do, they are far more interested in it than I am. They have the files, they have the computer. Or they know all about my ways, my preferences, my accretions, my little secrets – my gardens – be they political or sexual. And they are fascinated by it. They smell it like freshly mixed tobacco. They knead it. They manipulate it, they slobber over it. It justifies their lives . . .

INSERT

Home. Home, James, and don't spare the horses. Screaming down the tunnels of darkness, careening down the passages, going deeper ever deeper into the labyrinth; but I'm home now, maimed, diminished, splayed, with my vision impaired, my horizon narrowed, my reference points vague, obscure; and yet there is this total clarity even if it's only at the level of language, which is the surface, which is the superficial, which, by the definition of language must disappear to be allowed to exist.

When first I came out of prison I was thrown into emptiness and I found all space around me cluttered. For so long had I been conditioned to the simplification of four walls, the square of a barred window, a double square door, a square bed, emptiness, nowhere to hide the smallest illegal object, nowhere to hide the crust of bread to which you were not entitled, nowhere to efface yourself, or tuck away the soul or to protect your three dreams from prying eyes and acquisitive fingers, nowhere to hide your anguish: all these had been erased by being made apparent. It just became language. So that when I found myself ejected into what *you* would consider to be the normal world, I found it terribly confusing. Why are there so many people moving through the theatre décor of streets? How come the air is so bloated with useless words? Why on earth do people have so many objects in their houses? Why do they have to hang things on the wall, or have to have more than one set of clothes? Why do they collect possessions? You should know by now that one can never possess anything, and when The Law strikes you will lose everything anyway. And

I remember, because now it is passing, that whenever I entered a new space I lifted my feet very high and I pulled my head down between my shoulders from fear of the unexpected step or beam.

What else must I describe? Do you really want to know what it's like to be free?

Freedom is not knowing where to stop. It is a gargantuan appetite; it is a need to burn clean, with whatever is spicy and hot, the taste of dullness which has encrusted your memory and your appetite; it is the unquenchable thirst; it's the need to absorb, to take, to grasp, to experience, to renew and to drink, because it is simultaneously the necessity to deaden the nerve ends. I have not the slightest measure of what ought and ought not to be done and when and how. I should eat whatever you put before me. I read on the wall 'Mangez-vous les uns les autres', and I discover all kinds of lusts: a yearning for seafood; I must have mustards; I must have pickles. I must exercise the regrets and the shame and the guilt.

Ah, Mr Investigator, don't you think I'm guilty? Yes, I have the guilt of the survivor. All my friends are dead because they are still alive, locked in the cleanliness of asexual and dehumanized space. And I, I'm outside alive in the deadness of my surroundings.

I'm the Lazarus. I came back from that paradoxical paradise and have no life left. I have lived it. What remains is gratuitous, free, no attachments, no importance. I have no affairs. I have no interests. These too have been scorched clean.

Now I must get rid of the unreality. I must vomit. I must eject this darkness. I must plead with you, Mr Investigator, to not stop asking me questions. Do not desist, do not turn away from me.

The people? What about the people? Yes, I know, I'm the man who went down to the corner to buy cigarettes and who came back eight years later. Of course my return was a shock to my friends. I'm the 'happening' in the slur of their daily existence which gives it a different colouring. I'm the horse in the soup. And then very quickly I'm the invisible ghost, because their lives must continue as their lives had continued for seven years and had changed and had grown finally around the absence or the arsehole which I must have been for them, the way a tree grows around a knot in its fibres.

Which is why I turn back to you, Mr Investigator, Mr I, and I talk because you must give me sounds. You must allow me to regurgitate all the words, like the arabesques of a blind mind. I am the man on the corner, with dark glasses, waiting for your coin. I am the lift attendant in Security Headquarters. Don't ask me any questions. You don't have to. You will not be able to stop the answers in any event. The black vomit must be spewed out. See here, I hold it in my hands. I have the black gloves. Feel it. Feel the gloves. Look at the glasses. I know. I know what it is like to be black in a white country.

Freedom is the minotaur outside the walls.

2

About Where I Came From

No, you won't catch me, Mr Investigator. I know how
it is done. They let you sit down, they do not ask you
any questions; they simply say, 'Write'; and I've written volumes, volumes. My life is eaten up by words.
Words have replaced my life.

It is all surface. Nothing can be hidden there. My
life has been devoured by these insidious ants. But
don't you believe those documents. Do me the honour, extend only one measure of grace to all prisoners:
you must admit that whatever the detainee does or
doesn't do whilst in prison is done under pressure.
Never forget that the purpose of detaining and grilling
and convicting and then holding people, is to dis-
orientate them, to destroy their sense of themselves
and the whole field of unquestioned awareness of the
surrounding world, the whole cloth of relationships
with other people, all the tentacles of grasping and

understanding ideas, and finally to burgle and to burn down the storehouse of dreams and fantasies and hopes.

This is what they do. This is their destiny. The prisoner must be kept in a permanent state of unbalance. And the prisoner in a game of trying to outwit the 'other', the human being in front of him, the Man, the *boer*, the Gat,* isn't he only pulling the strings tighter and tighter around himself?

'Write', they say, and you write. Two sheets. 'What must I write about, sir?' '*You* know: just write.' And they come and they read the two pages, and they smile and they tear it up. 'Write', they say, and you write. You write the same two pages. You want to please them: you don't want to annoy them. They outnumber you. And inside you have the wildness of completely irrational hope: a miracle will happen, they will find out that they'd been mistaken. Daylight come an' I wanna go home. They'll let you go. Or they'll say, 'Oh, we know it's not really all that serious, you're just a prankster; we'll let you go.' They will say, 'So we've been naughty, haven't we? What's all this romantic nonsense then? Deathwish of the ineffectual intellectual? Trying to join in the dirty game? Well, Lord Byron, we will let you go home . . . Go, and sin no more.' One will be punished lightly but finally even the punishment will be a measure of reassur-

---

*boer, pl. *boere* – meaning 'farmer' or 'peasant' originally, but when written with a capital (*Boere*) it is also the way the Afrikaners sometimes refer to themselves – has become a generic name for policemen and prison warders and, by extension, for Whites; derogatory.

    Gat, pl. *Gatte* or *Gatta*, collectively *the Gat* – meaning 'hole', 'backside'. Used in reference to policemen; derogatory.

ance, as it used to be when very small and one's father felt the need to correct one.

But this wild beast of expectation is entirely caged in. Perhaps that's why he's so agitated. They know about him: they use it, they exploit the fact of their knowing. They stroke this beast through the bars of your ego. They pretend to feed it with promises of letting it go. So why not write? And so you write, again. What's your alternative? They will only keep you until you start writing. You yourself become the master of your time; it is *you* who will decide the length of your incarceration. There's nothing, there's nobody, no power anywhere in the world that has any say over them. They can keep you for ever. They can put heavy hands on you. They can break you down. They may even go red in the face and really let rip. They may have to use 'the telephone' on you, or 'the parrot', or 'the submarine'; they may have you leave through 'the Bantu exit'.* Do you remember about that Black employee of the Christian Institute whom they picked up on the street and took to the top floor of a building and how two men in tracksuits just kept on thudding into him all the way across the room, and how they dropped him on the street again, unconscious but unmarked, still without a word of explanation? Do you remember how the *boer* called 'Red Russian' broke down Wally Serote over a period of months? Shouldn't you cooperate? Besides, if you're innocent, what do you have to hide? Don't forget that you're innocent. It is all a matter of relativity. So why not write . . . and so you scribble. This time four

---

*Reference to torture methods. See note on torture, p. 467.

pages. And they come, and they take it, and they read it, and they tear it up. And perhaps by now they stop smiling.

Or they start asking you small questions about one or two little facts you may have mentioned in passing in your first efforts at writing. (You have to show your open-heartedness and your innocence by admitting to facts you *know* they know about. But how much do they really know? How did they break into you? For how long have they had you on a line?) How about telling us a little more about that, or about him, or about her? And you write. Hoping that you are still repeating the same story which you had invented and knowing that you are now deviating from it gradually, but not knowing how much. Because time, which for you has become the heavy encroachment of total obscurity, to them has no sense: they are not in a hurry. They can wait for you to start contradicting yourself, and they can relay themselves; you, you have to stay awake because you have to write, scribbling, filling page after page, repeating, altering, having it torn up, starting anew. *They* leave, they are replaced by two fresh interrogators and you sit there. 'May I go to the toilet, sir?' They do not answer, they wait. You write. You have become desperate. 'May I go to the toilet, please?' And you're accompanied to the toilet where you are stripped of the last vestiges of privacy or the dignity you may have thought you had, because you are not allowed to close the door of the closet and you have to do whatever nature calls you to do in full view of the cynical man standing there, observing you, picking his teeth. Not even sneering at your testicles.

You go back to that brown room giving off the stale

odour of policemen and again you're given more paper and you are asked to write.

So it went on continuously for forty-eight hours – a day and a night, another day, plus the first night, always the night, more and more the night; and then when it is dark again they put you in a car and they drive you through the deserted streets up to the portals of a building. Nobody knows my name. You were supposed to be in Rome by now. Your wife would have been waiting at the place of rendezvous. August. Balmy nights on the piazzas. The oleander and the laurel in bloom.

The Transvaal winter nights are bitter. Above, the crystalline stars. Comes morning the crystals will be deposited as white rime over the veld. The crust of time. You get out with them. They knock on a very big door. A small judas-eye is opened. You hear bolts being drawn. A door is unlocked from inside and you are let in to the entrance of Maximum Security Prison.

That first night I was too tired to count the number of gates through which I was led until I finally arrived at the cell where I was due to spend the next two years. I was handed over to a young prison sergeant. Later I learned that his name is Nit Arselow. A thin fellow, bristling little moustache, sharp very pale green eyes, wild look, tight jaws, ears sticking away from his head. A complete marionette, fierce and violent. He opened my door with a brusque gesture, pointed to my bed which was a bunk built into the wall, and said, '*Ek is die baas van die plaas* (I am the master of this farm). *I* shall make you crawl here; you will still get to know me.'

Yes, I did get to know him.

They locked the door and without taking off even
a shoe I crawled onto the bunk, onto the thin mattress
there, pulled the blankets over me; and then I couldn't
sleep. Not at all. Everything came tumbling back. I
couldn't control my body. I was shivering, my legs
were shaking; I couldn't even quieten my lips. And
in the background, all around me in this weird place,
I heard male voices; it sounded like scores of voices
singing in unison very rhythmically, very strongly,
what sounded like tribal music and sometimes like
religious hymns.

'Beverly Hills' the place is called in prison parlance. It's a prison for Blacks essentially though a few
Whites are kept there too. I sensed that first night,
and it was confirmed later on, that this was the place
of death; this is the shameful place to which people
are brought to be killed legally and in cold blood by
the representatives of the State. I saw so much. With
the ears only, since the eyes are confined by bars and
walls and steel partitions never more than seven yards
away. The whole place is impregnated by this one
overriding function: this is the reality of Maximum
Security. Terminus. Death house.

I lay there in the unreal tumbling condition between sleep and wakefulness, with the broken film
slapping in my head; not even daring to think further
than what was in my head at that moment, not even
allowing myself to imagine the pain and the shock that
my arrest must have meant to my wife and to my
parents. I couldn't even know—I had no way of
knowing—whether they had been informed. For all
the world I might have been wiped from the face of
the earth; I might have died in some mysterious accident. Nobody would have been the wiser ever. And

nobody would have dared suggest that I had been done away with by the police because that would have been tantamount to admitting that I was involved in illegal or subversive political activities.

The night must have passed. The door was unlocked in the morning. Arselow, who later on I got to call 'Red Shoes' because his shoes were of a specific red shade and always shining brilliantly – he spent nearly all his hours on duty boning them – Arselow called me out of my cell, took me down a short passage to a bathroom, told me to clean up. He handed me a bar of green prison soap. I undressed and got into the bath and he never left the bathroom. I had to wash my body and my hair with the same bar of quite strong-smelling soap; dried myself; dressed; was handed a razor by Arselow, with which I was told to shave. There was no mirror; just a metal sheet screwed into the wall. In this surface one could see a vague reflection of yourself. Just enough to shave by. Like looking at a memory of yourself through an opaque sheet of glass. I dressed in the same clothes I had on the night before. Neither hand luggage nor my suitcase had been returned to me.

And then very early the police turned up. They took me back to Compol Building.

The second day I started identifying the people interrogating me. I realized that this was a team specially assembled for this inquest. In the end they became quite familiar. We can say that we'd covered a fair amount of ground together. It would seem that political police from various centres in the country had been ordered to Pretoria to work on my case. There were two from Cape Town: a certain Hakkebak, and the infamous Nails van Byleveld.

Mr Investigator, if you are really whom I think you are, Mr Eye: how you would have loved to have Nails van Byleveld before you. What novels that man must have in the coffin of his memory! What a paradox, what joy it must be to unravel the skein of the apparel within which he goes clothed. Later more about him.

There was a tall young man from Port Elizabeth, a lieutenant; there were in the beginning two people from Durban; one from Kimberley; and then of course there were the locals: Colonel Huntingdon, the chief investigator, your colleague, your example, perhaps your master; with him Hendrik Goy, Derrick Smith, Koekemoer, the one with the brown skin and the black and white shoes.

I shall tell you more about them as I go on. I think I must stop now for a little while. Because it's a new day, a new loop of time, darkness, the night, streaming down the corridors of night, falling into limitless space, dying to be reborn so as to die to be reborn. . . .

3

From Room to Room

From room to room. Dying so as to be reborn. To die. To be reborn from room to room. From womb to space. From space to room. From room to coffin. From coffin to the density of space. From space to nothingness. From nothingness to seed. From seed to womb. From womb to pain. From pain to room-womb. To wombroom. To another tomb. Other worms. To another room. Into the car. Up the street. Screaming down the corridors of darkness. Through the door. Beyond the grills. Careening down the passages. Feeling the cement. Touching the steel. Hearing the doors closing. Tasting the salt. Experiencing the shivering. Listening to the chants. Lifting the darkness. Mumbling. Writing. Writing with eyes closed. Writing with black gloves holding the black pen through which the blackness flows where there is no light. Waking not knowing whether you're awake or whether you're still a dream feeling the ache of the mind. From room to passage, to bathroom, to corridor, through the grills, through the gate, by car careening down the narrow lanes of darkness past the blind man. From room. To room. To room. To room. . . .

It was the second day or perhaps it was the third, no, it was the first day. Then it was the fourth day, I mean it was the second day, it must have been the morning of the second day. On that morning, the morning of the third day, they took me back to Compol Building and the questioning continued. Nails van Byleveld came into the room. He has very big hands, he has very big ears, he has two very small brown eyes rather like those of a hedgehog the better to pin you down with. The skin of his face is very rough and porous. His skull runs to a narrow point at the top. Perched on his head he has, parted in the middle, a small neat oily patch of hair shorn close to the scalp above the ears and behind. Under his nose he has the faintest little reference to his master, Herr Hitler. He has a very big body (what a waste of meat!) which he props up against the wall or drapes over the table, casually. He thereupon produced and read to me the Terrorism Act in terms of which I was now formally arrested. This was just a small interlude.

The questioning continued. From time to time I was taken to the toilet. I made use of these occasions to splash some water on my face. Then back to the interrogation room. Here there was only one table and a chair and a second chair in which I had to sit. There was a window in one wall just slightly below street level outside. How weird it was to see the shoes and the ankles of people passing by in front of the window—so close, my God, so close—and completely oblivious to what was happening behind this very thick wall separating us. People on their way to work or on their way to some happy rendezvous with a friend or a lover, for a quick cup of tea.

The questioning continued. At one stage—it must have been the second day—on that morning of the fourth day, no, I remember now, it was the third day, I was taken into a second room, slightly bigger. At one end of this room, behind a table, three or four officers sat rather like judges having an imaginary meal. Very involved in what they were whispering in each other's ears. Nodding sagely at the wise advice. Never looking at me. Getting up. Leaving. Coming back with urgent messages, shaking their heads, tapping the table. And while this was going on I was put in a chair and a photographer came to take the official mug shots—from the front, in profile, with glasses, without glasses. Some of these pictures later on appeared in the press. I'm sure you must have seen them, Mr Investigator, but you didn't know they were of me, did you? Well, neither did I. And then, maybe they weren't of me. Those were the pictures taken of the hulk that they were excavating at that point, or of that man who was alive in that web at that time—and he has nothing to do with me. That is another room.

On my way being accompanied into this room of the fixing of images, I saw lying folded on a chair a fresh newspaper, and in passing my eye caught a headline and the first fat introductory paragraph which announced that some people had been arrested in Cape Town, that these included a university lecturer and several student leaders, and immediately I knew that the net had closed not only around me but also around the people with whom I had been in contact in Cape Town. I couldn't tell you, were you to ask me, whether this newspaper was left there by accident or whether it was done so on purpose to fuck around with my mind, because you must understand, you, being of the *métier*, that planting the doubt in a detainee's mind makes him that much more amenable to disorientation and to pressure. If others had been arrested, weren't they also writing away, each in his own little room? And if they were writing, what was it? Were we all building our own labyrinths, our own little palaces of ice, hoping that these would dissolve with the first rays of the sun? Or were they perhaps already beyond hope, telling what they thought would be the truth? The fools – don't they know that truth is a convention? Or could it be that this bit of information was left lying there as a warning, a friendly tip-off by one of the policemen, one of the Blacks perhaps? I'd noticed on my second day, or perhaps somewhere during the dark period between the first and the second day, that there were some Black security policemen working there also.

How stupid I was, Mr Investigator! I thought these blokes at least must have some sympathy left in them somewhere. Aren't they *black* after all, members of the oppressed majority? Surely they can't be complete sell-outs. Somewhere they must have retained some link to their own people and to their aspirations and their longings. And of course then they must know that I identify myself with these ideals, and then, *for sure*, they must want to help me . . .

It was perhaps that same day, or maybe the next, that one of the people on duty, Goy or van Byleveld, called in very ostentatiously two of the Black security policemen and said, 'Come, *you* tell him. You tell him what you think of Oliver Tambo and Johnny Makathini.' First one and then the other started laughing and said, 'What a monkey, what a monkey he must be to have believed that they would support him now that he's in trouble, to ever have thought that he could collaborate with them. They were only using you, white boy, they couldn't care a damn for you. We know them, they . . . are . . . our . . . own people!'

Yes, Mr Investigator, simple tricks, tools of the trade, I know, I know; but remember—at that point you are swinging over the abyss holding on to a very slender thread of sanity. It doesn't take much to split the last fibre and to have you plunging down screaming into the opening-up of completely empty space, a space which is at the same time crowded by voices singing their death, intermingled with voices whispering, 'Write.' Because to write is to celebrate death. 'Write why, who, where, when, with what. . . . '

Many more people had been arrested. Not just those with whom I had been in contact in Cape Town, but also all those whom I might eventually have wished to contact in Johannesburg and elsewhere, and even some people whom I had no intention of meeting, whom I didn't know, whose very names were unknown to me. This I couldn't know at that time yet. But it became obvious as we went along that the political police disposed of enough information to make the necessary cross-references, to plot all the actual and the potential courses. I remember that they tried to get me to help trap Schuitema who had entered the country with me and who had slipped through their fingers. They were aware of the liaison that we used, a person living in Pretoria whom we could phone and where we could leave messages. What they didn't know, of course, was that we had also established a danger signal so that when one called and was told a certain word he would know that the game was up. Thus I had to pretend to cooperate and a meeting was fixed with Schuitema in Joubert Park in Johannesburg, but naturally the message included the detonator so that there was no chance whatsoever of Schuitema going anywhere near the appointed place.

It was interesting though to conclude from these manoeuvres that they had not yet arrested our contact in Pretoria—for obvious reasons—and, more importantly, that my own arrest had not yet been made public. But It was also stupid at the same time, since the arrest of the people whom Schuitema must have known that I would have seen or met, had been announced. Even so it would seem that news of my arrest—exactly eight days after the fact—was made public inadvertently, in a 'gaffe', by the then Minister of Justice (known for his propensity to put his foot in his mouth), probably for short-sighted political goals: the Transvaal Nationalist Party was having its annual congress.

At night, every night, I was driven back and turned over to the gentle care of Nit Arselow, and my nights were populated and punctuated by the terrible outpouring in song of the so-called 'condemns' or 'ropes'. I wrote one day a desperate plea addressed to Snaaks, going in my words down on my knees, asking to be removed elsewhere because I couldn't stand this stench of death. But it was probably of the same effect as of praying to a god.

At this stage some of the other detainees were kept in the same prison where I was. I deduced this one night from hearing Karel Tip trying to converse with Glen Moss. I don't know whether they were in adjacent cells. Evidently they didn't know that I was somewhere close by. Poor chaps—they were completely bewildered. 'What did they want to hear from you?' one was anxiously asking the other. 'Oh God,' the other answered, 'they keep on accusing me of having been recruited to go to terrorist training camps in Algeria.' 'What? You too? They're onto me for the same thing, but we don't know anything about that.' That's how it went on. Indeed, it's clear that the political police were making me out to be a terrorist in the minds of those with whom I had been in contact.

You feel like laughing, Mr Investigator? You splatter. What? Am I not a terrorist then? No, no, no, don't get me wrong, I'm not denying that. I've accepted it. *Mea culpa*. (I am guilty in any event. All that's still lacking is the crime to fit the guilt. I'm sure you can help me there, Mr Eye.) I was accused of being a terrorist, I was brought before the courts in terms of the Terrorism Act, I was convicted of being one, I was sentenced as a terrorist, on my jail ticket where it asked 'sentence or crime' it was written, carefully, 'terrorism'; therefore, because this is the way we do things in No Man's Land, therefore I am indeed a terrorist. But at the time when these interrogations were going on it was still a secret to the minds of my young friends.

I shall not bore you with all the details. It must be like trying to teach the old grandmother how to suck eggs. Let us conclude with the reality that the written pages were piling up. It was a senseless exercise really, because it was so clear after some time that these gentlemen knew far more about me and my life and my lies than I could ever hope to do. They knew exactly when I was last home (because I had in fact left home several days before departing for Rome, and thence for Johnny's), what I did the last days hour by hour, whom I was frequenting.

It is a principle in underground work never to go directly to your destination, but to rendezvous or complete the preparations in a neutral area or in a sanctuary. In my case the Greys had obviously penetrated the sanctuary. I later learned that the South African embassies abroad had been alerted, several days *before* I even applied for a visa, to facilitate 'Galaska's' request. Although this may be part of the confusing game of disinformation, of sowing confusion and suspicion. You see, my story isn't finished yet.

What it all adds up to is that, at least as far as France is concerned, the Greys were either allowed to operate quite freely on French territory,* or that they benefited from collusion with–at least–certain 'elements' in the French secret services.

They had well-thumbed manuals with photos and *curriculum vitae* of the South African 'terrorists' and 'trainee terrorists' abroad–these they prized and brought up to date the way other perverts would care for their girly magazines. And their knowledge of the 'enemy' was quite astounding. They have files on senior ANC militants going way back in history and, quite apart from the mixing of fact and interpretation and imagination, containing enough incriminating information to have these act as time bombs within the

---

*After my arrest South African agents brazenly visited, and attempted to intimidate, several of my Parisian acquaintances. The letter-box at my studio was forcibly opened. In some instances the dirty collaboration would have drastic consequences: cf., my next section.

exile movements. If I were Tambo or Makathini, I'd not sleep easily.

They also had girly magazines, of course.

They confronted me with printed documents, in English, containing a breakdown and an analysis of the various organizations with which I had been in contact, including, for instance, Solidarité, which I had been led to believe was ultrasecret and safe. They had at their disposal lists of names, the *noms de guerre* – with next to these the real names – of people I had never met, people I didn't even know the existence of. They knew all about Henri Curiel. They wanted me so badly to admit to the name of Henri Curiel and I refused right up to the end, stupidly, as if by not admitting to knowing that the mysterious 'Raymond' or 'Jacques' or whatever was in fact Curiel I could deny my links to him. Naturally they tried to make out that this Curiel was a KGB agent. In fact, the line of questioning during the first few days, it must have been on the second day or perhaps the fifth that it became very clear, was that I too am a member of a highly specialized group working within the KGB, charged with the specific and dangerous task of eliminating certain people. We were supposed to have as our commander a certain colonel. The name was mentioned. I don't remember it, Mr Investigator, no.

Ah yes, these spies – I'm talking now of the people who have questioned me – they have such wonderfully fertile thumbs. I've always felt that they read too many, far too many spy thrillers. Take Blue Eyes for instance, rolling his shoulders, narrowing his eyelids, combing his moustache, swaggering when walking, muscular: the brute. How he thought himself to be James Bond!

I called him Jiems Kont in my mind. Excuse me for taking refuge in my own language: there's always another language behind the present one; there's always another world living in the shadow of the one we share; there's for ever another room behind this one and in this other room there's another man sitting with a little tape recorder whispering in his own ears, saying, 'There is another world living parallel to this one, there is another language on the other side of the wall being spoken by another man holding a little instrument, etc., etc.'

Anyway, if you have the lack of respect or common decency of not wanting to call a Black man by his own name you call him by the generic name of Jiems, our Afrikaans version of 'James'; and 'Kont', well, it is just the untranslatable Cunt.

He was so sure that he'd brilliantly stumbled across the master spy of the century that he could hardly contain his own excitement. (He saw promotion winking on the horizon. . . . I have a suspicion that the handling of my case got Huntingdon his promotion.) And when this didn't work, because even amongst them there are some cooler heads, they changed direction diametrically.

What was interesting to notice was that parts of the volumes of evidence which were piling up were analysed supposedly in an expert fashion by specialist groups presumably either within BOSS or working on a contract basis for BOSS. One of these groups produced a working paper which showed by analysis that I'm a CIA agent. Let me quickly explain to you, Mr Investigator, how they arrived at this beautifully self-evident conclusion.

There used to be an old man, Black, from the

southern States of America, living in Paris. A painter.
Beauford Delaney was his name. I believe he is dead
now. He died sitting upright in his hospital bed, oblivious to the world. I'm told that when one went to
visit him towards the end, taking flowers, he was apt
to munch away at the bouquet. That's beside the point.
He was a beautiful artist. I was asked by a friend,
Lewis Nkosi, who worked for a publication in London
called the *New African*, to do an article for them on
an exhibition of Beauford's paintings here in Paris,
which I did, and in fact round about the same time
James Baldwin also wrote an article on Beauford—
Beauford having been a friend of Baldwin's for many
years. And this article—the one that Baldwin wrote—
was reproduced by the *Classic* in South Africa: another magazine. Don't get confused, listen carefully
to my argument. We are in the presence of superior
minds. The *New African* was partially funded by an
organization called The Congress for Cultural Freedom, with headquarters in Paris. This organization
also to some extent funded the *Classic*, being printed
and distributed in South Africa. It came to light that
The Congress for Cultural Freedom was in its turn
partially financed by the Central Intelligence Agency.
It was a slush fund for them, a cover, or at least an
organization which they could use in the way spies
use whatever organizations they can. Like lice feeding
on whatever body they can get hold of. Such is the
filth that our societies have secreted, Mr Investigator,
be they from the West or from the East. This is the
real vermin living amongst us, the secret services, the
spying brotherhoods.

As I said (or as they claimed), since the CIA was
pushing money through The Congress for Cultural

Freedom which was funnelling money to various publications with the people working for these publications quite innocently benefiting from the lolly, and since I in my ignorance had written about Beauford Delaney whom Baldwin had also written of, it was therefore evident, surely *you* must understand that, Mr Investigator, that *ipso facto* I had to be a CIA agent.

I'm sorry, excuse me for the cheek of attempting to breathe, but it's true: that is the level of their deductions and arguments. Such is the house of suspicion which they inhabit. It is in terms of this type of reasoning that a nation's policies are being fashioned. It is with this grasp of reality and with this knack for clarity that they've walled in a people doomed to destruction. In this way they can prove that the whole world is against them and that they're the only ones who are right and brave and pure. God talks to them on Sundays. God spoke to them through Calvin, who said, according to them, 'Since we have the power we are *right*!'

Not all of them were of the same brilliant calibre of Jiems Kont. The two with whom I had to spend a lot of time, it may amuse you to know, were different. Jiems Kont always pretended, enigmatically, to know far more than he actually did, hoping that he would in this way lure you into giving yourself away. Huntingdon, on the other hand, is a slyer fellow, always trying to make out that he knew far less than he really knew, playing the role of the stupid one, saying, 'I'm just a simple Boer, I don't have the facility of you chaps playing with words.' He dripped sarcasm.

Certainly he was also hiding a personal complex. He was a touchy man, given to attacks of white anger.

Vain—natty suits, dyed hair, carefully repaired teeth; and pretentious—living in a 'better' suburb, insisting that his children go to university, frequenting *hogene mense* (higher-ups) like professors of Afrikaans; and fatalistic—'I know we shall die here, but there is *no* other way, and I shall be among the last with my pistol up in the hills'; complexed about his youth as the son of a poor mineworker; sexually obsessed; sensitive enough to get a kick of pain from the exercise of breaking people down; in awe of authority in a submissive way—'The Big Man' up above was God whose ways are by definition unknowable, but 'The Big Man' was also the judge; anti-Semitic—a hundred times he bitterly told me the story of the Jew who sold eggs from door to door in their neighbourhood when he was young, and who went on to become a millionaire; realistic—scoffing at the then Minister of Justice as 'that ridiculous little man'; and above all power hungry—'Don't forget it is *I* who will decide whether your wife obtains a visa to visit you. *We* have the real power.' Crawling when in the presence of superiors, tight-throated when talking to journalists, cold to his subordinates. A man of the church. Pious. Jiems Kont went down on his knees to him. Nails van Byleveld hated his guts.

Derrick Smith—ah, what a dilemma he must be in! English-speaking, not entirely rotten, working with this crew, having to listen—in my presence—to remarks made about the bloody 'Red Necks', meaning The English-speaking White South Africans. It was a measure of the insensitivity of his own colleagues. I can still see him blushing, and yet he continued the filthy work. I wonder why? In his way he tried to be nice to me. Maybe also trying to impress me—telling me about his youth among the Pondos,* showing off his knowledge of Pondo. Apparently he specialized in 'treating the ladies'. He became quite a friend of one of my co-detainees, the lady telephonist from Pretoria; even after the trial, during which she testified so abjectly, coached by him, he used to go and help her with her gardening problems. He was also the one who had to handle Moumbaris's wife when, very pregnant, she was arrested with him. (Alexander Moumbaris, a French national, was accused of smuggling ANC fighters from Swaziland into South Africa; he was sentenced to twelve years' imprisonment.) He claims to have become quite fond of her–and once showed me a rather brave statement made by her. Yet, I have respect for Derrick Smith, trying so hard to be 'one of the boys', a *real* South African.

There was Willem Koekemoer whom I think was truly lost; not a man of violence at all, a religious man, and I do not think he liked the work that he was doing. You must remember that some people become policemen, perhaps originally for fairly honourable reasons (really wanting to help society, and pushed into it also for economic considerations), however hard it is to understand, and it can happen that someone like Koekemoer gets posted to the Security Police without his asking for it. He was a sensitive, intelligent man. I remember the scorn with which he referred to Jiems Kont as a 'Christmas detective', seeing a communist behind every bush.

There was Hendrik Goy, tortured, chain-smoking, again ambivalent; capable of fierce hatred, a chip on

---

*A South African tribe, related to the Xhosas, many of whom live in the Transkei.

his shoulder, aware somehow of being a pariah in society, but being allowed to cover this knowledge with the veneer of the power of being able to terrorize others. I still hear him in his crude way trying to bring me to other insights, trying to argue into the silence that what they're doing is right. 'I don't mind them (meaning Blacks),' he said, 'I grant them the same privileges as I have; but how would you like to sit next to them in a bus, with their stinking bodies? Could you allow your wife having to live next to one of them seeing him standing on his lawn taking out his fat blue prick and pissing?' His favourite aphorism was that one of taking the *kaffir* out of the bush but never being able to take the bush out of the *kaffir*. The poor man.

There were the others, the more mysterious ones pulling the strings, the higher-ups whom I saw or rather who came to gawk at me the way one would look at a rare capture. Brummel, he of the one brown eye and the other green one, Mr Vanity himself with his three-piece suit and his moustache and his treatise on Trotskyism. Pulled himself up by his own boot-straps, he did, to the position of probably the third most powerful man in No Man's Land. Amoral. Living on cold hatred. Perfectly dishonest. A kingmaker. Embodying the Afrikaner suicide urge.

And Withart, the Commissioner, with his ticks, pulling up his trousers which he tried to secure with a very broad belt, his facial muscles stretching, his thin moustache twitching; a man who sleeps badly.

Others. Always others. A political detainee is in a private zoo for the *boere* to come and tease or touch. As during the trials, when there are trainee *boere* present, they come to get the 'feel' of a political. Also

to recognize him later? People come to talk shit to
me. To talk to me about trade unions or labour relations. Even (once, a rumpled, thick-glassed, 'intellectual' Grey) to ask if I would do a confession on 'the
role played by English-speaking South African writers'!

Then, the Blacks. The sad traitors having to live
in armed compounds among their own, trotted out
for the dirty work, being humiliated by the White
baas – perhaps in the way a necrophile is made to
fornicate with corpses in public – and, as I saw in the
offices, serving as tea-boys! Such a one was 'Snow
White' who had to uncover himself during the Moumbaris affair. Gladstone his real name is – truculent, living in fear from his own people.

But what does it matter, Mr Investigator, what
does it matter? I can go on forever evoking these
caricatures of mankind.

But, listen: they are *killers* down to the last man!
They torture and they kill, again and again. Sometimes you see them in daylight, caught in the glare
of another inquest after a 'death in detention'. See
their dark glasses, their ill-fitting suits, the faintly
laughable haircuts. Do you feel the menace? Do you
get the message? Watch it – they kill!

Let's get beyond that, let's move, let's get it over
and done with, let's get to the point. What about the
case, let's make the case, come now, give me the
charge sheet! Because once I'm given the charge sheet
I am supposed to be allowed to contact lawyers, I'm
supposed to be admitted to be alive to the outside
world again.

We shall come to the charge sheet. Two short little
things before the end of this tape. Today, it must have

been the first day, maybe it was the sixth, no, no, no, it was the fourth one after I was arrested, Huntingdon comes in with a little paper bag containing chocolates and a few packets of Gauloises. Somebody had sent in a parcel, knowing who I was—why else would it be Gauloises? I never found out who this mysterious donor was. Secondly, my one brother is allowed in to come and see me briefly and in so doing there's this terrible destruction of the love that I had for him as a brother, him, on such close terms with them, him taking exactly the same line they did, doing their talking for them.

Who is my real brother then? In what room sitting with what machine listening to what conversation? Ha, Mr Investigator, come closer now—don't make me laugh.

4

I Found Myself Confronted by

I think one of my most pervasive and naïve drawbacks must be that I always assume people to be reasonable. Maybe this is an elitist approach, or perhaps it is conditioned by the need to be accepted by others. Somehow I seem to think that if only people could sit down and give themselves the time to really think, or to see the situation objectively for what it is, they will come to reason. The implication is that seeing reason would be seeing it my way, and that would bring about ultimately that people would understand I do not really intend them any harm. This is a dangerous delusion on my part.

In Pretoria, what was perhaps the most disconcerting experience was that I now found myself confronted by, to my mind, entirely unreasonable people. They were and they are fanatically committed to their view of reality, to the justness of their analysis of the situation, and finally to their way of life. So, although we could smile at one another and joke, and although, after an interrogation session, I would be offered a cup of tea brought in by one of the Black Greyshits, deep down underneath there was the rock-bottom realization that we are irreconcilable enemies.

At times the atmosphere was quite relaxed, but at best it was the kind of relaxation of a cat playing with a mouse which is entirely in its power. Not for a single moment was I ever left alone; never was there a crack in their vigilance. And if by chance I had the impression of momentarily having established a privileged relationship with one of them, never could I be sure that this too wasn't just part of their intricate game of manipulation and disorientation. If for some reason the officer interrogating me had to leave the room, he would call one of his colleagues and ask him in an off-hand, affable way to *hou vas* for a moment, meaning to hold on to me until such time as he could return.

They are fanatic in the same way that the Israeli security agencies are, or so they claim; that is, not only do they believe their cause to be just, but so convinced are they that the whole world is ranged against them, that any and all methods used in breaking and destroying those they finger as the enemy are justified. But the Israeli society is not monolithic—looked at from the outside it would seem that it benefits from a vigorous democratic life, with at least 50 per cent of the people clearly anti-expansionist and probably also against some of the 'values' embodied or promulgated by their security experts and their militarists. (What a strange identification the Afrikaners have with Israel. There has always been a strong current of anti-Semitism in the land, after all—the present rulers are the result and the direct descendants of pro-Nazi ideologues. And yet they have the greatest admiration for Israel, which has become—let it be said to the eternal shame of some Israel politicians—White South Africa's political and military partner in 'the alliance of pariah states.' They identify themselves with Israel—as the Biblical chosen people of God, and as a modern embattled state surrounded by a sea of enemies. Which, they believe, justify aggressive foreign military adventures . . . Jiems Kont, alias Blue Eyes, proudly displayed a star of David ring on his finger, given to him—he insisted—by David Ben-Gurion himself, after a South African Israeli 'dirty tricks' operation presumably somewhere in Africa.)

The interrogating officers are also very conscious of their own image. Some of the worst moments were when they regurgitated phrases that I had used describing them in a poem or in a work of prose. For instance: they never forgave me for having referred to them as people with chewing-gum minds. And where in *A Season in Paradise* I described one of them as a lap dog—and in fact I was not even referring to a security policeman, but to a hanger-on accompanying them to the airport that night in 1973 when we left— that adjective or description kept on surfacing and being thrown back at me. Heine once advised that when you refer to an easel you'd better identify him by name—else too many people will recognize themselves in the allusion. In the same way Snaaks, with his tight little purse of a mouth, wanted to know from me how I dared call him a lap dog.

They were keen to know what the outside world thinks of them. 'We are the best, aren't we!' Huntingdon used to say. Perhaps the general disgust with which the people of South Africa regard them does get through to them. Even though they move around quite openly on their missions of terror, they still seem to feel that they live in the shadows, even that they are not appreciated as they ought to be. Therefore, when they get their hands on the sworn enemy, they tend to really let go to make up for all the pent-up recriminations.

They're dangerous. One always had the feeling that one had to placate them. Later on, with prison warders, I had similar experiences. One was not so much afraid of the harm they might do you on purpose, but that they may lose control of themselves and maim or exterminate you, as it were, by accident. (This risk was compounded with prison warders since they were also nervous from a lack of experience or training.) One was always trying to calm them down, not making any untoward gestures, not saying anything that would infuriate them. I'm often reminded of the story of the *tokolosh*, one of the enduring myths of our country. The *tokolosh* is said to be very small and very puckered and very unattractive, but also to be extremely sensitive about his appearance. He it is who will break and enter the house of a political prisoner to rape the wife. It is claimed that he sneaks up on one; but be careful if you are suddenly confronted by him—do not show any surprise, and if he asks you whether you were expecting him, be sure to answer in the affirmative and to make him believe that you had really seen him coming from a long, long way off.

They are dangerous furthermore because they live in a world of make-believe where fact and fancy mix, and their reactions to any stimulation become unforeseeable. For example, they are completely convinced of the conspiracy of the whole world led by the communists or orchestrated by them, to attack and destroy the citadel which they defend. They seem to think that the subversion of their republic is a number one priority of the masters of the Kremlin. They are sure also that what the communists really are after are the gold and the diamonds and the strategic materials in the subsoil of the country. They are not open to the simple, and one would have thought natural, process of altering their views according to their experience of reality.

This, of course, makes them ultimately dangerous to those who created them. I cannot see how the security of the country could ever be built on the analyses of professional security experts who have no means of separating simple facts from emotionalism and conditioning. They are certainly also a mortal threat to the politicians who suppose themselves to be their masters (this is a feature common to totalitarian states)—as their power is unchecked. They create the enemy and in the name of combating him they have usurped the powers of judge and executioner. They have learned to fabricate and manipulate information. They have learned the value of spying and collecting information on everybody, their puppet masters included. After all, in the State of Abject Fear and Taboos we are all guilty—we are just, sometimes, clever or lucky enough not to be caught.

They do not even seem to be able to recognize fiction when they come across it. Many years ago I had written a short prose work called *Om Te Vlieg* (In Order to Fly). It was basically the sad story of a perfectly absurd character called Panus who tried by any means, fair or foul, to acquire the art of flying. This meant sleeping in trees, dissecting locusts. Towards the end of that story he died in three or four different ways. But, when writing *A Season in Paradise*, I decided to resuscitate him and I imagined a meeting between Panus and myself in Cape Town. I then described how this man (more properly – this fictitious character) turned up at the place where I was staying; how old he'd become; how pathetic and bare his wings were. In this weird world of ours many things are possible, Mr Investigator, but it still came as a surprise to me to be interrogated by Jiems Kont about Panus. 'Who is he really?' he wanted to know. And especially, 'What is his political orientation?' No way could I convince him that this personage 'twixt prick and bunghole was simply an outgrowth of my imagination.

You'll understand why, under such conditions, the line between reality and illusion is effaced. For, to the extent that they believe something to be real and act accordingly, that thing does become real.

They are dangerous also because, despite the fact that they are conditioned to their work and believe blindly that they are justified in doing their thing, and questioning authority or the validity of an order has never been part of the Calvinist tradition, they are nevertheless very human with the same brittleness and the same doubts that you or I may have. The danger then comes from the internal conflicts they have to struggle with. The dichotomy is between doing what they have been conditioned to do unquestioningly and the leftover feelings of humane compassion, and – as they are not mentally or culturally equipped to resolve these contradictions or even to recognize them – they tend to become very violent in an unconscious effort to blot out and perhaps to surpass the uneasiness. However strange it may sound, Mr Eye,

I am convinced that some of the people they have killed in detention probably died when the interrogator was in a paroxysm of unresolved frustrations, even that the interrogator killed in an awkward expression of love and sympathy for a fellow human being.

They may be experts in riot control; when in their hands one must learn to become an expert in killer control. Don't upset them, don't talk down to them, don't play with them, try to foresee what they may want, try to forestall the anger they would experience when they make fools of themselves or are led up a cul-de-sac. Talk to them about the weather, get them talking about rugby, or motorcars, or *braaivleis* (barbecue), or sex.

But they can be much more dangerous than that. I learned, a few years after this, that Curiel had been assassinated brutally on his own doorstep in Paris. At that time I was already in Cape Town and a senior prison official on visit from Pretoria brought me a laconic message from Huntingdon to the effect that 'We got Curiel, you're the next'; intending it perhaps as a joke. But I remembered then, and still do now, their all-obliterating fascination with, and the hatred they had for, Curiel. As if by eliminating one man they could destroy what they considered to be a menacing network of conspiracy against them.

Much later, about two years before my release, I asked my lawyers to start proceedings against a Johannesburg Afrikaans daily that had abusively headlined my name in a transparent attempt to link it to that of Curiel and his supposed terrorist organization.*

*The matter was settled out of court to our satisfaction.

The tone of the article sounded very familiar indeed. Let us say it was an 'inspired' piece of writing. It was exactly the line of argument that I'd heard the political police use whilst interrogating me. In the course of our preparation for the legal proceedings I finally learned the essential elements of the killing of Curiel, or rather of the plot preparing the event. Some time after my arrest an anonymous article appeared in a French magazine which had connections with a South African publication of the same title – and I know that the South African magazine is used by the South African spying services. Not long afterwards, then, a cowardly French journalist became the mouthpiece of the South African masters and smeared Curiel. During the resulting polemics Curiel was isolated, consigned to house arrest by the French authorities, only to be released when the accusations were found to be groundless. But this was only part of the diabolical plan to put him up for marksmen. It was never their intention to have the French immobilize Curiel, but only to create a climate which would permit his extermination. Which it did.

There again one day the truth will have to become known. As for now, it would seem that the actual killing could have been carried out by elements within the French intelligence establishment, rightist groupings which are still there and which, naturally, collaborate with the South African fascists.

Mr Investigator, there are a few last little incidents and impressions that I wish to describe and which may help you to understand how it becomes possible for one ultimately to be like the rabbit assisting open-eyed and without kicking at one's own eating. (It is against the law to struggle when you are throttled.)

I've mentioned how these persons move in a make believe and a twilight world. An illustration of this would be the photos with which they decorate their offices. These are functional places with working tables, safes, filing cabinets, many filing cabinets, telephones—one assumes everything wired for sound, because they certainly don't trust one another. But I recollect being struck by the photos of themselves taken somewhere on the border. Like parties of big-game hunters. Yes, in their capacity as security policemen they also spend periods of service at the border. One wonders how their particular talents are employed.

The border, this mythical concept in modern-day White South African awareness . . . Not so modern after all. The history of the Afrikaner has been one of borders, of the enemy lurking just over the horizon, of buffer states used against the world wanting to take over the lands their ancestors conquered. They were proud of their periods on the border, of the hunts they participated in. But I think they conceive of their activities inside the country as just an extension of the same hunt and patrolling the same border.

Later, when in Cape Town, I often had a likewise impression from the prison warders: that looking after me was their way of combating and fighting communism on the frontier.

A similar myth, even more pervasive, more sick, is their obsession with sex; the sex lives of their victims, maybe even those of their colleagues and superiors. Like repressed puritans all over the world, the sexual dimension becomes a primary source of wonder and titillation and envy. So many of their questions turned around that aspect. When they talked to me about previous victims like Bram Fischer, or about fellow detainees such as Jim Polley, it was always the sex lives that fascinated them. Huntingdon described to me how he'd spent time hidden in a flat opposite that frequented by Fischer at the time when he was under surveillance, and what stuck (and festered) in his mind were the couplings, the love affairs, what he called 'the orgies'. I think, given his attitude of a voyeur, he probably would have spent even his off-duty hours behind his peep-hole.

Similarly they thought it very funny to have lured Polley into the situation where he believed that they would carry love letters to his girlfriend, Meagan, who had been arrested and was kept in a female prison. These letters were ˜f course the source of endless amusement to them. Meagan, though, was released not long afterwards. It must have been impossible even for them to make out a case against someone who so obviously had had nothing to do at all with Okhela. But they made sure that her telephone was tapped, and Huntingdon was furious, livid, had to be restrained from using his formidable powers for the sake of immediate revenge, when in one of the first intercepted calls Meagan was overheard to give her frank opinion of Huntingdon to a friend, explaining how he, Huntingdon, had made sexual propositions to her, which she rejected, not because he was a pig, to call the police by their American name, but because he was to her such a detestable and ludicrous male.

At one point during this period, I was taken to Compol as usual one day, and inadvertently shown into Huntingdon's office while he was still busy with Garfield Thurston, another of the arrested ones. Garfield turned round, had his back to Huntingdon, saw me at the door, winked broadly, and was quickly shunted off. And for the rest of the afternoon Huntingdon tried to regale me with tales of young Thurston's illicit homosexual love affairs. Again by quoting in length from intercepted letters.

Repression, power madness—two faces of the same coin. You cannot imagine how strange it is to live in that perverse world, superimposed upon the normal one but worlds away from it. And yet, how they love to flaunt their power to underline the inaccessibility of their charges, to brazenly parade them practically in public—knowing that they have the power of death and life over them. More, that they have managed not only to make lepers out of their victims, but to render them invisible. What greater kick can there be than to decide for the world, the people in the street, what they see and what they don't see?

I was summoned once from my cell and taken out of the front door of Beverly Hills. Huntingdon particularly was proud of the facility with which he could come and go in the prison, and he had nothing but disdain for the prison staff. Outside the front door, still within the enclosure of the wall with the electronically controlled gates, his car was parked, and in this car there was a young girl, perhaps seventeen years old. He introduced her to me as his niece, studying to be a teacher in Johannesburg. He then left her alone with me. She claimed to be a fan of my poetry and so emotional did she become at the thought of my plight that she ended up weeping. He was standing a little way off, hands in his pockets. When he'd enjoyed himself enough he came and had me escorted back to my cell.

On another occasion, one morning, having perhaps other fish to fry, he instructed van Byleveld and Hakkebak to put me in their car and to go show me the Voortrekker Monument. Imagine, Mr Investigator: here you have the terrorist held incommunicado, this danger to South Africa, and the newspapers were full of it – in fact the detention and the trials were run also as exercises in media communication by the security police, even to the extent of them inviting readers to try and crack the so-called Cuban code which Okhela had made use of in their correspondence. In any event, here, on a beautiful spring morning, I was driven to the holy place of Afrikaner nationalism just outside the capital. It was a normal visiting day; there were other people moving around. Van Byleveld and Hakkebak allowed me to stroll through this horribly depressing edifice to the warped history of the Afrikaner. Of course I was never out of their sight, but they weren't next to me either. Imagine passing by normal human beings in the marble hall, or as normal as anybody who visits the Voortrekker Monument could be. Truly, one was hiding in the light.

I had to lift my hat to them. It was perhaps the same principle that I was working on when I entered the country clandestinely: that it was so unexpected, so far-fetched for one to be there that one could walk by one's mother in the street without her recognizing one.

They were inevitably and duly moved. Their souls were touched by the barbaric altar in the crypt upon which it is said a single shaft of light is calculated to fall on a certain day of the year to light up the chiselled words: *Ons vir jou, Suid-Afrika* (We for you, South Africa). After that we went next door to the little museum and looked at a replica of an ox wagon, the dresses and utensils and firearms they used at the time.*

Van Byleveld had unexpected sides to him. He proudly showed me a photo of his little daughter in her ballet tutu standing on the kitchen table of their suburban house in Parow, and he told me of his great joy in driving back to the Cape from Pretoria, picnicking by the side of the road even when transporting a political prisoner, and going for a stroll — because his passion was to collect rare indigenous bulbs and plants in the Karoo. Recounting this, talking of the beauty of the sunset over the bare hills, would bring tears to his eyes. Killing a political suspect with his bare hands obviously did not.

But perhaps the most telling example of this cynical display of power must be the one Saturday morning when Huntingdon, accompanied only by his son, came to fetch me from prison and took me to his house. On the way there we stopped at the rugby stadium, Loftus Versveld, which was then being enlarged, and he showed it to me with great provincialist pride. I could see no other escort, but perhaps

---

*The first and only other time I'd seen the Voortrekker Monument was at the age of eighteen when, on my first visit to the Transvaal, I hitched a lift from Johannesburg to Pretoria from two Blacks in a little Ford Prefect. As we passed by the sandcastle the chauffeur asked, 'Have you ever visited *that*? No? Well, I've seen it. I used to be in a prison span [team] taken there to clean up the pigeon shit.'

they were there—invisible to me. When we arrived at his house, he introduced me to his wife, his two daughters, and in a very relaxed fashion conducted me around his garden, talking about the difficulty of establishing his proteas, the way any normal gardener would.

And my mind, Mr Investigator, my mind was in turmoil. . . . Their house is on the edge of town from where you can see the first hills and the empty space, and apparently there was nothing preventing me from running. What was this? Trap? Was that what he wanted me to do? To shoot me while I was trying to escape? Or, in his convoluted way, offering me the possibility?

We went indoors. He showed me his study with his hunting trophies on the walls: pictures of him and Ludi on either side of Bram Fischer going to court. In due time my picture would be there too. It is probably there now. . . . His two daughters came and asked me to write something in their little visitors' book; you know, the way kids, girls particularly, up to a certain age, have these books of mementoes. And I did. For the little one I even wrote something in French. Then his wife called us to table and I sat down, completely bewildered after these several months of not having used a knife and fork or even eating from a plate—since one got one's food in a plastic dog bowl in Maximum, scooping it up with a spoon.

I don't remember what we had for lunch—salads most likely. Weird, schizophrenic to carry on conversation with people, everybody pretending to be normal. And then, before the end of the meal, there was a phone call for him which I couldn't overhear, but he came back to the table smugly, told me that I could make use of the bathroom facilities, even use his toothbrush if I wanted to, clean myself up a little bit, excused himself that they now had to take me back. So we returned still with only his son riding shotgun.

And when we arrived at Maximum, instead of being taken through the clanging steel doors and grills, he took me to the left, down the wing where the officers were. And, without saying anything, ushered me into an office where Yolande was.

Mr Investigator – imagine, try, close your eyes the way I do now, and imagine what the effect must be on one. What a psychological shock! The completely cynical manoeuvring of the morning – because the intention, apart from showing his absolute power, must have been to try and create to my family, to my wife, the illusion that I was treated humanely; why, I'm even invited to his home! But further, to walk back into the house of death with that man accompanying me, and then to see, without any preparation, the person who is the dearest to me on earth. And not to break down. Not to break down. Not to make it more difficult for her. To try and comfort her. To reassure her. To pretend that it is less serious than it would seem. That there is still hope. To invent hope for her where there is none. And just to hold her hand. But feeling the gaze of this monster, avid for a strong emotional charge, hungry to partake of the plunging emotion of the pain so as to feel alive, and justified. He had to have that. He needs to abase himself even more, to rub the raw nerves so as to forget about the dead hole in his centre.

(RECAPITULATION)

I must know (he says). I must sniff out. I must uncover.
I must gut. I must reconstitute. I must comprehend.
I must *prove*. That is, I must allow it to reveal itself.
The secret secrets. Therefore I must ask. Do you mind
that I ask, I ask, I ask? Don't you know it's necessary?
That it can *never* be any different? That it has been
like this from the beginning of time—you and I en-
twined and related, parasite and prey? Image and
mirror-image? You are my frame and my field and my
discipline. I bring for you cookies in a tin—my wife
made them with her own two hands. In you I live.
Do I see all the evil concretized. Do I try to cherish
the little good. You must come to other insights. You
must realize the implications. You were used. You are
the pawn. Don't you know it yet? You are the sly one.
You are the sheep that strayed, you are the rejected
one, the excretion, the bosom-adder. You don't want
to know about me. I'm beneath you, am I not? I am
the rock, the flatfoot. I am stupid, not so? But you
know of me. Here we are, today, still today, still this
interminable dark day, days and days for ever. I am
with you. I never let go of you again. You are pro-
grammed. I cleanse you. I break you in. I break you
down to the pure outcome of spontaneous confession
and give-away and self-oblivion. Since I love you so.
Something that's barren in me goes out to you. You
are the dew in the chalice of my soul. Ah, what a
grand game this is.

I am the controller. I despatch you. I drive you
on. I manipulate you. You are my lifeboat. You must
open up, go open. You must just say. Say that which

I must hear. Tell that which I know. I know you so intimately. In such a profound way you will never know yourself. I nose around in your psyche. You are my excursions to wanton cellars. You are my book. I create your past. Your future is in my hands. I leaf through all the painfully constituted files on your comings and your goings, the records of your thinking and the organigramme of your associations. We are never free of one another again. I am your control. I am your handler. I squint up your arse. Relate your deepest fears to me, your best hidden desires. Forget about yesterday and tomorrow. The world knows only ending, ending. Pain is *now*. You are mine. You are the human. You are the bad. I am your present time, forty-two hours per day, from now on until all eternity. Come, I'll show you who you are. Look in this mirror, look. I bring you the image. Look how naïve you are.

I know already. I always know. But I must *prove*. You are the confirmation. You prove. You are of my making. I am the controller. I slit open, and then I sculpt. You make sense of my anxieties. You flesh out my dreams. You are, and therefore my life is not in vain. You flower. You are the true-coming of my prophecies. You are the product of my education, the crystallization of my heritage, the grail of my sacred task. Ah, what a grand game we play.

Talk to me! Write for me your cacography. We have time. Nobody will disturb us. There is no world outside. Night is pumping through the panes. You don't wish to walk in the night. We have come so far together. I know you. I know your private life so much better than you will ever know. Why do you resist? Why do you argue? You know that right is on my side now and this endless day and forever more. Our path has been traced for us. Accept what I give you. Be rich! Occupy the references I create for you! Are you surprised by my ability to induct? I know. I know all deduction and the creation of proof and all suscitation or alteration and all precipitation and all delay and all irritation and all stimulation and all the impulses and all transferring and all input and all feedback. I am the practitioner. I am your companion. I walk in your tracks. I am your tracks. I know of the eye before the keyhole, of the lens by the window, of the ear in the telephone or the ceiling or the floor or the tree, of the dagger in the back, of the explosive in the manuscript. I know of the stool pigeon and the provocateur. I know of the boot in the face when you're down. I love you so. I need you so. Don't you see? You permit me relevance, you give me my outline. You give me status. You make me accept myself. You make me feel that I know I *am*! Come, I'm your father confessor. Together we are the embodiment of the reality of my thoughts, my wishes, my anguishes, my existence. In me you are as safe as death. I have the two faces. Because you are, life is infamous. Because you are, there is sin. You make me humble. Through you I touch eternity. Through you I see that the looking-glass is true. You bring me to my knees. Because you are you and I am I, I am saved. There is relief for me in the holy hills before the shiny portals. **Ah,** how grand.

Do I go too far? Do I delve too deep? Are you ashamed of not having any shame left? Does it bother you to soil your pants? If you could only know how strongly it links us! Look, I am your safe harbour. You searched for me, you found me. I am your forever today still, and this day which will never stop screaming, which will never fade or lose its circles. I am your *reality*. Even of the most hidden things you need never be afraid again. Isn't it wonderful that you may share everything with me? Let go—I lead you to new dimensions. You don't think I'm just being curious? Do you not see the implications? Ah, what a grand game. I shall reveal all discourses to you and take them to logical conclusions, I shall point out every orientation. Surely you know that you are the old human nature. Come, I am the conductor. Trust me. Open up! I shall put together your prognosis. I am your proctoscope. You are my wondrous thousand and one nights. Describe your relationships to me. Tell me about what is veiled. Admit even to that which you don't know. Be glorious! I must test your credibility. I know everything. How lovely your confidence is. Don't struggle so!

I touch you. Why are you so withdrawn, so crumpled? Be dependent. *Talk* to me. But don't leave me! I am the controller. Don't you know me? Help me! Don't slide away like that from under my fingers. Resist! Be rich! Be! Don't leave me alone! I am the Afrikaner. Why dost thou not love me?

5

Then I am Presented in the Death Hole

Then I am presented with the indictment and the dance of the law starts. In the offices of the political police I am introduced to my legal team: Sam Norval, attorney; Pieter Henning, barrister. They were appointed, they said, by my family. Both of them were visibly very nervous, anxious even. It was only much later that I learned that it took great courage on their behalf to agree to represent me at all, that enormous pressure had been brought to bear on Sam Norval's firm, for instance, to try to get him to withdraw from the case. The firm of attorneys of which he was a partner also represented, amongst others, a major newspaper publishing concern (the chairman was a personal friend of Sitting Bull) which threatened economic blackmail, saying they would withdraw all future business from this legal firm unless Norval desisted from aiding me. It required the backstage intervention of some just-minded jurists to allow me to have any legal representation at all.

Huntingdon used to say to me, 'Why bother to have legal representation; why don't you leave it in my hands – I shall defend you.'

The charge sheet was a very hefty document indeed. It accused me, amongst other heinous crimes, of having smuggled weapons across the border, of having plotted violent acts of sabotage, of being involved in spying activities in the ports. And conspiracy! Conspiracy is a heavily punished crime in No Man's Land. The court is not so much interested in what you've actually done, but in what you *intend* doing, and especially the *implications* of what you were conspiring to do. (The Bible says that the end of time is near!) To be convicted of this the State only needs to show that you *associated* with known subversives. You should have seen the list of absent co-accused! So, on the advice of the legal team who so obviously operated within very strict parameters, bargaining with my tormentors was started. I had refused to give evidence against any of the other detainees. Things looked very sombre. If we allowed this indictment to go through unchallenged there was a very good chance that the prosecution may demand the highest penalty and the court may well grant it its wish. I myself was no party to whatever negotiating that took place, but I was aware of the intense insistence by Huntingdon and his cohorts, as also by the prosecuting team, that this case should not be allowed to become a political show trial – from *my* side that is.

You must remember that the trial took place during the 'secret' invasion of Angola by South African troops. What a heaven-sent gift, propaganda-wise at least, my capture must have been to the government! No wonder such a big fuss was made of it in the papers. (Poor editors – prevented by law from writing about the real war being waged.) If, as a bonus, I could be prevented from using the court as a political platform – well, then the good little Nationalists could really wag their tails. (And, come to think of it, when one now remembers how much back-stabbing there was going on between the CIA and the Greys concerning Angola, it becomes clear why BOSS was so uptight and anti-CIA.)

Gradually, also aided now by being able to look back on the events, gradually a line emerged. In return for my pleading guilty, and in return for my not insisting on making political statements from the dock, and in return for the freedom of the other arrested ones, the State graciously agreed to alter the charge sheet so as to delete any reference to violence, to not attempt to have me convicted under the Suppression of Communism Act, and it was agreed that the prosecutor would ask for the imposition of the minimum sentence, which was five years.*

My family was obviously and understandably trying to limit the damages. Sam Norval and Pieter Henning are certainly very capable jurists in the fields of their respective specialities – Civil Law and Corporate

---

*None of this could have been agreed to except, on their side, by the highest authorities – meaning Krüger, then Minister of Justice, and the Sitting Bull himself. After I'd done five years my legal representatives of the time petitioned the Minister for a remission of sentence, with arguments based in part on the pretrial agreement arrived at in 1975. Dr Yutar, the prosecutor, by now retired and back in private practice, went to see his ex-boss, the Minister, on

Law—but neither of them had any experience as a political lawyer. I don't think they could have designed the strategy for a political defence even if they wanted to, because they were far too closely integrated into the Afrikaner establishment. (By this I mean that the political police—the State for that matter—were not natural enemies for them.) I believe that they tried, mistakenly but with such solicitude, to do what they thought best for my interests at the time, and the atmosphere of terror created by the powerful political police was such that they felt we ought to tread very lightly indeed. During consultations Sam Norval used to be wet with perspiration and say, 'God, my God, we must be *so* careful!' I was aware that they were also having talks with the police and with the prosecuting team, but, strangely, all of this was quite beyond me. I was not aware—I don't remember now—of a formal agreement being reached, or how it would affect my future. I was numbed. To my mind the whole world was hostile (expressions of support were carefully kept from me, and the offices where I could consult the lawyers were bugged)—legal gown and policeman's uniform blended. All I wanted was to please. And in my cell I was alone in the house of dying.

One wanted to have it over and done with. I felt

my behalf. I was told that an extremely hostile Krüger warned Yutar that their conversation was being taped from the moment he entered the office, and then proceeded to deny any knowledge of the agreement (despite written confirmation from his Department). Yutar was shocked and humiliated; felt he'd never been treated in such a cavalier fashion in his life. In Afrikaans we call this *stank vir dank*, meaning 'stench for thanks'.

quite passive. I can understand how the mouse is paralysed although still alive whilst being eaten by the snake – celebrating with open eyes its own death.

But, Mr Investigator, let me not create the impression that I repudiate my lawyers. Had I instructed them differently, had I been strong enough to call the bluff of the interrogators, had I felt that I was entitled and justified to defend myself *politically* (which I did not: I was no ANC member, and Okhela was formed in support of a *faction* within the ANC so that a political defence would also have been an embarrassment to people I then still considered my friends), or had I been willing to make a martyr of myself – they would probably have outlined a different type of defence. I could not have been an easy client – that is the story of my life, Mr Investigator: not to be an easy client. As it was they advised particular caution – perhaps seeing the real dangers more clearly than I then did. And I went along.

I was asked to prepare a short statement. Without being political it was an attempt to explain how I got to be standing where I was, without rejecting my convictions. Read it – you will also hear the insidious voice of the controller in it. This was in the hands of Huntingdon a week before the trial commenced, and Vorster himself had it on his desk before it was read in court.

Mr Investigator, the public play is not really the part of the story which interests you most, is it? Do you want to dance? I think you'd rather like to know about what was happening behind the walls. (Are you also one of those who believe that the unsaid must be more truthful?)

The trial itself was a strangely muted affair. It took

place in one of the courts of the Pretoria Supreme Court building—wood-panelled with carved motifs, very morbid, very depressing. I believe the building served at one time as a synagogue.

The prosecutor was the attorney-general of the Transvaal at the time, Dr Percy Yutar, a small bald man with glasses and one withered hand. Worth his weight in gold to the Nationalist government he was, because he allowed them the pretence of justice and objectivity they so sorely needed. After all, a Jew— that is, a non-Afrikaner—in their service, being their henchman: surely, they argued, it must prove to the outside world that our justice is not a partisan one. (This coming from a party which supported Hitler during the war and which is still marked by anti-Semitism!) They used him only for the major show trials such as the Rivonia case or the trial of Bram Fischer. He served them well, Percy Yutar, he sold his soul over and over again and in the end I don't believe that he was paid in kind. His senior assistant was a tall supercilious man called Dennis Rothwell. (Long after the trial Rothwell came to visit me in my cell with Huntingdon. He then admitted to being a Satanist—seriously!—and felt we might have something in common there as he sensed, he said, an admiration for the Devil in me too!)

The judge was an old flunky going by the name of Silly, son of a minister of the Church of the Free State. It is curious how these fanatic Afrikaners, entirely biased, with tribal loyalties only, and therefore completely disqualified for the elevated duty of administering justice, succeed in hiding their rottenness behind a robe of respectability. Silly must have been an important functionary of the Broederbond.* He also most surely received instructions from Sitting Bull defining the line to take during the court proceedings and the type of sentence to be imposed. And yet he put in his daily appearance as if he were really an objective and stately elderly judge. He did once warn against people attempting to influence the decisions of the court— but I learned, much later, that he was referring to individuals from abroad who had sent telegrams in my support.

Despite the muted proceedings there was quite a lot of interest in the case. In the body of the hall I could see every day the senior security police officers sitting there. They are fascinated by the mechanism of a trial. They love to assist at the conclusion and the accomplishment of their handiwork. It gives them, in their own eyes, the appearance of legality. It is nearly as if, in this way, they feel that they are justifying in public, by their own appearance, the dark deeds committed in the sad cells and interrogation offices. But they are there also to observe, to advise, to control, to make sure that the noose fits snugly. The other State officials will not be allowed to forget that they are there. The investigating officer, of course, is part

*The Broederbond (League of Brothers)—an Afrikaner secret organization, started in the early years of revived Afrikaner nationalism, into which only 'right-thinking', influential, white Afrikaner males can be ritually initiated. Pretending to be a 'cultural organization'—most Dutch Reformed ministers are members—it in fact, through its occult presence and because you have no future in Afrikaner public life unless you are a member, directs Afrikaner political ideology and practice, as well as its economy and its cultural life. And, by extension, the country's.

of the prosecuting team. There are other, younger political police present, to allow them to become acquainted with the accused and the witnesses and inevitably with the politicized spectators who turn up in solidarity with the accused.

It became clear fairly rapidly that even though I had been tricked into renouncing any attempt to politicize the trial, the State, by mouth of Dr Percy Yutar and his assistants, was going to go all out to smear a few organizations which, up to that time, they had not yet succeeded in eliminating. I'm referring to NUSAS, the National Union of South African Students; to some of the more Christian elements in the churches, such as those then grouped around the Christian Institute; and even to dissident Afrikaner thinking as expressed to some extent in the writing of a few colleagues. I should add that I had been until that time an honorary vice-president of NUSAS, that several of the other detainees were involved in trade union activities sponsored by NUSAS, and one at least was a Christian Institute worker.

They did not bother to call too many witnesses. (Nails van Byleveld was asked to tell how he searched a house in Cape Town. He arrived at the front door, accompanied by a detainee.

Prosecutor: 'What did you do then?'

Van Byleveld: 'I entered the house.'

Prosecutor: 'And then?'

Van Byleveld: 'I went deeper into the house.'

Eventually he found a document hidden away in a book on the bookshelf.)

Of those they did call there were three kinds: one such as Mrs Röhmer, or Lewis, who went out of their way to wag their tails and ingratiate themselves with the prosecution to the extent that they would invent and ascribe intentions to me which did not even exist, with allusions to spying, to violent terroristic activities. (Mrs Röhmer, her head covered by a mantilla veil as if going to church for confession – yes! – when asked how she felt about her role, said, 'I think I ought to be taken outside and shot.' Lewis, I learned, was suffering from uncontrolled bowel movements, and appeared in an ill-smelling, rumpled suit. On his way back from the witness box, passing by the dock where I sat, I couldn't refrain from advising him to have his suit cleaned.) There was a second kind of witness who answered strictly and only the questions put to him. And then there was the third kind, such as Karel Tip for instance, who quite obviously was most uncomfortable in giving evidence and managed to convey that he regretted having to do so and that his loyalty to our cause had not changed. ('Could you describe the accused to the court?' 'He is of medium height.' 'Colour hair?' 'Medium.' 'Colour eyes?' 'Medium.')

I'd like to think that there were some people in detention who refused to give any evidence at all, but I bear no grudges against those who did. Why drown just because another madman did?

We on our side, when I say 'we' it means essentially the legal team, influenced and pressurized by the political police, decided not to call any witnesses. I myself was prevailed upon to enter the box to allow myself to be cross-examined, and during this passage the smearing tactics of Yutar came to fruition. Two witnesses were summoned for mitigation of sentence.

To my everlasting shame Huntingdon went up to testify to my cooperation. No 'uncontaminated' literary expert (that is, no literary figure of any standing) was willing to appear for me. So a young lady was called upon to talk about my poetic abilities and she read some verses in an embarrassingly dramatic fashion. And then we rested our case.

On the days of court proceedings I was fetched every morning at the prison by the political police. I'd managed to recover two of my own suits and borrowed a few ties from one of my brothers, and the security police would flutter around me, helping tie the knot around my neck, pretending to be concerned about my appearance. We would then drive down to the Compol Building which was obviously heavily guarded by armed policemen and there I would sit around waiting for them to take me to court.

One morning I noticed Huntingdon taking exceptional precautions about his own appearance, combing and recombing his hair, and patting one of his flashiest broad ties into place. He then nonchalantly announced that since it was such a beautiful morning we were going to stroll to court.

I was preceded and flanked and followed by a phalanx of Greys through the streets of Pretoria, with Huntingdon and his dark glasses to my right, and sure enough, as we approached the Supreme Court building the photographers stormed at us and started clicking away. The whole operation was stage-managed by Huntingdon to get his mug in the newspaper. He is a very vain man, but probably he also tried to convey the impression that the security police had the situation entirely in hand.

During the sessions, when I wasn't actually in the dock, I was kept down in the court cells behind a locked door. The court cells are watched over by an aged, idiotic functionary. Upon arrival one is handed over to him, but one's escort must have a 'body receipt'. If the police or prison officials don't provide food for lunch, this bald shuffler will do so: a slice of bread ('but the bread is white') and a mug of coffee. These court cells are atrocious places. The walls are painted black, they're filthy inside, the toilets are broken, and all over you see on the walls the scratched graffiti of desperate detainees leaving their messages of hope or their exculpations or just a curse or a threat. Never was I alone in any of these cells. Always there were two or three of the Greys with me. (It wouldn't do to be found hanging with Judge Silly waiting upstairs; the show must go on!) To them the proceedings were like a circus. One of them would leave the cell, go for a stroll around the building, and come back reporting that he'd seen Helen Joseph or Winnie Mandela. One was not aware, whilst in the court cells, of what was happening upstairs or even what the weather was like.

The trial of the SASO student leaders (South African Student Organization) was going forward at the same time as mine, in an adjoining courtroom. Sometimes, during recesses, I passed by them in the stairwell or the corridor. They were all dressed in complementary African shirts – very flashy. I envied them their warm and rumbustious camaraderie. Once, on my way in, I caught a glimpse of Rick Turner's red beard, sitting alone in the SASO court. He was to be assassinated not long afterwards. I shall have the chance to tell you about the echoes of his death as I heard them in prison.*

Upstairs then one sat on a very narrow wooden bench slightly higher than the rest of the spectators in such a position as to see the people in the hall. My father used to be among the audience, day after day, sitting half way towards the back, very straight, with his face entirely closed. How he must have suffered. His life was coming to a close, but his years of deepening shadows were not going to be easy. He had lived through the feuds pitting Afrikaner against Afrikaner. His father – my tough old grandfather – had been a labourer on other people's farms. He himself had worked with his hands: building canals, ploughing and planting, mining. His first son, my eldest brother, was (is) the commander of his country's crack anti-guerrilla special unit, a brigadier-general, a trained (and enthusiastic) killer, be it with knife or gun, a 'dirty tricks' expert for Military Intelligence; his second son was (is) a reporter, fellow traveller of the Greys, with decidedly fascist sympathies; and now there was me, a terrorist, vilified by many (but that didn't bother him, he was used to it, except that some neighbours stopped talking to him – although others, ordinary folk, would be heart-stopping in their continued support). Plus, he hated being in the Transvaal. My sister, who stood by him day after day, used to

*Rick Turner was an academic at the University of Natal. He was also active as an adviser to the nascent Black trade unions. He had written an important book (banned in South Africa) on the economic impracticabilities of the Bantustan policy, called *Through the Eye of the Needle*. At the time of his assassination he was living under a banning order.

remark that Oubaas (as we call him in the family) would get physically sick the moment he crossed the Vaal. My mother didn't come. It would have been too much of a strain for her. And we'd agreed that Yolande shouldn't be there either. Why increase the pain? She wasn't even living in Paris anymore. Never, until the end, did the *boere* stop attempting to implicate her – people like my brother and the writer, Chris Barnard,* concurred in this plot: they continued trying to use my marriage to her as a pressure point; and some of the fine and loyal people who offered her friendship and hospitality on her periodic visits to the land were confronted with photographic and other evidence of their association with Yolande in an attempt to blackmail them into working with the *boere*. But, being under the protection of the French embassy – representatives of a 'friendly' power – they left her alone apart from the obligatory shadowing and tapping of the phones where she sojourned.

From time to time I spotted the presence of other friends; so close they were and yet out of touch – moving in another world altogether. Although there were no barriers between us we were already irre-

---

*Their attitude seems to have been: she's Vietnamese, therefore she must be communist; she's considered racially inferior here and if we were in that situation we would have been embittered – she must be also, so she must be plotting against the State; she is intelligent and cultivated and we can't catch her, so obviously she is very dangerous. Barnard, the author, in a series of opportunistic articles in a popular Afrikaans weekly, *Die Huisgenoot* (which I saw later), suggested – or had it suggested to him – that if it had not been for Yolande I'd never have gotten involved in politics; that she instigated and probably master-minded my acts. Well, hen-pecked I am . . . but not to that point!

vocably separated from one another and I might as well have been dead. Once, during a break, a few fellow writers were allowed to come up and say hello to me. It was an awkward moment, for what does one have to say at a time like that? There was also an observer coming from Switzerland on behalf of an international organization of jurists. I tried to communicate with him rapidly in French whilst being taken past him, but that did not succeed. I saw neither hide nor hair of any of the more prominent literary figures. Fear was at their throat. Fear and *Schadenfreude*. They had rejected me entirely by then; they were not going to be identified in any way with a terrorist.

The State summed up its case and asked for the imposition of the minimum sentence of five years. Dr Yutar even allowed himself the luxury of advancing a certain number of grounds for leniency, in other words, justifying his asking for the minimum sentence only. My defence then made their final statements and on the same day, with hardly a break, the judge who had sat there nodding away in his sleep, pronounced my conviction and his sentence.* 'Mumble, mumble, mumble . . . ' he said; 'You are a very dangerous man . . . mumble, mumble, mumble . . . If we let you continue the results are unforeseeable, blood and death . . . mumble, mumble, mumble . . . ' And then nine years. Perhaps I should write – And: then nine years. Or – And then nine: years.

When someone says to you 'Nine years' like that (like saying 'the white cow'), it's like dropping a mantle

---

*But he did ask my age first, and then remarked that I was in the 'flower' of my years. I never worked out whether he considered this an aggravating factor when considering sentence.

of steel on your chest, and yet, at the same time, the sense of it does not penetrate. You cannot come to grips with it.

I was allowed to say goodbye to my father. I felt the need to console him. I didn't want the avid crowd of vultures hanging around outside—those sick ones who'd come to stare at the misery of other people—I didn't want them to see my father weeping. After that there was the indignity of having souvenir photos taken by my brother—of me, my father and a team of hunters all around us. Thus we have the beast, mated, tamed.

And then back down to the cells with the sad explanations deeply gouged into the walls. *To USSR with love,* or *A hippy was held here for no reason,* or *David Makwana was here for kak,* and *Kilroy is here for terrorism,* or *Make love to Jesus,* or the warning *All you murderers look out for justice Theron, he's got ropes on his brain, Good luck,* or, very succinctly, just *The palace of injustice.* And further *You Nats, today you have the say, but just wait till the Chinks get here, then I will laugh.* And sadly *Time is but the thought of getting closer to hell.*

I was escorted from the court cells to Compol, made to sit in a corner of Huntingdon's office. The door giving onto the corridor hid my presence. Huntingdon, like a hyena, had pretended to be aggrieved and surprised by the severity of my sentence, but now, as he sat there behind his desk, two of his colleagues suddenly came in, not seeing me, to congratulate him warmly on the success that he had obtained. They knew all along that he'd get me, as he said he would. There was some discomfort all round when they became aware that I was there. People came and went. Fellow-detainees were released and welcoming parties were gathering on the sidewalk. Released people had to be booked out, had to sign for the pawed-over, desecrated possessions returned to them. It took time. Interrupted lives could be resumed. A youngish BOSS agent who happened to be in the offices was asked to *hou vas* me for a while. He told me how one hunts jack rabbits by jeep and agile Bushman tracker in the Kalahari. Then he took me past the blind liftman to the toilet and conspiratorily poured me a large paper cup of white wine, a last one for a long time 'for old time's sake'. He handed me back into the care of Huntingdon and I was worried that he might smell the alcohol on my breath and punish me!

My interrogator then allowed a journalist by the name of Jack Viviers to come right into the heart of the fortress. It was time for the loyal collaborator to get his morsel of recognition and Huntingdon needed to preen some more. Jack Viviers was later to write a book on my two trials, so obviously inspired and dictated by the political police. He was their man doing the fetching and carrying and smearing for them. In return he would get his scoops and build up a reputation as a security expert. Mr Jack Viviers probably forgot about the possibility that the day could come when I may be out again.*

In this shocked state in which I found myself he came with the characteristic Afrikaans hypocrisy of softness and sympathy for one's dilemma. 'Please,' he

*At the time of dictating this (August 1983), Viviers actually works in London with the traditional cover of the flatfoot abroad: foreign correspondent. He had the cheek, some time after my release, to try and contact me in Paris!

said, 'won't you just write a few lines for me, person-ally, in memory of today?' And stupidly I did so. Of course, the next day this was splashed over the front page of his newspaper.

I'm then driven back to Maximum Security by Huntingdon. No longer can I look, hopefully, on Bev-erly Hills as a way-station; it would have to be home for as long as I could see into the future. No more excursions down to the court, no more winking at friends or acquaintances in the audience, no more private suits or soft shirts, all that was finished now. . . . He takes me all the way in.

In my cell the implications finally hit me and I have what one could only describe as a nervous breakdown – with this monstrous man sitting there in a chair, hidden behind his dark glasses, watching me, finally reaching the apotheosis of his own search for satisfaction. He goes all white in the face. To him it must have been like an orgasm.

Then he starts talking to me, telling of how he'd not always been like that, of how naïve he'd also been when young, of his hard life as a constable, of coming home on his motorcycle to a small flat and a young wife, of hitting the bottle too hard (and bottling up emotions), about being posted to the Illegal Diamond Buying Branch (which was an education in treachery and play-acting and greed), and then becoming the State President's bodyguard (so overwhelmed to still get the occasional postcard from him), but how this type of life, the life of an interrogator, Mr Investigator, how it has changed him over the years.

It was a miserable experience: this man with his stunted psyche needing the satisfaction of destroying his opponent and at the same time lucid enough to perhaps perceive the extent of moral decrepitude and corruption such an attitude implies.

INSERT

Somewhere in Sri Lanka, the ancient Ceylon, the even more ancient Serendip, where at present Tamil prisoners are being massacred by their non-Tamil jail-mates and where buses of Tamil passengers are stopped, the doors locked, gasoline poured over the vehicle with its trapped, gesticulating passengers, before fire is brought to devour everything (see how they dance, take a whiff of the stench, dear Mr I – that the compassionate ways of life of the Far East could not prevent such bestiality!) – somewhere in the highlands there's a temple with a mural showing Hare in the mouth of Lion. The lion does not close its jaws except, perhaps, gently, to save the little one from falling. It is said to be a picture of the goodness of Buddha. There is another one showing Crow flying along flip-a-flop with Fish in its beak, and a little further along the wall a whole area of skeleton fish. I have been told the interpretation of this one, but it has flown out of my mind. Man is a mythical beast.

On the door of the room where I work (the door is open to the breeze off the sea from Africa, it has no lock) the owner of the house has pinned a sheet of paper with an Italian text. It is called *da Una Certa Enciclopedia Cinese*,* and translates: 'The animals are

*A note to my translators: my corrupt translation, I learned later, was from a corrupt Italian text, which was a translation from Jorge Luis Borges' *Otras inquisiciónes*, which he had translated in part from the Chinese.

divided into (a) those belonging to the Emperor, (b) embalmed ones, (c) domesticated ones, (d) suckling pigs, (e) sirens, (f) fabled ones (or fabulous ones?), (g) dogs running loose, (h) included in the present classification, (i) which are madly agitated, (j) innumerable ones, (k) indicated by a pelt finer than the skin of the camel, (l) et cetera, (m) which make love, (n) which from a distance look like flies.'

6

Which from a Distance Looks like Flies

I understand, Mr Investigator, that you want me to go back in time a little bit to try to explain to you rapidly what this is all about, what Okhela was all about, and how I got myself into this mess in the first place. Well, I cannot give you the whole history, but I must indicate that what ended up in court started with an appreciation of the political situation which, forgive me for saying so, Mr Investigator, I still subscribe to. It further reflected, personally, the need of a person coming from a specific background, from a certain country, to become involved and to live out the convictions he had, based on a complex situation, on that appreciation, and naturally also on the dreams which he shared and still shares with the vast majority of the people in that country. I remain convinced, now more than ever, of the sickness down there, because I had the dubious honour of seeing it in effect very closely. I believe, more than ever, that the system existing in South-Africa is against the grain of everything that is beautiful and hopeful and dignified in human history; that it is a denial of humanity, not only of the majority being oppressed but of the minority associated with that oppression; that it is profoundly unjust; that it is totally corrupted and corrupting; that it is a system with which nobody ought to be allowed to live. It is to the honour of large parts of the world that they reject Apartheid, even if only half-heartedly so, even if for self-serving reasons, even if it is instructed by a false sense of being culturally superior to the 'Boers', even if the outrage is intended to divert attention from the dirt on their own doorsteps.

But what does one do if you are White, if in fact you are part of the privileged minority in power? When you come in revolt against such a system, how do you oppose it effectively? One of the effects – and perhaps it was intended to be so – of Apartheid has been that it has splintered the opposition to the system. The gulf between Black and White, or between Whites and all the others, is so enormous that in fact we are strangers to one another. The only common ground we share is Apartheid. But we interpret that ground differently. We are conditioned, each in his own way, by the privileges and the iniquities of the system. To pretend differently would be taking and mistaking one's desires for reality.

How could I, as a White man, express my opposition to the system, which means to the exploitation and the degradation, effectively whilst identifying myself with the cause of the Black majority? How could I relate to them? I could do so on the plane of ideas, concerning the absolutes of justice and dignity and freedom, even of socialism.

I repeat: my revulsion to Apartheid could not only be because of what it is doing to all the 'un-Whites', could not be really resilient if motivated by a 'do-good' approach, but because of how it was affecting *me*. The corruption of the élite is the corruption of privilege and ease and power and paternalism. The panacea found by Whites who have twinges of doubt and bad conscience is often Liberalism: disdain with a patronizing mask.

Man suffers because of his separation from the boundless, Anaximander said. If there is a life force, Apartheid goes against it. Surely what we live towards is a greater, even metaphysical, integration, however hazardous and dangerous. And just as surely we are inspired to do so by a profound sense of brotherhood. Apartheid is a mutation of *power* and *greed*. No religion can justify it, except that warped doctrine the Afrikaners have fashioned from their desert faith. Their god is a cruel, White interrogator.

I could relate particularly on the grounds of socialism. The commitment of a whitish citizen of No Man's Land can, to my mind, only be an ideological one. To the so-called Black it is dictated by the daily necessity of the struggle for survival.

Mr Investigator, I think you will realize that I am trying to describe to you a situation whereby I felt it necessary to become involved in the freedom struggle. But I cannot, could not, do so within the framework of the existing political organizations. I have since many years given my allegiance and support to the African National Congress which is the political formation representing the majority of South Africans. It is an African nationalist organization, forbidden in the country; its leaders are either in prison or exile or fighting underground. But it is also an organization working in alliance with several others, and in fact the pacesetter of these organizations is the South African Communist Party. The SACP actually has the nerve centres of the liberation movement in its control.

I shall be more specific, Mr Investigator. The SACP has in its hands the secretariat of the ANC, the financial structure of the ANC, the control over the armed wing of the ANC which is called Umkhonto we Sizwe. It constitutes the major link between the ANC and its foreign supporters, both on a government level, that is, support coming from the socialist countries, and on the level of anti-Apartheid organizations scattered all over Western Europe. The SACP evidently also controls, through its intervention and by dint of being the intermediary, the facilities offered to the ANC for the military training of its future soldiers. Above all the SACP has outlined and enforces the ideology by which the ANC is guided.

All of this I do not trot out as criticism or as 'redbaiting' or to pour oil on the fires of the South African strategists and warlords. I believe that a communist party is by its very nature and by definition a power machine. It is shaped and intended with that one goal in mind: to obtain and to exercise power. In South Africa the SACP for a long time was not exactly popular among the African masses, because of its flirting in earlier years with the White labour movement which, as you know, Mr Investigator, is profoundly reactionary and pro-Nationalist Party. The SACP represents numerically a very restricted number of people. It is therefore necessary and inevitable if it wants to guide the revolutionary struggle, that it should work within the framework of the liberation movement. The interests and the goals of these two organizations married in the Revolutionary Council which is, to my knowledge, practically exclusively in the hands of members of the SACP, even if they sit there as representatives of the ANC. The goals and the intentions of these two organizations overlap but whereas the ANC is open to ideological influence from the West, according to the speeches from the dock of Nelson Mandela at the time of his sentencing, and whereas the ANC is concerned primarily with liberation and the coming to power of the Black majority of the country, and whereas the ANC sees its task in attempting to accomplish this as being free from the dictates of class analysis – the SACP, on the other hand, and again to my mind quite correctly, sees the liberation, the throwing off of the yoke of Apartheid, as only the first step in allowing the process of a profound transformation of the South African society into one which will be characterized by a socialist economy and by pervasive State control of the kind that we see in the Eastern European countries.

The SACP, your Honour, is in principle and in practice a multiracial, non-racist organization. It has among its members people from all the various cultural and linguistic and ethnic groupings in the country. And this was exactly where I and my friends felt that we differed from them – not that we weren't yearning for the day when race or sex or language would no longer be a consideration when forming a political party, but because we thought that the SACP was papering over the real problems of cultural awareness (after all, we've had Black Consciousness in the meantime!). We thought that by grouping Black and White – in this way, at this level – in the same organization, one was diminishing the effectiveness of the militants by confusing the feedback and making it difficult for people (with their daily experience of harsh Apartheid, of differences between experiences) to identify with the Party. (What a long sentence!) We furthermore, perhaps due to diverse leftist experiences during the sixties, felt a strong opposition to Stalinism—because it needs also to be pointed out that the SACP, being the oldest communist party on the African continent, and perhaps because of its numerical weakness, could probably be considered as the most rigidly loyal supporter of Moscow's foreign policy.* To my shame as a South African I have to admit that it was among the first organizations lauding the Soviet Union for its invasion of Hungary and again later of Czechoslovakia. It is not a party which admits much internal questioning. It is finally, and that was another of our criticisms, not a very effective communist party, just as, in my opinion, the African National Congress is not a very effective liberation movement. (For the sake of power the party breaks the revolution. It occupies terrain which could be far more vigorously used by other formations. What happened in Zimbabwe must be a dire warning to the SACP. If ever there were to be an uprising, the party would in all likelihood be engulfed and lose its grip on the course of events.)

We were proud of the ANC's record as the oldest,

---

*Stalinism, or Stalinist, in this sense, means to be doctrinaire; to always follow 'Mother's' line, however often it may be revised or changed; and to be bureaucratic in the extreme. Also to be non-democratic by means of the astute formula of 'centralized democracy'.

most respectable, political organization in South Africa and of its kind on the African continent. Well, it is also by now the greyest, the most ancient, and perhaps eventually one ought to point out that it has squandered its assets and was only lukewarm in the struggle when more thorough opposition might have swung things the other way. But that is only a very superficial criticism because at the same time it must be admitted that after all these years of being illegal in the country – being in exile since 1960 – it is at this stage of its history more powerful and has wider support among the African population, among the so-called Coloureds too, than ever before. Is that not a victory? (These personal remarks about the ANC are made in passing: even if I were that capable I should not pretend to be analysing the ANC or its history here.)

Be that as it may. I repeat, our criticism of the SACP was coming from the left, and it was informed by the way in which we saw the profile of the Party *then*, clearly or obscurely. And the above are some of the objective causes for the coming into being of Okhela.

In practical terms: I was recruited during the early 1970s for the specific purpose of creating forms of aid to militant White opposition to the Apartheid regime in the country, of establishing these points of aid abroad, of helping the White militants in obtaining a basic training when abroad, permitting them to carry on the struggle clandestinely upon their return to the country. The people forming these organizations of assistance abroad, on behalf of the ANC, were grouped in an organization called 'Solidarité', with as its responsible executive a man called Henri Curiel. (I'm jumping in history: at that point of course I didn't know what his name was.)

I was told about the activities of Solidarité glance by glance, a little in the way one is taught to look in the mirror. Over the years I built up a fairly good working knowledge of how they operated. I may mention, Mr Investigator, for your footnotes, that Solidarité essentially grew out of a spirit of resistance during the Second World War. These people are imbued with the same thirst for independence and freedom, and tried to answer to the practical need of maintaining and propagating and continuing the methods which years of occupation had forced upon them. By the nature of their commitments they were in contact with liberation movements from all over the world and also with organizations representing political or social minorities in various countries, such as the Kurds or the Basques, in their struggle for independence from oppression.

I'm going to have to take short cuts. Everything I'm telling you now is known to the agents of No Man's Land. It turned out later on that they had infiltrated over the years both the ANC and the SACP, and Solidarité, and who knows, perhaps even Okhela. So I'm not giving away any secrets, but it's tedious to have to repeat this type of story (an interesting little turn-off from the path of our story is the fact that the court records of both trials, the first, and the second one we are coming to, disappeared from the Pretoria Supreme Court archives; I don't know who has them, I don't know for what purpose they are not available; mysteriously nobody seems to know where these records are if they still exist). But we won't worry, will we, Mr I, since I'm giving you these confessions. The blood of my heart.

During 1973, earlier, in '72, I created with a few fellow White South Africans in exile the kernel of a political formation which we called 'Okhela'. Very rapidly we organized some clandestine visits to South Africa and we were able to extend our support in the country in the same way as we were able abroad to extend the scope of our activities. When I was caught later in 1975 we were, however, still only in the beginning processes of establishing this organization and of defining, in consultation with those active on the ground in the country, the aims and the forms of our activities.

Nevertheless, for what it's worth, let me admit that during the few years of our existence we managed, *inter alia*, to penetrate the South African embassy in West Germany and to lay our hands on enough secret material to prove that the two governments – Bonn and Pretoria – were flaunting the international decisions of withholding nuclear research knowledge from the South Africans. In fact, we were able to show conclusively that there was collaboration with the Germans enabling the South Africans to start their own programme manufacturing, ultimately, nuclear arms. Similarly we were able to lay bare the machinations of several international oil companies in Rhodesia, how they circumvented the then officially applied oil boycott policy, and naturally the type of aid they were receiving from South Africa in particular. These are not negligible accomplishments. I am not so sure that we, at our level, in our context, were not at least as effective as the officially established anti-Apartheid groups and the representatives of the liberation movement abroad.

We had also succeeded in obtaining the promise of substantial sums of money directed to the nascent Black trade unions in South Africa and we were going to have our contacts in the country—who were instrumental in the formation of the Black unions, although not necessarily part of them—channel this money to the intended recipients. To be able to do that, though, we needed to establish a trade union office abroad, in Europe, manned by a Black and a White trade unionist from inside.

So, Mr Investigator, briefly, the purpose of my illegal trip into South Africa was, first of all, to recruit two such people and to make it possible for them to leave the country, most probably illegally, because it was expected that at least one of them would be a banned person and therefore not allowed to travel freely. Thus—to move these people across the border, to receive them in Europe, to install them, and to make it possible for them to function. And further than that my task was to go and see for myself what exactly the scope for Okhela-type activities was inside the country; to talk to our underground people there; to submit to them the proposed platform; to debate with them the basic issues: our stance, our attitude towards the liberation movements, our attitude to violence, how we see or saw our role in the White community, whether our intention of working in the White community only was correct, the need to stimulate and mobilize creative *alternative* thinking breaking the mould of Apartheid *thinking* and abetting the coming about of future structures by *conceiving* them), the function of culture, the link-up with outside, the strategy to be followed and the tactics we could allow ourselves – all the million little things which go into knitting a tight, loyal, effective organization.

Well, that is the nice Walter Mitty (or Robin Hood) side of the story; the darker side is that I was betrayed even before I arrived there. You can push me, Mr Investigator, you can tear this up and ask me to write again, you can fish for my tongue with a tuning fork, and still I shall not be able to tell you who exactly betrayed me. Yes, of course, I have my doubts and I have my guesses, and I know objectively in whose interests it might have been to do so. (Don Espejuelo taught me to *think* through the haze of self-deception and the smokescreen of grey disinformation by always asking: *cui bono?*) I can also divine the motivation of some people, perhaps even very close to me, who thought that in doing so, in exposing me, they could provoke a certain situation – a catharsis which would benefit the struggle. All I know is first: very few people, very few indeed, were in the know. Secondly: it was not my idea to go down there but I had to submit myself to the majority decision to do so. Stupidly vain, when told there were certain things which only I could do, it touched me, and I fell for it. And, of course, thirdly, I felt a moral commitment, a necessity to go. How could I pretend to want to lead an organization of which some of the members would have to do dangerous things if I was not willing to do so myself? (Yes, you see how inept, how inexperienced, how vulnerable to blackmail – or whitemail – I was!) I went, and I'm going back to the beginning of my story.

And I add to that beginning of my story this little subsidiary thought, seeing as how there are a few more loops of the spool left for this particular chapter, and that is: that my dear, ineffective, fat, institutionalized friends in the liberation movement who got me involved in the first place, those professional diplomats, those living off the fat of the suffering of our people back home and who've done so for years and will do so until they die, not really worried about ever going back, the suave politicians – they then dropped me as an embarrassingly hot potato the moment I was caught, and they avoid me now like the plague; because I am that of course: I am the plague. . . .

INSERT

Very fascinating reflections may flow from an appraisal of clandestine political activity or from the evaluation of any one underground political organization. Underground organizations, secret societies, seem to be a phenomenon of our time but they have quite a long history of course. Suffice it to say that nearly always the decision to go underground is imposed by conditions in the country where the political struggle takes place. Underground struggle is one expression among many of the continuing fight against fascism, totalitarianism, sometimes colonialism, even imperialism. As one of the characteristics identifying a totalitarian state is precisely that it prohibits any form of effective opposition to the party or class in power, one may say that therefore, the rulers of such a country make clandestine opposition to them ineluctable. They are the ones who make the rules, they create the conditions. But this is only partially true. There is and there has always been a line of thinking or *fascio* of theories that values underground action for its own sake. It is true that it is, as near as possible, a clean form of political activity divested of the more mundane horse-trading and compromising of everyday politics. There is a certain purity of thinking. There is often a heightened political consciousness because the awareness must be applicable to direct and nearly always immediate translation into action. There is therefore not the gap between theory and practice which so often is a debilitating aspect of political life. Clandestine activity imposes a rigorous discipline on those participating in it. It satisfies the Spartan urges we all seem to have. It brings about a greater confidence in oneself; you quickly become more aware of the value of confidence – where it is justified and where not – since people have confidence in you and entrust you with work which by definition is perilous, and you yourself have to continually test the canons of confidence, the extent to which you can use confidence in your relations with others. One finds great generosity among people involved in clandestine activity. Danger and fear tend to weave a more solid cloth of interdependence and mutual support among the various members. You may meet somebody passing through on a discreet mission – you have confidence in the contact who referred him to you, you abide by the rules of not asking him what his work is about or where exactly he comes from and where he's headed – and although you may not see him again, or perhaps *because* you'll never see him again, you are willing to do just about anything for him. Underground work generates loyalty. Sure, the training for it and the circumstances under which it takes place form a measure of conditioning. Unquestioned loyalty, discipline – these are some of the ways in which the conditioning makes itself felt. Since information cannot circulate freely you are willing provisionally to put the best face on even incomprehensible actions of a comrade. Pending an eventual explanation you withhold criticism; you trust him, you have to trust him because discipline, confidence, generosity, loyalty and trust are the basic components without which there can be no clandestine political work. It is true too that in such a milieu you may get to know a comrade whom you perhaps only meet briefly once a week far better than you would know lifelong friends. You may never find out the real name of this comrade, you have no idea of his situation in life – whether he is a priest or a doctor or an electrician or a soldier – but since your dealings with him will be direct and guided by the characteristics I have indicated, it will be as if the useless accretions normally clogging up and covering your relationships with people can now be jettisoned. When you are a mole or a shadow you cannot afford to lie to a comrade, and you know that neither can he try to pull the wool over your eyes. Your relations are based on rock-bottom mutual needs. Clandestine action teaches you to check and to counter-check every move you make: this is what it ought to do at least. You learn to think coherently, to the point, but not to trust your own thinking; to make up a mental checklist to go through again and again. You acquire, like a second nature, the instinct of being aware of your surroundings. When you book into a hotel you automatically look for the alternative exits, and you do not relax before you've checked out the quarter in which it is located, to get a feel of the topography, of the structure of your environment – where the danger points such as police stations are, how possible escape routes can be recognized. The same attitude of checking and counter-checking is applied in your communications and dealings with comrades: they know that you do this, they do the same, and the knowledge serves again to strip excess and unnecessary sentiments from the sinews of your relationships with others. Ah, what a grand game . . .

Some believe that underground work is of itself a transforming agent, that it slots in with, say, the theory of a *fuoco* as expressed by Guevara—that is, that the underground work of a small, dedicated group using effective means can, as it were, liberate specific areas of thinking and of appreciation, which may lead to them being exemplary and encouraging the establishing of other, similar zones of freedom. It—this work, or this type of action—is supposed also to form strong cadres for the future. True, to the extent that it inserts itself in a long and glorious line of historical struggle and similarly to the extent that it brings one into direct contact with all the implications of political action. It may well forge dedicated revolutionaries. It also favours convinced internationalism. You'll find, Mr Investigator, a tendency among clandestine action groups of various countries to help one another, even when they are not in total ideological agreement. I think it comes from a sentiment of fraternity, of being outlaws together, of being among the few just. Practically by definition underground organizations are small groups inclined to identify with other small groups elsewhere; and then too, the techniques made use of by clandestine militants are quite specialized so that one may find a situation, for instance, in which several groups tap the same specialist forger. But even beyond that, the very fact of having opted for such action usually implies that one has established a certain distance between yourself and the traditional, overt political groupings in your country. You are thus less bound by the nationalist symptoms that these groups may manifest. In choosing to go underground one moves out of the family constituted by legal or aboveground political parties. Frontiers become less important; one sees the struggle going beyond borders, growing from similar conditions in many points of the world. Also, you must not forget that clandestine work, as we know it now, is a distant descendant of the work and the theories embodied in various Internationals — the Comintern, for example, which was consciously internationalist. And then, as this type of action nearly always grows from a class analysis, it is understandable that it cannot be bound by the historical accidents which constitute different states. If we say 'class analysis' we are referring to conditions and objective agents creating similar classes and relationships between classes all over the world. We tend to call clandestine work a form of political expression proper to the working class. It has a history, as I've said, as old as the world itself though: from ancient secret sects through the Chinese *tongs* to the *illuminati* and the Italian carbon burners and the Bolsheviks. (Always there was the fascination of being a member of an exclusive group — the mystery of initiation — but too, the lure of concentrated power.) But do modern versions like the Tupamaros, like the Weathermen, like the *brigatisti*, have much to do with the working class? It is interesting when one looks at the continuous upheavals, revolutions, *coups d'état*, plots and counterplots, insurrections and uprisings in Latin America, to reflect that this may very well be the legacy that Italian exiles round about the time of Garibaldi took to that part of the world. I think we see it in its most baroque and sometimes absurd form there—*à la* García Márquez. In a certain way the relationship between clandestine activity and more open political action resembles the type of relationship between an avant-garde party and other mass expressions of political striving such as trade unions. Many of the theorists of clandestinity secretly hope to play the same type of leading role as a Leninist party is supposed to play *vis-à-vis* other fronts and political groupings.

But, and a very big *but*, must be: that all the above is a very romantic view of underground work. Is it really always necessary? Has it ever been successful, apart from, in some instances, making it possible for the clandestine activist to come to power? Does the need for such a type of action always correspond to a truly rigorous dissection of the conditions in the area you choose to operate in? Have all the other alternatives been exhausted? In South Africa, for example, we have a very poor tradition of underground work. We don't even have, as you'd find in Europe or Latin America, a generally shared code of conduct to be adhered to when confronted by the police. Our clandestine operators are amateurs; very often they have not been prepared for the dangers that face them when trapped. I was once told that, until quite recently anyway, the average time of survival for an underground militant in South Africa was barely eight days. But to come back to my argument: true, all effective political opposition to the Nationalist government has been outlawed, and in answer to that the underground organizations have opted for armed struggle. (To be generous to them one must hope that the armed struggle will make them, also individually, stronger.) But again – have we finally found it impossible to bring about change in any other way? Have we veritably thought *through* all the negative connotations and results of armed struggle, and the dangers to the political ideas, which we cherish, of underground work itself? Isn't it very often just a Boy Scout game? Adults carrying forward the excitement the child has when teasing fire or running round the garden for a game of hide-and-seek? Because it must be underlined that we have seen over the years the aberrations that clandestine activity gave rise to. We've seen, as in the case of the *brigatisti* or of the Red Army factions in Germany and Japan, how the means corrupt the men, how such groups become a law unto themselves, so infatuated with their own analysis, so turned in upon themselves and so cornered when these analyses prove to be incorrect that the only way out seems to be even more vigorous forms of terrorism. Maybe one day there will be a new analytical science called structurology, close to but not the same as structuralism. It would concern itself more with the study of the using of structure for its own end, the satisfaction derived from that. This – the need for structuring when involved in underground activity, because the matrix is a unit made up of cells, with information strictly channelled, with walls separating sector from sector, with a hierarchy which cannot be questioned– all this makes of underground work a very undemocratic process and it constitutes a structure which can be a very manoeuvrable vehicle for whoever happens to occupy the central nerve point. Cells, colonies of grave dwellers, are so easily exploitable. The hand demands no accounting of the glove. It is rather as if such a unit, to survive, must remain in quarantine. So we see the biological result that, as with other isolated cells, it loses some of its normal reactions against attacks from without. It becomes less immune to the sicknesses that every structure, every political party is subject to. It therefore easily becomes sectarian. And in a last analysis – what is it that makes an underground cell of militants any different from a spy cell, an intelligence network of the masters? Don't we here see the mirror and its own mirror image?

We should put our sights much lower. Maybe we ought to settle for the slower processes; maybe we must, very paradoxically, extend our confidence to the people and whatever mass organizations the people may throw up. Ah, but that means that we have to accommodate the very notion that our way, and particularly our goals, may be diluted or changed completely . . . since we shall be losing control over the evolution that we become part of. Isn't that what 'power to the people' implies? It is more important, I think, to know how to get from Long Street to Shortmarket Street than to go and write in the dust on the moon. The difficulty, Mr I, is not to learn to fly but how to walk on earth. So, if I may sum up: the struggle itself is a means of political awareness, of cultural awakening, ultimately of social and economic transformation. But to cling to the idea that we can make pure and honest militants is under-estimating human nature. It is subscribing to the fallacy of a theory which postulates that human character can be transformed, and that there is a measurable progress in the quality of human intercourse. The liberating concept is exactly to give over to the people the way a fish gives

itself over to the sea; and also, despite, or because of
the watery taste of failure in the mouth, to continue
struggling. *To do* without necessarily believing that
there ever was any sense in the doing. I agree, Mr
Investigator, here you also have the formula for your
most pure fascist who will kill or extort without there
being any reason for it or any sense to it. But that is
not quite what I'm turning over in my words. I mean
that a struggle for freedom and justice is such a natural
instinct that one fights for it, again in the words of a
Chinese writer, as the fish struggles for water. I am
intrigued though, by my interest for structures. What
I've just uttered with a twitch of originality about
'doing without believing that it's worth doing', or that
there could be an outcome, seems to show me that
therefore I am enthused by the form for its own sake.
By the word for its spine. By emptiness for its falling.
By the tree for its quality as an enclosure of light and
by the mind as an enclave of dark mindlessness. Why
do I bother to confess, to transcribe the confessions,
to package and parcel it in a book for you, Mr Investigator, if I believe that it has no use, that it would
not change a single gleam on a hair of a fly held in
the mind as the talisman of an image, that it would
not come up to the standards of aesthetics – beauty
and all that jazz – and that it will not even be a particularly searing human document, bringing nothing
extraordinary, nothing we didn't know or is not a banal
description of what has become commonplace in so
many countries? It does not unlock the passes to a
secret Tibet and does not have the flavour of one of
Sheherazade's reports to her lover late at night. Why
then? What is this obsession for feeling structures, for
flowing with the rhythm? Is it to escape objectivity?

Is it to get away from the strictures of treachery? Is it to loosen the grip that time may have on us? If I have no end I can have no beginning and therefore there can be no ageing. Yes, if there is nothing beyond the organic reality of pattern and repetition and illusion and rhyme and rhythm, then the idea of breaking a structure becomes exciting. The concept of the fuck-up is a liberating idea. Freedom is accepting unfreedom, denying that they are opposites, reading one in the other, and going beyond.

Today I am not sorry that I went through the experience, be it marginal, of deepening the consciousness of structures which underground activity implied. As a matter of principle I am not sorry about having been through any experience. What one has gone through becomes a new corridor outlining the innards of the labyrinth; it is a continuation of the looking for the Minotaur, that dark centre which is the I (eye), that Mister I: which is a myth, of course. The thing is to kill the devourer of virgins and not to forget to take down the black sails of the soul when rounding the cape of the home port.

Now, Mr Investigator, if talking shit was grass, I would have been through the donkey's arse a long time ago. Or if it were a sin, I would have been any old priest's lifelong joy.

I don't think I need to continue this exhibition of myself by weaving more tales about Okhela or about Solidarité and what they stood for. I'm abbreviating, but I must just briefly talk about three people I got to know in this way.

Some time after I'd been recruited for clandestine activity, I wrote, with a comrade called Yves, a paper on the aims and the methods of recruitment. Maybe I'll show it to you one day if I can find the hiding place where I've tucked it away. Still, I was recruited and the very concept of what I was to do was implanted subtly and gradually in my mind by my recruiters. The man directly responsible for me in the beginning, the 'elder brother' (in Intelligence slang he would be known as the 'handler'), was a young American whom I knew as 'Richard'. Was that perhaps why my name became Dick? It is a privilege, when recruiting someone, for the father or the elder brother to name the new member. He was about the same age as I was. He had been in the American Air Force in Vietnam, probably received specialist training while there, deserted and was one of those who found his way via Japan to a sanctuary in Paris. He had been taken up by Solidarité. He was bright, dedicated, thin but wiry, energetic and strangely effaced—or, more precisely, with the kind of face that would fit in and pass unnoticed anywhere. I saw him in different transformations. Not much was altered and yet he was a completely different nonentity every time. He left Paname quite some time before my débâcle, but before doing so it was he who conceived, at least in writing, of the Atlas groups for which I took responsibility and which were to be the underpinning of Okhela. What shook me to my socks was, when during my interrogation in Pirax, I was suddenly shown a photo of Richard. Well, two photos—front and profile—taken by the FBI in California somewhere. According to the date underneath, it was taken even before I'd known him, and chalked, you know, on that kind of false blackboard one must hold under the chin, was his real name. It makes me think that finally nothing is unknown. Perhaps somewhere everything is known about everyone and it is only plucked out and made to surface when the need is there to do so. So that underground activity becomes just an elaborate form of self-delusion.

The second person I wish to salute in passing, now for the last time, is Henri Curiel. Seldom have I met someone so single-minded and so warped by his single-mindedness. In my own vernacular I called him 'Spider', sometimes shortened to 'Spi'; because, yes, this theory advanced by the Greyshits and their colleagues elsewhere that Curiel was a KGB operative had crossed my mind too. It's not really so far-fetched. (He himself laughed when relating how he'd been accused, at different times, of spying for any and all conceivable foreign powers. But it is true also that some of his oldest friends quit Solidarité because, they say, he was using it as a vehicle to serve the Soviets.) He never made any bones about his total commitment to orthodox Soviet communism, call it Stalinism, and I often felt that he was a Secretary-General in search of a Party. Too, he did have his hands uncontestedly on an organization which, at its own level, was a perfect information-gathering machine, perched at the crossroads where many leftist organizations, particularly from the Third World, met. Not only was he in a position to know all about these organizations and to give them real aid – although I am convinced that Solidarité was never involved in violence, either for themselves or on behalf of others (Where does it start? What is the first step in the process ending in unavoidable violence? And was its non-commitment to violence why it was 'tolerated' by the French services?) – but it was also well situated to influence. Given

Curiel's ideals it is only reasonable to assume that he would have used Solidarité to achieve his goals, and I can't blame him for it. I would have done the same. I don't think he was trying to dupe anybody, though there were levels of confidence and there was manipulation: hence the 'Spider'. He was a fine and a subtle thinker, a master in the concrete ways to bring a mind to bear on political problems. He was an inspiring man: a limpid ideologue, and a man who remained committed to the better instincts in mankind. Never did he lose sight of the ongoing eternal struggle for justice and a slightly larger measure of freedom. Never did he waver in his belief that it is possible, if the right forces are mobilized, structurally to transform society for the betterment of humanity.

And the third, a man close to my heart, a Latin American romantic, the archetypal 'colonel'. Pierre was his name. Not his real name. Mr Investigator, when you write up your notes one day, take the pains to transcribe Pierre's story of how, as a dedicated communist even before the war, he joined the Republican forces in Spain and from there passed straight into the Résistance in France, which is when he attained the rank of colonel. He it was who organized the freeing of a number of resistance fighters, captured by the German occupying troops, from a prison in Perpignan. After the war he returned to his native Brazil and after some sojourns in Moscow, which were enough to disillusion him with traditional communism or the lack of it, and after disagreeing with the strategy of the Brazilian communist party, he, like Marighela, left and formed his own party called the Revolutionary Communist Party of Brazil. Captured by Brazilian police, he was very severely tortured. Together with nineteen of his comrades he was exchanged against an abducted Swiss ambassador in Latin America. It was one of the first incidents of its kind. They were flown out to Algeria, a country then still committed enough to revolution to want to accept them, and after living there for a few years he returned to France where he carried on his underground work. I met him there late in his life: a tall man, distinguished, beautiful grey hair, blue eyes, regal bearing, relaxed, full of wisdom and humour. He was still trying to enunciate what he called 'the laws of social transformation', but with humility, and a generosity and kindness and enthusiasm and a youthful spirit that I shall never forget. To Richard, in whatever deep cover, with whatever wild beard he has grown to survive, to Henri whose blood was splashed over the grey cement of Paris, and to Pierre,* who has lost his memory but not his peaceful enjoyment of life – I wish to pay homage. I embrace them.

---

*Pierre's son, who took over the reins from his father – not that the old man has ever retired – has adopted a little boy. Day by day the boy's genes are imposing themselves and he is visibly growing blacker. 'My grandson is looking healthier every time I see him,' Pierre laughs, 'and more and more like me!'

7

I am the Plague

My going, my being there, was contrary to all the principles of underground organization.

After receiving my false passport from Solidarité – Curiel was under the impression that I was going to use it for visiting Swaziland where I would be meeting White militants coming from South Africa – and after having arranged with him means of retaining contact during my absence, I flew off to Rome. I had also agreed with Schuitema, who had spent the period preparing for the trip in Paris and was going to fly to South Africa via London, also on a false passport, on the ways of coordinating our activities.

Before leaving I had a last meeting with Curiel who dramatically decided to tell me his real name. Like removing the last barrier between us. In one of those faceless apartments where we used to rendez-vous he wrote his name on a slip of paper, showed it to me, and then destroyed it. (He did not swallow it!)

Why am I now reminded of the kiss of death? We talked for a while. He had the knack of talking out of the side of his mouth without moving his lips – to frustrate lipreaders in public places. Over the phone he had a grey voice. He knew that he was being watched, of course. From time to time he changed the *centrale*, by means of which we kept contact, because it had become unsafe. Several people who had worked with Solidarité over the preceding years had tried to warn me off. They considered the group to be thoroughly penetrated. Watch, they told me, how they are 'allowed' to carry on their minor activities, but whenever they attempt a major operation it is always blown wide open. I was convinced that Curiel knew, or suspected, my true destination. At times, I thought, his hearing aid wasn't functioning very well. I shook his hand and found the stairs.

I arrived in Rome, where I stayed with one of our Atlas people. There I altered my appearance slightly, shaving off my beard, retaining my moustache, combing my hair differently and donning a pair of heavy-rimmed glasses. I went through my outfit carefully to remove any traces of my previous personality. Armed with my new, or rather used but altered, passport in the name of Galaska, I went to the South African embassy there and applied for a visa, which was granted to me without a hitch. I'd never met the Galaska who is the original owner of the passport – but a few days after my arrest Huntingdon, pleased as a cat who has been at the cream, showed me an extract of a communication they had received from Paris with the full particulars and the photo of the real Christian Galaska – an open-faced young man who never dreamed that he had a shadow who would end up doing time for terrorism. I booked my flight with South African Airways.

It was late July. The grapes were starting to ripen. My friend in Rome accompanied me to the airport. I was quite intrigued by the security check at the point of departure and watched the X-raying of my luggage, particularly since I had hidden in my luggage some very incriminating items. In the false cover of one book there was a copy of the proposed Okhela manifesto, and in another several newly printed blank passports of the kind used by Blacks only when crossing the South African border to neighbouring territories. We had thought that these might come in handy later, and in any event, they would have constituted a gift for our militants in the country, reinforcing their usefulness for Blacks who may have to leave the country surreptitiously. We had to win a place on the market. A very big, red summer sun was bleeding to death over the ancient city of Rome when we boarded our flight at Fiumicino airport. It made me think of Africa, as dust always does.

There was one stop-over in Portugal. What was noteworthy was that, after having been allowed to disembark and to wander around the airport, before being allowed back on board we were body-searched and our luggage was checked not by Portuguese security officials but by two South African security policemen travelling on the same flight.

It was a long, tedious journey. Some time towards the end, before arriving at Jan Smuts, while we were still flying over the withered Northern Transvaal, one of the air hostesses on board started a conversation with me, asking me where I was going and what I intended doing there. White South Africans are al-

ways keen to sell their country. I was acutely aware
of the security man sitting not much further down in
the back of the plane and pretended to be just a normal
tourist not knowing much about my destination. Her
name was Anna van Niekerk, and before landing she
gave me her address and telephone number with the
invitation to call her if I felt the need for anybody to
show me around Johannesburg.

We arrived and I passed through immigration and
customs smoothly enough, although my heart was in
my throat like a monkey in its cage. Now I suddenly
found myself outside the airport building, standing in
the shade of a pillar, trying to work out how I was
going to get into town. But I was light-headed. What
a sense of relief, of freedom nearly, after the long
night, after the tension of not knowing what was waiting for me. One could smell the thin, dry air. White
men in shorts and socks up to their knees and moustaches were striding purposefully through the halls.
Black men in loose-fitting, sloppy overalls dog-trotted
over the same floors, trying hard to pretend that they
were on an errand to somewhere specific. No Man's
Land. Another world. A world of genteel manners
and old-fashioned picnics. And a vicious world. A land
of harsh, dream-like beauty. Where you can feel your
skin crawling. Ever on that last lip of annihilation.
You had to shade your eyes against the glare of the
sun. It was with a sensation of incredulity that I found
myself there on a very bright, clear but slightly cold
winter's day. The three occasions on which I'd been
back in the country of my birth over the previous
fifteen years had always been dramatic. It had been
a shock every time to find one's feet back on that soil
and to recognize so distinctly the sounds and the

movements of the people. I changed some money, took a bus into town and found lodgings in the Victoria Hotel.

Then my foraging started. I went for a walk and, feeling that there was still too much of the old Breytenbach in me, I bought some dye to lighten the colour of my hair. Incidentally – that is how I later realized that the *boere* must have been on to me from the very first moment I set foot in No Man's Land – Huntingdon, after my arrest, told me of having found the very same bottle in the hotel room where I stayed. They must have been even quicker than the cleaning lady. I now had to find a way of alerting the person in Cape Town (who was the 'essential' link) to my imminent arrival. I did not dare to do so directly, so I had to set about finding a neutral person in Johannesburg who could effect the necessary communication for me. I also called Mrs Röhmer in Pretoria, who had been warned of my coming, since she had to confirm to someone in Europe that I had arrived safely. We agreed that I should take the train to Pretoria to meet her. It was wonderful to travel by train, jostled by the other commuters, an everyday face in the crowd; to flow with the movement, to stamp your feet the same way they do and to dip your hands in your pockets; to buy a local newspaper and to read the small ads page or the punter's tips for the afternoon races. Even, like a regular White, to find it perfectly normal that trains and station platforms and ticket offices should be racially segregated. I was home and nobody knew it.

This was the life! Yet, simultaneously, it was a disconcerting experience: I was the faceless face in the crowd, I was the invisible man. Around me there was the space of death. I was a zombie only, a visitor from another planet—painfully aware of pretending to be regular and accepting as normal the ways of an unruffled bigot. If someone had attempted to start a conversation with me, he or she would have found just emptiness behind the name and the how-are-you? What if I got involved in a street fight? The girl sitting in the same carriage as I (was it coincidence? Was she really innocently going to the same destination?) was a million miles away. My smile was dry and my chest made of paper. I was home and nobody knew it! It is perhaps just as well that I did not know, then, that I was shadowed everywhere I went, that I was never alone. Jiems Kont, ole Blue Eyes, told me later how he tailed Ashoop who had accompanied us to South Africa in 1973, how he loved to come as close as possible to him 'just to smell the fear'.

Röhmer fetched me at the station, we went for a drive, and I finalized with her the procedure for maintaining my link with Schuitema.

Days passed. I was at a loose end in Johannesburg. My part of the work was more to be in Cape Town, and then to follow up whatever developments might come from my meetings there. I phoned an old friend who was not related to my political work but whom I knew well enough to trust, conveyed to him the necessity of not saying anything to anybody about my being there, and made an appointment to meet him in the airport terminal near the main station. We met and got into his car. It was evening, with neon signs reflected on the pavement outside. We went to have a beer in a working-class pub, and it must have been as strange for him as it was for me to be standing there with the smell of stale alcohol and sawdust, men chucking darts in the background with grunts and whistling sighs, and to pretend that everything was just normal. He laughed and couldn't believe his eyes. (How much of my trip was to impress people like him? How much of it was an attempt to force a break in the contradictions in which I was caught up: the dreamer ensnared by political work—neglecting his art—and suffering from it; the exile who had never accepted the finality of his exile, whose roots were still in South Africa; the man, becoming a European, writing in an African language, with the world evoked by it, which no one around him understood? How much of it was suicidal? Or repentant homecoming?) He agreed to make contact with Paul in Cape Town and to arrange a meeting and a meeting place for me.

This was to take a few more days. In the hotel I received a call from Anna van Niekerk inviting me to go to the theatre with her. I accepted and had to play the role of someone being shown around Hillbrow, learning a bit about South African cultural activities and nightlife. She proposed introducing me to some friends of hers the following evening, to experience the typical South African *braaivleis*. She duly took me along to the house of two young homosexuals. It was a revealing and amusing evening. My story was that I worked for a publishing firm in France—I had to justify my interest in South African literature after all!—and they fed me snippets of gossip and conjecture about South African authors. (They also, to make me feel at home, played records of Edith Piaf and Georges Moustakis.) They were all three of Afrikaner descent and it was highly entertaining to hear them discussing (and disagreeing about) Etienne Leroux and André Brink and Breytenbach who, they said, was not living in South Africa but in China, being married to a Chinese

girl. Every once in a while, as South Africans tend to
do, they would leave off speaking English and converse among themselves in Afrikaans with me looking
the blank dummy since I was not supposed to understand a living word. I did learn in this way, though,
that Anna van Niekerk was having a very difficult love
life, since it would seem her husband had left her for
another man. Perhaps the two youngsters were friends
of her husband.

A day or so later – it was a Sunday – while I was
still waiting for my Cape Town connection to be made,
she took me in her Peugeot 404 for a drive to see
some sights of interest in the vicinity of Johannesburg.
Again I had this double-visioned experience of being
driven through a landscape seared by winter, the grass
all white but the sky so blue it could crack at any
moment, and yet to have to mouth the oohs and the
ahs of someone seeing this for the first time. So that
I sat there watching the land running through my eyes
and at the same time watching myself watching myself. (In what room, Mr I? Which brother? Listening
to what spool of the tape? Which closed circuit? What
empty mirror? What semiotic structure? Which or
what movement?) For the last couple of days I moved
into Anna van Niekerk's flat as she was away on one
of her periodic flights.

The Cape Town meeting was arranged. I was to
find Paul at a certain time on the steps leading up to
Jamison Hall on the campus of the University of Cape
Town. But first my Johannesburg friend invited me
to have lunch at his home with two other friends,
writers both, and for a few hours we all sat around
the kitchen table laughing and joking, with them being
amused by my naked yellow face, and not forgetting

to talk seriously also. Like self-respecting South Africans, they were wine connoisseurs and we smacked our lips; they stroked their beards and I my absence of one, singing the praises of this vintage or that one. We discussed books, your Honour. My friend is a fine cook and his wife is very shy. (One of them said, 'Perhaps we Afrikaners need a civil war again, with real shooting like during the Rebellion.') I was never going to make any attempt to recruit or even to inform them of the real nature of my visit: that would be abusing their friendship, but I knew instinctively and without even asking that they were going to respect my desire for anonymity. When later I was arrested and brought to trial they remained loyal to me and gave support to my wife, as they continued to do through all the years following. Whatever private doubts they may have had about my sanity or wisdom of the course of action that I chose, never did this interfere with the warm support and friendship that I got from them. I would step out of court with my hands in bangles and find them there, smiling and with their thumbs up. They are the Three Musketeers.

I flew down to Cape Town and booked into the Hotel Elizabeth in Sea Point. (The taxi which took me there was transporting another passenger, a middle-aged American on his way to some posh visitors' club. His presence irked me. But surely if he was what, in my paranoia, I thought he was, he wouldn't be getting into the same taxi with me?) From there, the next evening, I made my way first to town and thence by bus to Rondebosch and to the University of Cape Town, where I found Paul waiting for me, sitting in the dark on the steps.

It was a joyful reunion. We went for a walk through

the quiet lanes of that area (with dons dreaming in cool rooms of quantum and Darwin and Freud and de Saussure) as the *katjiepierings* – little cat's saucers, as we say in Afrikaans, meaning gardenias – softly spread their sweet-though-sad odour. I briefly sketched the outline of my mission. My young friend is by nature a very thorough and cautious person. He asked for time to think things over. I left the Okhela manifesto with him and it was agreed that he would facilitate my meeting several other White militants, some of whom we'd been in contact with before. I also asked him to be the intermediary between me and Thurston, which was no problem for him. Things were going well. (Those whom the gods wish to destroy . . .) Paul drove me back to the hotel on the back of his motorcycle and the wind touching our faces as we came over De Waal Drive was balmy. One could imagine, because it was dark, just out of sight in the bay, the lurking island where Nelson Mandela and Walter Sisulu and the other Black political prisoners were kept. I have a nostalgia for the smell of the windswept Parade late at night, perhaps with some oily papers in the gutter. I have Cape Town in my bones. Long Street runs down my spine.

Between meetings for discussions with Paul and other militants I found that I had quite a bit of time on my hands. It was early August, the vineyards were blind, but the weather so beautiful that I could actually go down to Graaff's Pool and sunbathe and have a dip and watch the old naked sun lovers who sit there leathering themselves like seals the whole year round, wondering whether the ocean liner whose white breath they espy on the horizon may be making its way to New York, and idly speculating about stock market prices. I did notice one young man watching me rather intently but ascribed his attention to other less pure and certainly not security motives. And once I went down to a protected cove. I was going to miss my regular European summer, but this was even better, brighter. And no one else was around apart from the whirling seagulls, a few municipal workers raking together and carting off a rich harvest of seaweed and a bored office worker in black glasses stealing the day.

Here the ocean could get very turbulent, a green-and-white rage making furious rushes at the coast and the grey clouds scudding along, whipped by a keening wind. But today, that day, both water and land were as calm as the stretch and the glitter of a smile. White sand. Waves gurgling at the jokes whispered in their ears by the rocks. A tape of laughter. I lay back, rubbing warm sand over my belly, losing my eyes to the impenetrable sky. Looking for shells I found nine perfect examples. I gave them names. The number nine has magical connotations for me. It denotes Buddhistic infinity. It is also the number of the years that Boddhidharma spent facing the wall of a cave after his notorious interview with the anxious Chinese Emperor whom he told, in effect, 'You big-shit-no-sound; you mistake merit for bread. Who I? No-know.' I made a few scratches on my mind, reminding myself that I must try to reinterpret the resulting scars in(to) a poem. I thought that, as one sees in shells, emptiness is the rich heritage from the sea. I thought of my father.

I also phoned, and subsequently met in town, another old friend, the Swami, and spent an agreeable evening at his house in that part of town which borders on the old District Six before White greed bulldozed that into oblivion, into dust-devils, and real estate developers started building 'quaint Cape cottages' on the slopes. With him I discussed a topic we had explored earlier during one of his trips to Paris, the possibility of starting a literary magazine which would group the work of South Africans both in the country and in exile or banned. I met his girlfriend briefly. Wind screeched down from the mountain. The weather was sickening for a change. (It is said that, during the Second World War, White soldiers passing through here on their way to the front sometimes had their sex protuberances sliced off with knives wielded by dusky whores in the dark alleys.) On another night I had an appointment with them on the terrace overlooking the winter-closed Sea Point swimming pool, eerily deserted in the moonlight.

There would be, it seemed, no problem to complete that part of the mission which consisted of finding two militants who would be willing to come abroad to take care of the trade union office we intended to open. I very much wanted Paul to be the White one, although he was also becoming more and more a very important figure for us in the country due to his abilities and his clear insight and his extensive network of contacts with the live young political forces. But he was seriously considering our offer. The Black person whom he had in mind to win over was none other than Steve Biko, and we were to travel to the Port Elizabeth area to meet him. I sometimes wonder if, had we succeeded in our plan and had Biko left the country with our help, the course of political developments in the country would not have been slightly different from the way it turned out after the murder of the leader. History is seldom changed by a single man. Biko was a powerful figure though, a natural rallying point for Black Consciousness and non-ANC forces.

But at the same time that things were apparently moving smoothly, with very interesting reactions coming from the chosen few who had a look at the Okhela manifesto, at the same time I started feeling that I was perhaps pushing my luck. Maybe it was the opening of the fourth eye. If it was, it came a bit late. I decided to change hotels and moved to another one, in Three Anchors' Bay, ideally situated in that it was less public but with a good way out the back.

One day—it must have been about ten days after my arrival in the country—I was due to meet Paul together with one of the NUSAS leaders he wanted to introduce to me. We were to rendezvous along the main street running through Sea Point and, as I'd done several times before, I went for a walk, roaming the streets, passing the time.

There was a little coffee bar that I had visited once or twice. As I walked in there that morning I overheard part of a conversation between the girl who might have been the manager or the owner and a client: they were talking about being harassed by the cops and it sounded to me as if she'd been approached by the police quite recently and was very reluctant to collaborate with them. When one lives like that, the way I did, one's ears become keenly attuned to any anomaly, but one has to keep a tight grip on oneself all the time so as not to go around the bend utterly.

One says to oneself: after all, not every policeman in town is on the look-out for you particularly, and there must be many coincidences. I was close to the corner, near to the crow. I remembered how, the night before, whilst wandering through the streets, I came across a Coloured man doing the same thing, that is, nothing, and how we both watched from a distance a party going on in a hotel 'for Whites only'. We rested our chins on the wall surrounding the hotel and exchanged a few bitter remarks about the poor looking in upon the well off, how it's the same the whole world over seeing as how it's the rich that get the gravy. (And the geese.)* Then we turned and looked out across the bay at Robben Island, which is like a ship of ghosts patrolling just offshore along the Cape coast, like a knife thrust of conscience, like a warning. With him, that anonymous Brown man, I could speak like a native without a name, not having to pretend that I'm a foreigner with this slight French accent. But there too, afterwards, I asked myself: how did he find himself in my way, as if by accident? Wasn't he planted there? And earlier still that same evening, when I was taking a stroll along the promenade running down the seafront, a car stopped just as I was about to sit down for a drink in one of the beer gardens open to clouds and stars, and two men got out. The older one of the two (looking like a seedy Jean Gabin) turned to me, gestured at the glorious sunset which was turning the sky into a mother-of-pearl shell from which the moon would grow anon, nacreous and globe-shaped, and said in French, 'How beautiful! What a pity that it will all be covered in

*In the Boland area there was the case of a labourer one night stealing and eating a certain farmer's very rare, imported black swan. Before being given a tough sentence for 'theft and wilful destruction of valuable property' the magistrate enquired after his reasons for taking the bird. 'I was hungry, *baas*,' he said.

blood.' And my first reaction was: how on the bloody earth did he know that I would understand French? What was this—a warning? Or simply a slip of the tongue? And what about that girl, the barefoot art student, I started talking to one night while queueing to get into the cinema? (The place was booked out: I never did get in.) I had been there earlier the same evening, killing time, idly taking some photos of myself in the Self Photo booth in the cinema's foyer. Perhaps I wanted a record of this fugitive person with the moustache like a black grin, staring back enquiringly at me from the eye-level mirror facing the stool. How come Snaaks, later, knew all about the girl and the photos (which I'd torn up two days later)?

In any event, I'm trying to describe to you. Mr Interrogator—sorry, Mr Investigator—that I was in a constant state of jitters, suspicious of any and everyone, expecting my good luck to come to a disastrous end at any moment and now, after ten days, intensely aware of my isolation and my helplessness if something untoward were to happen. Suddenly I could measure inch by inch the enormous distance between the southernmost point of the African continent and far off Europe which had become a haven of security.

Walking along Main Street, waiting for the hour of my appointment, a young and scruffy White man accompanied by an equally sloppy Brown girl came to me asking for money, pretending to be Portuguese— 'You know how it is, these people here don't consider us Portuguese as Whites'—and I gave him some. The funny thing was that later, after the fall, during the interrogation, Hendrik Goy wanted very badly to know who that contact of mine in the street in Sea Point was, the man they had on the photo with me. And what was it I gave him, perhaps a roll of microfilm, a capsule containing the secrets of life and death? But again—was he just trying to twist my mind? Wasn't he in reality one of their staked-out agents? Or was there competition?*

Sea Point is in some ways like a foreshortened illustration of the South African folly. The rich live there in retirement with their little scented dogs (there's a shithouse, exclusively for dogs, built on the esplanade), the hippies or the bohemians populate some of the less well-appointed flats, and in the backyards you find a myriad of Blacks and Browns working there, particularly servant girls who often fill their spare time by being prostitutes, and very boldly so I may tell you, since they seem to be quite accustomed to the fact that every White man prowling that area is on the look-out for easy nooky. I heard, after leaving the Brown man the night of our brief encounter, how he tried to pick up one of these girls. But she knew the colour of the hand in which money came to her. Very tartly she laughed at him, saying in a sing-song voice that she didn't 'fok ghoffels' (meaning Browns). The Whites living there mostly belong to a party which supports the idea of a decent minimum wage for servants; at the same time they form residents' associations to pressure the authorities to remove the Blacks, to

*Schuitema claims that months after his first clandestine visit to South Africa (eighteen months earlier) the CIA tipped off the Greyshits that he had been there. From that time on the *boere* would have been keeping Paul, whom Schuitema had seen when there, under surveillance (did the CIA give their South African counterparts a complete breakdown of Schuitema's contacts then?), and so they were inevitably right on top of me—still according to S.—the moment I met Paul. Seductive explanation, but it doesn't quite fit.

'clean up the beaches' (meaning to have zoning and segregation enforced) in the name of 'combating crime' and preserving Sea Point's good standing.

My two friends turned up. I got in the car. We were going to talk while driving, and immediately upon leaving Sea Point we realized that they were there. Paul saw them first in the rearview mirror and alerted us coolly. They were making no attempt to camouflage themselves. There was this big white Ford sitting on our tail. We tried shaking them, accelerating down around Clifton and tearing through Camp's Bay, up one side street and down another. Patiently they waited for us to re-emerge on the main road, and whenever we did, there they were again. We took the road hugging the coast towards Cape Point and crossed over to the Indian Ocean side of the Peninsula by Chapman's Peak. Let me assure you that we were quite panicked, our NUSAS acquaintance especially so. Paul claimed that this little game was nothing out of the ordinary, that it happened often enough. I wanted to believe that it was not for me that they were there, that since both Paul and Glen Moss—a person I was meeting for the first time—were known activists intercepted by the police from time to time, the tail was just a routine check or silly harassment or curiosity on their part about who the third fellow (looking like a lost spy) with the two students might be. On the other side of Constantia we decided to return to town, to suspend our intended discussion, and that I should by all means try to escape from our pursuers. We went back via De Waal Drive at a terrific speed with them never very far behind, and upon arriving in Cape Town I made use of a red light to jump out of the car and run into one of the big stores in the centre of the city. I had in my pocket a little red knitted woollen cap. Rushing down to the basement I put this on, took my raincoat off, and went out a different exit; and then, on foot, tried to get as far away as possible from the place of ill luck where my friends had dropped me off.

Late that afternoon I made my way back to the hotel on the edge of Sea Point, changing buses, going uphill and downhill, like one of those mental cases one sees sweeping up his own tracks, and of course my mind was now seething with doubts and questions. We, that is Paul and myself, were at a point of concluding our preliminary discussions with the other comrades in Cape Town, and we had made an appointment with Schuitema, who was operating in the northern provinces, to meet him in Durban. We were due then to take the Garden Route for Port Elizabeth and ultimately for Durban. It was important that we should do so if possible, lest all of these plans be abandoned or postponed for too long. I was to confirm the next morning whether we were to go ahead or not. Back in my hotel I paced the room, nervously glancing out the window at the sea, which was grey and stormy. Cape winters can change rather abruptly from one day to the next, and obviously now a storm was in the offing. How many boats had come to grief here? What treasures the waves must be turning over, and what skeletons! How the voices must have been choked! The foam there, can it be the residue of confessions? And when it's dark—what ghost ships, islands and whales bump into each other there?

It became dark and then, luckily, before I thought of putting on my light I peered out the window again. I noticed a car parked a short distance away from the front entrance of the hotel. There was the glowing tip of a cigarette. The white Ford was back!

I watched them from behind the curtains, two gorillas sitting there patiently and obviously not being able to withstand the temptation of sending up a little time in smoke. (Their doctor should tell them about the dangers of nicotine.) Which was a dead giveaway. Who would be spending a stormy night in the dark in a car along the sea front, not even fondling another's sex? But it meant that matters were far worse than I allowed myself to imagine. Our afternoon escapade was not a coincidence. It wasn't Paul or Glen Moss they were after, but Galaska, the albatross. Or Breytenbach. (But surely not me!) Did they know that I was in the hotel? And if so, what were they waiting for? Was the idea to give me more rope or to see what other contacts I may have? Much later in Pretoria I was to learn that the two ghosts in the car were severely hauled over the coals for their blunders.

I was supposed to have dinner again at the Swami's that night and when I didn't turn up a call came for me to my hotel room. I could give him nothing except a lame excuse that wouldn't raise suspicions with those listening in. Remember, I was Galaska. Your men out front there are making a big mistake! I can't remember what I said. Rain lashed the windows, the wind was blowing in force outside and the sea was rising behind the black wall of night to come thundering against the cement ramparts protecting the street running along the sea front. Would that it could rise up and swallow my enemies!

I spent my night destroying as much as I could of whatever notes I had. I had to lighten my luggage. Above all I had to get going. Come on now, do something! What are you waiting for? But I was strangely apathetic. First my stomach had to get used to the new situation. My mind was flowing with the storm. Does destruction exercise a fatal attraction? What was the best way again of getting rid of compromising documents? The hotel manager was not going to like these repeated flushings. Reluctantly I decided to leave my nine perfect shells, my beautiful nine lives, behind. It wouldn't do to be suspected of receiving messages from the deep. Did Skapie Huntingdon ever find them? And in what laboratories were they analysed to dust? I tried to work out how I was going to get out of the trap. There is a saying that someone is so weak he can't even fight his way out of a damp Kleenex. They never budged. They were burning up their salaries. Once, to test them, and without my dunce's cap, I risked it a few yards outside the front gate: the car immediately growled. I didn't leave the hotel in the dark for fear of attracting undue attention from the night staff (what, leave without paying?), but with first light I went down with my bags. It was a Sunday morning. No, I won't wait for breakfast, thank you. I precipitately settled my bill and then went out the back without being seen. But Sundays, dammit, the back gate is locked, so there I was scaling the wall and throwing my bags over to the other side. What an undignified way for a gentleman to leave, like a guilty lover! From there a very steep road was going up the hill, crossing several side streets before it ran, near the top, into the road used as a bus route from and to Cape Town City.

Grey was the morning, mournful and empty. Rain still came down incessantly, like it was going out of fashion. I had had no sleep but it wasn't only the cold that made me shiver. Water in the stomach. Was the intention to trap me with my cheeks bulging with marmaladed toast? Or weren't they sure that I was there still (my windows dark) and were they waiting like decent Protestants for first light before bothering the landlord? (Afrikaners aren't popular in those quarters.) Did they not know about the possible back exit? Or were they satisfied that no one but a servant would use it?

They must have found quite soon after my departure that the bird had flown the coop because suddenly, in these deserted early Sunday streets, I could hear their car going from one side street to the other. I managed to hide behind a hedge as they came round the corner and when they were out of sight I made my way to the upper road and to the first bus stop I could find. Trying to make myself small behind the bus stop, with hunched shoulders. Misery. A bus, luckily for me, turned up not much later and I got in with my cap pulled as low as possible over my eyes. And found to my discomfort that I was in a bus reserved for non-Whites only. There were a surprising number of early morning workers aboard, probably domestic servants going into town to prepare breakfast for their masters. How they move and watch while the Whites still sleep. Since none of them seemed to mind I just slouched down in my seat, hoping not to be thrown off by the conductor for being in contravention of one of our Apartheid laws. That would have been too funny. ('I'm just a stupid, colour-blind tourist, finding my way back to respectability after a night's whoring in Sea Point, sir.')

The bus terminus was near the Parade in the centre of town. I got off, and hardly had I started walking, my bags slung over my back, when the white Ford emerged screaming with fury from one of the side streets on to the Parade. I ran. They spotted me and as I was dodging between the rickety fruit stalls, empty now, they started weaving in and out, trying to corner me. Take this down nevertheless, Mr Investigator. It was like something out of a very corny third-rate movie. Rain swept the plaza, the deserted stalls, the squashed fruit and vegetables underfoot. There the false Coloured who is a false Frenchman who is a false South African goes running hell for leather with his possessions in a bag of which the strap broke soon enough, and here comes this powerful automobile like a blind beast howling around the corners, slashing through the mush, and actually pushing over some of the stalls. Smoking slows down the reactions. I managed to get away from the Parade. That part of town with its many one-way streets has a lot of arcades joining one street to the other. It turned out that I succeeded in losing them quite close to Caledon Square, which is the police headquarters.*

But now, what was my next move going to be? I found a public phone booth and tried calling the one person I considered safe and on whose aid I could count—I had him up my sleeve like a last card—but all I got was an empty ringing tone on the other side.

---

*And manage to lose them I surprisingly did. Years on in my sentence I met a fellow-prisoner with a natty appearance, shoes a-shine, etc.: an ex-cop. He told me how he begrudged me having to get up one cold winter's night in the East London area, to help man a road-block when they were looking for me. They were searching for me all over the country. I was lost—like Mr Eliot's cat Macavity.

I could not even think of reaching Paul. If they were
so furiously trying to get me they probably already
had him or otherwise would be waiting there for me.
Sunday morning in Cape Town. No one around. The
masters are having their breakfast. One sticks out like
a sore thumb with a red cap on. Staying close to the
walls, flitting from entrance to entrance, I worked my
way uphill past the last mosque left standing in the
naked District Six and on to the Swami's house. I rang
the bell. Had to ring again. Hard. Had to insist.
Thought: my God, what if he too should not be home?
But eventually aroused him and was allowed in. They
were still in bed in a darkened room but in his honour
I must say that he evaluated the situation immediately
and never for a moment vacillated in his warm acceptance of my being there and in his willingness to
help.

I was given a bed, a glass of brandy and a cup of
coffee, but of course I couldn't sleep. The same shivers
ran down my back. It was a feeling of utter lassitude
prefiguring the situation of a few weeks later when in
another bed I would be lying, shivering with all my
clothes on. I used the bathroom for removing my
moustache which, strangely, took more time and was
more difficult to shave off than the beard. Regretting
it rather. I thought I was quite the dandy with my
Latin American macho emblem under my nose. The
question was: where to now, and how? Not long after
my arrival the Swami's phone rang, but when he took
the receiver there was no one on the line, or at least
no one willing to say good morning and discuss the
weather. He informed me that he had had several of
these anonymous calls over the preceding days, so it
was clear now that a check was kept on him too.

There aren't, when you think of it, that many ways of getting out of Cape Town. Imagine yourself, Mr Investigator, in a similar situation at any time, and suddenly you realize how tough it must be for the camel to get through the eye of the needle. You're a marked man. Anybody can take a pot shot at you. And what normally seems such amiable disorganization suddenly becomes strictly controlled entrances and exits.

The Swami went to the airport to find out about the possibility of a flight out. We'd agreed that we couldn't try doing this by phone since a glum controller was obviously listening in, and he came back saying that the place was crawling with Greyshits. The port? Perhaps. But what boats were there? None was due to leave, and anyway, you have to go through police control again before getting into the port area. So the train then. But if they are at the airport and the harbour, surely they'll have the station covered also? The Swami had the brilliant idea of smuggling me out of town in his car to the first mainline station outside Cape Town. He was quite willing to drive me all the way to the border. Had I but taken up that offer! But there were good reasons not to. If he was being watched, as seemed to be the case, his absence would only confirm their suspicions and get him into really deep trouble. Also, how was he to explain his sudden absence to his employers, and how could he leave his family on such a foolhardy mission? I felt it incumbent upon me to refuse with my hand on my heart, bowing slightly. (In my mind, Mr Investigator, in my mind, much later, when I could afford to be polite.)

The Swami left the house and returned with, for

the first time that day, some encouraging news. He'd been down to the station and he'd bought and booked a seat for me, a ticket in the name of E. Christie. I have since often asked myself why he chose that name. Was it an obscure reference to his past as a Methodist minister? The astute idea he had was that I would not be getting on the train in Cape Town but at the first stop along the line to the north, which would be Wellington, my old hometown.

We waited until fairly late that afternoon. I felt cornered. Although I hadn't slept the night before, I was in no condition to sleep then: my nerves wouldn't allow me to. As it started getting dark, the Swami brought his car as close as he possibly could to the house, scouted up and down the street, and when we saw nobody I scurried out and hid myself between the back and the front seats. I think we were all very wound up. There had been several more of the mute phone calls during the day. But I was finally on the move. We drove out of town and tried as rapidly as possible to lose ourselves in the flow of traffic. In Paarl we stopped, waiting for time to pass, because we were too early, and after walking around for a while on the outskirts of the town we even dared to stop at a Portuguese greengrocer's to buy some fruit for my trip. We continued on to Wellington. The Swami had the consideration to drive past the house of my parents. They were no longer living there—they had retired to Onrus—but the big old boarding-house, 'Grevilleas', was still intact and lights were on in the windows which used to be mine and those of my father and mother. We drove by slowly. I stared, feeling the tug of memory at my heart and not knowing when I'd be seeing that house again, if ever.

At the station we had to wait some more. We were parked off to one side of the deserted lot in front of the Railway Hotel where some local dignitaries entertained my wife and me in a welcoming reception during our 1973 trip. A dog came to bark his heart out. This was certainly, as far as I could judge, the last time that I was going to be in the Boland for many years to come. One feels inexplicably safe and at ease there. Maybe the looming walls formed by the mountains have something to do with this feeling. But even that the people in power managed to desecrate. A very prominent and very ugly monument to the Afrikaans language (to Afrikaner power, in fact) had been erected on Paarl Mountain not very long before. The original movement for the recognition of Afrikaans had spread from the Paarl area. I never saw this *Taal-monument* but one of the fancies of the security police which I found very difficult to contradict was that I had attended the inauguration of this monument several weeks earlier, disguised as a woman. God only knows how that denunciation or observation got into the omnipotent files of the Greyshits. I assume that I was supposed to have been wearing one of those Voortrekker dresses reaching down to the ground and a *kappie* on my head – as these deep, sinister sun bonnets are called. How else could I have disguised my hairy legs and my moustache?

It was time for the train to arrive. I took leave of the Swami and the girl who'd assisted me so bravely, negating all personal danger in doing so. I must underline, Mr Investigator, that their aid was inspired strictly by humanitarian instincts. Truly, they are the kind of people of whom it might be said in biblical language, 'I was hungry and you fed me, I was ill and you dressed my wounds, I was in prison and you visited me.' It was an emotional farewell.

I didn't want to appear on the platform: I wasn't so sure that the station master or one of the railway workers on duty would not recognize me. Didn't I grow up with some of them?*

I got on and there was the whistle that I'd heard so often when I was a boy sleeping on the verandah during the hot summer months. That mournful whistle would evoke then all sorts of memories and vague desires. It is as if the whistle of the train opened an inner eye, or a little window inside the mind, on a wide expanse, but an empty one. The conductor came by, studied and nicked my ticket, and I settled down to sleep for the night. The Swami had made sure that I had a *couchette*. There was one other passenger in the compartment that I was booked in; I never saw him until the next morning. Perhaps I must have dozed a little, or perhaps I just drifted off to that in-between state when one is neither awake nor asleep.

When we woke the train had already entered the Karoo, that huge, central area of semi-desert that you come upon when you cross the Hex River Mountains from the Boland: as if going through a little window opening the mind to a naked land. But the Karoo is not naked.

Now there started for me a dream time, maybe corresponding to what the Aborigines in Australia would call the 'walkabout'. The land is magical. It was winter.

---

*My one uncle worked as an 'assistant electrician' for the railways. His job it was to take the lightbulb from the Black helper and to pass it up to the man standing on the ladder to replace the dead light. I also had a cousin, Kowie, working as a train driver.

The colours so subtly blended into one another that one believed everything to be washed and grey. Far on the horizon there sometimes showed a mountain range, discernible but unreal, and nearer one had the prehistoric figurations of hillocks and then the veld, as far as you could see the veld, with here and there mysteriously, seemingly without there being any cause or origin, a fire burning unattended: little red flames licking at the crystal-clear air. There weren't all that many animals to see. Even fewer people. Very occasionally, if the railroad stretched for some distance along a farmroad, one might pass a little Brown boy ostensibly on his way back from school, skipping along, lifting his bare feet very high so that one saw how nippy it must be outside. The train would stop at even the most insignificant little siding—a quaint name evoking some hunting feat, some flowers, a few dusty shrubs, a water-tower, the office of the foreman or the station master, an outhouse with a painted door, waiting rooms for White and non-White. The farm labourers one saw had the slight physique and the physiognomy of a vanished race: pale yellowish skin, prominent cheekbones, slanted eyes set deep in folds and wrinkles.

But people got on, stayed with us for maybe a hundred miles before they got off again. One such itinerant entered our compartment. He had no luggage, he was dressed in khaki pants and shirt, and the face with the ruddy skin of an outdoorsman was drawn and pale. He had red hair. It soon became evident that he was in pain. He would groan and clasp a hand to his waist. Eventually, to our horror, we saw a reddish stain spreading over his shirt. He opened it, removed a soaked plug, and showed us what I could only describe as a hole in his stomach. It was probably the result of a very recent operation. As he spoke only Afrikaans and I was not supposed to speak any I could only deduce that the old man had discharged himself from some hospital, desperate to get away from the theatre of pain, or perhaps only to get back home. Or was he on the run from some prison? It became so bad that I went to look for the conductor who helped him off the train and presumably handed him over to the local station master at De Aar. Maybe the conductor had phoned ahead from some small halt because the De Aar people were waiting when we pulled in. Another old wanderer joined us for a while. In broken English he engaged me in conversation. Suddenly he took from his pocket and showed me a box of South African matches, grumbling about how the boxes contained fewer and fewer matchsticks all the time and how – 'Look, see how easy they break?' – the quality was deteriorating. He gave me his address in case I ever needed any assistance: he was from Pretoria! (There are many drifters, wandering over the face of South Africa – burnt-out cases with defective matches.) I had to think of another old one I came across in Pretoria a week or so earlier. (A week only? So much had happened since then!) I had stopped off on a bench there to greet the sun. There was nobody around except for this old body, sitting in the shade of the statue of President Pretorius. He watched me for a while, and then produced some soiled items of underwear from a voluminous coat pocket (he had no luggage), trying to flog them! I was not in the buying market that day.

I did not converse with my fellow pilgrim, and time stood still. Nothing happening in this vast land on the other side of the windows. One was edging all along the rim of the world and one could see in that limitless sky all the graduations of blue, from a very dark, nearly black canopy right down to the white haziness above the distant horizon. Night came. Maybe because the land is so flat it seems to spread very slowly and nature was exhibiting itself in a peacock tail of colours as the sun came to rest behind the earth. There were bands of blue and then green interspersed with vivid orange. We were crossing the Orange River into the Orange Free State and the sky looked to me very much like the flag of that old republic. Under the high bridge dusk was gathering among the pillars over the water. One couldn't see much anymore. Bloemfontein. I've never been to Bloemfontein. I don't think I will ever get to Bloemfontein. Not that I regret it particularly. There must always be places on earth that one never visits so that they may remain embalmed in history books and discoloured chronicles.

And the next day we arrived in Johannesburg. The station is huge and cavernous. The Swami had had the foresight to lend me a coat and a pair of shoes in Cape Town, partially as protection against the cold of the northern provinces, but also because I felt the need to attempt to alter my profile and a shabby, longish South African overcoat of the kind that one takes to rugby games on a Saturday afternoon was about the best I could do. These I now put on; the shoes were too big. (I returned a few mornings later to deposit the Swami's possessions in one of the luggage lockers—maybe they're still there?) At least I wasn't reduced yet to selling my underpants and my socks. Skulking, but trying not to look as if I was skulking, I made my way out of the station, convinced that at least some of the beady-eyed gentlemen in the arrival hall, frozen in their watchfulness, must have been from the security police. Johannesburg station is a sad place with a few desperate prostitutes plying their trade, some down-and-outers trying to bum a drink and white-faced gentlemen trying to take a look (as long as possible) at your penis when you're having a pee. Security police complete the picture nicely.

In town, in Hillbrow, I booked into a cheap hotel still using the name of E. Christie, holding thumbs that I would not have to show any identity papers when registering, but it wasn't necessary and I made it safely to a temporary haven. What was I to do now? I could not even begin to evaluate the extent of the disasters that had overtaken me. I'd left Cape Town in such a hurry that there had been no chance to make contact with either Pretoria or anybody elsewhere. (I did succeed, thanks to an intermediary, in leaving a message of warning for Schuitema, cancelling our plans, but I didn't even know whether he was still free.) I didn't know whether or not Paul and the others in Cape Town had been captured. We had agreed, you will remember, Mr Investigator, we were on the point of travelling via Port Elizabeth to Durban and in fact we already had an appointment in Durban with Jan – which is the pseudonym Schuitema used – and together we were to finalize the Okhela manifesto in the light of reflections and objections made by the people I had been seeing over the previous weeks. All that was blown out of the water now. I didn't dare try to reach my friends in Johannesburg. If they knew so much about me in Cape Town, didn't it go back further and didn't they also know about my friends in the north? But to get to any border I would need help. Also, I was running out of money; my ticket was one of those excursion ones, which meant that I had to wait until a certain date before using it. You can imagine how isolated I felt, Mr Investigator. How I now longed to be the invisible man I had imagined myself to be in the beginning. Now I felt myself only too obviously standing out like a fool with a red cap over his ears. I even felt uncomfortable going into the street. It is one thing to be invisible – it is quite another to be a bat outside in daylight.

One night I did go for a walk through Hillbrow, though, browsed through a bookshop and, becoming convinced that I was being tailed when seeing the same man with twitching ears hovering near me for too long, started going uphill and downhill again, retracing my steps, using one-way streets, and eventually slipping into a cinema.* The film showing was one of those kung-fu pot-boilers starring Bruce Lee. Never in my life had I seen a kung-fu movie before, but one is never too old to learn to fly or to win the lissom heroine's hand by stopping bullets in mid-air and chop-chop eliminating three hundred and ten adversaries. (The Swami's shoes on my feet would have made my high kicking too clumsy though, too much like the final shiver a dying person may shake out of his trouser leg.) Before the main picture, as is customary down there, they showed a few newsreels and some documentary or other. The documentary turned

---

*No Man's Land with its sexual taboos and political paranoia (everyone being either a *boer* or a terrorist) can be confusing for the isolated, for those on the run. You don't know whether you are being picked up by a pervert or a policeman: the dividing line is so often non-existent anyway.

out to be on the so-called Recces, that is, the reconnaissance units, the first of which was commanded by my eldest brother John Wayne himself. So I found myself in the utterly incongruous situation of hiding away in a dark cinema hall watching my brother and his men on the screen jumping from aeroplanes with their parachutes blossoming in the sky like cherry trees in a Japanese chain verse, blowing up gullies and skewering blackened dummies with the audience applauding patriotically. We were ready for the Ruskies, the Chinks, the Yankees too, and all the *kaffirs* of Africa.

I remembered being told by Anna van Niekerk before going to Cape Town that she and her two friends intended spending a few days in a holiday resort in the Drakensberg Mountains. Not knowing where to turn, not knowing what was burnt and what not, I now went to her place, found her there in the presence of one of her colleagues, a steward working for South African Airways (and again the question crossed my mind whether such an unexpected presence was coincidental or whether I should read anything more in it). But I decided to push ahead and joined the party that was leaving later that same day for Natal. I could not broach the real reason for my wanting to go there. To them I still had to keep up the facade of the slightly cynical Frenchman who'd been down south and who'd come back minus the moustache this time – but still in his very own underwear – and who was keen to see where the White Voortrekker heroes had crossed the perpendicular mountain walls from Natal into the safety of the Transvaal (obstacles strengthen xenophobes) and maybe even where the Zulus carved out their kingdom.

It was quite some trip. Night overtook us. We were travelling in two cars. Van Niekerk's developed some engine trouble. I took over the driving and after leaving the high road we started climbing up the mountain, going along very badly kept earth tracks in the fear that the car might stall at any moment. We once passed some Africans along the road who tried to motion to us to stop when the headlights of the car fell on them. I was on the verge of doing so because it looked to me as if they only wanted a lift – perhaps their car had broken down – but I was surprised by the absolute panic the very idea of stopping seemed to provoke in Anna van Niekerk. The Whites live next to the Blacks and as long as the sun shines and the cars don't give any trouble and the roads are well frequented they feel no fear, but when night hides the face of light and the conditions worsen and one seems to be lost, the White seems to be convinced that the slightest contact with a Black would inevitably mean rape, if not mutilation, murder and mayhem. Brother, do we know one another!

When you go up into the high regions during this time of the year, you can very often see mountain fires. One whole valley seemed to be burning. (*'And the mountain a haze of flames. . . .'*) It was like looking down, from very far up, upon some mythical city, some prehistoric necropolis perhaps, a place where the spirits of the ancestors gather for an *indaba* and where they make little fires to warm their cold bones against the frosty breath of a winter's night. The next day you will see only windblown ashes.

The place we arrived at is just a hotel high up in the mountains above Bergville. There was nothing special about it. A big dining room overlooked the flanks of the purple mountain. But one could rent horses there and go for a ride up the canyons, accompanied by a guide. The Lesotho border is not very far away. This was what was at the back of my mind. (I have a mind crisscrossed by borders, the knife edges between safety and death.)

So we went riding, climbing higher along narrow trails. Still I could not take anybody into my confidence. Could I be sure that there weren't any super-*boere* around? How much room was I to leave for the little animal of suspicion fouling up the lines of my mind? Anna van Niekerk had told me of how she and her colleagues had been pressured by 'security people' to act as spies on exiles when abroad, even on in-flight passengers. They had been, she said, dismayed by the very idea. But surely such an overture meant contact, and the South African system is one of back-stabbing and blackmail. Was she really as naïve and as ingenuous as she seemed to be?* And besides, for once I had no confidence in my own evaluation of how people might react if I asked them to help me get across the border. They were good, loyal Afrikaners—never really doubting the wisdom of their masters, never openly questioning any of their decisions, conditioned to apathy and despair. I forgot myself one night over a meal and argued with them, telling them that they didn't know the Black at all, that they were driving

*Gordon Winter, ex(?)—BOSS operative, in his book, *Inside BOSS*, claims that van Niekerk was simply one of their agents. Her then later marrying my second brother bears out the point, he seems to think. Birds of a feather . . .But Winter's book is a sagacious and judicious mixture of real fact and true fact and false fact and non-fact and fancy and . . .disinformation?

around in the dark with defective vehicles, that, after all, the accumulation of injustices perpetrated against the Blacks must make any hope for a future of the White man inconceivable. There was no way, I said, that the ultimate conflict could be avoided. Remembering only from time to time who I was supposed to be, I would spice my arguments with references to French colonialist experiences in North Africa and in the Far East. The march of history is inevitable. Maybe it is not as mechanical as the phrase seems to imply, perhaps it also takes far longer than the human mind can sometimes conceive of, but I must continue to believe – if I want to retain any sanity – that such obvious and blatant iniquities as the South African masters impose on the majority, make their system anti-historical. Natural forces will eventually wipe it away. It was sickening to see my companions sitting there like beaten dogs thinking only of going to die in a desert.

An old man with a quizzical expression sat not very far off in the nearly empty dining room, listening to this, and eventually in a quiet way he just had to intervene. He was not at all of my opinion, although he could take a slightly more objective view than his South African cousins, who were stupidly squandering their future (maybe, he was implying, because they are *boere* and we all know what *they* are like). He was from Rhodesia, he said. He had come down to Natal in fact to prepare his retreat from Rhodesia. There was no more hope for the White man up north – the good sense came too late and because they weren't fighting the war the right way. They were now giving away too much, or not in the right way. They'd gone soft on the *munt*. (The gist of his remarks was,

I think, that the Blacks had—because of the Whites' shortsightedness—started calling the tune; they should only be taught to whistle psalms really.) He seemed quite a civilized sort of chap, perhaps equitable and humane in his personal relationships with his servants, but nothing could remove from his mind the etched conviction that the White man was entitled to rule because White equals civilization which equals progress which equals uplifting which equals doing God's work which equals being recompensed for it which equals wealth and power over others for ever and ever for their own good which they would accept if it hadn't been for the communist snake in the garden of Eden. ('Africa for the Africans? Not in our time,' snorted good old Smithy.) I had to be careful not to unmask myself in a fit of demagogic enthusiasm.

But these were futile splutterings. Everything was coming to a close; the various pieces of the jigsaw puzzle were being fitted together and, perhaps fatalistically, I felt that it was no longer possible to fit the odd-shaped blank piece that I am into any other hole than the one that seemed to be preordained for it. Choices were being made, held up to the light, and discarded. I was not going to reach the Lesotho border on horseback, not alone in these unknown mountains, nor with the help of these conservative young Afrikaners. I couldn't ask them to take me to the Swazi border either, for the same reasons. And if I wanted to use my last exit line, which was my return ticket, I would have to do so soon. So, maybe with death already in the soul, I decided to go, booked a seat on a flight leaving on 19 August, and then spent the last day sitting in the sun on the side of the mountain above a little swimming pool they'd built there, lying back, dozing, absorbing myself in the blue sky, stretching my arms up as high as they would go: it is surprising how long you can hold your hands in the air when lying flat on your back, seemingly forever – they just do not tire.

We drove back to Johannesburg the next day. There was no trouble with the car now. I recollect passing a road sign that said 13 kilometres to Jan Smuts Airport and the wave of superstitious fear that flooded me. Why the hell 13? Why now? Nevertheless – in the same way as, they say, the body knows about a pending heart attack quite a long time before it actually takes place, and in the same way that one senses an oncoming cold several days before it manifests itself, by the mental depression which foreshadows it – in a similar fashion, I think, I was already entering the loop of time which would carry me forward and deposit me at the feet of the interrogators. To play with for some time before feeding it into the grinding prison system.

I do not subscribe in any way to the theological concept of predestination. I do not think that man is a blind maggot with no choice except that of digesting more or less putrid matter, no; but I know I'm experiencing the law of Karma and in prison I learn about that of Reti but this comes later in our story, Mr I. Karma is not just a simple matter of cause and effect; it is an ongoing process without beginning or end, or rather, the beginning is the end of what went before, as the end is the beginning of what comes afterwards; and within this intricate and interdependent network of history and free will and sheer accident which together form a structure we call life, flowing always, flowing forward, the obscure stream penetrating the dark land, creating it by depositing its reflections and gnawing away at its crumbling banks, invaded by emptiness – part of all of this, I'm sure, is the fact that you can and do prefigure to some extent your own future: you cast a spell over yourself, you can confess things into happening, and I had been moving to the pulpit of Judge Silly and Colonel Huntingdon's subterranean cavities of morbid fascination for quite some time.

I asked Anna van Niekerk to mail for me some material containing notes of my travels through No Man's Land; I had already left with James Polley in Cape Town the first outlines of a series of poems called 'The Journey of a Guilty Fool'; and now I was quite divested of most of my baggage. I was ready. It was August 1975. I had arrived earlier that evening at Jan Smuts Airport, on my way back to France. I had known even as I arrived that I was blown, that they knew about me, and rather in the fashion of a small child closing its eyes hoping that in so doing the hideousness will go away, I'd hoped against hope that I'd be able to slip through the net which had been closing around me for some time. As I booked in at the departure counter, Mr Investigator, you took shape in me –

INSERT

The other night I dreamed that I had to return to prison for the outstanding two years I still owe them. What a calamity! My pluck was gone, my heart sank like a fish going down to the bottom to die: night was not deep enough to hide my defeat.

But what was it that mortified me so? The idea of

losing my freedom? No–I have learnt that a wall is a point (and a joint) of relativity. There is no more freedom outside than inside. Mine is total. The sadness of being separated from a loved one? No–seven years had taught me to be like an ox before the plough with each hoofplod like a lightburst of the heart they can never destroy. And I was a fatalist: I knew they have the might to lead me away again. I was not afraid of prison.

What then? My spirit waned at the thought of having to start all over the process of creating a liveable world for myself behind bars. Everything was gone. Like a philanthropist drunk with largesse, I'd liquidated all my assets upon release. My tobacco I'd given away to Doug, Mossie inherited my precious flask, to Piet I entrusted the task of distributing my carefully hoarded muesli, and the few books I had struggled so long to be allowed to obtain I now left to the 'public domain', our common library. *Nulla bona!*

I had to start all over from scratch and what a tedious process that was going to be! How long before I'd make A-Group again? With what was I going to buy a broom from the storeman, or a 'suit of clothes' that would fit? Naked as a shorn lamb, I was going back.

Except . . .All I had left was an inkwell that Yolande had given me, old-fashioned and beautiful even though the bottom was uneven so that it sat before me at an angle. But it was empty! Inside it there was only an evaporated reflection of blue. Like a memory of sky . . .

Part Two

A MEMORY OF SKY

which shows us the first person learning about the fact that Death is structured; passing through a second trial, wherein a writer emerges with raised finger; how the reader learns with pained surprise of the extent some people will go to to deprive others of their lives, but also how strong the urge to survive can be; bringing more news about security policemen and other monsters; in which said reader enters by the way of understanding the mazes of boop; showing that there is always action in non-action (wu-wei) and that one has to penetrate to the non-heart of movement to be still, for to be decay is to deny the law of decay; consisting of fourteen sections of which six are inserts:

1

The Maze
Have no fear: Death is here.

(THE ENTRY)

Nature has turned its face away from me.

It is 25 November 1975 when I am sentenced. I shall not be seeing the stars again for many years. In the beginning I don't realize this; I don't miss them; and then suddenly it becomes very important, like chafing sores in the mind—something you've taken for granted for so long you now miss the way you'd miss a burial site if you died in space. It is not natural never to see stars, or the moon for that matter—it is as cruel as depriving people of sound. I see the moon again for the first time on 19 April 1976 when, at about twenty-three minutes to four in the afternoon, I am in the largest of the three exercise yards, which has towering walls, making it rather like a well. I looked up and to my astonishment saw in a patch of sky above a shrivelled white shape. Could it be a pearl in my eye? Was it the afterbirth of a spaceship? No, it could only be the moon. And they told me that she'd been hanged, that she was dead!

The sun and its absence become the pivot of your daily existence. You wait. You build your day around the half an hour when you'll be allowed out in the courtyard to say good morning to the sun. You follow its course through the universe behind your eyelids. You become its disciple. The sun knows not of the justice of man. You know exactly where it touches at what time—winter, autumn or summer—and if you are lucky, as I was for some time, to be kept in a cell just off the main corridor with windows giving on to the catwalk which was not closed to the outside, you would have a glimmer, a suspicion, a hair-crack of sunshine coming in during certain seasons, but never reaching far enough down for you to feel it. I used to climb on my bed, stand on my toes on the bedstead, and then, sometimes, for something like two minutes a day, a yellow wand would brush the top of my hair. Of course, you develop an intense awareness, like a hitherto unexplored sense in yourself, for knowing exactly when the sun rises and when it sets without ever seeing it. With the first shivers of the very early morning, even before the call for waking up sounded, I used to get out of bed and try to position myself in that one spot of the cell where the warder could not see me directly and then for half an hour sit in *zazen*, and I could always feel in me a very profound source of light inexorably unnighting the outside; with eyes half closed I could feel it first tipping rose the roof made of glassfibre, giving shape to the trees one knew must be growing not far off because the birds talked about these trees, and then jumping over the walls

which were made of red brick, and generally investing
the day. It was the quiet moment then: the *boere* for
the morning shift hadn't arrived yet to come and stamp
their feet, and those who'd been on for the second
watch from twelve at night were nearing the end of
their turn of duty and so they were sleepy, perhaps
dozing with the FNs in their hands hanging limply.*
On summer days when you were cleaning your corridor you could see through the grill clouds passing
along the blue highway above the yard wall facing
you: boats on their way to a dream, bit actors always
dressed in white being taken to an empty space where
Fellini would be filming a saturnalia, a wedding feast.
There was wind which you never felt on your face but
which you got to know through its aftermath – the red
Transvaal dust you had to sweep up. There were the
most impressive summer thunderstorms tearing and
rolling for miles through the ether, slashing and slay-
ing before big-rain came to lash the roof with a million
whips. It was like living underneath a gigantic billiard
table. Behind the walls with no apertures to the outside, behind the screen of your closed eyes where you
hid from the *boere* – you still saw the stabs and the
snakes of lightning. There was also the defiance of
those singing their death.

Excuse me, Mr Investigator, these are discordant
thoughts, but I need to start with what is the most
striking in prison. When your sentence starts you are
first of all aware of being buried; that you entertain
the fancy of still being alive is of no consequence.
There is no death. You are buried to what you know

*FN stands for 'Fabrication Nationale'; it is a Belgian rifle produced
under licence in South Africa.

as normal life outside: the rhythms of day and night, of the seasons of the year, the rhythms of intercourse and communication between people with hands, between butterflies and *croissants* and dolphins, the million little things which weave the cloth your life consists of. This death world is filled with sounds you never imagined, steel on steel, fear and rage; with the pervasive smells of not very clean men (with no joy) cooped up in a restricted area, of evacuation and badly cooked food, of clothes worn for too long by too many different bodies; with the sights of nearness—grey, brown, grey-green, brown-green.

So let me try to be more organized. When you are sentenced your city clothes, your private clothes, are taken away from you. If your stretch is less than two years these are stuffed in a property bag and kept somewhere up front for the day you are released; if longer, your people have to fetch them or else they are destroyed on the premises. That is, of course, the theory. In practice over the years I very often saw private clothes either being claimed by the warders or smuggled back into circulation inside—in fact used as means of exchange among the prisoners.

(Maybe this is the moment to regale you with the way in which my friend Jerry got a bit of his own back. At the time of his arrest the *boere* stole nearly all his possessions. During his trial he wore a flashy jacket to court every day, with a blocked pattern, and this he handed in upon being sentenced. Very rapidly though, being an old ape, as we say, he managed to sell the jacket for a few packets of snout to the Coloured prisoner working in the reception office. Came his release after a few years and he wanted to reclaim the jacket, which of course was no longer there. Now, since it had been entered on the books, countersigned by Sergeant Prins, and as he was doing less than two years, he insisted that he should be paid an amount equivalent to the price of the 'bootiful' garment. Naturally he also claimed then that this was a very unique, hand-tailored, made-to-measure piece of clothing imported from France. After many months and threats of laying a charge for theft, the poor old sergeant just had to fork out the sum of money that my friend insisted on. I must add that the jacket had been bought off a hanger in the OK Bazaars.)

You are then given your prison outfit with a printed form on which your kit is marked. In Beverly Hills it was:

Jacket, moleskin	1
Trousers, long green	1
Shirt, green	1
Shirt, safari	1
Shorts	1
Jersey, brown	1
Socks, pair	2
Shoes, pair	1
Raincoat	1
Blankets, grey	3
Pillow	1
Spoon, stainless steel	1
Mug, plastic	1

I never saw the raincoat and in the beginning I was allowed to keep my own underpants. No dixie was provided because in Maximum Security one eats out of a plastic bowl. You could keep your mug to drink water from during the day.

Your hair is cut to regulation shortness. Since I was kept in isolation, mine could not be cut by a fellow prisoner and one of the *boere*, more often than not Nit Arselow, had to take this task upon himself.

You are issued now with your prison identity. In normal circumstances your booking in takes place in the reception office but in my case I was privileged enough (or exclusive enough, or enough of a sight for sore eyes) to have a warrant officer displace himself especially to come and enrol me in the ranks of the people of the dark. The initiation consists of one being fingerprinted and one's complete physical description being entered in a really gigantic book looking like the ledger one imagines St Peter — or whoever keeps the records in Heaven — has ready for all us sinners on earth. Literally every birthmark or scar must be written down. The beautiful side of this — administration getting ensnared in its own regulations — is when one sees them or hears of them having to spend days describing laboriously and with tight tongues all the various tatoos on an average Brown gangster being admitted. Depending on the gang and the length of time you have been a member, you can be covered virtually from the hairline right down to every single last toe and the balls of the feet by an uncountable number and an unimaginable variety of designs.

Reception offices are segregated, of course. From the moment of arriving there the process of 'breaking you' starts. White warders take their own sweet time. The prisoners are screamed at. Don't think you arrive in prison to be processed just like *that*. (The tall German who did time for murder with us in the Cape came with his lawyer to see the Officer Commanding a week before booking into the prison to ask what he should bring with him. The officer smiled, 'Of course Mr Humferding, by all means bring your sports gear and your electric shaver.' When he did arrive the reception *boere* laughed until the tears came as they kicked his tennis racket, his running shoes, his shaver and his radio around before locking them in a vault.) If you are transferred from one prison to another you may very well spend a day and a night and the major part of the next day in the reception cell, or the court cell as it is also known, waiting for the *boere* to finish all the necessary procedures.

Sometimes there is confusion, particularly in the Cape, over whether a prisoner should be considered as White or Brown. I've known people who've done time both as Brown prisoners and as Whites, and the majority of them prefer to be Coloured. The Coloured prisoners are 'stauncher', they say, more loyal to one another. One, Skippie (of Portuguese descent), went on a hunger strike of protest when he was dragged out of the Coloured prison (called 'Medium') and put in with the Whites (called 'White Males'). It happened in the Cape that a prisoner was 'demoted' to a Coloured prison. Ghana, as we knew him, maybe because of his dark colour, had organized a written petition to complain about the dictatorial ways of Tattie Swart, the section sergeant, and was promptly isolated and moved across the street. There was also the case of one man being booked and nobody being able to make out where he should be shunted off to. Until the sergeant in charge shouted in his frustration, 'Now tell us what the hell you are – Black or White?' And the man answered, 'But of course I'm White, my *baas*.'

These books then – because there also has to be one for your private possessions – were dragged up to the office in C-Section, and I was born. As prisoner 436/75. A card is made out with your number. In South Africa it is numerical, every institution (with its name on the card) starting the new year with No. 1. They later introduced a letter after the number which would make it clear that you are White or Coloured or Black. When I was moved to the Cape I became No. 573/77/W. On this card, which you must have with you at all times – it is your birth certificate and your calendar – is marked your name, your alias, the Church you belong to, if any, the nature of your crime, the length of your sentence, previous convictions; and convictions you may further receive or be subjected to while in prison will be inscribed there too. It also has – the one date you watch – your day of release. The poor 'indeterminate sentences' have no dates. Their whole struggle in prison is the attempt to obtain one. I had at least that. But my card stated ominously: Sentence: *9 yrs no remission of sentence*.

You are now a member of the clan. No longer are you Mr Breytenbach, if you ever were; you are now the fucking dog, the *bandiet*, the *mugu*, the mother's cunt. A prisoner awaiting trial is theoretically treated a little more leniently than a convicted person. You may receive food parcels from outside, you don't wear the outfit, and the warders are less strict when it comes to scrubbing floors and walls. But that, of course, changes dramatically once you have become a permanent resident, a 'hard labour'.

As a political prisoner you are supposed to spend about three months in Maximum Security in Pretoria, during which time you are visited by various prison officials specializing in what is called 'observation'. They may be psychologists or officials responsible for studying privileges, also the warders whose duty it is to make you fill in all kinds of stupid forms, after which, without any reference to the forms, it will be decided what kind of labour you will be allotted to. This decision, as also the decision about the prison to which you will be sent, is made by the Prison Board, consisting of senior officers – in previous years the nominal chairman was a senior retired prison officer or even somebody from another State Department, offered this sinecure for his declining years – the psychiatrist, your social worker and the spiritual worker or chaplain. That is the set-up for normal prisoners. For a political there can be no choice: he can only be sent, if White and male, to Local, and the work in Local is very restricted in kind. And again, a political normally has no truck with the chaplain. And they don't trust politicals to consort with social workers either (who are perhaps not security conscious enough?). I once accidentally met a social worker in a front office of Pollsmoor and jokingly asked her when I'd be getting to see 'my' social – after all, was I not human too? Was I to go through all these years with my soul in perdition and my family life in tatters without any aid? She blanched and said, no, they had strict instructions not to see me, and if ever I asked, they were to inform Pretoria, who would then fly down a brigadier to come and feel my troubled heart. But this comes later.

Your three-month 'observation' period is the occasion for teaching you the ways of prison life. South African prisons have the pretensions of being organized along military lines: you fall in for various 'parades': the 'sick parade', the 'work parade', the 'roll-call parade', the 'food parade', the Saturday 'cinema parade', the 'sport parade'; and in the criteria they impose for your personal appearance and the appearance of your cell they try to follow the military tradition too. The initial period is, then, what corresponds to boot camp for the marines when, quite consciously, your personality is broken down, to be reassembled in the right way, the 'reel Sot Efrican' way. The *boere* would say that you learn to keep your place, which is at the bottom; you learn about your privileges – which are few and will have to be worked and compromised for very hard, since you have to acquire the knack of wagging the tail – and about your rights, which are none.

For me it was going to be different. My 'observation period' was to stretch into nearly two years. I was also in complete isolation. Isolation meant never seeing another prisoner except when I happened to be taken down the main corridor and passed by the flunky employed there as a cleaner. It meant, naturally, never being able to talk to another prisoner. It also involved the warders not being allowed to converse with me, so that the talk was restricted to orders on their side and requests on mine.

Up above my cell, on the catwalk where I couldn't see it, there was a notice threatening the warders with prosecution under the Security Laws if they were to communicate with me. A sympathetic youngster on night shift once read it down to me, in a whisper. When I subsequently complained about the restriction to Brigadier Dupe, the sarcastic and uncertain man in charge of everything pertaining to politicals, he climbed the stairs with great show and feigned surprise at finding the notice. And when later, during the second trial, General Bliksem – small, slicked-down hair—was questioned by my advocate about the reasons for keeping me isolated, he was most indignant: no, no, no, he exclaimed, the prisoner was never put in isolation; he was just 'segregated'.

There have been enough studies made of the effects on people of long-term isolation. For my part I think I should like to divide it into two kinds. One is the obvious kind—parts of you are destroyed and these parts will never again be revived. You are altered in your most intimate ways exactly because all objectivity is taken away from you. You watch yourself changing, giving in to certain things, becoming paranoiac, staring at the wall, living with an ear at the door and yet cringing at the slightest noise, talking to the ants, starting to have hallucinations—without ever being able to ascertain the extent of these deviations or this damage precisely because you have nothing against which to measure it. And this damage is permanent even though you learn to live with it, however well camouflaged. You have seen them, Mr Investigator, those who have been through camps and salt mines and 'breakwater-building' (as we refer to No Man's Land's jails), and you marvel at their serenity and their conviviality. But just make them jump and you'll see how brittle their eyes are. You don't really know what they do behind closed doors, do you, Mr Investigator? You don't know of the bitterness under their tongues. Of how they watch the doors. Isolation has made me sick of myself, and sick of others.

Then there is the second kind: by being forced to turn in upon yourself you discover, paradoxically, openings to the outside in yourself which you have not been aware of before. You grow rich with the

richness of the very poor; the smallest sign of life from
outside becomes a gift from heaven, to be cherished.
You really see things for what they are, stripped of
your own overbearing presence. A blanket really is a
blanket, and though it is grey, it has a million colours
in it. A bird, when it comes to nest at night in the
gutter running round the outside of the roof, really
does make a very wide range of comments and it has
a rich relationship with its partner. You roll and smoke
a cigarette and its aroma is worth all the valleys of
Turkey. You find a brown chrysalis in the small courtyard, like a finger of gold – already it is wriggling. You
take it inside and you watch the fascinating birth of a
death's head moth; how it waits, still tame to the touch
of the world, for its wings to dry, and when it takes
off a whitish spot the size of a one cent coin is left.
No king was ever as blessed as you are. The days
aren't long enough! You learn how things, appearances, fit together. About illusion. About stopping and
space and you yourself just one vibrating pretence
among many. That you outline absence by placing and
fixing anything. You look at the wall and you see the
battles between Saracens and Christians for Jerusalem
and you see a beached whale and how it is burned
down for oil and you realize your eyesight is weak-
ening. At night you lie looking at the weak bulb very
high against the ceiling (you get to know the placing
of that bulb very well) and someone comes into your
cell. It is Fyodor Dostoevsky, scruffy and unshaven,
with black dirt under his fingernails, wrapped in a
coat so sloppy that he must have filched it from some
locker in a station, and he never says a word. You
describe your cell and all your little utensils to him

(how crowded your life is!) and it becomes too much because you must then also enumerate everything which isn't there: isn't thereness relativity? You tell him minutely about what has happened to the world since his departure. He utters not a word. Night passes like a whispering. You promise to finish for him that poem in *The Brothers Karamazov* which he never got around to writing, that one about the return of Christ. You learn about rhythm and about balance. How nothing is sacred or personal because *boere* come to *skud* you (shake you down: cell search and body search) three times a day, turning everything inside out. You learn that all is sacred, since everything regains the value of having been touched, despite the repeated desecrations. You lose interest. You sleep and you dream that Kasyapa sends for you to reveal to you the Teaching of the Sky, a dynasty of patriarchs passing nothing from generation to generation – taking care not to lose it. You dream that the mattress is emptiness. You wake and in the dark you write a poem to the man who held up a flower by way of transmitting the it, the only-all. You enter the temple to help him by holding down his head when he goes for the final somersault. You wake. It is quiet. Everyone is awake. Not a sound in the night but for the lone voice singing. You remember that this week only one is due for hanging. What a shame to choke off such a beautiful voice. 'Lord, I'm coming home. Coming home, coming home, never more to go . . .'

'You're taking liberties, hey?' the thick *boer* in charge of the night shouts. 'You're bloody lucky you're hanging this week, *kaffir*. Else I'd have charged you and seen to it that you got spare diet!'

(THE LOCALITY)

Maximum Security, or Beverly Hills, is a building all by itself. It often goes hidden under the name of Pretoria Central, but Central is a whole complex of buildings within the perimeter of the prison compound, which contains, furthermore, the houses of the staff, their club buildings and their sports fields. Until a few years ago the grounds were freely accessible; now prisons are more and more becoming armed camps, not so much as a security precaution against the inmates wanting to go for a spin, but as forts in a sea of uprising around. During the 'riots' in Cape Town it was a common sight to see carloads of warders, armed with shotguns, go tearing off. And when I left the workshops in Pollsmoor were producing rotating machine-gun nests, the first of which was to be installed on the roof of Maximum there. Pretoria Central is now closed off by huge, manned gates, and strategically positioned television cameras sweep the terrain so that 'control' can at all times watch the staff and the visitors moving about their business.

There are four prisons in the compound. First the original 'Central', dating from the last years of the nineteenth century, parts of which have been renovated. It has an imposing entrance: the gates of perdition. Some wings still have no toilet facilities apart from the ubiquitous slop buckets. There must be quite a few nooks and crannies because people sometimes manage to get on to the roofs to be shot down from there. That building is called 'Big House'. All male White prisoners who pick up more than two years in South Africa have to spend a few months in Big House first, for their observation period, before being redirected to various other prisons elsewhere. Short-timers and some long-timers do their whole stretch there.

Then there's the female prison where both Black and White women are kept together. Then Pretoria Local (over-)populated by the people awaiting trial—the so-called *stokkies*, meaning 'sticks', perhaps referring to their being 'behind sticks'—which also had, and has again now, a special section for political prisoners. That part has recently been rebuilt, after the break-out of Moumbaris and Jenkins and Lee, into a super-special high-security sector. The new place, I believe, has (for instance) artificial light only.

And there is Beverly Hills, sitting on a slight incline behind the others. The cherry on top of the cake. If one had windows giving on to the outside, one would have had a lovely view over the city of malediction, Pretoria. But there are no windows to the outside and there's also a very high wall encircling the building completely. In this wall is an entrance gate which is electronically controlled by a *boer* sitting, in fact, in the wall itself. You drive in, gates slide open before you, you are in a space between two gates, those behind you close before those in front of you open. Sure, there are also watch-towers on the wall. Congratulations: you are now in the space between the wall and the prison building—immaculately kept with lawns and shrubs and a few wild deer they allow to roam there. So peaceful. The approaches to the prison and the grounds around it are constantly observed by rotating television eyes. When I left they were to proceed with the installation of television eyes in the corridors and in the ceiling of every cell. Mount the few steps to the entrance. Don't be shy—knock! Use that big brass knocker. A little judas eye will slide open and an eye and ear will inquire after the nature of your death wish. Now a small door in the portal is unlocked and you are among the chosen few allowed inside to tread the sacred soil. Look at how clean everything is, listen to the quiet: like being at the undertaker's. Oh, you're not very far inside yet, only in the space separated from the foyer of the building by a grille. Once your identity has been ascertained by a man sitting behind a table, keeping his big ledgers, balancing his columns of death and life ('You have an appointment?'), with death winning hands down because surely not even one percent of all those admitted ever leave the same way again, the grille will be unlocked – not by him but by a warder whose sole duty it is to unlock grilles from morning to night. Keep a stout heart. You are at present in a corridor-like space with grilles blocking off either end. If you're just a visitor to the slaughterhouse, a spectator from another prison – warders from elsewhere can, by special permission, assist at hangings (once all the members of the Prison Orchestra were entertained in this way: some puked and others fainted – what fun!) – or one of the hangers-on of death (a lawyer or some such), you can turn left and move into the wing where the offices of the personnel taking care of the administrative functions are. Down there too is the room for legal consultations. Or you can turn right to where the officer commanding the prison has his office full of carpet and pass other rooms where warders on duty or off duty spend their time. You are welcome.

But you, as a prisoner, have to go straight on through a gate in the grille which has to be unlocked by the key carrier. Up a few more steps and now you can turn either left or right depending on whether God (which is the Nationalist Government) made you Black or Brown or Asiatic or White: left to C-Section for the Whites, right to A- and B-Sections for the others. Another grille. Sounds vary from gate to gate. (You could, lying in your cell, follow the progress of an officer through the building just by the foot-stamping of his underlings.) One of the clowns who passes for a warder has attached to the top of this grille a small *pawp-pawp* hooter of the kind you sometimes fix to your bicycle and this is then squeezed to obtain the attention of the *poisan*, that is, the Black warder whose task in life it is to look after that particular gate – 'He won't get away from me, *baas*.'

You are home. C-Section. Of course, you will be taken even deeper into the labyrinth to your *own* room. Another steel-plated door will have to be opened to let you into your small corridor and from there your door has to be unlocked so that you can finally find yourself in your cell. There is a corridor, similar to the long one making up C-Section, running down the other side of the building, from which A- and B-Sections lead. On that side there are many more cells, big ones too, for all the Black prisoners condemned to die are kept there.

Both these corridors have at the other extremity doors locking off the access to the stairs leading up to the gallows. Sometimes I was employed in cleaning that end of the corridor (travelling to China in my mind) and I'd go right to the fatal gate. It was a sombre area. People believed that it was haunted. 'I'm not afraid of any ghost,' a young *boer* on night duty once said to me, seriously, bravely. 'If I see him, I'll shoot the shit out of him with my gun here.' The steps lead to a room called the 'preparation room', where the final little touches are put to those being prepared for departure – pulling a shirt straight, making sure that a hood fits snugly (neatness counts, you know: it forms character), and from here, this antechamber, this terminus, the door opens in to the execution place itself. Back of that again, but at ground level, is the area with big washbasins and tables with little furrows allowing blood to run off them. This is the space, then, where the bodies are sluiced down and dissected if necessary. In any event, the doctor assisting has to make a little cut in the neck to verify the cause of death. Here too are the big ice boxes in which the bodies can eventually be kept. Beyond that there is the workshop where the bodies are put in coffins. From entrance to 'over-and-out' not more than, say, 200 yards. Functional, Mr Investigator, what?

For your unpublishable information I add that a catwalk frames this whole area. The catwalk covers the corridors (it is a grid) and from there the alligators (as the *boere* are also called) look down into every cell. Down a part of C-Section the catwalk is open to the big yard, and if you are in that part, the winter wind will fill the cells at night with its bitter cold. Windows, set high in the walls, giving on to the catwalk, have to remain open. The catwalk *boere* are armed with FNs. (Black and Brown *boere* are issued with ·303s; from warrant officer up, the staff are entitled to pistols – all of these apart from the shotguns, riot guns and light machine guns locked away in the arsenal.) They used to have walkie-talkies too – and kept one awake the whole night with their obscene chattering – but the whole place has since been equipped with a two-way intercom system.

Let me give you an example of why their inex-

perience made me nervous. One winter night a poor
sod up there complained of the cold, and to illustrate
his point he passed his firearm down through the narrow window, barrel first, just holding on to the butt.
'See, if you touch the metal, your hands will stick to
it, frozen stiff!' . . .All it needed was a good tug. (And
then: I'd shoot my way through the door shoot my
way through the grille shoot the *poisan* shoot my way
through the grille shoot the *poisan* shoot my way
through the grille shoot my way through the grille
shoot the nightshift-member-in-command shoot my
way through the door shoot right through the television the wall the night go shoot Big Chief Sitting
Bull himself so that the blubber and the sighs leaking
from him can blot his miserable volumes of repressive
decrees. . . .But they are given only six bullets at a
time, I believe.) Set in the floor of that part of the
catwalk, about 50 cm. wide, overhanging the cells,
were small, oblong, bullet-proof windows through
which the *boere* could observe the 'blind angle' area
underneath.

Finally, to give you an idea of the Hills' accom-
modation – it holds probably up to about two hundred
and thirty people at a time, nearly all of whom are
Black – that is Black and Brown and Asiatic – and a few
Whites. I don't think there are ever more than four
or five White 'condemns' at any one time. Plus the
politicals in observation, again never more than one
or perhaps two. Stefaans is also kept there – Tsafendas,
who's been there since the beginning of the sixties
without ever having been tried, and who has not a
dog's hope of getting out as long as the present regime
lasts. Apart from the warders manning the watch-towers, the television room, the entrances, the catwalk,

there is also permanently at least one warder locked
up in every sub-section (C2 for the Whites) where the
'condemns' are held, to keep them under twenty-four-
hour surveillance. The particularity of Beverly Hills,
if you are a White prisoner, is that, for the average
of five *mugus* they had there during my time, they
had a day staff of fifteen *boere* looking after us. Bored
stiff they were. Polishing their shoes, telling dirty
jokes, chucking a ball about the yard, just getting up
every now and again (in force) to go and take a prisoner
and his cell apart.

On two occasions during my stay other White prisoners were brought up there. (There is always one
White cleaner, a short-timer from Central 'lent' to the
Hills.) These were the so-called 'Springboks', escape
artists who had 'taken the hole' more than once from
other institutions and were considered to be either
very dangerous or else were sent to Maximum for
more severe forms of punishment. A rough lot of chan-
cers they were. It was amusing to listen to their
stories – since they were each in his own single cell
they had to shout to be heard, and one profited by
this; you were, in a manner of speaking, sitting in the
circle. (But like hawks the *boere* watched me to prevent me from participating.) They would moralize,
'We should have been beaten with sticks when we
stole our first bicycle, then we wouldn't be here now!'
Or reminisce about films they'd seen (nearly always
in prison), depicting the Second World War, for instance. And patriotic! One informed his mates that he
knew for a fact that South African fighter pilots are
the best in the world. 'Did you see in that war flick
the way they drive their planes sitting *outside* the
cockpit, just like that? They fly them bareback, I say.'

Or brag about their achievements in sport. One claimed to *skommel* ('shake', meaning to masturbate) for Western Transvaal's second team! And in this way too I heard about how one of them stood out one morning during the 'requests and complaints' parade and handed in a written request asking to be released for two weeks only (and to be issued with a rifle) 'to go and kill Idi Amin'. Since these fellows were deprived of cigarettes, we worked out by sign language – right under the nose of the *boer* accompanying me to the bathroom which was down their corridor (C3) – a way for me to leave them some *entjies* (little ends: cigarettes) and *scratch* (matches). Their dirty clothes were thrown in a corner of the bathroom. I'd have the necessary articles in my pockets, undress (with the *boer* watching me glassy-eyed), put my pants on the same pile, and after washing just put on another pair of shorts.

There were always empty cells enough to take in detainees falling under the control of the security police, but who were in fact also having to submit to the prison regime and the prison staff, as happened during the detention of the people involved in my trial. Once, and once only during my stay there, five or six Black political detainees were lodged in C-section. A *poisan* was then stationed in the corridor, basically to eavesdrop as they were talking to one another from cell to cell in Sotho or Zulu. I believe they were from an outfit called the Azanian People's Organization, and I don't think very much came of their trial: their detention was probably already the intended punishment. They kept up good spirits while there, exercising in unison under the leadership of one of them, engaging the *boere* in talk quite often. They were all students, way above the intellectual level of their keepers, and it was funny to hear them manoeuvring the *boere* until they had them talking about their motorcars or about their girlfriends.

It was a period when I lodged in the 'suite' on the main corridor – someone else was occupying C1 – so that for my ablutions I had to be taken past the cells where the Blacks were kept to the bathroom of C3. It was quite a palaver. Their windows (that part of the door which was barred only, and the small window each cell had looking onto the corridor – because there were no windows to the outside) had to be blocked out with newspapers every morning before I could pass. This was to obviate any possibility of our communicating or even seeing one another.

I was kept in two different cells during my stay in Beverly Hills. C-Section consists of a long main corridor running down the length of one of the wings of the building, with three side corridors, called C1, C2, and C3, leading off this main corridor to the left. To the right were the offices used by the warders, the store room, the visiting rooms and two other rooms which in fact were used as cells also. In earlier years these served as dormitories for Black warders going on duty or coming off duty at midnight. I was kept either in C1 or in one of the cells giving directly onto the main corridor. The side corridors are separated from the main corridor by a steel plate reaching about 13 feet high, with just enough space at the bottom to allow one to slide one's spoon or one's mug through.

Upon entering C1 there was a bathroom immediately on the right which also had a toilet used by the warders, and then two small single cells. On the left were two single cells and a third door which gave onto a slightly bigger space converted, incongruously enough, into a little chapel: two wooden benches, one wooden pulpit. At the other end this short corridor was barred by a steel door plus a steel grille which, when open, gave access to the small walled courtyard which was exactly 6 yards wide by 9 yards long. It had running round the four sides cement paving, and the centre consisted of what could only pass for a little handkerchief of soil: a minute lawn and four flower beds. In one corner there was a white rose bush and in the other a red. Despite the most scientifically dosed mixtures of tobacco and water I never quite managed to rid the roses of plant lice. In between these two I had some carnations, flourishing in the shallow sandy soil. They never stopped flowering. Religiously every night Arselow picked one flower which he carefully fitted *inside* his cap before putting it back on again. I assumed that he wanted his hair to smell nice, but in fact he was smuggling out the flowers to offer one every day to his (illicit) sweetheart. I also had a tomato bush bearing small sweet fruit. I remember eating a tomato the morning Engelbrecht and Fourie were hanged, how fresh it tasted, and my being very aware that they would never eat tomatoes again. But after I'd mentioned the existence of the tomato bush in a letter to my mother, the brigadier had it removed immediately.

I was the gardener there. One learns quickly to try and make your time outside stretch by any possible means. When I had to water my little kingdom it had to be done by bucket, which I had to fill up in the bathroom, so naturally I took as long over this as I possibly could. In the same way when it was the season for planting, because it was never the season for harvesting, one would spend as much time as one could wheedle out of them turning over with a stick the soil which was only about a foot deep—underneath there was cement again—making your little holes, planting your seeds, doing all you can to dissect time with your fingers the way one would eat a fish off its bones.

The brick walls around the courtyard reached as high as the catwalk, and they were closed over the top by a very heavy wire grid resting on steel beams and crossbeams, so that you never saw the sky unimpeded, but always blocked off in small squares. These apertures were just big enough to allow a bird as big as a dove to be able to enter, looking for seeds, but it could not go out again once it was inside. In this way we caught several birds which had hurt themselves attempting to get out. One of these I was allowed to keep for a short while as a pet. For a few days it lived under my bed, sharing my food, watching me with a smooth eye. The wagtails though had no problem in getting in and out. Cheeky chaps in their grey morning suits, like ushers for a high-class wedding. Or slightly navicular lamps for burning oil in ancient shrines. In reality they were quite tame and flew right into the prison, emitting the most eery and beautiful tones which I learned to imitate. They are very inquisitive little beasts. When you lure them by making the same sounds they come as close as they can, tilting their heads, trying to find their mysterious Mr Bird. They never tired of the game. I wondered sometimes whether in some obscure part of their imagination they actually saw me as just a very obscene, bloated bird without wings. Maybe one of them was even trying to woo me!

On the C-Section side there were three courtyards: the small one which I described to you, belonging to C1, also had a small balcony protruding above the wire grid. On this a *boer* would take position with his firearm when I was in there with another *boer*, doing my exercises. A second, slightly larger courtyard, was for the use of C2, that is the 'condemns'. And then a fairly large one for C3. That one, perhaps because it was so big, was not wired over. The courtyards had not always been covered. That only happened after the one and only escape ever from Maximum Security – by an ex-policeman, due to be hanged, called Franz von Staden, who made his way from the C1 courtyard on to the wall, and from there he got away. At that time the wall around the building didn't exist either. Even so it was believed that he had been given a help-me-up by one or more warders. His freedom did not take him very far since he went straight to the station where an off-duty policeman recognized him and re-arrested him promptly. He also was among the many who tried to commit suicide before his execution by diving head first from his bunk into the cement floor. Not successfully so. This is one of the reasons the death candidates are watched continuously while waiting to be killed: so that they do not deprive the State of its rightful vengeance.

The cell itself, because I want to invite you right inside, Mr I, could not have been much larger than 6 feet: I could just barely brush the walls with my arms outstretched. In length it must have been about 9 feet. But for what it lacked in floor space it made up in depth: it was a good 16 feet high, with just open space for the last 6 feet, blocked off from the catwalk by a wiremesh. It had a steel door with again, from chest height, meshed openings between bars. The cell had one bunk set into the wall itself, with on the bunk a thin mattress. At the head of the bunk there was another small wooden plaque bolted into the wall, on which you were supposed to fold your clothes neatly. Next to that, hollowed out in the wall, was a small water fountain. You pressed the knob in the wall above it and water squirted into the receptacle. Next to that there was the toilet bowl, without any lid, activated by a wire loop just protruding from the wall. You hooked a finger through and you pulled. (On Sundays, immediately after lunch, the Black prisoner cleaners used to gather on the other side of that wall for a religious sermon, led by a visiting preacher – probably telling them to accept their fate, that the White man's ways are mysterious because they are the ways of God – and they sang the saddest dirges. One of them could wriggle the wire leading to my throne. I would bend and squint down the wire through the conduit and just barely perceive, pressed to the other end, a friendly black eye. I would jiggle it and he would respond likewise. It was like touching a finger. We communicated. It was also like a monkey groping behind a mirror after its own image.) The floor cement. The walls painted an off-white.

The whole prison was sagging slightly: it had been built not all that many years previous to my arriving there on a site which apparently had been used as a rubbish dump, so the foundations were not very solid. There were already cracks in the walls.

The other cell, the one on the main corridor, was much larger – consisting in fact of two rooms communicating. In one room there was a bed, a small table with a chair, and a little wooden cupboard. The other room was entirely bare except for a wash basin and a contraption they had built specially for toilet purposes. They'd given me a bucket which was inserted in some kind of a box that one could cover. In the mornings then, I had to take the bucket and, accompanied down the corridor, I had to go and empty it in the toilet of C1 bathroom. I don't think they particularly appreciated my referring to this morning ritual as 'bringing the Brigadier's breakfast'.

Those were my two living spaces. The floors of the two-roomed apartment, if I may call it that, were covered with plastic tiles of the same kind as those in the main corridor, and these had to be polished and kept shiny. But so also had the cement floors in C1. You had to be able to mirror your face in it. That was my Sisyphus task: making of my floor a mirror which could capture and return my real face—which would immediately be walked over and sink back into greyness: washing it, taking off the old polish, putting on some new, using the brush first with swaying shoulders, and then moving over it again and again on your 'taxis', which are little squares of folded blanket. We used old blankets or old mats for that purpose. I've travelled many miles, Mr Investigator.

(THE WAY)

Your whole life in prison is regulated by rhythms, and the breaks in rhythm, the exceptions to these. You adapt yourself to the rhythm. (You have no choice but to.) Adaptation becomes a factor of security: it is part of the process we describe as 'institutionalization'—meaning that the ups and downs and the reference points of every day become your territory and you hate any intrusion, anything out of the ordinary happening, even if under other circumstances this happening would have been felt as something pleasant, like an unexpected visit. The routine existence becomes a shell and you withdraw into it. The *boere* know this attitude and they know how to play with it. By making you skip one meal they in fact destroy your peace of mind for many days. When you are used to being unlocked at a certain time and suddenly you're not, everything is upside down. You go grovelling for the most insignificant thing—in fact for security—for your hand-holds on reality. You lose face. You become weaker *vis-à-vis* the warders. I've heard a 'condemn', Skollie, due to be destroyed in two weeks' time—and the inevitability of death apparently did not disturb him—go into a screaming and weeping fit, banging his head against the door, because he didn't get, that Wednesday, the Louis Lamour westerns he'd requested, but some other junk like Tolstoy. He read only westerns.

Rhythms—understanding them, to some extent using them—these also are your means of survival in prison. It is the way you chop up time in manageable entities. There is the rhythm of every day, that of the weeks, that of the months, and then the years. Living from pulsebeat to pulsebeat, recognizing the salients particular to the unit, be it a month or a year, is a way of putting these behind you, allowing the possibility to say to yourself: so many down so many more to go. And you live for these recognizable points; you look forward to them.

But one's conception of time is not an immutable faculty. Some periods are far longer than others. The first days, for instance, as you lie there 'eating head', are interminable. You never expect to survive the first month. The first year, once you've been given your go, rears up in front of you like an unclimbable mountain – and you say to yourself: if one year is as bad as this, how in the name of King Kong and I am I going to survive the other eight? (Prisoners are obsessed by time. One 'does time', or you push it. You are a 'timer'. The best wish you can emit is: *roll on time!* We used to say that magistrates and judges are most spendthrift with other people's time: they are time stealers. We also described prison officials attempting rehabilitation as baboons trying to repair broken watches.)

Still, the same events coming around again, the rhythms being repeated, the familiarity of your situation – these deaden you to the passing of time. You look down from the bridge and you don't remember any water having passed under it. The past has the taste of water and you can't imagine now why it was so traumatic then. You haven't aged: the years were empty. People come and go, the equations remain the same. You forget perhaps that you were then a different person, that you have become that entity which inhabits this time which consists of clearly defined patterns, repetitions, the same again and again and again. You yourself are purified or reduced to some other personality.

This, the texture of life in prison, the absence of texture, or at least the way you experience it, will be different from one jail to another. It will depend on the stage you have reached in your time. There will also be regional differences between, say, the Transvaal and the Cape. What remains the same is the diet, the clothes you wear, and inevitably the type of relationship you have with authority.

*   *   *

In Pretoria Maximum the day started off at 6 o'clock when someone would be coming around to switch on your light and take a peep at you through the bars on the door. You get up, make your bed the regulation way, dress, and maybe half an hour later two people would be doing the rounds again—this time to count you. The door between C1 and the main corridor is opened with a bang, a voice shouts at you to 'stand to!' and you show your face behind the bars. You also say, 'Good morning, sir.' Once this ritual is completed, provided the figures check with those of lock up time of the night before, the *boer* on duty would return and unlock you. You now proceed to the bathroom with your toothbrush, your soap and your towel. You have recovered your shoes which had to be left outside your cell door for the night. (When I was rooming off the main corridor and had to be taken to C1 for a bath, I always used to see—during a certain period—a shoe and next to it a *leg* and shoe parked in front of one of the cells. The temporary resident there at that time, obviously minus a leg, would remain locked up until I'd finished my ablutions and had disposed of the Brigadier's breakfast. This *bandiet* one day casually told the *boere* to have a look inside his artificial leg, where he had squirrelled away R25.)

The warder hands you the razor which was kept in his office, and under his supervision you wash, shave the reflection in the dim metal plate, brush your teeth, and are taken back to your cell to be locked in.

Another half hour would pass and again there's the whole rigmarole of unlocking you. This time the cleaner confined to the main corridor would deposit your morning graze just outside the main door. You could see his pimply prison feet in the gap between steel partition and floor. On the one foot was tattooed *lets run* and on the other *to hell*. The door is now unlocked, you take in your breakfast (stealing a quick look up the corridor to try and see another inmate going through the same motions), take it to your cell and eat. Personal rule No. 1: always eat everything you're given. You never know when the world is going to explode. You would have taken your spoon which overnight is wedged in the wire mesh covering the bars on your door. Your food will consist of a plastic bowl of 'pap', a porridge made of maize, and some milk already poured over it. There will be a second bowl with an exact measure of brown sugar, an exact measure of jam (the same mixed-fruit jam year in and year out), an exact measure of margarine and two slices of brown bread. Also a mug of coffee. You lick your bowls clean, break wind and go through the fetch-and-carry process in reverse. I soon learn to hide away some of my precious brown sugar, to dampen it at night and eat it on my evening bread which would be served without anything.

Now the warder normally leaves you unlocked (if he doesn't, you're in for a troublesome morning) as you have to clean your small kingdom: your cell, the bathroom, your corridor. Cleaning means sweeping up whatever dust there may be; dusting the window sills, the ledges, the bars of the grills; scouring the toilet bowl and the wash basin and the bath; polishing with Brasso all the copper appurtenances such as door handles and light fixtures. When needed, which was about three times a week, you would scrub the floor with water and ordinary soap, dry it, apply fresh polish with a little rag, go over this first with your brush, and then commenced the ever on-going process of shining the surfaces with your 'taxis'. It is a good time of the day. The morning is fresh, and with your ears you try to steal the news from the magical world beyond the partition. Working close to this partition you could, through the crack of the door joins, catch a glimpse of the office across the corridor. Often Stefaans would be taken there, haggard and grey, to complain of his worms and to plead for a special diet. They – the *boere* – would laugh and play around with him. Sometimes they would pretend to be solicitous and accommodate him. For a time his lunch consisted of only one whole carrot and nothing more. Once I even hit the jackpot: the cleaner came to rub away just on the other side of the door and whispered his dream to me. He was going to profit from his time inside (he was innocent, as all prisoners are; it was a frame-up that got him there) and have all the necessary operations – get his back straightened, have all his (perfectly sound) teeth pulled and replaced by smart dentures, get glasses (for his perfectly sound eyes) – and then, upon release, he was going to buy and put on an electric blue suit, buy a real electric guitar (which he couldn't play) and nonchalantly strut into a swanky restaurant, dragging the guitar after him. Man!

At any time after 9.30 and before lunch, which on a normal day is at about 11.30, you will be allowed out into the small courtyard for your half an hour of exercise. Prison regulations prescribe that you ought to have half an hour in the morning and half an hour in the afternoon but very often the afternoon session was skipped with the excuse that the warders were too busy doing something else or that there were not enough of them: one of the perks for the staff was that they could practise sport during service hours. The grille leading to your little courtyard is unlocked, then the outside steel door; you are let out with a warder accompanying you and the grille behind you is locked. There's a second warder standing on the balcony looking down on you. They time it very exactly. Now you do your Tai-Ji or whatever you can to profit from the fresh air, and if you're lucky, if it's the right season and the right time of the day, also from the rays of the sun entering the courtyard. You get to recognize every pebble and lost twig there: they are your friends. After exercise you are taken back in and locked up.

Lunch time: same ritual as the one you went through in the morning. You knew in advance what food you were having, on what days.

To save space, Mr Investigator, let me finish the food (story) once and for all. Prisoners' diets, it is claimed, are worked out scientifically by dietitians. You can survive on it. It is boring and bland and you often are hungry. The time between your last meal of the day and your first one the next morning is very long. Supper is handed out at 4 o'clock – Sundays often at 2.30! It is my experience that if you have to live from that only for any length of time, you end up with a vitamin deficiency. I started having trouble with my hair and my skin and my eyes. Suddenly I developed boils and cold sores. (In Pollsmoor I employed a fellow convict – since I couldn't circulate in the prison – to buy for cigarettes as many pieces of fruit as people were willing to sell after the weekly issue.) Regulations prescribe the exact amount of food a birdie should receive. A White prisoner, all in all, receives 210 grams of bread per day, 120 grams of meat on meat days, five eggs per week – three of which disappear in the dough

of Friday's fried fish. (But then, while I was in Pollsmoor, it happened several times that one F-Group
warder or another, kitchen *boere*, got caught stealing
eggs by the dozen and selling them to their colleagues.
Not that anything much ever happened to them: they'd
be transferred elsewhere for a while before returning
to the kitchens.) These diets are not the same for White,
Black and Brown prisoners. For example, White prisoners are entitled to one fruit per week, which the
Blacks or the Browns never get. White prisoners also
receive a small portion, 60 grams, of peanut butter a
week, on Wednesdays, and similarly 30 grams of cheese
on Sundays. Again Blacks and Browns don't qualify for
these. Blacks and Browns will get more 'pap' than
Whites do, and boiled-down fat in the place of the
Whites' margarine. The Blacks are also given *puzlamansa*, or *magou*, which is some kind of fortified soy-
based powder that can be made into a paste or, when
more liquid, into a drink. They do not get much bread.
The Coloureds on the contrary get more bread. Blacks
and Browns get less meat than Whites do: the bread
and the *puzlamansa* are supposed to replace it.*

The only time Blacks or Browns are entitled to the
same food as Whites will be once they have been

---

*It is, I believe, the Prison Department's policy gradually to elim-
inate the discrepancies in diet among various prisoner groups, as
also the differences in clothing. Some Brown prisoners in the Cape
even sleep on beds now—no mattresses yet: 'Let them first for a
year or two get used to not falling off the beds.' the Store Master
sneered. And, just as I left, it was decreed, despite the tenacious
opposition of the storemen, that Browns and Blacks can wear un-
derclothes too. Only certain categories to start with: those employed
as waiters, the cooks, those working as 'monitors' in White warders'
houses, and the sick in hospital.

condemned to death when, immediately, they qualify for the so-called 'White diet'. This holds true until the ultimate meal when again a White will be getting a full chicken for his last meal on earth – cooked in the warders' mess – whereas the Black will receive half a chicken only.

These different diets provoke a continuous smuggling of food. Whites try to obtain *puzlamansa* because it is reputed, if prepared in a certain way, to have a slightly intoxicating effect. The Blacks and the Browns of course, particularly those working in the kitchens, steal and sell and trade items like peanut butter, which they cannot lay their hands on otherwise.

For breakfast you have, five times a week, your *mieliepap*, and twice, on Wednesdays and Sundays, it will be oats. I've already mentioned the rest, and that every Sunday is Christmas because of your finger of Cheddar. Your lunch on Mondays will consist of two boiled eggs, your vegetables, either *samp* (which is mealies) or broken rice, also called 'mealie-rice', and a mug of tea. For the other days of the week that the good Creator made, the same, except that the eggs are replaced by meat – either pork or chicken – and on Fridays you will always get fish. We, the prisoners, at least in the Cape, say the year has two seasons: one season is cabbage and one is carrots. Many a time people used to 'stand fast', dixie in hand, disgust or incredulity written large on the features, to complain: mostly about the meat. At one stage our pork (which we'd get uninterruptedly for weeks, and then chicken for weeks) used to consist of whole pigs' heads slung into the pots, boiled, and then crushed. Some *mugus* found within a week or two enough pigs' teeth in their plates to make necklaces. As for the chicken

— it came in either one of two ways: 'smashed chicken' or 'chicken *à la* fuck-up'. We knew the officer's reply by rote, 'You think this is a five star hotel, hey? You should have worried about this before coming to prison. And what do you have outside anyway? Fuck all! You come here and eat up the State's food. Lot of fat *skelms* (crooks)! Who pays for it all? *I* do. And *I* don't eat as well.' And then, as often as not, the complainers found themselves charged for being 'agitators'.

Your evening meal will consist of a *kattie* of bread. (*Kattie* is short for *katkoppie*, cat's head, which traditionally was the size and the shape of the measures of bread baked in the ovens of Pretoria Central Prison when they still functioned; this custom was stopped to prevent the prisoners stealing the yeast which is an indispensable ingredient for fabricating any alcohol.) So at night you get your *kattie* — four slices of bread it is, and a mug of soup.

After lunch: in your hole. If you are let out, it will be for a short period just before lock-up. If not, you may score a short end of time to give the floor a final going over. Lock-up on weekdays just before 4 o'clock. The lights are switched on, the process of counting takes place all over again, you 'stand to', you are checked off on a list, and now you have a whole lot of nothing to do until lights out at 8 o'clock. You hear the warders patrolling on the catwalk, and every once in a while one of them may stoop to look down on you and, if he is bored enough, to exchange a few words.

The interruptions in your day's rhythm will be when the warders come to ramp your cell, or when you are called out because some officer wants to blind you with the 'irons' on his shoulders or the 'doveshit' on his cap's peak, or because you have to have your hair cut.

Your weeks are marked by three days: Monday, when you get your clean clothes and fresh sheets; Wednesday, which is when you get your two permitted library books (joy! bells peal in heaven!); and Sunday, when for lunch the cooks make a little effort and still using the same basic components, try to provide a salad or attempt at least not to mash up the meat too badly. Sunday was furthermore distinguished by the fact that we had our meagre supper much earlier and often found ourselves locked up for the night by 2.30 in the afternoon. Weeks were also marked by the weekly inspection, on Sunday mornings, by the head of the prison or sometimes the officer commanding the Pretoria Prison Command, and during the week on a Wednesday or a Thursday by the visit of the chaplain, an old gentleman called van Jaarsveld. The week's rhythm could be destroyed by a hanging. This normally meant that I would see the very short doctor, who had to assist at the execution and made use of the occasion to visit his other charges also. Or the lulling routine could be interrupted by one's not receiving one's library books (this was catastrophic!). Or, again, by being unexpectedly called out for a visit by some psychiatrist or higher-up, passing through on his way. (They also had to show that they actually *earned* their salaries.)

The months were marked by three major events – important because they constituted one's contact with the outside world. Once a month I was allowed to receive a letter and to write one. Once a month too, I was entitled to a visit lasting half an hour. And at the end of every month the prisoner could – from his 'private cash', that is the money he has on his name up front, and for a limited amount fixed by the authorities – buy a certain number of items from the local 'tuck shop' or canteen. Until such time as he becomes A-Group, these will consist of toilet articles and tobacco and writing material only.

The letter, both that going out and that coming in, could only be 500 words long and naturally had to be very bland – not referring to any specific conditions or events behind the walls. These were censored by the section sergeant first, then the officer responsible for security and, in the case of politicals, certainly also by the security police. (Anybody else handling it along the way also perused it as a matter of course. When I knew a letter had arrived for me, and tried desperately to obtain it before the end-of-month deadline, I often felt like asking, 'May I read it *also*?') The visit took place in one of the tiny visiting rooms leading off the main corridor. You were separated from your visitor by a thick glass and you spoke through a trumpet-like contraption inserted in the table before you. There was at all times at least one warder present on your side, breathing his stale hamburger breath down your neck, and one present on the other side. These visits, although the Prison Department always strenuously denied it, were taped, and I assumed that these tapes or their transcriptions were vetted again by the security police. Actually I have objective proof that my visits were taped.

One's month could be ruined by the alteration of any of these salient features: a letter not arriving on time or a visit being interrupted because one spoke about forbidden things.

There are other rhythms, Mr Investigator. There are the movements of light and darkness down the walls. There was the coming back of the swallows once every year, rebuilding their nest in the same place under the eaves. Seasons change and one morning one is issued with a heavier jacket and with long pants. You know that winter must be burning up the veld. It gets warmer, the sun grows a beard, thunderstorms: summer. You start to capture also the rhythms of your own body – the depressions succeeded by lighter periods, the recurring dreams, the touch of rheumatism you have in the right wing when it's damp. And in this way, bit by bit, you go through the year, and then another, and you learn that the years have a routine of their own also. There is at least Christmas to use as a benchmark, although it is a very sad occasion for prisoners. Christmas: the time of the year when there are the largest number of attempted suicides and escapes.

Rhythms, routines, elements of your understanding and experiencing the self and the environment; fetters which make you weaker: but, as always, within the weakness the strength already lies – and so they become the ways in which you destroy time.

INSERT

In this room the corpses are taken to the fathers for embalming. (One goes to visit the deads from time to time, talking to them, telling them about how Aunt Agatha lost her favourite speckled hen. It entertains the dream of immortality.) The visceral parts, the heart and the lungs, will have been removed and kept separately in a container on the mantelpiece: 'For the best mum in the world – your loving son.'

The naked corpse of the deceased remains for several hours in a bath of arsenic – quicklime is cheaper but it removes the body's natural colouring and thus plays havoc with the system of having everyone in his rightful place. Thereafter it is locked away for eight months in a stagnant cell behind a closed door. Just to give it the right patina of ageing. Food is pushed through under the door. Only now will it be taken out on the roof or a terrace, to dry out in air and in sun.

Look, there they are – dressed in their best greens. See, there a bullet nicked a scalp or here a knife creased the stomach. The weal? Oh, that's the bite of the rope. Have mercy on them. They are in heaven. Their angels incessantly look upon the face of our Mister Father who is in heaven too. Prison is just another heaven.

Mr Investigator, I hope you realize that it's not easy for me to talk to you like this, with an open heart. I'm trying to stick to a simple principle: to tell everything, hodge-podge, be it a clapper-clawing or a whining, whichever way it comes. Naturally I have forgotten a lot – I wouldn't be human otherwise. That is why I try to structure my mind – the one incident carries the echoes of others – like death. There is no composition like decomposition: not just a rearranging or a falling apart, but verily rotting to the bone to bring to light the essential structure. The further you go the more you realize that there are no finites; just movements of the mind, only processes.

But it is not easy and neither is it pleasant. The only comfort I allow myself is the thought (or the

hope?) that recollecting all the events will also allow
me to put them out of mind forever. I am hoping for
a purge. (That is why it is so important to dredge up
everything: what one leaves behind will, like the
bloodsucking head of the louse you remove from your
skin, start festering.) So one must burn! The mind—
this *mélange* of mindlessness and memory and me-
tempsychosis (which is only a metathesis?)—is ever
groping for the meridian where it can moulder in
motionless meditation.

Maybe there are strong forces which object to my
talking to you, Mr Investigator. Force has no moral
dimension. The fact that they're evil doesn't make
them less potent!

My skin is packing up on me. It is peeling over
the shoulders. In my moustache and between my eyes
there are rough patches, like winter blisters. In the
folds of my thighs I have a stubborn rash: I talk to
you and I perspire and the sweat makes me burn all
over. (I waddle along with legs wide apart like some
old goose in heat.) So one must burn! Is the need to
vomit the surfacing past a rash on the brain?

Madame la Générale washes up after supper and
inexplicably lets fall eight plates to smithereens in one
go. (She who has such sure hands!) My watch no longer
works; when I shake it, it sets off again, sweeping a
cat's paw over its face, but it watches and when I'm
not looking it loses time as if I have nine years of it
to spare. The mosquitoes keep us awake at night.
Sluggish flies circle in the kitchen: I go after them
blindly, but there are always others to take their places.
Three kinds of ants invade the house like water seeping through cracks. I pour boiling water down the
cracks in the walls. The acrylics I've made of masks

and of men being hanged in heaven's gate as a warning to the angels – these fall off the wall. So now I shall have to make a painting of falling paintings. When I talk to you the tape is ruined by quarrelling neighbours, each reciting *Finnegans Wake* at the top of his voice.

On Sunday four young urchins try to steal the car we've been lent. I see them from the balcony just as they are moving away with it from under the trees on the Square of Pawnbrokers: I point a stiff arm, lift a trembling white beard, and bellow, hoping to give an imitation of a wrathful priest. (Imitation, all imitation.) They scamper off into the Street of Flying Chairs. We recover the car, but they (or their elders) have already succeeded in stealing the battery, so we are left with the carcass. I have to buy a new one and have no way of knowing whether the natives are taking me for a ride. No one saw the culprits. I shall not recognize them: they all look alike. Eyes slide away from your face. Don't know, don't know. It is life. Even at this level *omerta* works, efficiently. (What have *I* learned about the law of silence?) And then I say to myself: if they were caught, what then? A first step on the way to prison? Is that what you want? Of course not! You've just come from there – what is it that you're thinking of?

There are portents and omens which I hesitate to read, but I dread them. (Ignorance is no protection.) The thuds and the febrile light of fireworks outside the city over the mountain where the resident guardian saint lies on her side in the cave she occupied during her life, now coated in gold. On two occasions lately I've crossed muttering nuns in the street. It is said that one should never travel on a boat with nuns on board – the waves will become wild because the nuns resemble them too much. A bird flies upside down. A fat beggar curses me when I refuse to give him alms. There must be a warship in the bay: suddenly there are scores of Egyptian sailors in the *sukh*. Over the television screen flit grey images of inscrutable Japanese divers bringing from the deep speared living things (coral?) called 'crowns of thorn'.

We drive down to Little World and the only available parking space I can find is in front of a house numbered 13. On the beach I see a pair of twins with silver reflections where their eyes ought to be. I also see a hunchback, who leers at me. And a poor child who is so ugly you instinctively make all the ancient signs to ward off calamity. At least I haven't come across any midgets. Another judge is gunned down on the steps of the court. Fantastic wreaths cover the blood. A mother holds the head of her nine-year-old daughter under the water of a bathtub in a *pension* until the girl has stopped quivering, and then wraps her in a shroud fashioned from a sheet: she had to 'wash the child's soul'.

Back in town I decide to break the silence. We're supposed to be incommunicado—to get this over and done with—but we contact the *centrale* twice a week for any messages. He tells me that he's just had the unexpected visit of a midget! So that too is done.

But we must go on, mustn't we, Mr Investigator? See, now that I've told you about all of this, I can forget it. One must burn! Maybe, once I'm finished, there will finally be neither you nor I left . . .

And, as one of the *boere* used to say grimly when whatever mishap befell him, be it the death of his first-born or the roof caving in, 'It is still better than being in prison.'

2

The Writer Destroys Time

I am the writer. I scribble. I have, stuffed in my pockets, old envelopes, small folded pieces of paper, the torn-off edges of newssheets. These I fill with cryptic notes. I scratch them out. I write over them. I ride them down. I fill in every blank space. I lose them. I find them and I'm incapable of deciphering a thing. At night, after the lights are turned out, I can't sleep. I used to be a night bird. Now I'm just a jail bird. It's too early for me. Winters, when it gets quite cold in the Transvaal, I lie on my bed with just my hands outside the blankets. Cement and steel concentrate the cold. In bed I keep my socks on. I have a chess-board with pieces, given to me during the time of my detention, and I have been allowed to keep it. But I have nobody opposite me to crack a game with. You are not there. In the dark I put the squares next to my bed on the floor, set up the men, and start a game. I put my soldiers in the dark. It is a schizophrenic experience, playing white against black, I facing I, me against Mr Investigator. I cannot lose. I cannot win. I am free.*

In the dark I am not in the way. There is nobody to look over my shoulder. I am relieved! Then, like an irrepressible urge, there would be the need to write. In the dark I can just perceive the faintly pale outline of a sheet of paper. And I would start writing. Like launching a black ship on a dark sea. I write: I am the writer. I am doing my black writing with my no-colour gloves and my dark glasses on, stopping every once in a while, passing my sheathed hand over the page to feel the outlines and the imprints of letters which have no profile. It makes for a very specific kind of wording, perhaps akin to the experiments that the surrealists used to make in earlier years. There is the splashing of darkness, the twirled sense. Since one cannot re-read what you've written a certain continuity is imposed on you. You have to let go. You must follow. You allow yourself to be carried forward by the pulsation of the words as they surface in the paper. You are the paper. Punctuation goes by the board. Repetitions, rhythms, structures, these will be nearly biological. Not intellectually conceived. Ponder for two beats and you're lost. It is very much, Mr Investigator, like me talking to you now with my eyes

---

*Jerry tells me later of a chess game he watched, while imprisoned in Czechoslovakia, between a fellow inmate and one of the guardians. Whenever, during the course of the game, the guardian was called away elsewhere, the inmate would swallow one of his opponent's pieces. It is a hard struggle to survive.

closed, seeing behind my eyelids the words moving by as if on a screen. Sighs looking for an orgasm. You write on in an attempt to erase.

In this way one plunges directly into a dream. I remember now that I am in the Hills – rowing down the main corridor in a little boat. In this boat there are my father and my mother and my wife. All the doors leading off to the side corridors are closed and the water is rising slowly but steadily to the point where I no longer need to use an oar. I can push the boat forward by using my hands against the ceiling. We need to escape. We need somehow to fit through the small space at the top between the steel doors and the ceiling itself. But we are heading deeper into the labyrinth. The Minotaur has drowned. His bloated body must be tumbling along somewhere, bumping the floor. My mother's hands clench the edges of the boat. Already she is as grey and as sad as the very water.

Writing becomes for me a means, a way of survival. I have to cut up my environment in digestible chunks. Writing is an extension of my senses. It is itself a sense which permits me to grasp, to understand, and to some extent to integrate that which is happening to me. I need it the same way the blind man behind his black glasses needs to see. But at the same time I soon realize that it becomes the exteriorization of my imprisonment. My writing bounces off the walls. The maze of words which become alleys, like sentences, the loops which are closed circuits and present no exit, these themselves constitute the walls of my confinement. I write my own castle and it becomes a frightening discovery: it is unbalancing something very deeply embedded in yourself when you in reality construct, through your scribblings, your own mirror. Because in this mirror you write hair by hair and pore by pore your own face, and you don't like what you see. You don't even recognize it. It won't let you out again. . . . Who am I? Where and who was I before this time?

I have no common mirror during the first period of Maximum Security. It is only something like a year and a half later that Arselow, for some reason only he would know of, one day brings a mirror to my cell—a real one. I look at this naked-faced yellow monkey looking back at me. In an adjacent corridor the young Jewish security guard who attempted to take over the Israeli embassy in Pretoria, shooting a diplomat in the process, and who is now kept here under permanent surveillance, one late afternoon breaks a mirror and starts slashing his own wrists and stomach. I hear the warder with him screaming hysterically, banging against the steel partition to be let out. They save him. They save the prisoner too.

Even during the period of detention I had been allowed to write. It was something I could not ignore. A voice said, 'Write', and I wrote. And the more I had to enter the slithering area of confessing to and for the Greyshits, trying to pin down and imagine life, and becoming aware in the process of the ridiculous aspects of my illusions and my pretensions, the more I experienced the need to write what was 'true'—to communicate with someone else, not always with the enemy; to create, even if only precariously so, in the towers of verse the other world, the one where I could withdraw with my wife. And so I was allowed to write poems. These all originated over a period of hardly six weeks and were published not long afterwards under the title of *Voetskrif*, meaning 'Footscript'. The very existence of this volume was exploited by Huntingdon. He saw herein one more way to manipulate me and simultaneously improve his image and, he hoped, his acceptability to the literary community among the Afrikaners. He did not want to be known as a cultural barbarian, and in any event he was intuitive enough to understand that the real threat to the Afrikaner would come from within their own ranks—so, far-sighted, he already had to lay the first lines of infiltration into the ranks of the Afrikaner writers from whom he suspected subversive ideas or rebellious noises in due time to come. He insisted quite brazenly that the volume of verse should be dedicated to him. It was a naked instance of horse trading: you dedicate this to me and I allow you to have it published. But it had to be censored by him of course. One complete poem bit the dust. Let me quote it to you, Mr Investigator. The title was 'Help', and the body of the text consisted of 'Help!'

It is absurd, thinking back on that period, that my nemesis, the man who was—however insidiously—trying to have my guts and to flip me inside out, at the same time acted as my literary agent—in fact creating or giving me the possibility of survival. By means of their men in Cape Town I recovered the poems left with the Swami. I still have the envelope in which these were forwarded to Huntingdon in Pretoria with, written on the outside, 'These are the poems he left with so-and-so in exactly the condition we found them in.'

During this period also, at the beginning of my time in Pretoria, *A Season in Paradise* was published.*

---

*The first edition, a censored version, was published in Afrikaans by Perskov, during 1976.

The Greyshits knew all about it long before publication. They are very keen connoisseurs of literature. In their impatience they will intercept a manuscript between author and publisher. They may even read a book before it is written! I mentioned that I was interrogated partially about material contained in that book. I felt, as every prisoner does very strongly, the need to be able to contribute something to life outside. There remained the urge to communicate, to shout, to get on to the roof and wave your arms and say: 'I love you,' or just 'I'm here; I'm dead but I'm here — be sure not to forget it!' But also there was, knowing how difficult life must have become for Yolande outside (or suspecting it — she was too discreet and considerate to refer to troubles) the strong desire to be able to help her in whichever way I could. Therefore, in order not to have my voice cut off entirely, I urged her to arrange for the publication of the manuscript which had never really been finalized to my satisfaction, and I agreed to certain cuts being made in the book on condition that these were supervised by people whom I trusted entirely and also that the integral version be used for any translations and publications abroad.

There is an important principle to underline: in a repressive State inimical to the writer you will never find the perfect conditions for freedom of expression, but it is essential to continue, even if only with the minimal demands of integrity that you impose on yourself and on your umbilical cord with the outside world. It is possible to falsify for some time the thrust of one's words by inserting them in an environment controlled by the enemy, but eventually — if what you write is 'true' to yourself at that moment — it will be-

come evident and be rectified. (Even if it is true only
in its absence of truth and its fumbling for checkpoints
and references.)

Over the years, while I was in prison, several works
were translated. There were volumes of poetry in quite
a few European languages and there was *A Season in
Paradise* in English and in Dutch. For a long time I
was not allowed to receive any of these publications
and never could I participate in any way in the preparation thereof. For instance, I was not allowed to go
over previously unpublished work – that is, pre-prison
time texts – to alter anything in them. (All I could do
was, by means of my contact with Yolande, to try to
advise her, and through her the publishers, about
what material to use and to some extent in what order.)
The ostensible reason for this was that any such participation while in prison is considered by the Prison
Department, very narrowly, as continuing economic
activity, which is forbidden by law. (Although you
very often will find instances where businessmen, in
some camouflaged way, are allowed to keep running
their affairs. Prison lore will tell you about C, murderer millionaire, who continued directing his multiple business concerns from inside; also about how
generously he paid for prison sports facilities, etc.;
and that he was released after doing only five years
of his twelve-year sentence, for 'exemplary conduct'.
In Cape Town I knew a fellow convict who was regularly and often visited by his business partner – an
Indian – for consultations. But he had to grease the
palm of an officer to obtain the privilege.) In P'town,
then, I never was permitted to read my own published
work. The one occasion when I did see some of my
books was when I was called in to the Commanding

Officer's office and told that as the result of a petition
to the minister I was allowed to take cognizance of
the existence of some books. I was thereupon sent
back to my cell and told to sit on a chair before it,
and with a warder sitting facing me I could take in
my hands and leaf through a copy of *A Season in
Paradise*, a copy of the French verse, and my collected
poems united in two volumes printed in Holland, on
condition that I did not attempt to *read* these.

But I am the writer . . . I need to write. . . . Soon
after my sentencing I applied in writing, as always in
prison, in duplicate, to the authorities for the permission to paint and to write. Without my knowing
about it similar requests were being made from outside, emanating from the South African milieu of writers and academics. People who absolutely rejected
me and my ideas and what my life stood for but who,
perhaps from an obscure sense of uncomfortableness,
if not guilt, and also, surely, because of a true concern
for my work, applied to the minister to allow me to
continue writing. 'For the sake of Afrikaans literature.'
Was it a way for some of them to establish in their
own minds their evenhandedness?

The request to paint was turned down with the
excuse that too often painting or drawings are used as
means to barter with in prison. (Perhaps also because
someone, somewhere, had realized that to paint is
truly to escape: it is a healing of the hands and the
eye.) The officer telling me this had hanging on the
wall behind him several paintings made by prisoners.
Writing, he informed me, I would be allowed to do,
with the following conditions attached to the permission: that I would not show it to any other prisoner
or warder (that went without saying since I had no

contact with anyone); that I would not attempt to
smuggle it out of prison; that I would hand it in directly upon completing anything or any part of any
work; that I would not hoard or keep notes for the
work and would destroy these immediately after fin-
ishing the work. In return I was assured that the work
would be kept in safe-keeping for me.

A bizarre situation, Mr Investigator, when you
write knowing that the enemy is reading over your
shoulder; when you have to write as deeply down in
yourself as you can because you need this to survive;
writing in a desperate attempt at communication with
the outside, with the world, with the people closest
to you, knowing beforehand that it cannot reach them
and knowing also that you are laying bare the most
intimate and the most personal nerves and pulsebeats
in yourself to the barbarians, to the cynical ones who
will gloat over this. Bizarre situation also when you
cannot remember what you have written before and
you have no means of recovering the previous jottings
so that you do not know whether you are writing in
circles, raking over cleaned soil, coming back to sniff
again and again at the same old sour vomit. You wanted
to write a metropolis of anthills and now find yourself
lost among the ants. You collected seashells hoping
to find the sea. Thus you start erecting elaborate structures in your mind and filling in the blank pages one
by one, building a tenth floor before you do the second
or the basement—and since you write your dreams
and write in your dreams and dream that you are
writing, you do not know what you have actually written and what you have only imagined. You write your
mind. That is perhaps, Mr Investigator, why or how
I have become so sensitive to living structure. Also

to the objective existence of that which has been exteriorized. (I'm not saying exorcised!) That you are not only writing your past but also your future: you are cutting open new lanes to the heart of nothingness but you are also papering over cracks and blocking off routes. Much later, for instance, I realized that I had foreseen in my writing the experiences that my father was still to go through. There was the recurring image, surfacing through the words of that time, of an old man all alone with his head exploding in a thousand tears. It became only too true when my mother died and he remained utterly isolated – to later suffer a stroke and become paralysed and mute. I also recognized only afterwards that long before there was any question of my going south, there already appeared in my writing the mountain, the magical mountain, the manifestation and mirror of life which the mountain would become to me later on in Pollsmoor.

We were in 1976. It was – naturally I could not know this at the time – the time of Soweto. But I sensed that something was afoot outside, that there was mayhem abroad. (In No Man's Land one always lives with the expectation, the foretaste, of Apocalypse.) The *boere* were uncommonly tense. There were out-of-the-ordinary goings-on at night. Hooters blared. Shifts were doubled. I heard rumours of other prisons being over-crowded. I heard one *boer* say to another, 'Let's play Putco-Putco (the name of the bus company serving the townships), you be the bus and I'll burn you!' I overheard stones being referred to as 'Soweto confetti'. And once a young warder threatened that he was so fed up at being underpaid that he had a good mind to go and park a lorryload of stones by the roadside to sell. I thought I could smell acrid smoke in the dark. My mind was filled with images of fire. I heard voices crying over the desolate veld. My poems became vehicles of apprehension and destruction and bitterness. There was a singing death.

During this time I wrote what later would become *Mouroir*. I also wrote the feeling of a mirror looking at itself, a kind of essay (ecstasy) on what writing means to me, called 'Driftpoint'. This essay called for a continuation which I started on in Pollsmoor, giving it the title of 'On the Noble Art of Walking in No Man's Land', and quite naturally these enclaves grew into a third, which is 'Pi-K'uan', or 'Zen in the Way of Being a Prisoner'. It is a reference to the nine years Boddhidharma spent in his cave.

Was I ever going to get these texts back? Was it even important that I should? Writing took on its pure shape, since it had no echo, no feedback, no evaluation, and perhaps ultimately no existence. I had to try and get some recognition from someone, somewhere, admitting that these things did in fact exist. I kept note of whatever I handed in to them and informed Yolande accordingly. We soon tried to get them to recognize the fact that they had these by asking my lawyers to approach the authorities with the request of obtaining copies of the work, using the pretext that we were worried about what would happen if, say, the prison burned down. Sure, we knew there was no chance of their granting the request, but in the process we at least had a confirmation in writing from them that they were indeed in possession of so many pages. It was then too, that they formally undertook to return all of the material to me on the day of my release. This promise was kept.

But over all these years I never trusted them. It

happened too many times that solemn promises were ignored; too often had one been duped and fooled. I've seen far too closely the basic falseness and hypocrisy and duplicity of the civil servant or the man in power ever to have confidence in them in any way. Don't ever trust a *boer*. His two faces are the result of a tragically flawed culture. Don't put your faith in any other category of South African either—the system of the *boer*, the elemental presence of discrimination and oppression, have tainted and corrupted one and all. Truly, South African culture is the picture of painted putrefaction! Don't believe, don't trust—navigate! Survive! (And tenaciously recommence and continue the struggle for social and economic justice.)

So, naturally, all along I continued trying to find alternative means of saving the material—smuggling it out of prison. A part of the story became known during the second trial. Other channels, Mr Investigator, that I am sure you will allow me not to talk about. Why embarrass the people who were kind enough to help me? They may be needed again. The struggle between prisoner and guard is always that of the captive trying to dig or find holes (to breathe through), and the keeper trying to fill them up. Why expose the furtive means? The attempts did not always work. One has to take many risks in prison and you have no way of making sure that your connection is a safe one, or that the person into whose hands you have given the work will not steal it for his own benefit or to impress his girlfriend. You cannot trust anybody: that is the first law; and the second one equally strong: you cannot survive at all without trusting some people to some extent. It is not a luxury. Conditional and limited trust is a precondition for any life at all.

Material smuggled out in the early days was used as evidence during the second trial to validate the charge of my having used illegal means of communication with the outside world. After the trial I was called one morning to the office of the commander and found there a general, lolling in a chair with his tunic unbuttoned. With the crossed sabres on his epaulettes and the carefully coiffed grey locks, he looked the spitting image of the idea one has of Custer. This was his only stand. He told me that it had been their intention to cancel my permission to write in the light of the abuses that came out in court, but that they had been put under persistent pressure by the literary establishment to allow me to continue doing so. If ever he thundered, if ever I misuse this privilege again, well, then Afrikaans lit-tera-ture can go to stinking hell!

'Culture' is in any event considered a threat, or at best an obscure pastime, by the Afrikaners. A luxury. Something indigestible. The people (and who are the 'people' if not the police, the warders and the prisoners? Certainly they are more 'people' than the intellectually long-haired writers!) are aware of the divorce. Often warders or prisoners would say to me, 'Of course, we don't speak proper Afrikaans.' And be half-proud of the fact that they read only the popular detective stories or Konsalik or Wilbur Smith. 'Why not?' Why indeed not? Poetry is a closed book. 'Do you actually mean to say you write it just like that, without copying it out of a book?' What to do when you have been subverted by other tastes? For years, in the various prisons I frequented, I tried—with limited success—to obtain 'alternative' books (Hemingway, Faulkner, Turgenev, etc.) through the library.

Religious or educational books, yes; literature, no.
'You don't need them – you can write your own books,
can't you?' an officer once asked me sarcastically. Even
later, when politicals were permitted to subscribe to
magazines, I never could get a literary magazine, not
even the most conservative Afrikaans one!

I was the writer, but I was also the scribe. In prison
everybody eventually finds his own function in terms
of his usefulness to the inmate community. You may
be the one 'sticking' the others, meaning that you
decorate them with tattoos (you should have seen the
infections!); you may be only a cleaner of cells and a
washer of clothes; you may perfectly illegally be making cakes, or 'boop puddings' as they are called, and
selling these for a measure of tobacco; you may be a
'grocery rabbit', that is, flogging your dubious sexual
charms in return for some tinned food; you may be a
'boop lawyer' (often after having been a real one outside, to counsel the law-obsessed); you may be an
interior decorator, if I can call it that – meaning that
you go round offering to decorate people's artificial
teeth by drilling small holes in them and inserting bits
of coloured glass filed down smooth – you should see,
Mr Investigator, how flashy some smiles behind the
walls are; you may paint and sell pictures, using coloured toothpaste as pigment, or you may carve little
objects from the prison soap and then stain them with
prison polish (what a patina!); you may do needlework,
embroidery, patiently building boats and houses from
matchsticks (all of the above will periodically be confiscated and/or destroyed by the *boere*); or you could
be the bookmaker, or be running a gambling school.

But I was the scribe. At the outset it was strange
that people should approach me and ask me to answer

their letters for them—it impinged upon my sense of
privacy. I soon learned that a letter in prison is public
property. Those who do not get any mail, even the
poor 'social cases', can thus also vicariously have an
outside dimension to their lives. No major decisions
concerning love or family problems are made without
being discussed widely among the prisoners. (One
could also be a love consultant.) Often this brings
about an amount of degradation. I have heard with
my own ears how Dampies, lying in the 'bomb' (the
punishment section), sold his fiancée for three packets
of tobacco to Dexter lying in the next-door cell.

Nothing in prison is free. (If a fellow strolls by
your cell giving you a broad smile, he is sure to be
back within the hour to ask you a favour in return.)
You cannot render a service for free either; you
must enter into the customs or else become very suspect. So I had to submit—don't think I objected
strenuously!—to being given fruit maybe in return for
the writing that I did for my fellow prisoners. Once
I even scored a dictionary from the deal. It was left
as payment by an old man whom I had helped, com-
posing his appeal for mercy when his case came up
for review. Can you not understand that a man wants
to go home and die in peace, Mr Investigator? (This
was my line of attack.) He was one of my most successful clients. He left for court. It was just before
Christmas that year and the judge, perhaps in a benevolent Father Christmas mood or subject to a faint
recurrence of compassion-weakness, released him immediately. He came back to prison to pick up his thin
suit, absolutely elated with the outcome and, true to
his nature, begged to borrow a tie off a fellow
prisoner—the tie being down in the reception office

— so as to present a decent appearance upon coming out of the catacombs (barflies don't wear ties, and barflies may be refused admission to drink-holes), and of course he never returned it. I came across the same old gentleman again. My success was not to be crowned with permanence: he was back inside not very many months later, looking quite the worse for wear. He obviously had made up for his years behind the walls by hitting the bottle with gusto. (And he reminded me about the valuable dictionary—which had been confiscated immediately on orders from crazy Colonel Witnerf—and wondered if I, as an educated man(!), could perhaps help him in . . . but I moved away sharply.)

Among my more noteworthy successes I must cite two instances when writing bore visible fruit. The one was when an old lag going under the name of Pirate came to ask if I could refer him to anyone outside. He was due for release and he was in need of some money to, he said, buy tools. Tradesmen must have their own equipment. I knew for a fact though that, inveterate punter that he was, he was convinced that he had worked out the foolproof betting combination. Be that as it may. I wrote a poem, requesting the addressee (in rhyme!) to help the bearer out with R50. This he 'bottled' (you must know, Mr Investerrogator, that 'arse' in Cockney slang becomes 'bottle and glass'). He was duly discharged and after giving birth to the poem in freedom, presented himself to the consignee and did collect the immediate royalties.

The other instance was more problematical. Bames approached me with the request of giving him a hand with a translation. He was starting a new gang (a difficult undertaking) and he wanted them to have tattooed on their backs the Praying Hands of Dürer – an evergreen favourite with the pious time-pushers – and the Latin version of 'live and let live'. But no, man! I protested – I know not of Latin. But yes, Professor Bird, he insisted. Was I to lose face? I warned him that the best I could come up with would be an approximation in corrupt Italian (not even the vulgar form). Good enough for Bames. And before I left I could see his acolytes circling the exercise yard, like sandwich-men, with the respectfully folded hands on their bare backs, and written large and indelibly underneath. *vivere e lasciare vivere.*

Dampies, however, had worked out his own motto. With a fine disdain for the niceties of grammar he commissioned the tattoo artist to write above the dotted line around his neck: 'my last words is a rope around my neck.'

People came and asked for love letters; for poems – particularly poems; or they wanted me to write requests to the *boere* for this or for that, or to help them apply for jobs outside when the time for release became imminent and parole depended on their having a job. So I was continuously inventing their lives too, Mr Investigator. Imagine – here I am, so-and-so, applying for the reasonable position, entirely rehabilitated, you see, having understood the errors of my ways, a trustworthy and honest man willing to break my balls and give my all for my prospective employer, who would be missing the chance of his life if he passed me up, and I have in front of me while I'm writing this a poor bugger who has no intention of working and no capacity for it either . . . I wrote requests for parole, for release, for transfer, for interviews. You name it. I am the writer. I wrote the personal histories of chaps, that they had to submit to their social workers. A prisoner would come and say: well, *you* know, just write that I'm OK, you know what to put in, I'm sure you know better. In fact, they were quite convinced that whatever life I could invent for them would be far better than the one they had. Some, the saddest cases, came wanting me to write a letter of contrition to a loved one. There were always references to having broken a mother's heart and seeing now, when it was too late, the ways of evil that their feet had been on. But Your Honour, my love, it was really all the fault of my friends. And some came and wanted me to write their life stories. One small-statured *robaan* (slang for robber) said to me, laughing with a big toothless purple mouth like the fig's overripe burst, 'If only I had the time to tell you my life, what a novel it would make!' And I'm sure it would have been true too. There are as many novels in there as there are human beings going to hell.

One tall distinguished multiple murderer (but he had the pasty mien and the stilted movements of Frankenstein's fix-me-up) with the name of Jakes, claimed that he'd gone through every possible trick to try to get to the same prison I was in. He had been in Paarl, in Victor Verster Prison, he said, and had even feigned a heart attack in the hope that they would be sending him to Cape Town, to Pollsmoor, for medical care. Because, he said, he had this unfinished manuscript which I must help him to complete. After more than ten years in prison he had come to the conclusion that the only real job for him outside would be that of a successful writer, and as he had had these incredible experiences as a mercenary in the Congo, surely all it needed was for me to help him divide the material in paragraphs and, you know, pop in the commas, and we would have a masterpiece on our hands. It was all there, ready to be poured out. All it needed was my say-so. He ultimately showed me the manuscript too. It was clear at that stage, judging only from the hand-writings, it had already been written by five different people – all giving free run to their diverse fantasies.*

It's not such a bad idea, Mr Investigator. Like a *cadavre exquis*, but in writing. Why not have several people all letting themselves go in one work? (Did I hear you say something? No?) The problem is that with prisoners these fancies and fantasies are extremely predictable and second-hand, and all of the same kind – the hackneyed prison images.

What people wanted were the same things. What they believed of themselves and of others were along the same lines. If I had to typify the genus 'prisoner', I'd say that it is someone who is socially weak, who has no control over his own desires and impulses, who has really no means of making a separation between the real world and the imaginary ones. (This predic-ament the prisoner solved by taking everything as real whereas the Vedantist would see all these words as *maya*, illusion. As a Zennist I would say, 'Oh, officer!') He is also of course someone without the slightest sense of responsibility to anybody else, and no feeling for originality, or 'property'. 'Look here,' one of them said to me seriously, 'I've decided to be a writer too. I'm going to take all those old books people no longer read and rewrite them, just changing the names.' And

---

*I have managed – don't ask me how – to conserve a number of poems written by prisoners, and given to me over the years. Some are quite revealing. I intend to publish them in 'Pi-K'uan'.

in Pretoria (I hope I'm not confusing you by this jumping from the Hills to Pollsmoor and back) I was most
impressed when Skollie sent me a poem, just before
being topped, of quite outstanding originality. It was
addressed to God – a simple conversation in which he
announced that he was looking forward to making His
acquaintance soon. The poem, hidden and re-hidden,
survived for years with me. I was going to do something for the defunct killer's literary reputation. I was
going to rehabilitate the gallows bait. So much worse
then my disappointment when some time after my
release I came across the identical verse written by
an American soldier in Vietnam.

Why do we have this obsession with 'originality'
though? Why do we accord such value to what is
'unique' – as if anything could ever be that? Admittedly, our senses are jaded and we appreciate someone throwing fresh light on old questions – we like,
through the medium of the artist, to 'look' at something and to 'feel' it anew: in fact we want to experience the unexpected or to unexpect the already
experienced. Isn't it more a matter of wishing to make
the experience of the object really *mine*, exclusively
so? Isn't that why such disproportionate value is accorded to the 'new'? Is 'originality' not just a bourgeois
vice?

Sometimes there were funny letters. One man came
to me asking if I could please convince the authorities
to let him have a three-hour visit with his wife. When
I asked why (wanting to fulfil my task conscientiously),
he said he'd had a letter from the Army asking him
to return his rifle, and he needed three hours to explain to his wife where in the house the rifle was kept
and how she was to go about returning it. Another

wanted me to put in a request for him to have his
religion changed. He said he wanted to become a
Buddhist because it sounded like quite a nice religion,
far-off and unknown enough for no one to give him a
hard time about it, and he was sure that he should be
getting better food as a Buddhist. But please could I
write it out for him because he didn't quite know how
'Buddhist' was spelt, and also one had to give at least
the impression of knowing something about it. When
I asked him for his real reasons for wanting to change,
it turned out that a friend had sent the *Kama Sutra*
to him but that it was blocked 'up front' (by the cen-
sors) and that the only way he could obtain permission
to receive it would be to prove that it was a religious
work used by the faith he subscribes to.

I was the scribe not only for my fellow inmates
but also for the *boere*. It started in Pretoria. Brigadier
Dupe, very soon after I started doing my time, came
to ask me if I would translate a certain number of
French texts into Afrikaans. I was only too glad to do
so, basically because in this way I could obtain paper
which I would hide away for my own writing needs.
And reading French, any French, was like being 'back
home'. These texts turned out to be reproductions of
articles published during the Boer War in the International Red Cross reviews of the time: reports written by their envoys in the Transvaal and the Orange
Free State. Fascinating material in that it described
not only the nature of the wounds among the warriors
and their rudimentary medical care, highlighting the
fact that far more people died of dysentery than ever
did of wounds, but also because it contained reflections and criticisms on the conduct of the forces in
the field. It pointed out the anarchistic way in which

the Boer forces went to war and their lack of discipline – the bravery very often but also the abject cowardice of people inflicting wounds upon themselves in an attempt to opt out. It underlined the marksmanship of the *burgers* of the time: the majority of casualties among the English apparently had head wounds between the eyes. (Most of the fatal wounds inflicted upon the Boers were in the back!) I learned that the material was a subject of dispute between the South African authorities and the Red Cross. Brigadier Dupe and his colleagues were hurt by demands made on them by the International Red Cross Committee on behalf of political prisoners, and true to their own nature accused the Swiss delegation of being biased, of being anti-Afrikaner, and saying, I assume, that never would the Swiss do or have done anything for the Afrikaner in the way they were doing now for the enemy of the Afrikaner. ('The whole world is against us. The world is sick.') At which point it would seem the Swiss submitted the proofs of their previous aid and commitment to the Afrikaners. To the disgust of Dupe my translations bore out the Swiss position.*

I had to write love letters for the *boere* too, or applications for promotion. Another one of my successful cases, Mr Investigator, was when I managed to have a *boer* in Pollsmoor transferred from the sections (looking after us in the building) to the workshops where at least he could be taught a trade.

---

*I was told that some senior Afrikaners – not the top boys: these would have run away to Argentina or Taiwan before the crunch – are indeed worried whether, 'one day', the IRCC will be as solicitous of *their* fate, when *they* will be on Robben Island, as they are now about the Black prisoners. *Deus misereatur!*

Sometimes I was asked to write essays for their kids. Once, I remember, it was on the history of the Karoo. I absolutely lapped it up, sir; I loved it because I could use their need to obtain, illegitimately, material on the subject they wanted me to write about. Sometimes I would be asked to do their homework for them. Quite a few were attempting to finish matric or to obtain their junior certificates by correspondence courses, and I would complete their tasks. I became involved to the point of holding thumbs when it eventually came round to examination time, and analysing afterwards why 'we' did not succeed; agreeing very much that it was entirely unfair, that if one could only find the right person to send a bottle of brandy or a leg of springbok meat the decision to fail us might perhaps be reversed.

But there are two instances in my profession as scribe of which I'm not very proud, Mr Investigator. They remain etched in my mind. Both of them took place in Pretoria. The first was one night when a *boer* brought me over the catwalk a request from Johan, one of the 'condemns' due to be hanged not very long afterwards. He was asking me to respond, please, to a letter from his girlfriend. How does one refuse somebody who's going to be dead soon? So I sat down and I composed a letter, trying to put myself in his position. I must buck up the girl. Encourage her. Invent a future for us together—which all the time I knew there was no possibility of. A second letter came. Johan sent it along to me, and gradually it was as if he fell away. I grew into his skin. The contact between me—the Johan on the page—and the girl, living in poverty with her parents on some small farm back of beyond, became direct. And then came the time to die. Then the moment to take leave. How far, Mr Investigator, can one push duplicity? I was doing something filthy, surely, and yet at the same time I was extending a last hand of human solidarity to Johan, the shadow, who called me 'the Professor'. Don't think that the possibility of playing a mirror-game of chess with death never crossed my mind. What if I should continue writing to her, still pretending to be Johan? Communicating from beyond the grave? Or would it have destroyed the rosy memories glowing in her, that one major event in her life perhaps, when a man, with the black taste of daybreak already on his lips, poured out his last thoughts and sentiments, his last protestations of innocence and his deep commitment to a pure life ahead?

The other instance was even stranger. I was approached quite early on during my stretch in Pretoria, by the then head of the prison, asking if I would help him write a letter, in English: he did not trust his own. The letter had to answer an imperious demand Pretoria had received from the Clerk of the Transkei Supreme Court (the Transkei had acceded to 'independence' not very long before) to produce, before a certain date, two accused and convicted persons before the said bench. The hitch, Mr Investigator, the damn nuisance fly in the ointment, the slight technical fuck-up, was that these two gentlemen were no longer with us in the land of honey and milk and sunshine and mind movements. They had arrived condemned to death in Pretoria a month or so before Christmas. Things go rather rapidly immediately before the season of love to man and peace on earth. The hanging services are closed down over the festive period; the High Courts too. In this way, according to the letter

I was asked to transcribe, as these two natives refrained from informing the prison authorities of the names of their legal representatives, and since they were quite illiterate and did not leave the addresses of their next of kin (we all know what complicated and unusual family ties these people entertain), nobody knew whom to inform when their demise became imminent. It is with much regret, the letter was to continue, that we now learn that an appeal had been lodged against their convictions and that said appeal is to be heard by Your Honour, the Judge President of the Transkei Supreme Court. But it wasn't really our fault, Your Honour, (*we err in a no man's land of ant-empires*), you must understand that there are language barriers and the warrant officer on duty the day they were booked into the foyer of Heaven perhaps forgot to do the necessary checking, so, inasmuch and herewith notwithstanding, with all our respect, sir, we the undersigned, etc., always your willing servant.

Mr Investigator, I often lay there thinking that these two men who had jerked their heels could still have been alive. I dared not show the depth of my revulsion to the head of the prison and the warders. I don't remember that they themselves were particularly affected. When you process humans by paper, a wee slip 'twixt last breath and noose is, alas, always possible. To err is human. And I think that the multiple hangings would have blunted them already. I could not then make any notes of the event, but for a long time I remembered the two names. Then one slipped away and now I have only one left: Sizwe Bethani he was called. I repeated to myself: this you mustn't forget – *Sizwe*. Just think of Athol Fugard's play. And *Bethani* – wasn't Jesus also reputed to have

been to a certain Bethany? Ah, Mr Investigator, with
all due respect we regret that writing can be used as
topsoil for burying mistakes. Notwithstanding, I'm sorry
if I sometimes forget that it is at the same time the
maggots which lay bare the structure. . . .

The mind produces its own blackness from the
dark. Light comes at first from other sources. There
would be the monthly letter. Before my conviction
Yolande had to write to me via Colonel Huntingdon
(yes, he controlled that too). Now, processed and
stamped, I looked forward to my 500 words. The mar-
tinet responsible for 'security prisoners' in Pretoria (I
think the authorities even now still refuse to talk of
'political prisoners'), a relic of the Habsburg empire,
a boop-bellied little grey monster with an enormous
handle bar moustache growing into side whiskers, the
veins in his neck permanently swollen, shorts down
to his dimpled knees – used to wheeze up the hill to
see me every once in a while. (His base was Local,
where the politicals are kept.) *He* now handled my
mail. A letter I'd written to my mother was refused
because in it I referred to *tronk* instead of
gevangenis – the familiar 'jail' instead of the fancier
'prison'. Exceptionally I'd be allowed to rewrite the
letter, omitting the offending word. 'But watch it.
Don't you try and be a *mister* with me. Here you're
just a fucking *bandiet!*' Another time he came, proudly
fluttering his handiwork: my mother, not quite used
to having a son inside, and loquacious by nature, had
tried ducking under the 500-word barrier by writing
ever smaller towards the end of her page (like whispering), but Major Schnorff had cut her off in mid-air
with a pair of scissors, exactly at the 500-word mark.
(Do you see my power? And do you tremble?) (In

Yolande's letters words were blacked over or simply snipped out.) And once he came to play cat and mouse with me. Called me into the office. I sat down. 'Get up!' he screamed. 'Who the hell gave you permission to sit down like a . . . like a *mister!*' Then took his time. I watched his hogshead of angry purple blood. Waited for the ire to subside. He, harrumphing and fiddling around with a few sheets of paper, 'Sit down.' A letter he had there for me, from a concerned lady in Johannesburg, Suzy Lang Tak. Chinese, would it be? (Squinting at me from behind his fierce glasses.) Very Christian, very worried about my soul. 'Do you want it?' I was keen for contact, novelty, yes. Kind sir. Then came the slow leer tasting its way through the white hairs of the whiskers. 'Of course it would have to take the place of your wife's letter.' (As if to say: what's the difference between one Chinese and another anyway?)

Never mind about Schnorff, Mr Investigator. I only knew him for a short while, I only knew his moustache. (When younger he had a beard because he'd made a vow never to shave until the advent of the Afrikaner Republic. And he looked religiously after the bullet-pocked wall in Local where Jopie Fourie had been executed as a rebel during the First World War: to him it was a shrine.) To him we, the politicals, were all just communists, scum and vermin that ought to be exterminated to a man. I, of course, was furthermore a traitor. (He refused my Afrikaans. Spoke his quaint English to me.) Others can testify to how he made life a misery for them. He was kept on way beyond retirement age by the Prison Department, exactly for that reason. Now he's gone. Dead perhaps. In the eternal *laer* of white-tented wagons. Having lived long enough to see Afrikaner *baasskap* (mastership). No retribution. Why should there have been, since there is no God (except his kind), and man's justice is much slower, much more tentative?

Never mind about oom-pah-pah. We prisoners always say: there's one thing they can't do and that is to stop time! And however many hands pawed and drooled over my monthly letter—however much they taunted me, holding it back for weeks sometimes (it was a constant complaint of mine to the Red Cross and once it needed a written request in duplicate from me, announcing that I wished to lay a charge for theft, for them to 'find' my letter—minus the date—where it 'had fallen out of the post bag, under the counter in the post office')—eventually I would get it. Not to read it immediately, no sir! (One learns to space one's joys; one learns how to spoil oneself.) Just to carry it around in your pocket at first. To decontaminate it. Then, eventually—after lock-up tonight—you would unfold it, sniff the faint traces of perfume, and the walls would recede. Blue sky. A million words between her lines. Her voice—laughing . . . scolding too! My hunger would come and sit on my chest. Too soon the end. Maybe a P.S., a snippet of news. To carry me into the night and forward for days and days. Back into the envelope. Careful now—don't open it too often lest the sweet breath be dissipated. One or two stamps—those reproducing the paintings I keep for myself, for my own miniature art museum—will go to the friendly rapist in Cell 3, the obsessive collector, who pays me a jar of peanut butter every month. (The next day—I'm in the Cape now, you understand?—Shorty or Mother Hubbard or Oldface or one of the other trusties and office cleaners—'stink-

ing of Boer' we'd sometimes say, unkindly—would
sidle up to me in the food line. 'See you had a letter
from the wife. Everything OK still? Shame . . .' Or,
'Sorry to hear that.' Or, 'Jeez, prices have gone *up* in
Paris, hey?' The ant hill.)

INSERT

I walk downhill. It's cold. The streets are empty. Once
every now and then there's a dog trying to lift its paws
as high as they would go possibly because of the cold
paving stones. The bridges over the river have a thin
white layer of frost. The river itself is of a brownish
green colour, flowing fast; it is swollen, nearly washing
over the banks. Down in the kernel of the city there's
the old City Hall—the light-blue slate roofs, the green
statues cut out of the skyline, green with combustion,
and above that a very pale blue sky. I look up and
like a memory another vision superimposes itself. Already now I know that there will be this blotting nostalgia, other scenes darkening under what the eye sees
at the moment. The slight blue, the sniff of wind in
the air, and the green figures having the shapes of
movement make me remember that wild and desolate
coast along the Atlantic Ocean with the primeval wind
sailing over the dunes bending the grass to prayer,
and that same light blue allied to white. I can taste it
on my tongue. When later I walk up the hill again
there is a folding into evening and outlines fading fast.
Winter. But the light grows daily: already it stays
luminous until nearly half past six. Unbelievable still
every night to be taking another route. Walk up the
straight streets so well remembered and yet so com-

pletely new. Everywhere, all over town, there has
been a renewal, a take-over of little shops, small res-
taurants. And as you stroll by in the dusk you can see
people sitting behind the glass panes quietly waiting
for the first customers of the night. There's life behind
the façades. It is an ant hill of the living. You suspect
the space of courtyards behind the buildings, the spi-
ralling shells of staircases winding up to rooms all
askew under the roof, you know that there are rooms
behind these rooms, someone is putting on the light,
the floors are tiled, a fly buzzes around the bathroom
bulb, on the settee (or an armchair), the evening paper
open at page three, gathering dust on the floor behind
the settee (or the armchair) the leg of a broken doll,
one cough flew through the room. People are living
there. It is the very . . . crust of life. And below that
more life pulsating. Contrast it with that other place
in No Man's Land having the attributes and the gestures of life but in fact being a labyrinth of death. In
the thin alleys leading off these streets the lampposts
start revealing the first yellow globes of darkness. Unseasonal fruit. Sky clear but smoky. And when you
get to the highest promontory near the cathedral you
can see the horizon falling away in the distance all
smudged and stained like a receding battlefield. That's
quite a nice image: the gunsmoke of struggle fading
away. I look up and lo and behold above the spires
the shiver moon on its back, curled because it's cold,
and very slight again because it's so cold. This cold
leads you by the nose. The buildings are dipped darker
in darkness. In some rooms, breathing into the streets,
there's still some mysterious activities going on. In
some rooms the blind don't see that night has fallen;
they listen for the moths. In some rooms vegetarians

with pale thighs are wrestling in the dark, goosing the
furniture. Suddenly I imagine hearing a rattling noise
and again falls open in that inner man which never
forgets a memory of an image of dusk-coloured grey
with a verdigris glow over the mountains and he lis-
tens to the whirring sound of the gallinaceous birds
with slate-blued white-spotted plumage that lived
around the prison. We tried in many ways to capture
these guinea-fowl. Fellows used to get hold of a length
of string which meant unravelling one of the government blankets and tie to one end a few maize pips
and these they would lower through the narrow slits
of the window hoping that one of the birds would
swallow its stupidity and then perhaps the string would
be strong enough to hoist the meat up to the window
and twist its neck. And then who knows. Maybe one
could prepare hidden-hidden a meal. Please to eat my
blanket and come into me. But it never worked. And
one's nights were marked by the repeated chattering
of the birds. A convention of spinsters. Other flying
animals too. Bats. Plovers perhaps with their stretched
plaintive cries as they whip over the prison; or (but
that was earlier, in Pretoria) the wild doves coming
to nest in the gutters along the roof, humming and
cooing at the dying sun. At other times, very late when
everything was quiet, one could sometimes hear an
owl thataway and one crossed one's mental fingers
because superstitiously one thought that the hoooot
announced even more sadness. And regularly once a
week the *piet-my-vrou (Notococcyx solitarius)* would
return for a few weeks, shy to the eye but you could
occasionally see him jotting against the skyline, de-
lineating with repeated cries like beautifully crafted
droppings the territory within which he hoped to charm

a mate. Or during the long days one used to walk with one's ear along the busy lives of the little wagtails. They would enter the prison itself, flutter around the catwalk, perch on the windowsill and project the mirror of an eye down at one. I used to sing to them. *Wagtail bag snail how come no mail?* I also placed bets with myself, reconstituting the image of my wife while sitting back against the wall in a corner, feeling nightfall fall, fall around the grey fortress, layers of darkness silting up, and saying—if that bird, that little grey one, makes again that fluting noise it will be a sign, for sure, that she is also thinking of me at this moment. Come, little feathered friend—puke thy whistle! Your days are made of crystal. You become very attached to any form of life around you under those circumstances. One day, in the big yard, the one where we tried so hard to cultivate a lawn (how many times I broke my back carrying buckets of fertilizer, carting in wheelbarrows of sand to level the surface, watering, weeding, digging up the lot and starting all over—in vain: death had left its blight on that grey-walled enclosure), I watched a dove struggling to save its young. The young bird had just started flying and had landed in this courtyard not being strong enough yet to fly up and over the walls. Now its parent was trying to get it to flutter to freedom, and actually took position below the young one attempting physically to lift it, with awkward wings, higher against the vertical wall, again and again. There was the other one, the beautiful one, wood-pigeon or stockdove, with its red-rimmed eye and its coloured neck resembling some object of Egyptian mythology, which had entered the smaller courtyard outside my cell, the one covered with the steel crossword, and, in its fright when I walked out into the yard, it damaged a wing trying to get out. I caught it and was tacitly allowed to keep it in my cell. Where it became quite tame. Living under the bunk. Sharing my food. Venturing forth to watch me with a little black eye when it thought I wasn't noticing, extremely curious as to what I was doing. But unfortunately it didn't survive very long. There were too many shadows. One day, when I was called to the visitor's cubicle to see my wife (like a beautiful bird behind the reinforced glass partition), I must have left the door of my cell ajar and Lukas, the horrible cat belonging to the head of the prison (called Lukas too), must have entered and found the flip-flopping prey under my bed. There were only blood smears and feathers when I returned. . . . Droplets of blood. Images. Images are not confined to a place or to a time, they are now, thousands of them, even as I talk to you here. Images like birds, always present everywhere. We intrude upon their world. In the Cape, for instance, there were always seagulls riding the wind, being blown about, tattered and torn, uttering the most awful imprecations, swooping down on us when we were in the courtyard, probably hoping for a gizzard of food (craziness! what *bandiet* would ever leave a morsel?) and screeching at us, cursing the day. In the north, sometimes, very high, when one looked up from within the sunken well of the courtyard where you were allowed to walk the distance of half an hour a day, you could see floating vultures, nearly invisible to the eye, moving over the city. There were words flying about too. Although I was not allowed to participate in the talking, I could hear the thrumming and the rustling in the corridors behind my wall. And it struck me that these words were visible. And how senseless they were – some form of pollution dirtying the air, clogging up space. In a way I was quite happy to be deprived of words. I could be the monk chewing my silences. I realized how many unnecessary words one produces in the course of a day. Not even counting those scurrying around inside, unuttered, like ants, being the mind. Birds and words and other forms of life may be striking one so forcefully because they are seen separately, in isolation, and therefore imbued with far more penetrating importance. Later, down in the Cape again – on clear, early spring days – we often saw people practising hang gliding, jumping off the crest of the mountain behind the prison, feeling around in the air for the warm up-currents which will carry them higher, describing a wide arc over the valley, go whistling over the fortress, and land in a field not more than two hundred yards away. A beautiful sight indeed – the strong-coloured wings with the minute human being cradled below it. We tried to attract the attention of these flying humans. I wonder whether they ever saw us. I wonder if anyone outside ever sees a prison. Perhaps I could give you an example, Mr Investigator, of the evolution of prison language. You know how *dagga*, or marijuana as you know it, comes in various quantities – the smallest being a 'blade' and then a 'finger' and then a 'hand' and then an 'arm' and the jackpot being a 'bale'. As we were there on a Saturday afternoon all bundled up against one wall of the courtyard, to glimpse their parabolas and to try to see over the wall where these hang gliders would land, some of the *bandiete* started shouting: '*Kak 'n baal! Kak 'n baal!*' ('Shit a bale! Shit a bale!'), meaning, 'Why don't you throw us down a bale of *dagga*?' And

this went on for quite some time, every weekend,
until in due time the word for hang gliders in prison
jargon became *kakkebale*, 'bale shitters'.

What is *my* name? *You* choose it. Take your word.
A name is exactly the absence of definition. I've told
you that I'm called Bird, *Mister* Bird if you don't mind,
which means the jail bait. I've also explained to you
how I involuntarily took a vow of not using words,
because the words cluttering up the spaces on the
other side of the walls of my cell were like birds without wings. Can you imagine anything more obscene
than a bird with no wings? And yet it is exactly what
I'm giving you here. I'm stuffing this confession of
mine with all the other wingless birds. Perhaps it is
the stuffing coming undone which brings with it un-
asked for visions of wings and sand and sea, and others
of tame guinea-fowl mocking us from beyond the walls,
moving through the evening becoming more opaque
in their ever-repeated mating dance. Sounds, images,
birds, insects, wirds and borms and names—the mul-
tiplication and manifestation of nothing.

3

A Separate Section

Mr Investigator, I'd like to open a separate section, a veritable visitors' book, for the various tourists one meets in prison. We prisoners have a very simple way of dividing them. A visitor is either a friend, at least potentially so, or an outright enemy. The friends are few and far between, and there are many false ones, but that falseness stems more from the hope which springs eternal in the anxious breast of every jail bird. When a senior general, for instance, visits the institution, there will always be some demented souls who cling, starry-eyed, to the conviction that by bringing their complaints to his attention things will change radically.

Seven years is a long time, and now when I try to greet again clearly in my mind all the trotters who passed through those citadels of misery during the seasons that I spent there, I realize that they add up to quite a crowd. So, to simplify my discourse, I shall try to categorize them for you. (All along, of course, there were the Greyshits who never stopped coming to see me regularly until May 1977, when I was formally charged again and the proceedings for the second trial started; and even afterwards, much later in Cape Town, there recurred a few odd visits.)

(1) All those who actually work within the prison system: the doctors, the psychologists, the chaplains and the preachers.

(2) Those who are part of the system but whom we do not see very often: the ministers, senior officers of the Department, judges, magistrates.

(3) Those favoured by the system and allowed special privileges when they want to visit someone inside: the 'personalities'.

(4) Those who in a larger sense are still part of the system but as a loyal opposition to it from within, or even as critics of the set-up: they inspect the prisons to help the authorities foster the impression of a democratic administration.

(5) The outsiders who have objective reasons for visiting the prison, resented by the authorities – but they're obliged to tolerate them: here I'm thinking of the International Red Cross Committee, the French ambassadors who came to see me, and naturally, also, my lawyers.

I have already said that Huntingdon never stopped coming. In fact, Mr Investigator, the interrogation never ceased and the first trial with its conviction was just one step in the ongoing process of dissecting and undoing the psyche and washing the brain. More often than not he would be accompanied by Jiems Kont. There was no urgency. It could not be that they wanted any information. What was there to be had from me, locked away from the world for months already? Although they kept on testing, prying and prodding. No, I think it was more out of a morbid and sadistic fascination with agony, a preoccupation also with their own mirror-problems. We seemed to be locked in an embrace of hate and mutual dependence. But one should not underestimate the ritualistic aspects either. The Calvinists have a strong belief in sin and preordained doom, and equally strongly do they believe that one must be brought to an acceptance of one's fate. The notion of the acquiescent victim is an important one. And the victim must be humiliated to the ultimate grovelling cry of recognition: to save all our souls, Mr Investigator. . . . I am reminded of that Company of Whites which came into being in 1541 in Palermo, during the Inquisition, consisting of 'gentlemen and honourable persons', who had the noble task of preparing the victim for the Great Step, convincing him by subtle or not so subtle (but infinitely absorbing) means of persuasion (or perversion) to willingly and liberatingly participate in the 'spectacle of justice'. For the just man to use base methods is an act of abnegation and purification, of becoming a blind tool in the hands of God. To preserve our security, Mr Investigator. . . .

In a way their visits were more relaxed. Yes, I even looked forward to these breaks in my dull daily routine. Huntingdon would have a few sweets in his pocket and these I appreciated. In that weird way he had, he would convey to me that we were conspiring together against the Prison Department. Prison officials were just a lot of stupid cabbages, he said. But we have to play the game, since I'm in their hands now. He would make me understand that we should

be careful about the electronic bugs in the office where
he used to meet me. Simple games destined to create
a bogus sense of complicity.

It was also through him that I had confirmation
that my monthly visits were being taped. He knew
the process and one day actually asked me to say,
during my next visit, a few kind or admiring words
about him, knowing full well that the transcript would
end up in the hands of his superiors.

Sometimes he would bring a senior member of the
Security Police along, I suppose in an attempt to impress this visitor with his tamed political pet. In this
fashion Withart, the Commissioner of Police, came.
As also Zietsman, the second-in-command. He brought
along Percy Yutar who became sentimental, wept, and
told me that the day I'm released and reunited with
Yolande he will don his best hat to go and give thanks
in the synagogue.

But then there were also his colleagues and the
others of BOSS who came, hoping to learn something
useful in the conversations with me. Jiems Kont one
day informed me that Colonel Jan Snaaks was now to
retire to a smallholding he had acquired somewhere
in the Northern Transvaal and that the service was
throwing a big farewell dinner for him. He had the
cheek to ask if I didn't feel like writing a small poem
which could be read at that occasion. He thought it
would be really funny, a nice joke. The two of them,
Huntingdon and Kont, once even brought along my
eldest brother. In they strolled with their hands in
their pockets jingling cents and balls, and visited my
little courtyard and my cell. Although my brother is
a hail-fellow-well-met type, the hearty soldier, I think
even he was somewhat embarrassed that day. For me

it was quite an experience to see him and Huntingdon together, obviously with much mutual admiration. Real equals. At that point they had the same rank. (It must also, subtly, have been the chance for the flatfoot working as a flunky from an office in the capital to humble the soldier – engaged in 'dirty tricks' behind the lines – whom he was so jealous of.)

Huntingdon probably considered his finest achievement during that period the letter that he got me to write to Withart, offering my services to the Security Police, and motivating this offer in the name of the preservation of Afrikaner culture. I thought I was clever, Mr Investigator; I thought I could still manoeuvre and try to catch them at their own game. But those were the desperate delusions of the trapped animal as, without my knowing it yet, the pieces for the second trial were being assembled.

The visits of the Greyshits became rarer. I never saw Huntingdon during the second trial: I am still not sure of his role in the affair but it could well be that he was not the instigator of that episode and that the inquiry and prosecution was led by rival elements within the Security Police. But he still kept a grip on my case – after the trial, when it became too much of an embarrassment for the authorities to hold me in Pretoria, it was he who came late one night to the prison, pretending now to be even more wary of bugs than before, to inform me sarcastically that it had been decided to send me to a place where I can see the 'mountain' I keep on crying for.

In later years, as I said, I had some further visits from these people. Once Nails van Byleveld turned up: the same pig's eyes glaring from deep sockets, the same quivering little worm passing for a moustache (he probably thought himself to be the replica of some movie hero of the 1940s), the fingertips as hard and as square as ever. With him he had three admiring colleagues. They were ostensibly investigating an attempted escape. It was not long after the exposure of Williamson as a South African spy in Switzerland, and he literally crowed with pride. 'Did you see how we got you all? You must admit that we are fuckin' strong!' I answered by reminding him about the 'Info Scandal' – when so much of their overseas subversion was uncovered – and the brutal murder of Steve Biko. He went red in the face. What you lose on the round-about you win on the horses. . . .

At a later time the pale and scheming Huntingdon himself came down from Pretoria. Schuitema had in the meantime returned to South Africa and had given himself up to them and they now made believe that they were going to try him. Huntingdon's visit was supposed to be with the purpose of asking me whether I was willing to give evidence in a possible case against Schuitema. When I asked to be allowed to consult my lawyers first, he left in disgust, muttering, 'Just as I thought.' Hendrik Goy then followed, again accompanied by several cold-eyed Greyshits. He'd forged ahead in the meantime, was now a colonel himself. He talked to me quite a bit about Schuitema in prison, and eventually admitted that they were not going to prosecute him. Seeing Goy after all those years had, strangely enough, the effect on me of meeting an old acquaintance to whom I had become indifferent. There might even have been a touch of gladness at seeing him again. (He brought me some chocolates 'for old time's sake'.)

Let me dispose of the Schuitema case immediately. Many of my friends are convinced that it was he, Schuitema, 'Jan' as we called him, who had shopped me. Even while I was still in prison I learned of an inquiry launched by people close to me, and the envoy sent to Europe to investigate returned with the verdict that Schuitema was the man. The facts I *can* vouch for are the following: After my arrest he managed to skip the country and return to Europe. Remember— according to his own words—that he had been tracked by the CIA during a previous clandestine visit to the country and, one must presume, under surveillance ever since (see my footnote to p. 126). So, again presumably, the police must have been aware of his every move in the country. Back in Holland he was pushed from his position as Secretary of the Dutch Anti-Apartheid Movement. A Communist coup, he could claim later. The existence of Okhela had exploded in the Liberation Movement;* the Party was tightening its control and purging non-Communists from the supporting organizations. Plausible. With the help of Curiel, Schuitema then tried to refloat his reputation and credibility, working from Brussels. (Already he had been branded as the infiltrator, the man who had fingered me.) Failure and fiasco. He was with Curiel up to shortly before the latter's death. In Scandinavia —and later in Holland too—he still managed to raise quite a bit of money. Okhela split in two factions— ostensibly on pro-Breyten and anti-Breyten lines. (Both factions have been in contact with me since, both

---

*'Liberation Movement' in this context refers to the alliance of Congresses—that is, the ANC, the Coloured Peoples' Congress, the Indian Peoples' Congress, the South African Congress of Trade Unions (SATCU) and the now defunct Congress of Democrats.

claiming to have remained true.) He had to leave Europe and first went to Britain where he became involved, he claims, with the Irish Nationalists. Expelled from there, he went to America. By now he feared for his life, and asked for protection. Times must have been tumultuous. From New York he arranged for his repentant return to the Republic of No Man's Land. He said, afterwards, that he'd returned to offer himself in exchange for my liberation. Huntingdon received him at the airport. The Greys held him for a hundred days. A veil descended. And then they released him. Because, they—the *Gatte*—said, the international oil companies whose sanctions-busting operations Schuitema had helped expose from Holland during the 1960s, when there was supposed to be an embargo on oil to the then Rhodesia, now preferred not to be involved in a case against him! Let it be. Some time after his release, he left for Zimbabwe, with a girlfriend. They were arrested there and handed back, in murky circumstances, into the care of the South African intelligence agents. Who promptly let him go. In interviews during this period Schuitema admitted to having given information to Craig Williamson, one of the South African spies abroad but, he asserted, only from 1978 on, and then only to counteract the communist domination of the Liberation Movement. And yes, Mr Investigator, he's been to see me since. Twice. Right here in Paris. Admitting to regular contact with, and/or control by, various South African security services. Particularly with Huntingdon. Playing Peter against Paul. And he sends me the weirdest epistles, written in a jargon of his own, consisting of a jumble sale of analyses and theories. It is British Intelligence, he now declares, which is at the root of his personal persecution and which is using the Black Liberation Movement as a stalking horse to abort the revolution and extend its imperialist influence in Africa. The only solution, he postulates, is to resist as Afrikaner nationalists, particularly in conjunction with the extreme Rightist neo-Nazis. Spy? Tragic fool? Tool? What is true is that the man is a broken pawn in this sordid game. But dangerous— because he must end by either trying to destroy me (which could have been his mission all along) or, in a paroxysm of frustration and self-hate because of the tangle of contradictions, by blowing himself up. . . . I leave the judgment to you. . . .

As my story continues unfolding, Mr Investigator, even when we leave the prison, there will be a few more shady characters whom we will come to in due time. The only other one I want to mention for now is an elderly English-speaking gent who rolled up one morning to Pollsmoor and had me summoned. Dressed in his immaculate blue striped suit, looking like a prosperous travelling salesman, he tried to hide behind an affable exterior in the office and in the presence of Colonel Witnerf. He proceeded to show me two albums filled with photos. Some were close-ups, others were obviously taken in the streets of maybe Johannesburg, when the subject photographed was not aware of it. It was not exactly an Asterix comic strip. He wanted to know if I recognized any of these people. I most certainly did not. He remained convinced that I most definitely should. Another dialogue of the dead. Obviously they were on some false track again. I believe the photos were largely of FLQ militants. (And how the Quebec Liberation Front—does it still exist?—fits into this story, I'll be damned if I know. You might as well have my eyes sucked by wild ducks!)

The Greyshits are the masters of No Man's Land's system. Together nowadays with some military people, they can come and go as they bloody well wish in any penal institution, and they can materially affect the conditions of your detention. I'm not sure that over and above the continued 'normal' control they kept on me by visiting me and by means of reports from their agents among the staff and by monitoring my letters and analysing the transcription of tapes, that they didn't have also undercover agents among the prisoners. It was clear that my slightest moves and gestures were known to them. I worked out with a fellow prisoner doing time for fraud, about to be discharged from boop, a very simple method by which he could let me know whether he'd been approached by them after his release. He had been – in Pollsmoor – in a big communal cell down my corridor for about a year, and during that time I saw quite a bit of him. To outsiders it might well have looked as if I had confided in him or that we'd become close friends, and sure enough, the day he was released and taken to the airport to be deported from the country was also the day that the Security Police confronted him with our association.

But let me tell you about the other 'foreigners' breaking the dull routine of our existence. There were the doctors, a group of individuals, it needs to be said, whose professional consciences, when working for the State the way they do, do not seem to suffer too many qualms. In reality they have become rubber stamps for the penal system.

Immediately after being sentenced, I was visited

in my cell by one old fellow whose duty it was to give me a check-up. The results were presumably to be entered on my files and made available to the Red Cross when they asked for them. These files also served to protect the State in the event of one complaining later on about a bruise here or a break there. He had me lie on the bed and started prodding me in the ribs. All I remember about him was that he trembled, that his fingernails were long and dirty, and that the shirt cuffs protruding from the sleeves of his jacket were frayed and filthy on the inside. I felt quite soiled after this inspection, but I didn't see him again. The doctor normally responsible for the prisoners in Beverly Hills was a very stocky young man called Burns. He was of a friendly disposition with a penchant for minor operations. No surgeon, but he loved cutting and he didn't rest until he had me on a makeshift operating table in one of the offices, to get rid of some warts and other excrescences I had. As a doctor he was quite competent, but he also fancied himself to be an amateur moralist. One morning he tried to convince me that our prison set-up is the best, particularly when it comes to executions, at which he assisted. (And where he could allow himself the joy of innumerable small surgical interventions: it was his task to slit open the necks of the warm deads to visually establish the cause of demise.) I would never credit, he said, the contentment with which people go up to the gallows to be hanged. Convicting them to death and leaving them about a year – it was the average delay – in which to repent and give their hearts to Christ, was, according to him, a very humane procedure. How they were converted! How happy they were! How they sang! How touchingly they said goodbye in that last chamber before the inner sanctum and how they proffered a 'Thank you, *baas*'! I could not help but remark then that in that case you were hanging not the person you'd convicted but in fact a transformed and repentant sinner.

In Cape Town I had to do with two doctors. These apart from the several dentists I had the occasion to consult over the years and the eye specialist who once came to check me out. In normal circumstances any prisoner needing specialist care is taken to the hospital under guard, or even to the rooms of the specialist, but for me the poor man had to transport whatever instruments he could carry to the prison itself, the mountain coming to Muhammad, and he excused himself for having therefore to use very outdated equipment. The dentist one could theoretically have access to once a week. Sometimes there were long gaps: the regular appointee from the Department of Health and Public Welfare had many other mouths to peer into (those of reform school kids, inhabitants of old-age homes, etc.), and had to be replaced by a young man shakily doing his military service, or the dentist's chair would break down for a few weeks, or there wouldn't be transport available to truck the patients to the main prison in the same compound, or there wouldn't be enough warders to serve as escorts. And then, in Pollsmoor, the *boere* started making it more and more difficult for one to get there, since, quite correctly, they understood that people 'put their names down' for doctor or 'head-doctor' or dentist with the flimsiest of pretexts, really wanting only to be let off work for the morning, or to visit the other prison building — which opened up possibilities of smuggling! So they announced that the dentist would be there for 'pulling' only, not for 'drilling and filling'. Thus I saw some chaps, bored or desperate enough, with a perfectly good mouth of teeth, stand out for the dentist, to return round about lunchtime spitting blood and without a tooth left in their heads.

The two regular physicians, with one of them coming in nearly every morning for an hour or so, were Barnum and Pagel. Barnum picked up a bit of trouble with the Department after once prescribing the wrong cure to one of the members of the staff who nearly died from the medicine. He was suspended awaiting the result of an inquiry. He it was who gave me aspirins for a skin rash. Of Dr Pagel I became quite fond. He had been thoroughly impressed by the contact he was obliged to have with the International Red Cross. One member of the Red Cross delegation is always a medic and the collegial discussions between Pagel and his Swiss homologue sharpened his awareness of the important task he had been entrusted with – taking care of a 'political'. From time to time he would have me sent for and he was always very keen to let me have pills or syrups or antibiotics even – which he once prescribed for a cold. Anything, it doesn't matter what, as long as it could be written down on the big yellow medical card so that he could show the year thereafter to his honourable overseas confrère visiting the prison how conscientious he'd been concerning my health. When it became evident that periodically I was going through valleys of depression, he gave me a long talk, the gist of which was that there is nothing quite as good for a depression as trying to transform certain Bible stories into plays.

But for being talked to we had psychologists, the parasites living off our twisted souls. I had the occasion to meet some of them from the very outset. The big boss of the prison shrinks himself deigned to come and visit me immediately after my first trial ended. Master Basie, that is his name. At that time he was a short, fat, bald fanatic wearing glasses, but quite young still – younger than I am. He has travelled a long way since then and is now doing just fine, thank you. He sported the rank of brigadier-general and was soon after to rise to that of full general. He was made Assistant Commissioner. At that young age it was clear that he had been earmarked for the highest position in the Prison Department. It was not to be consummated however, since it wasn't commensurate with his burning ambitions. After a short flirtation when there was talk of his entering representative politics, he switched departments and went to Interior Affairs, and from there was promoted to the Prime Minister's advisory council. I believe he now occupies what could be considered the dominant place on that body. He is a dangerous man because he is a clever diehard and endlessly power hungry. Do not underestimate his intelligence; after all, even in the Prison Department it took a measure of grey matter to reach the rank he had at his age.

He was the instigator of what we in prison lingo call 'psycho city', which is a special wing for psychopathic prisoners in Zonderwater Prison. I talked to people who'd been through there. They had no privileges at all – no letters or visits, for instance. These had to be earned again and again on a points system based on Pavlovian principles, it would seem to me: if you are good you are rewarded; if you are bad you are punished. One of my informants was aghast at the fact that the 'psycho city' boys, when playing soccer against other prisoners, had to stand up and applaud vigorously when the opposing team scored a goal. Very unnatural behaviour for any prisoner, let alone the psychopaths.

When he first visited me together with Colonel van Holbaard, the resident psychologist of Pretoria Central Prison, Master Basie had with him a recently published article from a newspaper which claimed that one of my poems was prophetic in that I had foreseen my own arrest and imprisonment way back in the 1960s. Master Basie, I think, was intrigued by me. He came back several times and I could sense that he wanted to communicate. Perhaps he really wanted to find out what or who lived behind the name. Like Huntingdon, he was very publicity conscious; he loved showing journalists around some of the Prison Department's strong places or exhibiting his few words of French when showing the IRCC into my cell on one of their visits to Pollsmoor.

The last time I saw him was in Pollsmoor when – late one night at about ten o'clock – he had me brought from my cell to where he was sitting in an office with only his bodyguard present. Both of them kept their coats on: they must have been on their way North, perhaps after visiting Robben Island. The bodyguard chomped away furiously at his wad of chewing gum and kept on caressing the bump in his trouser pocket while Master Basie gave me a spine-chilling but quite coherent exposition of his own political beliefs. (The eyes of the chewing watchdog flicking with uncomprehension from Master to me.) I should not say beliefs – maybe these were more in the way of reactions. He was curiously needing to justify and defend his position, although I hadn't said a word. It came

down to the old line: we are living in a dramatic period
of exceptional importance, having to face and combat
extraordinary challenges; we cannot afford to be man-
acled by concepts such as 'democracy' or even 'decency'; we—meaning *them*—need to be strong to go
all out in a total answer to the total onslaught concept;
our fate is fatal; rather suicide in the desert than . . .
than anarchy; and Apocalypse, of course. (What else
do the Afrikaners live for after all?) I think it must
have been the first time that I came across this 'total
onslaught' idea (meaning that the whole world is united
in a communist coordinated conspiracy against South
Africa) which has since become a favourite stalking
horse of the Prime Minister. At that time Master Basie's conduct was inexplicable to me. It was only later,
when I learned that his name had appeared on a list
of 'enemies of humanity' published by the United Na-
tions, that I understood partially his need for self justification.

I saw van Holbaard more often. Sometimes he
would turn up in his colonel's uniform and at other
times in civilian clothes. He was very young still and
very inexperienced, the cap on his head unfamiliar
and his mind still creaking with greenness, so everything he did had to be by the book. He had me go
through the gamut of outdated tests, the Rorschach
blots and blobs, squiggles and various IQ examina-
tions. Naturally I was never informed about any of his
deductions. I was the guinea pig. These perverted
practitioners of the spurious science of psychology do
not have as their first priority to help the prisoner
who may be in need of it. They are the lackeys of the
system. Their task, very clearly, is to be the psychological component of the general strategy of unbal-

ancing and disorientating the political prisoner. Their
learning is at the disposal of the investigators and the
interrogators. I quite liked pointing out these contradictions to van Holbaard. Perhaps it was not nice of
me to be amused at his discomfort—he was so young
still and I could sometimes literally hear the clicks in
his mind when he recognized in my behaviour the
answers corresponding to bits of knowledge he'd underlined in a manual during his studies. I once told
him that it would be impossible for any officer in the
Prison Department ever to be an effective psychologist or a psychiatrist (spychologist maybe, yes) because
in the mind of the prisoner he will always be identified
with the oppressive authority, particularly when he
has on that ridiculous uniform with the pumpkin peel
on the peak of the hat.

Once he attempted to lead me through the free-
association process. A dream that I recounted to him
now surfaces in my mind again. . . . I was in this
enormous building. Something, something of moment
and of import, was happening outside and I just had
to get to a vantage point so as to find out what it was.
Maybe fire in the land. Maybe a mountain. Mount
Maybe. The building had no windows—just an interior
staircase—and there was no one else around. There
would never be light again. I climbed the stairs and
could hear the ring-neighing echoes of my boots on the
metal runs. One floor, two floors, three floors. Going
up. And up. I lost count of the number of storeys. Until
I eventually emerged on the flat roof and walked to the
parapet. I raised my eyes and I looked out, and as far
as I could see there was an absolutely dead-flat landscape with not a shadow moving on it. Utter and complete desolation. And then I looked down at my limbs

and saw that I was dressed in grey, in colourless clothing. I had become grey, as grey as grey. The upsetting
part of the dream was that I was entirely indifferent
to what I saw, both out there and inside me.

In Cape Town there were a few more of these odd
fellows with studies on prison conditions–done, by
others, in English–hidden in their briefcases. They
needed to talk, they needed to be comforted. It must
be hard for them: their field of study, however limited,
must bring them into contact with alternative visions,
even with the spectre of freedom, but their job and
the society within which they evolve always force them
back to the straight and narrow. No deviations could
be condoned. The *norm* was all-important and had to
be applied, and it was Calvinist, authoritarian, repressive. Some of them would spend a few years in
the Service (which was a sinecure after all), but I think
the reality of their incompetence and the absence of
any grip on the hard matter of prison life eventually
forced them out.

I made the acquaintance of a clinical psychologist
called Zorro towards the end of my time in jail. He was
not of the Prison Department, but in his capacity as
director of a psychiatric institute he was used very
often by the State for examining certain prisoners and
reporting to the courts afterwards. It was as a result of
a request by the Red Cross that I be given access to a
psychologist that I started seeing him. I liked him. At
least he was not one of 'them', although he could never
be one of 'us' either. Not being one of them reduced
his effectiveness within the framework. If, as happened, he insisted on one of his patients remaining in
the Cape Town area for continued observation by him,
the Prison Department showed no reluctance what-

soever in removing this person. In fact they needed to impose their authority: the longer a prisoner remained in the (occasional) care of someone like Zorro, the more he tended to become a *mister*. (A 'mister' is when the prisoner forgets his condition and starts having illusions about being human. Prison rejects this violently.) With him I felt more at ease and freer to talk about the true conditions of confinement and isolation, and I found in him a man with a firm measure of common sense and not too many pretensions.

Chaplains—our next category—chaplains and pastors and dominees and preachers and bible-thumpers and lay converters pollute the South African prisons. Again they are only functionaries of the penal system—the chaplains, I mean—proud as punch of their uniforms, their purple headbands and their purple epaulettes, and insisting on being addressed as 'Major' or 'Colonel' or whatever and to be saluted by their inferiors. Not exactly, one would think, the best persons to look after the well-being of one's soul— provided, of course, one has such a luxury item. In Pretoria it was old man van Jaarsveld, an old Afrikaner, true to type, fascinated by any illness or physical deficiency, by medicines and by operations. Out of curiosity, I think, he came to look me up regularly, only to launch into long and detailed descriptions of his bodily functions or malfunctions, opening his shirt to point out a scar or a weal. He was an old-school racist, regretting only that he was too decrepit now to be sent to the border with a machine-gun to kill *kaffirs*. As an afterthought he remembered that he was a minister of the Church and hastily embarked upon a prayer, cajoling and scolding his God. An old busybody, but a friendly one.

The one in Cape Town, Colonel Flêbê, was altogether a sadder case: a dry little man, a bigot who refused to live near the prison because the surrounding neighbourhood was English-speaking and he wouldn't want to have his children grow up in such an environment. He also refused to let his children take karate lessons because, as he said, when they finished their sessions with a moment of silence, *that* is when Satan entered their souls. I remember how he came one day into the General Stores where I worked, to whine about not yet having received his service pistol. We were very busy just then. The police and officials of the Department of Cooperation* had rounded up several hundred Black squatters on the Cape Flats – people forced by hunger to come and squat around the city – and we were issuing blankets and spoons etc., since they were to spend time in jail before being repatriated to their 'homeland'. Clergymen of various denominations were trying to save these poor people, protesting, paying their fines, acting like Christians. The Reverend Col. Flêbê cracked a feeble joke about *kaffirs* coming to prison with babies and with dogs. All *he* wanted was to obtain his free firearm. One felt sorry for him. After hearing him preaching to the inmates once or twice, repeating the same words, which consisted fundamentally of: You are sinners, you have sinned, that is why you are here. Repent! Repent! Repent! – I felt that if I had any religious feeling I ought to be praying for him to find some juice, some joy, some faith.

Yes, there were others too. A Salvation Army colo-

---

*Department of Cooperation and Development, previously known as the Bantu Affairs Department.

nel used to come in every second Sunday, as thin as a dried fish, jolly in his dark-blue uniform, hoping very much to find a few people willing to come and listen to his ranting. Not much success there, but at least the people he did lure were entertained by his lustful singing. I woke up one morning in my cell in Pretoria to the very forceful braying of Afrikaans hymns. My first thought was that perhaps the government had finally arrested some of the extreme rightists around Hertzog* for political subversion. There were several men singing and they were obviously defiant of some authority. But later that morning I learned that someone who'd been in death row for quite some time, so quiet that I was not even aware of his existence, was hanged at daybreak, and, being a member of some fundamentalist sect, he had obtained permission for his lay preacher, accompanied by a few elders of the church, to walk the ultimate steps to death's door with him. This then was the singing I heard. Van Jaarsveld, I imagine, must have been most upset at these intruders. He loved executions. He enjoyed the stab at the heart when walking the last fatal steps arm in arm with the candidate of darkness. It must give one a feeling of spiritual cleanliness and immortality.

(Sad to reflect that a White prisoner had to import singers from outside, whereas a Black prisoner will always be carried to death's gate by the supporting voices of the other Blacks.) Even the Reverend General in command of all prison chaplains came to see me. I thought that it might have been out of concern for my soul, but unluckily it was only because he was

*An ex-Cabinet minister who had broken away from the Nationalist Party to form a new grouping on its right.

on his way to West Germany for some conference or other where, if asked about me, he wanted to be in a position to say, 'I've seen the man myself. He is doing just fine, don't you worry. We are taking care of his soul.' His ignorance of prison regulations, however, was staggering. He told me of how a German pastor, locked up in isolation during the war years, had retained his faith and his sanity by scratching verses from the Bible on the walls of his cell. Was I doing the same? he wanted to know. In what fanciful world he lived! Did he expect one to get away with wall-writing in a South African cell, inspected daily?

Soon afterwards an English-speaking Methodist major, purple cap and epaulettes well in view, asked to see me. In the privacy of my cell he invited me to call him by his Christian name, Hartford, but please (he said), I shouldn't forget to address him as Major Keen in the presence of the prison staff. He wanted to make himself acceptable by claiming to have known two friends of mine, ex-Methodist ministers both— Jim Polley, and Don Morton who was a founding member of the germinal Okhela.

In Cape Town I met two holy men—Father Murphy and Mr Smith. Father Murphy was the Catholic priest allowed in every second weekend to attend to the needs of his flock. I listened to a few of his masses, nearly accidentally so: since there weren't enough chapels in the prison, the Catholic service sometimes had to be held in my cell. At that stage I occupied a very big cell all by myself. I managed to remain there when he came. This was something else. First, the Catholic prisoners are of a slightly different background from the others. Most 'birds' come from very diminished economic and social backgrounds, but the

Catholic ones are even poorer than the others. They are more often than not English-speaking, from depressed 'mixed' areas, and something of the Catholic Church's condemnation of racism must have rubbed off on them. Father Murphy, one sensed immediately, was that rare outsider who was on 'our' side and not on 'theirs'; he never had to specify this, since it was so clearly implied in every phrase he uttered. I asked officially to be allowed to attend his services, not for any religious reasons but because the ritual attracted me and because of the kind presence emanating from Murphy himself. Ritual is a social necessity. One needs some form of it, even if only to evacuate one's fears. And he had a way of bringing Jesus into my cell and having him take up a position just behind my little table (used as an altar) where the slanted shaft of sunlight touched and ignited the drabness.

He (Murphy), on his side, similarly applied for permission to come to see me during the week as he was wont to do with the other prisoners, preparing them for the fortnightly mass. Both our requests were summarily turned down. I was furthermore expressly forbidden to continue attending Murphy's services, and not long afterwards these were suspended altogether in any event. It could be that 'they' were on to some of the favours he was rendering to his flock – the messages he carried out or the times he'd arranged for a fine to be paid.

Mr Smith was no Catholic but a Methodist lay preacher. I remember him for stopping off at the barred window of my cell whenever he came in on a Sunday, to shake my hand and to ask after my health and that of my wife, and to tell me about his small problems: how age was catching up with his legs and how his car wasn't running nearly as smoothly as it ought to, but he was going to put the purr back in a jiffy, just as he'd done with the lawnmower, and life was a great joy anyway, yes, it was a real pleasure to be alive especially since he was going to Heaven. All of this he conveyed with true human warmth.

I have said, dear Mr Investigator, that there is also the category of visitor who may be an eminent personality (a noble ass), part of the system but not necessarily of the good Prison Department. Had you come to find me down there, you probably would have been in that group. One is never told in advance who the VIP coming around will be, but you soon learn to recognize the symptoms of a pending visit. It is absolutely panic stations for the personnel; they run around like chickens with their heads in the dust, ordering prisoners back and forth, trying to get the place as spotless as possible – even those areas through which it is most unlikely that any visitor will pass. A whole new face is put on for the sake of the Man who provokes trembling, a false face, for sure, because all the defaults are hidden away for the duration of the visit. The misery is white-washed. Even some inmates are tucked away. Prisoners will get carefully prepared food that day,* perhaps with a sweet to follow, and everybody will be on standby. (And sometimes the visit is postponed at the last moment, to the next day,

---

*'False' food is not always meant for consumption. Pat M., a *langana* (a long-term prisoner), relates the story of how he was chosen to play the role of a prisoner in an eating scene of a documentary film on prison life, made for local television. Beautiful steaming graze (food). Take and retake. And when they said, 'Pretend to eat,' Pat did eat. Only to be charged afterwards for having eaten illicit food.

and then maybe to the next again: for days hysterical *boere* will be squinting at mirror-floors while we prisoners stand grumbling in our uncomfortable moleskin jackets behind the bars.)

The first time I experienced this type of visit was not long after being sentenced, when 'that ridiculous little man', as Huntingdon described him, the then Minister of Justice, Jack-in-the-box Krüger, was due to inspect the Hills. Prison warders anxiously asked me what form of address they should use when saying, 'Ja *baas*' to a minister. As it turned out I never saw him. All I heard from behind my closed door were rapid steps going tip-a-tapping down the corridor.

My next experience of a similar kind was when the then Commissioner of Prisons, General Du Preez, came sightseeing at the Hills. But thereby hangs a tale. I'd started having trouble with my scalp. One gentle morning I asked Arselow for permission to cut my hair short so as to be able to apply the ointment which the medical orderly had provided me with. He lent me his pair of scissors and, profiting from a moment of inattention, I started cutting off my hair entirely. When he returned and saw what was up (or off) he was horrified and immediately stopped the operation. The head of the prison was sent for. I was to be charged, but after a long argument it was decreed that the rest of my locks would have to come off too. I couldn't very well be allowed to walk around like some Cherokee warrior with a half-naked skull. (Punk was not yet the fashion.) Arselow completed the operation with curses and threats, and late that same afternoon, with a head as shiny as a lovingly polished egg, I had to stand to attention in front of my cell when Du Preez with his entourage came

through on their rounds. The man was quite taken
aback.

Let me tell you, Mr Investigator, that it is not an
unpleasant experience at all not to have any hair. One
forgets what a joy it is to pass your hand caressingly
over a deliciously sensitive area which is normally
hidden to hand and eye. And with one fell swoop you
have become another person. Gone was Breytenbach,
gone was Galaska, gone was the Professor or Bangai
Bird—there we had the birth of the Billiard Ball himself! But having one's hair off is also an act of penitence
and of submission. Years before, when I was accepted
in Sensei Deshimaru's *dojo* in Paris, and after I had
made the vows of a *boddhisattva*, a lock of hair was
ceremoniously snipped off too. It's a cleaning process,
a casting off of dead matter, a mental undressing, a
way of taking leave of the world and becoming strong
by making yourself vulnerable.

Another visit which caused me a bit of discomfort
was when I was told one day by Arselow, without any
explanation why, that I was to enter my cell and lie
on the bed. Lie there and don't move! This happened
during the afternoon. My cell was then locked and so
of course also the steel door giving on to the main
corridor. I heard, perhaps half an hour later, some
steps going up the corridor (I couldn't see anything
and nobody could see me) and when I was tired of
lying down I got up and started moving around my
cell. The *boer* on the catwalk however, probably did
see me because that evening, before lock-up, Arselow
came and shat all over me for disobeying his strict
instructions. It was only much later that I understood
that a journalist had actually entered the Holy of Ho-
lies escorted by the public relations officer of the Prison

Department, to take a peek at Stefaans Tsafendas.
Rumours had apparently been circulating for some
time already that Stefaans was ill-treated and in bad
health, and the visit was arranged as an exercise in
lie control. Or truth-masking. Stefaans was as happy
as a child with a Christmas toy when they showed
him the subsequent article in the newspaper, illus-
trated by a photo of him sitting there with his smile
like a yellow carrot, sipping tea with these visitors.

All the visits have the same purpose, Mr
Investigator – to put up a façade by which the Prison
Department may cover the ugly face of everyday reality; to comfort the Important Man by showing him
what he expects to find, making it possible for him to
stand up in Parliament or wherever and claim that
South African prisons are beautiful, clean, humanely
run institutions of rehabilitation. Unlike similar places
in Egypt or Turkey or France, or Russia particularly.
As he himself could swear to – having been there (the
prison obviously – not the world).

The only minister I actually met in this way was
Le Grange. That was later, in Cape Town, when I
was already working in the General Stores of Pollsmoor prison, which is where he found me. He was
brought there by Du Preez, the Commissioner – chain-
smoking as always, an elegant man but with the nervously shivering hands and the scented breath of the
alcoholic, and he was showing the swellings of skin
cancer – and the local yokel, or rather the brigadier
commanding the compound with its four penitentiar-
ies and the land around and some further outposts
(like a warlord), whose name was Swart Piet Vangat.
Le Grange, I believe, has the nickname of 'Clark Gable' among his colleagues, a name he is probably in-

ordinately proud of—although I consider it to be an insult to the intelligence of the regretted real Clark Gable. The man is obviously satisfied with himself, with his neatly combed moustache and his stylish silvered and parted hair (he has the upper-lip growth of a minister—carpets also vary in size depending on the level of the civil servant), though perhaps less so with his low forehead. His is a cold, bone-imprisoned, police-directed, sinner-and-saved mind with strong prejudices taking the place of any thinking. Scheming not excluded—even *de rigueur*. (Thinking is an obsolete luxury, seditious by nature, a communist technique.) The purpose of this visit was to make it possible for him to answer his detractors in Parliament by saying that he'd actually seen me personally, that I was living all by myself in a large cell (at my own request) and that by implication any criticism of the government's treatment of political prisoners was unfounded and evil-intentioned. (He did actually declare this at a later date in the House, without ever having been to my cell, of course.) The few questions he put to me were intercepted and answered by either Du Preez or Swart Piet. In this way I learned to my stupefaction that, after work and during weekends, I went back to the White Male Prison, where I benefited from the extensive sports facilities. When asked what kind of sport I practised I did manage to be faster on the draw than the two intermediaries by replying, 'Chess.' The fact of the matter is that there were then no sports facilities of any kind whatsoever for White prisoners at Pollsmoor.

Other senior and cynical officers of the Prison Department would pass through on a rapid tour whenever the moon was blue, and once a year there was a general going-over by the Inspectorate, led by a senior officer. When this circus arrived the inmates were called together in the dining hall and, standing there, drawn up in ranks, we would be addressed by the hoity-toity visitor. Always beforehand there would be so-hear-me-God threats and mutterings among the prisoners in the warrens and overflowing into the corridors. This time, kiss-my-thumb, they were going to stand out, they were going to bring to the attention of the visitor the bad food, or the cruel behaviour of our keepers, or the lack of fresh air, or the fact that there was no music, or whatever, and particularly the fact that – by individual reckoning borne out by patient and endless cross-checking – the original sentence was unjust and, taking into account parole and remission, we should have been released long since ('I am being sequestered by the *boere* and the world has wiped its arse on me!'). But then, when the crucial moment at last arrived and the general or the brigaboer asked if there were any requests or complaints, a dull and sullen silence would go humming through the hall. The few misguided sods who did stand out would be marked people forever afterwards, they would be *misters* or *slimmetjies* (clever little ones),* and long after the visit they would find themselves punished without understanding what caused the sudden harsh treat-

---

*There are basically three kinds of prisoners (in the classification system of the *boere*, but prisoners have adopted the order): the *slimmetjies*, i.e. those who pretend to be clever or who are cheeky, and are heading for a fall ('they will run *knop*,' meaning 'knob'); the *dommetjies*, i.e. the little stupid ones, the half-wits, or those pretending to be thick; the *malletjies*, i.e. the little mad ones, but truly so – because quite a few mental cases do walk behind the same walls as the criminals do.

ment. In any event the requests which did go forward would more often than not be entirely ridiculous ones.

Periodically there would be a delegation of judges or magistrates and prosecutors coming to play the reality game—still part of the bigger one of self-delusion. I suppose the people who actually sentence one to such a place must feel the need to come and have the wool pulled over their eyes and to pass inane remarks, or to stroll down the alleys of sadness, whinnying with their hands in their pockets. It is striking that no senior visitor ever attempted to find out what was really going on inside any of the prisons that I was in, whereas the International Red Cross people would very systematically and very objectively try to form a coherent picture of the situation and the circumstances.

I must mention one judge who did impress me by her reaction—Judge van der Heever of the Cape Bench. She at least was aware that she was being lied to by those accompanying her. As he introduced me to her Swart Piet Vangat stroked his authoritative girth and bared his gums in a mockery of smiling to remark how well fed I looked, how fat I was getting, and she sharply intervened by saying, 'Well, then he must have been a spaghetti when he entered prison because he is certainly not looking very well fed now.'

I mentioned that magistrates and prosecutors didn't even bother to pretend to be interested in what they were shown. They would stand around for a few brief minutes, licking their pocket-smiles, and one would maybe ask you superciliously, 'Well, everything fine then?' and turn off his mind and look at you down his law-and-order nose through vitreous eyes so that you could answer seventy-bags-of-potatoes-and-one-dead-

rat and it would make not the slightest impression on
him. But that had been my experience of magistrates
all along. After the numerous deaths in detention, Mr
Investigator, the political police eventually conceded
to detainees the privilege of being visited by a magistrate once every so many weeks. This government
employee, scared to a standstill even at the very thought
of hearing something bad about the security police,
would come with a writing pad and a frown and pretend to take down whatever complaints or requests
you may have the temerity or the stupidity to present.
The one coming to see me in Pretoria for some inexplicable reason was always shadowed by an inter-
preter, who from long experience in court, had lost
all respect for the man of the law: he would hop about,
sniggering and pulling faces – literally a court jester.
Or he would try out his few words of French on me.
The magistrate never looked me in the eye. Whatever
pain I gave voice to would be swept aside with a
muttered, 'This is not of my concern,' or 'I'm not
entitled to say anything about that matter.' No, don't
talk to me about magistrates, Mr Eye – they are there
only to give the illusion of legality to the system of
oppression. The chapter is getting long, I know, but
I must still talk to you about those people who are
benevolent to the system without, normally, working
within it, at least not in a narrow sense – the 'personalities': those for whom the doors would be opened
wide and the red carpet rolled out. In this way I met
Christ Barnard, the heart-plumber. I was summoned
to the VIP visiting room in Cape Town one afternoon
and, to my astonishment, left quite alone without any
supervision in the presence of this doctor. He was
very friendly, with a smile like a slice of bleached

watermelon which he could neither swallow nor spit out but kept flashing like an advertisement for watermelons. The purpose of this visit was to convince me to allow myself to be interviewed for a film about South Africa that he was in the process of making for French television. Everything had already been arranged with the Prison Department, he said. And smiled a mile.

Again then the iniquitous choice one is faced with: the possibility, however faint, of communicating with the outside world (and remember that the filming would in any event be a break in the rotting away of everyday life in prison), but at the same time it could be a trick to use one for propaganda purposes. I therefore asked for permission to consult my lawyers before making any decision, and this was granted. I wrote a letter asking them whether they knew anything about the project, who was it made by, for whom was it intended, and how come—if it was, as Barnard claimed, really on the level, that is, that I'd be free to say whatever I felt necessary—the Prison Department allowed him such easy access to me. A few weeks passed and one afternoon Swart Piet Vangat had me fetched from the General Stores in a great rush. In his office he told me that I was to prepare myself immediately for the filming because the professor (before whom he literally grovelled) and the French crew were already on their way. But I hadn't heard anything from my lawyers, I objected. 'Very strange,' he clucked in sympathy. 'They can't be very serious about their work, can they now, because we have forwarded your letter. But *I* can assure you there's nothing underhand about this proposed film and besides, just think, these people are coming specially all this way for you. It's too late to stop them *now*; I can't even reach them. Think of all the expense!'

I should have known better, or been stronger, but I allowed myself to be bamboozled into the farce. Swart Piet himself, striding with legs wide apart, took me to the section store where our clothes were kept and had one of his underlings, a lieutenant who was literally standing there on shaking knees, run over to the Female Prison at the double with a brand-new outfit over his arm, to have it pressed.

The television crew turned up. Barnard saw me alone first and told me that I would not be allowed to speak to the Frenchmen in any circumstances, and that anyway I was not to speak French in their presence. The sequences they wanted were filmed with me receiving Barnard in my cell. Tattie Swart, the section sergeant, had arranged for a bedspread to be thrown over my bed and wanted to bring in a carpet too, but I objected to these foolish attempts at masking the bareness. Barnard, preening as usual, then proceeded to interview me with very hostile and very slanted questions. Whenever there was a break in the filming he would switch off the little portable tape recorder he carried – he was evidently taping our talk for his own private purposes too – and say to me softly, 'You know, I agree entirely with your views. I don't like this government either. I support you wholeheartedly.' And when the cameraman was ready for the next take he would go back to his mouthings of pro-South African government drivel. Swart Piet and his entourage of senior officers were lurking just outside the cell door. When it was over they bowed and scraped and invited the professor for 'a drink and a bite' which, miraculously, had been laid out in the officers' club. (Knowing how these things are arranged, I'm sure that the prisoner-cooks must have been sweating for hours to get everything ready.) Barnard disdainfully declined. You should have seen their faces fall, Mr Investigator!

So upset was I after this charade that I wrote to my wife asking her to intervene with the lawyers in an attempt to have the broadcasting of the film stopped, and at the very next visit I had from my father I told him all that had happened. He went to see Barnard with the result that the professor returned, trying to reassure me that the film was not anything like what I thought it might be. Many months later I learned that efforts to stop the broadcasting of the film in France were only partially successful. By court order it was to be preceded by a statement by the lawyer who represented Yolande and the Breytenbach Support Committee putting the film in context. Only then did I learn that the film was in fact made for the Department of Information – part of one of its very aggressive schemes to sell the South African anti-communist line abroad. (And the letter to my lawyers was quite simply never forwarded.)

Barnard came to visit me twice more. I must grant that these were pleasant occasions – except that I could never get a word in edgeways and he seemed to have a desperate need to impress with his possessions, with his successes, with his talent as an author (we were colleagues, he said) and even with his wife's knowledge of French. (Except also that his visits were 'contact' – not behind glass – and that they were in fact of the 'red-carpet' type, whereas I couldn't obtain the same privilege for my wife or my father.) Still, in his own tortured way he did sincerely attempt to put in a good word for me, whether by means of his weekly newspaper articles or (I imagine) in the course of his direct contacts with senior members of the government. I understood clearly enough that it was a two-way process in that Barnard's concern for me and my fate gave him a good image abroad, particularly in France, where he had been approached by French writers concerned about my situation.

We are coming at last to those visitors who are critics of the system or people who can be depicted as the loyal opposition from within, notably members of the Opposition political party in Parliament and first among them, of course, Helen Suzman. On two occasions during my years inside she visited the complex I was in, but I never met her. Maybe she was refused permission to see me, or maybe she didn't know that I was there, or perhaps she didn't consider it of any importance. I'm not sure.

I don't think it would be excessive to say that the prisoners, both political and common-law, regard her as Our Lady of the Prisoners. She is indeed a living myth among the people inhabiting the world of shadows. The quality of the food suddenly improves? Out of the blue a movie is shown on a Saturday afternoon? People have been sleeping for years on mats on the floor – 'sleeping camel', as we said, because the skin of the hips eventually becomes callous – and now beds are made available? Prisoners would look at one another and nod their heads wisely and say, 'You see, Aunty Helen did it after all.'

At the same time she was, or is, considered the final recourse for any prisoner, the ultimate threat of retribution or redress one would brandish when trying to get something done. I once heard old Johnny Blik in an exercise yard in Cape Town shout, beside himself with fury, at one of the warders that he was not going to take things like this any longer, he was finished with this eating-shit business, he was going to go to the head of the prison and, if that didn't work, to the brigadier ('I'm not afraid of anybody!') and beyond that he would insist on seeing the Commissioner himself, just let him come down here. And if he didn't get satisfaction by Jesus he was going to write directly to Helen Suzman. The remarkable thing is that it had the desired effect on the warder. It happened many a time that an old lag would sidle up to me to ask, out of the side of the mouth, if I had Helen's address, please.

During my spell in Cape Town one prisoner actually slashed his wrists while in the court cell below the courtroom one day, in an effort to force the authorities to allow him to see Helen Suzman. He was guilty of rape but he expected her to work a miracle and change his guilt into innocence. If I remember right, she did see him and advised him to accept his fate.

They, the *boere*, to put it mildly, didn't like her overmuch. They detested her sharp eye and her sharp tongue and her fearless criticism of whatever wrongs she saw. A fellow inmate who had spent time in Kroonstad Prison (or Crown Town, as we knew it) once recounted to me how Helen Suzman came through there once. Since, however, the institution was at that time somewhat over-populated — not an uncommon occurrence — a good quarter of the prisoners, among whom he found himself squeezed, were actually hidden away so that she would not notice the lack of living space. Ernie Wentzel, one of my lawyers, similarly tells with great glee of how he himself was visited in prison during the early 1960s when he'd been arrested as one of the young Turks of the Liberal Party. He had had a finger wagged at him beforehand, and been duly warned that he was not to talk about the conditions of detention in any circumstances. When introduced to Helen Suzman in the presence of the commanding officer, he turned to the poor victim and inquired loudly and clearly in his most humble way whether he had indeed understood it right when told that he was not allowed to mention that the food is of very bad quality. And the officer, going red in the face, 'Yes, you are not allowed to talk about that.' And Ernie would say, 'And I'm not supposed to mention anything about the dirty bathroom, am I, sir?' 'No, you are not allowed to talk about that.' 'Or about the fact that we have no visiting facilities?' 'No, certainly not!' 'Or about the cold floors and the moth-eaten blankets?' And the officer, apoplectic, five furious frogs in his throat, 'No, I told you, *no* talk of *any* prison conditions!' Ernie with deference, 'Thank you, sir, I just wanted to make sure. . . .'

The only time I actually saw her was from the back as she walked briskly over an empty courtyard behind the workshops. The stores I worked in then gave onto the same courtyard. She was surrounded by a cohort of nervous and angry prison officials, grinding their teeth in impotent rage and hoping to shoo her off as rapidly as possible. The sergeant looking after me, Hansie Cripple, hobbled to the window to look at her retreating back and hissed, 'The bloody bitch!'

Near the end of my time in the president's palace I was visited by Van Zyl Slabbert, the Leader of the Opposition, but I shall have something more to say

about him by and by, Mr Investigator. For now I just
want to enter the remark that if, as happened supposedly when God wanted to destroy Sodom and Go-
morrah, if it ever were to become necessary to find
three just and good men among the Afrikaners to save
the tribe from extinction, I would have no qualms in
proposing Van Zyl Slabbert and Johan Kriegler and –
this may surprise you – Charles de Fortier as candidates. (Of course I know a few more just people who
happen incidentally also to be Afrikaners. Very few.)

Finally there were the outsiders, the foreigners,
those who had nothing to do with the Prison Department except that they needed in some way to fight
it. I was once told by a sergeant who had spent many
years working in the notorious farm-prisons of the
Boland* of how, when years ago the first international
delegation of investigators came to visit South African
penal settlements, all the Coloured prisoners there
were suddenly given brand new guitars (whether they
could play them or not). Needless to say, they were
overjoyed; needless to say too, the warders were most
perplexed by this unprecedented largesse, spoiling
the *bandiete* right into the ground. The visitors must
have been bemused by the widespread musicality of
the locals. But then the whole idea could only have
been to create the impression in the minds of the
visitors that our farm labourer-prisoners are a happy,
singing, music-making lot.

---

*These are rural prisons in the south-western part of the Cape
Province – there are similar outposts in other agricultural areas of
the country. The inmates are rented out by the Department as
farm labourers, under the armed supervision of the farmers and
their foremen, and a warder or two.

The years have passed and the members of the International Red Cross Committee who came to see me were certainly never going to be fooled by such a ridiculous attempt at eye-blinding. One cannot but have the greatest respect for their dedication and their competence. Besides, what a joy it was once a year to meet a group of people who did not attempt to manipulate you, who took and treated you as a normal human being, and to whom you could speak French for a few hours! They would measure your exercise yard, test your light bulbs, listen to your heartbeat, taste your food, talk to your medic and go with you down their check-list of questions and observations – and the year after there would be the follow-up, when they'd inform you about their requests and the results achieved.

They were thorough; they knew what they were doing; they knew what they wanted to obtain; they were realistic about their chances of success; they never wavered in their commitment to justice and in their patiently pursued efforts to obtain more humane conditions for those prisoners they were allowed to see. So objective were they in their approach, sir, and so careful in their work, that even the South African Prisons authorities could not entice them away from the facts. Whatever privileges we South African political prisoners had or have are nearly exclusively due to the work of the IRCC.

Of course, they very often did not succeed. Quite early on during my sojourn in boop they tried to let me have an electronic chess player to alleviate my solitary confinement, my moves against an absent I. Years of fruitless negotiating ensued – the Department throwing up as excuses the supposed fragility of the apparatus, the absence of an electric plug in my cell, the risk that one may be able to fabricate a bomb from the thing's innards (that's why I was never allowed a record player or a tape recorder either)—and then endless trouble again to retrieve the gift from the office of a senior official who'd probably hoped to 'inherit' it. Years it took too finally to obtain a flask. A-Group prisoners are entitled to a thermos flask for the coffee or tea they are permitted to purchase once a month. In my case, despite efforts by the IRCC, it was considered too dangerous an object. I could secrete missives in the isolating space between the glass of the inner bottle and the outside cask, Colonel Witnerf argued. Or smash the thing and use the shards either to break out or to kill myself (which would mean damaging State property). So, Witnerf claimed, the flask would have to be dismantled daily by his men for security verification and in the course of their work they might well accidentally break it, in which case I'd go complaining again to the Red Cross with all the resultant embarrassment for the Department and the sacred cause of South African survival. . . . Serious attention was paid the matter by the pompous Witnerf and by Smoel, his red-headed security henchman (because the IRCC kept on coming back at them): alternatives were considered—maybe a flask made of Tupperware and thus without the glass casing, maybe one with a mouth so wide you could ram your paw down it to finger the interior, or, it was suggested, maybe a regular flask after all, but locked away in the section sergeant's office, and once or twice a day I could be let out of my cell to go and have a sip there, under supervision. . . . It took a change in commanding officer and, I suspect, palavers at the highest

ministerial level for the matter to be settled about a
year before my release.

The plant, the bit of greenery, the small locus of
life, of *other* breathing matter, that I so repeatedly
begged for (a request forwarded and supported by the
Swiss delegation) – there we failed. Most long-term
prisoners have some plant or other in their cells at
Pollsmoor. The plants are naturally bought and sold,
stolen, fought for and looked after by several inmates
when in a big cell. (They sometimes, illegally, also
have small pets: a derisory attempt at imitating 'normal life'. More about that anon.) Once I thought I was
on the brink of success (I could already divine the play
of light on leaf, in my mind I was going through the
ritual of watering, the incalculable freedom of caring
for someone or something *else!*) – the soft-bodied head
of the prison foolishly said yes after I tried to talk
reason into his eyes for the umpteenth time, and Yolande had my sister deliver a beautiful bonsai at the
place of steel girders and concrete. But no, Witnerf
screamed – how could we risk security in such a fashion? Again he patiently explained that his men would
have been obliged to unearth the creature daily to
check that I hadn't hidden anything among the roots,
a pistol perhaps, a grenade, a vial of arsenic, a sword,
a guided missile or a poem; and in any event, he
considered, the bonsai was out because the pebbles
used decoratively to secure the roots can be (he seriously did say this) dangerous weapons. And Smoel
solemnly nodded his complete agreement. We were
living by our wits. Total onslaught. God knows what
the Japanese may think of next.

The mouth organ my mother sent me I did eventually get. I knew it had been sent but that it was kept

in some office somewhere (although my mother was told that I'd received it). You see, I had my spies working in their offices. So the Red Cross came and I brought up the matter. The officer locally responsible for me at that time, in our section, that is, was Captain Sodom. Small, compact, clear blue eyes. The Red Cross, after the visit, had a first talk with Swart Piet Vangat, officer commanding Pollsmoor Prison Command and adjacent territories, etc. Swart Piet (knowing it was going to get to the Minister's ears) called in Witnerf and copiously covered his underling with verbal excretion spiced with threats of death, destruction, damnation—who knows, maybe even prison! Witnerf, with his head-wobbling red-haired sidekick Smoel in tow, went to locate Sodom and buried him under the type of shit that can only be provoked by gut-twisting panic. And so Sodom came into my cell. He was speechless. European with rage. Not knowing what to do with his cap. The thing kept sliding around on his trembling head. So that he eventually threw it down on the cement. (Smoel similarly once destroyed his recently acquired green-banded hat by jumping on it in a fit of anger.) I did all of this on purpose, Sodom swore, his blue eyes practically crepitating. I did it because I'm a *mister* and because I wanted to trap him so as to destroy his career! But he's no fool, he assured me. He knows what goes for what. He's no doll and he wasn't born under a turkey either. He had the little mouth organ fetched (it used to belong to my toothless old deceased Uncle Koot), and made me sign a paper admitting to my having received the said object. He went back to the office and banged his fists against the walls and returned and had me unlocked and stormed and raved some more. He would have killed me on the spot if he could do so without complicating the ownership of the false musical instrument. (In later years, late at night, fellows in the next door cell would request me to play them a favourite tune: more often than not it would be 'Blue Eyes Cryin' in the Rain' or 'Somewhere Between Your Heart and Mine' – the latter was very popular because of its line: *there's a wall so high it reaches the sky. . . .*)

The same Captain Sodom not long after had me charged for being in the possession of a dangerous weapon. I was still a pipe smoker then, Mr Investigator, and Jerry – my crooked Czechoslovakian friend who worked in the metal-working shop – made and offered me a pipe scraper made of lead. The material could not be sharpened. I could not even cut a slice of bread with it!

Sodom left for Medium (Coloured) Prison, was badly bludgeoned over the head with a brick swung by a prisoner in the sick bay, and returned to us with a scar and the star of a major. We were apprehensive about his cell inspections every second weekend when he was on duty. In prison one is issued with chunks of green soap ('soap, green opaline', in the storeman's parlance). You wash everything with it – floors, your armpits, walls – and in the corridors you always encounter its pervasive odour. It is good carving material. Out of boredom one Christmas I cut a little Buddha from it, seated in the cross-legged posture of *mokusho* or *zazen*. It lived on my bedside locker. In walked Sodom on his Saturday rounds. Picked it up. 'And what the f-f-f- hell is this? Don't think you can make a – f-f-f- *fool* of the State. Soap is issued for you to wash yourself with, not for making d-d-d- *dolls*!'

And turning to the section sergeant, 'See that he's charged for damaging State property.' I destroyed the I-doll by washing it away gradually. Which was a good lesson: thus ought one to erase one's attachments, the same way that the mind must – like a blade – be sharpened down to nothingness. What a clean cut!

Many international agencies try to be of succour to political detainees. And often they destroy their credibility, and impair their effectiveness, by going off at half-cock or acting on half-baked information. (Deeper causes for their lack of success may be their ideological intransigence and the fact that they are often more concerned about the peace of their own consciences than about the conditions of those whom they are ostensibly trying to help.) They can learn a lot from the IRCC, which is precise in its approach, discreet, persistent and objective, and which individualizes its methods and its goals.

The other objective, non-system visitors I had were, towards the end of my time, the French ambassador to South Africa, Bernard Dorin, and – when Mitterrand came to power in France – his successor, François Plaisant. The French government (I learned later) had been attempting for some time to obtain my release. It also managed to alleviate my situation by getting permission for its representative to visit me once every six months. During one of Bernard Dorin's first visits Captain Smoel, who had to be present to take notes and to work the taping system, went even redder than usual in the face because we had exchanged a few words in French. (The *boere* hated the French visits and were always on the very point of being frankly discourteous to the visitors.) That was the occasion when Dorin gave me a short review of world events. I felt as if I was emerging from a profound cave. My mind was sitting there with its mouth all slack. In fact, I realized then how blunt and dull I had become. He told me about Poland and Afghanistan. And, in passing, Benin. Benin? I did not dare ask where it was but assumed that it must be a new African state. Were they reshaping the world while I had my back turned? Where was my time?

During his very next visit we were informed that it was forbidden to talk politics. It was likewise forbidden for me to talk about prison conditions. So we exchanged our mutually shared passion for literature. And I told Monsieur Dorin about *Mouroir*. (I grabbed every chance I could to tell visitors about my writing: to establish its existence objectively, which, so I hoped, would ensure the Prison authorities' returning it to me eventually.) I must also have told him that my biggest need was to keep the mind breathing.

The embassy, negotiating with the Minister of Justice, tried to help me by having French books sent to me. The Minister and the Commissioner of Prisons would diplomatically accede to the request, but the people lower down would systematically block the granted favour. Eventually I did receive some French classics translated into English—Balzac, Zola, Gide. . . . But the one Malraux among them *(The Fate of Man)* was eaten up by thin air. When I complained ('stood fast' or 'pressed up', as we say in boop slang) I was told by Smoel, staring at me from his small red orbits, that I couldn't have it because it contained too much . . . sex!

And I felt reassured when I was told by one of the cleaner-prisoners working up front that it happened, when Yolande came on a visit, that she was chauffeured to the compound in an official black car flying the tricolour from its bonnet. Whoever protected and helped her would be my friend for ever afterwards.

Because, Mr Investigator, there remains the last category of visitors – the most important – which cannot be categorized: my wife and my parents. Whenever Yolande came to see me or, during her long absences in Europe, when first my parents came and then – after the death of my mother – my old man, all alone, straight as a pine tree, hat on the head, then time would stop . . . only to flow away with a painful rush. You look at them through the glass panel and you see the contained sorrow. In Pretoria you had to bend forward as if with heartache and speak through a kind of funnel. You were one huge deaf ear. In Cape Town it was at first by telephone, over a crackling or buzzing line, taped, staring at one another from a distance of 4 inches. Like being in the mirror! And later, in the White Male Prison, again we had to talk through a temperamental squawkbox made of steel. These visits – once a month at first, more often when we obtained permission to group them during Yolande's stay in the country – were so deeply upsetting that I understood why some prisoners refuse to have their loved ones come to the prison at all. Why disturb the dead? Why come and prod the pain? It is better to forget that outside, unimaginably, another world and other life exist. And yet, if it hadn't been for these visits I could never have survived.

You know more or less when a visit is due. (Mine always took place either on a Friday or a Wednesday – the other weekdays were for visitors to those detainees awaiting trial, and weekends were for the 'hard labours', and the authorities went to great lengths to prevent an occasional outside visitor from accidentally catching sight of me. I always had my visit alone – apart from the obligatory guardians on both sides – whereas the other prisoners saw their people in lots of several at a time.) You live forward towards it. Then the day dawns and you smell its freshness and you put on the clean, pressed greens you have kept aside for exactly this; you polish your shoes and you try to keep the shine by rubbing the toecaps against your socks, and you shave carefully; you even use some of the deodorant you bought for tobacco off a fellow bird. All vanity! The visitor can neither touch nor smell you and will see you only dimly through the scratched and much talked at partition.

The agony starts too because life goes on as if this were not a big day. You can't talk it over with anyone. Morning passes and nothing happens. Anything wrong? An accident perhaps? Or maybe your lady or your parents have called the prison to postpone the visit or to explain about the hold-up – and of course 'they' will never bother to relieve you of your anxiety. They tell you to go and work. You can't refuse but you panic because you know how complicated it is and how long it takes to bring you back in when summoned from work. (Because you must be double-guarded and transported in a closed van.) And they don't care, obviously. Why should they? In fact, you are convinced that they would purposefully have the visit ruined by accident. You hate the idea of your visitor(s) having to wait, not knowing the cause for the delay. The warders know that you are on tenterhooks. They sneer at you. They think they're funny. An old sergeant once expressed his conviction that 'She won't be coming any more – she's sailed away on a ship with a big black *kaffir* ' – certainly expecting me to be insulted by the racist slur. Or they try to get intimate information. Who? What for? How does it feel? 'Rough, hey, when she's so near and you can't touch her!'

At last a call comes to your place of work. You can't hear what's being said but your sixth sense knows that this is it! Your eyes are glued to the lips. You are to be brought back. Visit! You stand around like a sick crow, waiting for your escort. They torture you. There's no van available. The warder riding shotgun cannot absent himself from work just now (always there must be an armed warder present when you are transported, even for the 150 yards from building to building within the same walled-in complex) or he doesn't want to. It's not his turn, he says. In any event, they will not be rushed – else you may end up forgetting that you're just a *bandiet*.

Or, if you stayed in, Smoel would come to your cell and wordlessly indicate that your wife is there by making the rude sign by which a woman is indicated among prisoners: imitating the tits by the thumb of a closed fist.

You go with the knot in your belly and the sea in your knees. You take your best hidden smile with you. You also have a little 'shopping list' of matters that must be discussed. Into the visitors' room. Wait. Warder with you. (You try to forget him.) Steps in that corridor leading to freedom beyond the grille, audible through the glass. Familiar, so familiar. A previous life. In she walks (with a warder – you try to forget him), the colour of the sun on her skin and the breath of mountain and wind in her eyes and a handbag I know and a new dress, no? and a ribbon in her hair and and and and another and. And in one hundred and twenty miserably minute seconds the accorded forty-five minutes are finished, over, done, *klaar, pelielie, flêbê, oppela*. . . .

Sometimes it happened that they would interrupt her visit just to be bastards. In Cape Town, during the reign of Witnerf, she wasn't allowed to bring her handbag into the cubicle. Once an officer came in to take away her watch because, I assume, it might have contained, what? A camera? A recording device? Another time they took away her pen. Same pretext.

You fight for the last second. Time has dropped out of your body like a birth. It is done. A smile, fluttering like a butterfly looking for the flower of the face, leaves the room. Steps fade. You are kept in until she, or they, are out of reach of a desperate hand through the bars separating day from doom. Then back to your cell or back to work. You aren't present, of course. You chew it this way, you take it out and breathe it in all over again, and then you chew it that way.

Tonight, back inside, an office cleaner will come and report what he saw where you couldn't see—who brought her, what they looked like, how long they had to wait, what the officers mumbled among themselves—and maybe he will tell you that he 'scored' a few cigarette ends in the visitors' waiting room, real Gitanes. 'Strong stuff, hey?' He would ask whether she's your daughter. You would say yes. He would inquire, 'The oldest one or the littlest?' You would tell him where to get off. 'The oldest one, of course! What do you take me for, an old goat?'

And then I would retire and have a long chat with my old companion, Don Espejuelo from Pretoria, who was with me even in the days when I dwelled in the valley of darkness with a nothingness head. He would smooth down his grey hair and rub his chin with slender fingers to hide a cynical lip-twist. He would engage me in a conversation about culture. Or try to get me to define the ethics of resistance – in the No Man's Land context, naturally – or to identify the elements of a South African identity. There may be silences. There will certainly be silences. The moon outside the bars will be curled like a cold white caterpillar, but the cold white light will be copious nevertheless, and white and cold the inundated world. Don Espejuelo's eyes will be closed to slits against the acrid smoke of the cheap snout he used to roll his pills (cigarettes). 'Homesick?' he would ask. Crack a joint. 'Home? What home? Where . . . ? What a debilitating concept. Fool! Fool!'

INSERT

It is certainly true that the whole process of punishment, the inordinate insistence upon punishment, the proliferation of prisons, the amplification of the concept and its applications until you have a penal universe, an alternative world, a culture of darkness – it is certainly true that all this ties in with the Protestant ethic. I don't know off-hand of any other culture where you are, as in No Man's Land, born guilty to die guilty except (very rarely: Heaven is a tight joint) when you are, provisionally and arbitrarily, saved by the Investerrogator. With luck (or if The Law does not cover enough ground) the Greyshits, His soldiers on earth, will desist for the time being from punishing or terrorizing you. The dichotomy is 'guilt'/freedom. Where freedom does not exist except as a subversive idea.

It is not only the cadre within which you evolve. The dichotomy has its objective existence also inside you. You are guilty even when you do not yet know of what. You are the mirroring of your environment with all its broken monkeys. Where freedom does not exist except as a subversive idea.

It can be said that we have to do here with real democracy. You are a consciousness-generating, surroundings-expanding force, the way the termite is. You are a twinge of the Conscience. And the Conscience, the great Justification, is the *State*. The State *is* in reality the earthly shape and the terrestrial abode of Him, the Interstigator. And Minister Krüger said, 'The highest good is the security of the State.' (Can we allow the killing of God? Let us all unite to combat evil . . . which dwells within us. . . . To suicide, citizens!)

The State lives inside you. You are its condition. Except that the State is pure though jealous. Thou shalt have no other idols or urinations or blots. There will be no dissidence. You will not prostrate yourself before any other idea. Who else will be able to punish you? What other security can compare with the foot on the neck? There is no freedom (*that* is a fart of the heart) – there can only be guilt in its million convolutions and revelations. There can only be the twitching of many moustaches.

But the celebration of guilt can only take place in secret places. That too is part of the ethic: the need to hide, the need to pretend. It could be that other cultures, at other times, made a public display of their intimate rites – that they broke and burned their heretics on the market place. We, in our twisted ways, have to be subtle. We are not to be known, we can only be raped. We have built the mazes, the high walls from behind which we stare at the blocked-off sky. We take with us the images. We have to go down corridors, we have to have keys, we must shout and plead at the gates for guardians to let us through . . . to lead us ever deeper into the inner sanctum. To where the noose of the penitent waits. To where the altar of the State is erected. In the final heart of loneliness. We are the wind and we are the birds, and the singing, singing of the rope.

It must be like a wall. Very often – no, all the time really – I relive those years of horror and corruption, and I try to imagine, as I did then with the heart an impediment to breathing, what it must be like to be executed. What it must be like to be. Executed. Hanged by the passage of breath and of words. Sure, I remember the ritual preparations, the singing of those in 'the pot', the final leave-taking a day before when the weeping and the wailing of the mothers and the wives reverberated through the sections, surmounting even those high barriers which separate the bereaved from the doomed, and how the Black 'condemns' would regroup in the corridor after those last visits to return singing to the 'pot', the cell of the condemned ones, stamping their feet, rattling their chains and raising their voices in a rhythm of life and of sorrow so intimately intertwined that it could only be a dislocation of the very notion of the body of God; sure, and the next morning then when the cool light of daybreak envelops the prison and it is still dark in the tunnels, the voices behind the wall breaking with the poignancy of warm, breathed harmonies, the bursting of the pomegranates, the breaking of the fast and the rapidity of exhalation, and then the indecency from man to man of handcuff and hood and rope and trapdoor – the earth falling for ever away: we are the wind and we are the birds, and the singing, singing of weighted ropes. . . . .

Yes, of course. And yet I don't know. You have made of my mind a misery of images which I shall never be able to express.

It must be like a wall, I say to myself. One must come to it like a white wall beyond which the unimaginable resides. Beyond which you must imagine the silence of the minotaur.

I think of the occult powers which deliberate death. I think of how they erect that wall and my thinking is like bricks which will be covered with plaster. Because the judgment and the killing is the work of men. There is probably subtlety there. The expiation, the weighing, the sending off to the abattoir, the words about the neck – these must have been refined to the gestures of lifting an eyebrow and moving a pen. They must experience a deep, reverberating pleasure in *deciding* death. The means is the murderer. In this way does writing destroy reality, to replace it. I close my eyes and I cannot face the darkness. I cannot go to sleep except if I fall behind the membranes of my eyelids. Like a wall soundlessly giving way before nothingness. I imagine. I go. I position myself on the edge of the precipice, on the lip of saying, and I jump. Or the earth lurches to steepness and starts crumbling and shifting: I cling to plants which tear and become limp in the grip of my hands. And then the hazy views recede before the opening up of majestic vistas – all the past is there, and all the future and the never-

changed and the never-same which is always the same,
the immense green patterns of sorrow. Where freedom does not exist except as a subversive idea. A
falling, this falling, *forward* into the void.

Then also the dreams come. By night, when darkness has descended like a veil so that the eyes can be
open like the looking of mirrors, then the dreams
return. . . . I enter this tall building, this tower which
has no windows or apertures; weighted down, heavy
with the pack of a parachute on the back and straps
constricting my limbs; into the lift where many red
buttons indicating unidentified stages are flashing; another conscript there, a poor sod, a fellow. 'How long?'
I ask him; 'Two years,' he says; and us not knowing
whether we are going up or down; but we emerge on
the flatness of an endless roof under a canopy of so
many pale stars; we walk stiffly; to departure; we are
pilots about to be shot off into nowhere; and we turn
around–there's no lift shaft behind us, no stairwell,
no door: no going down ever again. . . .

We are moving from prison to prison; in fact, we
are to be released, we are released already; and are
being transported in a lorry along a road crossing many
high bridges; the wind, like ropes, singing, so that it
moves our hair and flutters through our garments of
prisoners; over many high bridges; far below us the
sorrowful pattern in green and brown patches (and
spirals and whorls) of prison compounds and lands
where pumpkins are cultivated; old Charlie–we are
free now–old Charlie is worried because he has no
clothes for freedom; will his freedom be restricted?
where will he go? we argue, he says no, he must go
back for clothes to be discharged with–how else can
one enter the world except through the skins and the

rags of anonymity?—and he jumps from the back of
the truck; I see the wind bulging the clothes of his
confinement as he twirls, falls, spirals back to earth;
and my throat is sore and swollen with tears because
I see, far below, how the ants receive old Charlie like
so many words, of how he will never be let go of
again. . . .

I am free now; yes, I'm on my way in a car—to an
airport? wedged tightly between two quiet mous-
tached civilians on the backseat; in front, the grey-
haired conductor with the jowls, the emissary of the
highly-placed person; who will take me to the destination where freedom starts; I have my own clothes
now, the suit unfamiliarly tight; up and over, and
down a steep incline then so that it gets darker; is it
raining darkness? a river at the bottom that we must
go through? people in the valley? are they shouting?
a riot? throwing stones? and the blind windows shatter
like a splurge of silver tears, dribbling, coursing; already we are rocking; we shall never reach the end
of the road. . . .

I am so hungry; the building is huge: it is a palace
made of glass, which may shatter at any moment,
disappearing with us when boundaries are effaced; I
live in it as in a dream; there is a throng of I's, of
convicts all lining up for food; pumpkin-and-potatoes;
but *boere* walk down the line, grabbing hold of our
dixies and throwing the yellow food on the floor; and
they laugh with ruddy faces and teeth shining through
the moustaches. . . .

They tell me to come to the office and they give
me back my own clothes which feel so strange to the
body; I'm to be transferred, they say, but they give
no further explanation; and I find myself on my way

back to Big House; many prisoners in the truck, an old friend of years ago too – old One-Eye Longtimer; how much we have to tell one another! but do you know why they're taking me, I ask him; surely because they want to release you, he says; if not, why else the clothes? but nobody says; nobody knows the troubles I have; and arrived there in the yard we are told to wait to one side; warders on a raised platform processing so slowly those to be discharged; Arselow among them, fatter than before; names are called out, mine not among them; what shall I do, I ask One-Eye – do you think it's good to ask? because as long as you're ignorant the worst will be postponed – and he assures me that I ought to – after all and if not, I can only be there to be freed; up I go; to speak to Arselow; who smirks and says, 'Ah yes, ah yes now; you just be patient – we have special plans for *you*. . . .'

It is the time of freedom – all to be released; the day is dawning like a sigh in the trees across the river; all go, all go; darkness recedes; quickly now, all ready, go! go!; I see them going, crossing the yard which is already growing its shadows, disappearing in the trees across the river, a singing in the air; I see them going, they are gone; the place is empty; all I need to do is get these bloody clothes on; now, I try; I try; my limbs are growing more and more dumb; I try; I'm getting caught forever in sleeve and in leg; already the outside is fading. . . .

4

Some Angels

Back to my cell. And the mountain a haze of flames. But for the time being the mountain is entirely in the mind.

And the mind produces its own darknesses. Darkness floods the dreams and taints the waking moments. Mind flooded by anguish. The darker it grows, the tighter it is wound, the more obscurantist and superstitious it is too.

I have retained a pig-eared pack of cards somebody let me have during my detention period. At night, in that slice of time between lock-up and lights out, I squat on my bed and I pack out the cards. Pale faces look up at me. I've started to ration my smoking—one pipe in the late morning and two after lock-up. So I can tamp down the tobacco now, and light a match. In the dark it doesn't taste the same. I've never truly learned the rules of solitaire but it doesn't really matter. In this way I can stretch the probabilities without having to sustain the knowledge of cheating. I lay bets against myself: if I succeed in 'playing out', it will be a good omen. And I go on and on, trying to succeed. The failures I forget about immediately, saying to myself: I wasn't really ready yet, that last game was only a dummy run. The mind trying to move the mountain. Groping blindly for interstices, for faults in the façade – desperate, like the rat in its cage sniffing at every crack, gnawing at every hole, for *any* form of escape. I can't lose and I can't win. If I succeed in my endeavours, then I'm jubilant. If I fail: well, who believes in these superstitions anyway? This is what Don Espejuelo tells me when he enters my cell. He makes a few acid remarks. He shakes his head. He chuckles. But I go down deeper into darkness.

Sometimes I continue playing long after the light has been turned out. I shuffle the pack and give myself the chance of drawing any card. Spades are bad luck– especially the ace of spades. It makes me think of Big Chief Sitting Bull. Of death. Hearts are fine. Particularly the nine of hearts. It means my lady love is thinking of me. The meaning of the other colours I have forgotten. I re-shuffle and draw and I say that the number on the card will correspond to the number of years left before there's a chance of release. If it's too high, I make it months. Or I translate it as being the number of days before I shall get a letter from Lady One. And when everything fails, when it is dark all over and the lettering on the cards is even blacker than the gloom in my cell, black like old coagulated blood, then I can at least remember the saying: unlucky at games, lucky at love.

The ears become the most important sense organs.

You use your ears the way a bat employs its radar—to situate yourself, to detect danger, to find some security in this environment you cannot escape from. You learn to interpret the sounds and the sudden silences, the banging and the rustling; by listening you unravel the rhythm of daily activity. Voices you hear repeatedly take on shape and colour, become personalities. There are some people, like the 'condemns', whom I never saw—and yet I still have the impression that I knew them intimately.

(But at other times you wake, you listen, and the rumours you hear are indecipherable. Your ears lead you up blind alleys—they do not interpret. The noises confuse you. They are the exteriorization of your confusion. You want to shout to identify yourself, to pin yourself down. What is this? Where am I? Am I awake? Your silence is sucked through the bars. You fight for sense. At the bottom end of the mirror-smooth corridor you hear Pablo Casals sawing his cello into sad brown sounds. Rats as big as police dogs pad from cell to cell, smelling the cracks. As they rub along the walls their fur makes a whirring sound. Your mind lives outside you. The whole world has burned down.)

The warders shout at the convicts and they shout at one another. When on night shift, they don't even respect the sleep of those about to die, exhausted by this waiting for death. Why should other people sleep when *they* have to work? Their mouths are filthy and the wit is poor. Perhaps they are only pretending to be real he-men so as to survive in these circumstances of decay and degradation.

Sometimes you hear them hollering from one guardpost to the other, insulting each other's forebears, vilifying their origins. 'Your mother just threw you away when you were born,' one would intone with glee, 'and then she raised the afterbirth instead!'

'Nah, and you?' Number Two responds. 'Your father shat you out on a stone and that's where your mother found you!'

'Why don't you go and suck the elastic of your old grandmother's bloomers?'

'*Your* grandmother doesn't even wear them! You have to suck her bloody old cunt!'

'Your father's prick, man!'

'Look here, I'll come and chop a hole in your chest so that you can cough.'

'And I shall climb down your throat and shit on your heart, man!'

'I shall kick your child off.'

'I shall clout you on the head to make you fart and then I'll give you another one *because* you farted, you pig!'

And so it would continue endlessly. They thought it funny to try and put you off your food. When one was brought some mess of indeterminate origin for lunch and inquired after its nature, the answer was apt to be, '*Poes, pap en rape*' (cunt, porridge and radishes). Or when there was a hanging earlier during the day you might be told that you're going to be served some minced *kaffir* pricks.

Gradually I got to know the *boere*. There was Nit Arselow as always, cock of the coop, proud of his skill as a boxer. In the office he had two pairs of boxing gloves and it was his entertainment to don these and invite some prisoner to a 'friendly' bout. There was his elder brother, Ghries, a strong man who played rugby for the 'Prison's' first team. (The brothers Arselow hailed from the Marico district along the Botswana border – Bosman country.* In their area, they said, Blacks still had to dive off the road when the 'old master' (their patriarch) passed by, and any wrongdoing was punished by beating them with a length of barbed wire. 'The *kaffirs* only respect you if you keep them in their place.')

There was Daaf the cricketer – fat belly, thumbs hooked in his belt. With Buggerit – a truly impish fellow always up to some trick or other – Daaf would spend his time in the yard, throwing a tennis ball around. A less experienced fellow warder (such as Lucky the Pimp) would at times be invited to join them, only to be told that he's 'throwing the ball like a small puppy trying to learn how to fuck'.

There was Turkey, the red-headed young turnkey from the Kalahari, stupid as an egg but quite touchy nevertheless, avid not to be made a fool of, living in his own world of imagined heroics, pacing the yard or the passages, oblivious to the rest, pointing a finger at the wall and making pistol-shot sounds with his mouth. (Later, during my second trial, they gave him a real pistol and private suit and had him sit among the spectators, presumably to squash in the egg any attempt at escaping I or my friends may be hatching.) There was Droopers, fat and jolly and obsessed by sex. He was from the Western Transvaal where, he said, the land is so flat that you can see your pension come crawling on its belly towards you from a long

*Herman Charles Bosman (who'd spent a few years, during the early 1930s, in Big House for manslaughter) a South African author whose archetypal 'poor White' farmer characters lived in the North Western Transvaal.

way off. There was Sampie, not so young any more, homosexual and suffering, with a good baritone voice, who used to sing on his rounds and sometimes, when he took pity on you, would throw down a morsel of *biltong* from the catwalk.* There was Sucker Snor who was caught one hellishly hot Saturday afternoon, snoring away on his back on the catwalk, stark naked, with his gun next to him and by his head a blaring portable radio. There was Irons van Wyk, the body-builder, who never wore shorts because he had delicate feelings about his thin legs. There was Soutie (Salty), the red-neck, the only English-speaking *boer*, who got caught up—it was alleged—in one of my escape attempts. There was Badweed, cap tilted over one eye, avid for money, always playing the horses, reading the sky and the stones and anyone's utterances for portents of winning (always just one out in his combinations), who actually offered to help me make a break if I would arrange for R20,000 to be deposited in his account. And there was Lucky the Pimp—of whom I shall have more to say by and by.

Gentlemen all, Mr Investigator. Pious too. On a Sunday they will be dressed in their best, and off to church. Believe in God, fatalistically. The end of the world is nigh. (I knew a warder who would answer to any remark one might make about the weather, the unseasonal cold or the early heat, the wind or the smell of snow, 'It's all written in the Bible that there will be signs and omens during the final days. . . .') Gargantuan meal for Sunday lunch, of course—pota-

---

*Biltong—wind-dried meat, originally of game, now often beef. A way of preserving meat the colonists adopted from the indigenous hunters.

toes with rice and pumpkin and sweet potatoes to go with the meat and the other vegetables. Perhaps, if 'mummy' is accommodating enough, a taste of nooky in a darkened back room. (They all call their wives 'mummy'.) Nit Arselow was so keen on promotion – which he could obtain only by cringing and hard slogging, as he sadly was passed by when intelligence was doled out – that he made sure it was marked in the 'incidents' book when he came to visit the prison on a Sunday evening. For conscientiousness beyond the call of duty. With his blue suit and his watered-down hair he would move through the sections, his little three-year-old daughter on the arm. Was it to taunt us, love-starved for the voice of a child, behind our bars? Or could he not afford to take her to the zoo?

I'd forgotten old Smizzy, Mr Investigator. How could I do so? He was such a perfect specimen! A stutterer, red face ruined by acne, ill-fitting dentures getting in the way of his tongue. His father was in the Service, as were two uncles and his father-in-law. His only brother had been a warder as well, but he'd accidentally killed himself playing Russian roulette in the barracks when bored. Smizzy's wife had been employed by the Department as a typist. His son? The little boy was interested only in becoming a guardian of people one day, he said.

You will find much in-breeding there. They live in the compound. They have to, to be on stand-by. And they never earn enough to live elsewhere. (There are special units – of fellow-warders – who, when the sirens summon them, will raid their houses at night to make sure that they don't have Black servants illegally 'sleeping in'.) Their whole life is that of the prison. They adopt the stance and the accents of their charges. The old ones will tell you that they have done 'the coat' (indeterminate sentence), when they have been in the Service for fifteen years or more. When they leave on holiday it is to a bungalow in another prison compound.

One sees young fellows of sixteen (fifteen even) arriving in the Service, not shaving yet, the caps still sliding over their brows. Are they happy? Well (they say), it's a safe job – you can't be sacked; and at least there's a good pension waiting for you. They were never going to make it through school. One is born not for happiness but for a guaranteed pension after sixty. The real reasons are probably that in this way they escape military duty on the border, that it is the only 'uniform' branch they could get into without any qualifications, that they are from a poor rural background, that it has become a family trade. And where else can a young dimwit obtain some self respect by being given (armed) power over people?

During my time I've met some warders who should definitely have been in an institution for the mentally retarded. On their shoulders they all wear, in polished brass, the letters GD–PS–standing for *Gevangenisdiens–Prison Service*. They themselves, with a total disregard for spelling, read it as *Geduldige Poessoekers* (Patient Cunt Hunters).

Among the prisoners you will hear many crude and derogatory jokes about warders. Such as the small boy asking his father whether a homosexual couple of men can also produce children together, and the father answering, of course, where else do you think the *boere* come from? Or the one about the father coming home from the first day of work in the new place of work he'd just been transferred to, only to be told by his son that the neighbourhood minister or priest had been around during his absence on a contact-making visit, and had asked what line of work the father was employed in then. 'And what did you say?' 'I told him you play the violin in a whorehouse, Dad.' 'What! How could you tell such a terrible lie?' 'But, surely I couldn't say you're a prison warder, could I?'

The warders can also sometimes laugh at themselves. One of them told me the story of the farmer who was suffering terrible depredations from a troop of baboons among his crop of stones. Everything was tried to scare them off—nothing worked. A reward was offered to him who could succeed. And a young fellow presented himself and went down into the lands to talk to the baboons. The farmer, sitting on his *stoep*, followed the proceedings through his binoculars. The youngster called the baboons together and apparently addressed them earnestly. Suddenly they all burst out laughing, holding their tummies, rolling in the dust. The speech continued and now, as one man, they were weeping bitterly. But all at once, lo and behold, they jumped up and ran hell for leather, tails between the legs, right over the range of hillocks, never to return. Well, when the victorious young candidate came to claim his recompense, the farmer was evidently most curious to know what happened. 'I told them that I'm a warder,' the fellow explained, 'and they all laughed. Then I told them what I earn and they cried with sadness. So I told them I'd been sent to enrol them in the Department of Prisons!'

5

Back in my Cell

Prisoners have unexpected and inventive ways of communicating. In C3 the 'Springboks' (the escapees) were housed, as also were all those sent up to the Hills for special punishment. They were lying in single cells, one next to the other. There must have been about ten of these down the one wall. When the man in, say, No. 1 cell wanted to talk to his mate in No. 10, he would shout 'Telephone!' down the passage. No. 10 would empty his toilet bowl; No. 1 would do the same, removing all the water with his mug, and they would then stick their heads down the porcelain pots. It is surprising what an effective, resonant channel can be established in this way.

People would send messages to one another, or tobacco, or maybe some other illegal article, by means of 'cables'. Any length of string would do: a thread picked patiently from your blanket, shoestrings and belt tied together—and this cord, with the buckle or a hook of some kind at one end, would be shot out through the slit between your door and the floor. Your neighbour meantime would be doing the same. You soon learn how to perfect the art of casting and fishing in such a way that the ends of these cables overlap and hook. Contact! Once the link up is made the rest is easy – provided that a warder doesn't come across the goods lying there in the corridor, and you on all fours with the lifeline in your hands. One gets to learn their rhythms too, at what moments of the day they are not likely to be passing through – and besides, the end cells act as 'early warning posts'.

People would send messages from cell to cell by hammering against their toilet bowls or on the separating walls. When taken to the office or to the bathroom one would leave a little note maybe, or some 'snout' and 'scratches' (tobacco and matches) somewhere, on a ledge or in a crevice or hidden in the cleaning materials or even in the food, knowing that your mate going down the same road will surreptitiously collect. It even happened that a prisoner would catch and tame a mouse, and using bread or some other delicacy as bait, the little animal would be taught to go from one cell to the other, again with some *dagga* or tobacco strapped to its body.

Nearly any part of the body of man or beast can be used for hiding and transporting illicit articles. In Beverly Hills it happened that a prisoner would wrap his small share of smuggled *dagga* in silver foil, tie a string to it and swallow it with one end of the string around a tooth. People would tape hacksaw blades to their bodies. I myself was caught once with a book stuffed down the front of my pants and I passed many a tense moment at some gate with a newspaper cutting in a shoe or inside my underpants, or even a complete (stolen) newspaper underneath the jacket down the back and into the belt. I once saw a young Black convict being caught after having smeared peanut butter all over the parts of his body which were covered by his clothes. (Blacks aren't entitled to eat peanut butter, but have to carry the big drum of peanut butter from the lorry in the yard into the stores. Can you imagine how strong the temptation must be?)

The most popular carrying bag, or hidy-hole, is of course the anus. When something is hidden away there we say it is 'bottled' – the anus in prison slang is called the 'bottle and glass' after the Cockney rhyme for 'arse'. Mr Investigator, it is absolutely eye-popping when you see what objects can be hidden there: blades, knives, letters, money – which is then called *holpond*, translating literally as 'arse pound'. Anything you can think of, always wrapped in plastic. These 'banks' are important in the black economy of a prison. In Pollsmoor, for instance, the cooks and some privileged cleaners had quite a racket going. Blacks were getting nearly no meat at all. But if they had money they could buy a dixie of pork for R1. This money was collected by runners and smuggled, as *holpond*, to the roof where the tailors were installed. There this money would be washed and ironed ('dry-cleaned', as by the Mafia in the outside world), the *boer* in charge would take his cut, and the rest would be used, *inter alia*, to buy young prisoners with, for R15 each. (The money was given to the warrant officer responsible for deciding in which cells prisoners would sleep. Young first-timers would be raped, and *wyfietjies*, 'little females' made of them.)

The warders know about these hiding places, naturally. The 'span' (teams) going out to work in the workshops, when coming back at night, will be searched from top to bottom. It is called the 'balls parade'. If in doubt the warders will have you frog-jump with legs spread wide apart. And if it is suspected that you are carrying something up your rear end, they will have you internally searched, which in our language is referred to as being 'finger-fucked'.

Clothes too are excellent hiding places. I remember now, when I was sent to the 'bomb' in Pollsmoor – that is, the punishment cell – for having contravened the Prisons Act, I carefully undid the seam of my jacket the night before and secreted away an amount of very rough salt that I had managed to have smuggled to me from the kitchen. The food you get in the 'bomb' is neither salted nor sugared, and every day I would undo a small length of the seam to get at the life-giving salt. ('Bomb', by the way, is a good example of typical prison linguistic ingenuity: in the old days one was fed only rice water when in the punishment cell – rice water had the association of India, India of Bombay, and Bombay became simply 'bomb'.)

In the same way the cell itself is one huge hiding place. In the 'bomb' it will be absolutely empty during the day – with neither blanket nor mat inside, just the empty toilet bowl and your Bible – and still one succeeds in finding some crack in the wall, some slit in the floor, some protruding ledge around the window, the rim of the toilet bowl itself, to hide your precious, minute split matches, or your little twist of tobacco.

Here is where you learn all about the usages of toothpaste. It can serve as glue: in the 'bomb' a 'connection' (friend) managed to get some 'twak' (tobacco) to me by sending the *boer* to my cell with his Bible, the only reading matter allowed. Between two pages a minute quantity of tobacco was glued with the paste. Or it can be the paste you use (mixed with soap) to camouflage a crack in the wall in which you have something hidden. It is even a seasoner: the only way to get the tasteless 'bomb' food down is to eat tooth-paste with it. Some prisoners use it, with ink, as paint for their artworks, which they then sell.

The cells, and your person too, are of course reg-ularly submitted to a 'skud' (a search). At any moment of the day you could expect the *boere* to burst into your cell, or you would hear the dull thumps and thuds of a neighbouring cell being 'ramped'. Once they're gone you will hear fellows inquiring from one another whether so-and-so or such-and-such has 'survived'.

'I say, did Oldface survive?'

'Ja, it's cool, man. No sweat!'

Nearly anything can be used as a weapon. In the Cape area, for many years now, the Black prisoners have had no handles to their spoons – the reason being that these could be sharpened for use as knives.* The metal of the fittings around the light bulbs, the strips

---

*The result was that Blacks, humiliatingly, had to eat their food with their fingers. Vangat and Witnerf particularly had the habit of punishing the community for the transgressions of a few. We Whites had all our beds taken away because two 'awaiting trials' used the transversal slats of one bed for grappling hooks, attached to sheets, with which they escaped. Spoons have handles now again, for a bureaucratic reason. Every year there's a general stocktaking. Steel implements have no admitted lifespan. But spoons without handles have to be condemned by the conscientious stocktaker. And condemned spoons – Head Office demands – must be sold as scrap metals . . . at the weight of complete spoons. Dilemma! Hence handles are no longer cut off.

holding down the neon tubes, the tin dixies out of which we ate – all of these could be, and were, used as lethal instruments. One could take a sock and collect as much soap as one could get hold of, of the rough big green blocks with the consistency of stupid brains, and stuff same down the sock; left to soak for a while it makes an excellent cosh. Or you would tie the end of your towel to your tin mug and fill that mug to the brim again with soap: you have something particularly dangerous to hit with. A weighted-down garment can serve the same purpose. Ropes are fabricated to strangle people with. Poisons are concocted. Finely broken razor blades may be hidden in your bread. A blanket can be used for smothering you. (It is often employed, thrown as a hood over the victim, so that he cannot see who or how many hit him.) But the knife remains the favourite means, the mythical instrument. When a gang condemns someone to death, the tool – the knife – will be indicated. It is to be left somewhere by someone designated by the *kring* (circle: the commanding council) for the use of the executioner. It, the knife, is called a 'coal', because it is said that it will be burning hot and can only be quenched by blood. There is urgency. The killer has to go and pick up his coal, and *move* with the thing in an ecstasy of initiation. People are killed that way month after month. But the violence is not always directed at others. In the Hills I learned for the first time how longtimers would maim themselves in sheer desperation. If they could fabricate or get hold of anything that would cut, they would sever the tendon just above the heel, never mind if it meant being crippled for life. There were blokes who would wrap toilet paper tight around their legs and then put fire to this. There were people who would steal Brasso and find the means of injecting themselves with it. If nothing else worked, one could procure a needle and thread, impregnate the thread with one's own excreta and then insert this under the skin by means of the needle. Left there for some time it was guaranteed to rot the flesh.

Some people provoked gangrene. Others perforated their own ears. Others again would smash their hands against the cement walls. One young convict, who could not have been much older than twenty-one or twenty-two, was in Beverly Hills with a spoon in his stomach. Young Burns, the keen quack, showed me an X-ray taken of the insides of the spoon-swallower where you could very clearly observe the whole thing, except for perhaps an inch or two missing from the handle. And this was not the first spoon he had swallowed either. It was claimed that he had had a homosexual affair with a warder in Zonderwater prison, or that he had been raped, and that was the cause of his transfer to the Hills. He had in fact been given further punishment for making 'false' accusations, they said, and it was clear that he had been moved to Maximum Security in an effort to squash the affair. The spoon-eating was to protest against all this. You kill yourself because you sense that they are trying to kill you. It is finally a matter of acceptance. (In the quiet of the night you could sometimes hear a grown man weeping in his cell.)

The various forms of self-destruction are all just efforts to attract the attention of someone or to escape from the horror of being in Beverly Hills – to be moved to some hospital section in another prison for instance. Another favourite way out, if I may call it that, Mr Investigator, was to eat blades. The desperate prisoner would ingurgitate a number of broken razor blades, wrapped in toilet paper, with the hope of getting these down without shredding himself to ribbons inside. 'Blade eating' provoked intense abdominal pains and after investigation by the doctor one would normally be permitted to go to the sick ward, or perhaps even be taken to 'outside' hospital. Naturally there were some who miscalculated and in this way deaths were provoked. I remember how one young prisoner died in Pollsmoor, horribly bleeding to death internally. . . . But this opens up the whole chapter of suicides proper, which perhaps need more attention.

Mr Investigator, suffice it to say that when that dark bell tolls, when you yourself become one enormous muffled sound of mourning, anything at hand can be used for making the final transition: hanging by belt or by shirt or by strips of blanket twisted into a noose, cutting the wrists or making slits under the armpits or slicing through the main artery of the neck, or carefully hoarding or buying or stealing enough pills to constitute a lethal dose, jumping from the bunk head-first on to the concrete floor. . . . You will not believe how many different ways, how many different roads, lead to the escape of death.

Meanwhile the royal highway of execution was used unremittingly. Martin the Brain died. Johan and Skollie were taken up hand in hand. At the last Skollie tried to thwart the course of events by asking for the case to be reopened, claiming that he was the sole killer and that Johan was entirely innocent. But it didn't work. And I'm afraid that, fond as he might have been of Johan, the intention was not to save his life, but to gain a few more weeks—another day, another hour—for both of them. They died. Skollie, so

I had been told, was tattooed from head to toe. I wondered afterwards how long it would take for the blue body-writing to fade from the corpse. . . .

Lying in my cell I was obliged, as we all were, to assist at the horrible final leave-taking, since sounds from the visiting cubicles flooded the corridors – the wailing of the wives and the mothers, the screaming perhaps of a baby who had, exceptionally, been allowed into the prison for that last visit. Johan and Skollie, before leaving that fatal morning, each sent me a cigar. The deed was accomplished. They became silently reverberating bells. I was let out in the yard. The tomato bush planted in one corner of the well-like space had small dew-speckled fruit (as red as flesh), which I was to pick and give to Arselow. I stole one and ate it and felt the incredible taste of redness, knowing that never again would Skollie or Johan eat anything else except earth.

More and more I got to know the *boere* and the other prisoners through my ears. In my mind they took on shape, each with his own history. Cocky was hanged in silence and indifference. I can't even tell you what he was like, since I never heard his voice. He was there for having raped and killed one or several small boys, and the warders were always teasing him cruelly. ('What would you say to a little boy now, Cocky?') From what I heard about him later, it would seem that he must have been at the very least a mental case. Without a word he went up to heaven.

Some arrived anonymously and left anonymously for death. Sparks moved into Death Row and shook the fibreglass roof with his exuberant diabolical laughter. Lasher came and started fighting for his life. When I left he was still in Death Row and by then he was trying to convince the authorities to allow him to have a hair transplant. (I don't know whether he eventually had to settle for baldness, but I heard that he came to within a few days of being hanged before his sentence was reduced to imprisonment for life.)

Every Friday night, lying on our bunks, we could listen to Stefaans, off at one end of the prison, doing his weekly nut, entertaining us with his songs: always starting with 'Sarie Marais' and then going on to 'Roll Down the Barrel'. He had a slightly hoarse, urgent voice. I could imagine him behind his bars, bellowing his songs to the empty passage, or maybe lifting his head to the high ceiling like a dog howling its primordial fears at the moon. He would be cheered wildly by everybody else in the prison – we were the world's most enthusiastic audience – and some *aficionados* would scream for an encore. But that was the extent of his contact with his fellowmen.

Time passed. Time itself became the grey matter of my existence. I would surprise myself sometimes on my bunk, having been there perhaps for hours in a supine state, staring up into space, not knowing what I had thought or whether I had thought anything at all. We call that condition *kopvriet* (eating head). During one period in the Hills an outside span came in every day to paint the walls and the railings of the catwalk. The team must have been made up of old apes, long-timers knowing the ropes and the aisles and, as I learned for myself in due time, these old prisoners get away with murder (in a manner of speaking). Perhaps they fitted in so well with their environment that a type of symbiosis between them and those who are their keepers came about. (Old prisoners fade into the walls. But there is also an unspoken

complicity among old *langanas* to 'break in' young
warders; to shape them to the needs and the laws of
the environment—our world; to corrupt them. The
old Coloured *bandiete* particularly have the knack of
sapping the *basie* (little master) with an ostentatious
submissiveness, until he is entirely in their power. In
No Man's Land the white skin is the most effective
rotting agent.)

The painters could not have been too closely supervised. One grizzled old fellow, with uncountable
folds in his face, hissed down at me from the catwalk.
He wanted me to exchange one of my cigars, a Toscani
that I still had left from my period of detention when
Yolande managed to get a few packets to me via Huntingdon, for something 'very special'. Some of the 'real
stuff', he said. We solemnly agreed. The next day,
like a cat, he was back. Hiss! Hiss! 'Hey, Whitey!'
(Every White prisoner is called Whitey by the others.)
Down he snaked his cable. An old bird will always
have a cable tucked away somewhere in his body.
(Also, somewhere on him, a rudimentary 'lighter' consisting of a bit of burnt rag—which ignites easily—in
a hand-decorated tin, and a minute chip of flint dis-
simulated perhaps in a button.) I tied my cigar to his
cable, he hauled it up and then chucked down into
my cell a good thick *zoll* of Transkei *dagga*. (I walk
through pastures of green peace. . . .) From any busi-
nessman's point of view he had made a stupid deal—
his *dagga* must have been worth at least ten packets
of cigars—but he was happy and so was I.

I already told you, Mr Investigator, that I had
started making the acquaintance of some warders. (They
are also known as 'guardian ghosts' or 'alligators'.) One
day when I was in the bathroom for my ablutions,

Arselow was summoned to the office and I was left in the care of the catwalk *boer*. This individual tried to squeeze part of a particularly ugly face through the narrow opening of the window looking down into the bathroom and started whispering at me. He wanted to know whether I was indeed Breytenbach. A metaphysical question admittedly, but I took the risk of saying yes. He said that, actually, he originated from the same part of the country as I did, and then he introduced himself. I said, 'Ah, yes?' He said, 'Yes, ja', and furthermore made it evident that if I needed anything done, any favour, he would be at my disposal. The scenario was repeated several days later, this time in my cell, and bit by bit Lucky the Pimp impinged upon my consciousness. He didn't like the Service, he said, and they couldn't stand him. And he didn't like the Transvaal. How could he, coming from the Boland? And it was a shame the way they kept me like a dog, locked up by myself. He would go mad if it were him. And I must be really dangerous, hey, because they weren't even allowed to talk to me. But he didn't care, he said. I could talk to *him*, he said, he was okay. Only, I mustn't tell anybody, else he'd be in the shit.

He was indeed not a pretty boy: he had the quality of which it is said in the Cape that it is not a question of being so *big*, but built in such an *indecent* way. He had the irritating habit of shuffling his bridge of false teeth around the mouth (like a petrified curse), taking it out, squinting at it and licking it clean. And he was sloppy – the headband around his cap was filthy. He gave the impression of bursting out of his tunic and his shorts were too tight. His shoes were seldom clean. No wonder he was always in trouble with the officers.

But I was going mad, Mr Investigator. Anybody willing to talk to me was welcome.

Another young warder on night shift would, after carefully checking out that nobody could hear us, engage me in a game of chess – he standing on the catwalk peering down and I making the moves for both of us. He was, he said, the champion of the Pretoria Prison Warders Chess Club, and to my satisfaction I beat him. But the one who constantly came back was Lucky the Pimp, and always he had questions. Fat with curiosity, like a cat. To establish an aura of 'confidence', or to impress me, he would tell me tall tales about trips he claimed to have made through Africa as a hunter or in the Namib desert as a diamond smuggler. He had the imaginary life of a cheap novel. He said that he'd read my books, particularly *Om Te Vlieg* (In Order to Fly), for which he invented new episodes and a far-fetched ending: the late lamented Panus who dies by suicide in my mind, in Lucky's book ended up by joining the Air Force. And, of course, he was endlessly inquisitive about my past.

There you see me, Mr Investigator, standing hands behind the back, peering from the depths of my well, or pacing the floor because it is winter and cold, and listening to this young fool on the angel's gallery – talking to him, talking him to death, talking death to him: that is what is known as 'the valley of death'. Only, it is not a valley, it is a cell. He was willing to forward letters – in fact, he provoked the situation which would make it possible. So I wrote to my wife, to Jim Polley, to André Brink, to my publishers suggesting the creation of a grave for the unknown poet, to Tom and to Dick and to Harry, to Schuitema even. With the pencil stub he'd smuggled in I started making drawings and sending these out too. The Pimp could scarcely conceal his disgust when I gave him another love letter or drawing to carry out. Obviously the channel was supposed to be used for hard political matter, not romantic slush.

Marius Schoon had arrived in Beverly Hills in the meantime, together with T. The two of them were coming to the end of their twelve-year sentence.* They were now to be released and therefore separated from their comrades in Local for the last few months so as to blunt the contact between 'inside' and 'outside'. Lucky the Pimp informed me of their presence. Marius, it would seem, had withstood quite well the corrosion of dead time, but T. (the Pimp explained) had gone round the bend. He would spend his days lying on his bunk, intermittently smoking thick *zolle* rolled in newspaper, squinting through pebbly eye glasses at a book. He wore an eye shade which he'd fabricated himself from cardboard and elastic. Sometimes one could hear him howl in the night. . . . Years back, twenty years ago now, I used to share a flat with Marius in Cape Town, and all the time that he'd been in prison he'd been in my mind too, so now we were exchanging letters, carrying on old ideological arguments or just gossiping. The exchange was illegal obviously – the Pimp was the postboy.

The Pimp was not the only one with whom I had this type of contact. There were other contacts best

---

*They had been members of the African Resistance Movement (ARM) and sentenced for attempted sabotage which had been masterminded, in fact, by a Security Police *agent provocateur*.

not mentioned. I remember, however impossible it may sound Mr Investigator, obtaining some rum one night from Soutie. Soutie, with his kind heart, had managed to smuggle in the liquor which he was feeding by means of a plastic tube through the wire grid masking the door to a 'condemn' due to be executed the next morning, and I got some of it also. I remember how it flooded the veins of my head like a sun rising after years of ice, and how anxiously he tried to *ssshhh* me because I was singing and dancing with myself in an ecstasy of letting go. There were others for whom, in exchange for a few sweets, I would make–from a snapshot–a drawing of a girlfriend or write a letter. One or two, from their unspoilt young *boere* hearts, were willing to forward signals of life, cries of desolation, to the outside world. The head of the prison must have discovered that things were leaking out. He tried to trap one of these warders by convincing a prisoner on Death Row, with only a few weeks left to live, to strap a tape recorder to his body and to provoke the suspected warder into talking about taking out letters. The *boere*–policemen, detectives and warders–just love *trapping* the suspect, or the innocent for that matter. They would go to inordinate lengths to *provoke* a crime, and South African jurisprudence does not provide for the possibility of the accused being protected against trapping. I've often wondered what could possibly have motivated the prisoner, at such a late stage in his life, to allow himself to be used as bait.

And then the Pimp–which in prison language doesn't mean the procurer, but the one who tells tales, the betrayer, the tattler–took off his hat, squinted around, and started whispering at my window, with a leer so wide that his gums showed up pink, about escaping . . . and my mind took up the embroidery which constitutes the dreams of all prisoners. It was nice to lie there in the dark, hands tucked under the armpits, and to scheme about sawing through bars, climbing over walls, stealing cars and breathing the killing air of freedom. I shall not tire you with all the hare-brained plans, Mr Investigator. One of the nicest versions was that the Pimp would get hold of the keys of my cell while on night duty, unlock me, and hide me in the gallows room where the bodies are cooled; I was to stay there until the shift changed and, when going off duty, he would have stolen around the back of the building with an extra uniform to whisk me away. But I am going too fast – forgive me. Much of what I'm mumbling about now was invented and was consecrated as 'reality' only during the course of the second trial.

Did I know that Lucky the Pimp was planted on me? Yes and no. *No* to the extent that one is always in the dark and one is always hoping for the impossible to be provoked into happening, for the crack in the inevitable. Your world is so small that there are no longer any limits to it: the walls receive, the mirrors cloud over, you do not know who you are, or whom you can trust, or even, sometimes, what really happened to you. *Yes* because the man so obviously faked a life; he was so entirely unreliable, so desperate to impose himself, to stay as close to me as he could get. I would be in the yard for exercises and he would be responsible for looking after me; he'd come up as close as he could and ask me to tell him again that story about the comrades outside. In the natural course of swinging my arms and bending I'd move away from him. And he would follow, sweating, bothered. It was practically as if he was saying, 'Please talk into the microphone,' the way I am talking now into this microphone, Mr Investigator. It was so obvious and somewhere in the ruins of my mind I naturally knew it, and I was feeding him ridiculous information. I think I wanted to see how far it would go and if it would rebound, I wanted to know what they were up to, and *who* was up to what (since Skapie Huntingdon was still coming to see me 'normally' all through this period), and in any event some signs of life were meanwhile penetrating the walls. I was going mad.

Gradually, I think, the Pimp and his controllers realized that I knew what they were up to; the game was no longer worth it. He disappeared for a while. He had been down to the Cape in the meantime, taking letters for me. Then, one Sunday, he turned up again. It was quiet. The silence of desperate men lying in narrow cubicles breathing their bitterness and their imprisonment. The sounds one heard might as well have been in your own head, the washing of violinists, the slow shattering of mirrors. Not a soul about. Must have been in the region of two o'clock when suddenly the door giving on to the main corridor leading into my section opened. No voice. Me up from the bed, ears hurting from listening behind the opening in cell door covered with wire mesh. Who? And Lucky sneaking up, unlocking me. Held out a pistol to me, butt first, whispering urgently—*here now is your chance quick all is safe there's no one around look I've got the keys you can go go go!* But I had been warned, Mr Investigator, between the lines of another letter. Throw up your arms all ye who enter here; you are now going into the valley of oblivion. And the chilly foretaste of death was now coursing down my spine. Remember what happened to George Jackson when they shot him, supposedly because he had a pistol tucked away in his Afro hairdo? Time locked in silence. A million years. Man, God's gift to creation. And to history. I knew that if I touched that weapon I'd be *morehond*, carrion, I'd be a gift to the maggots and the worms. I refused. He insisted. I refused. And he left. That was the last time I was to see him until we met again in court.

Silence. Brigadier Slappes, commanding Pretoria Prison Command, when coming by on inspection, insisted upon informing me that I could apply for the privilege of writing an 'extra letter' if ever circumstances merited it. Irons van Wyk unexpectedly gave me a printed document entitled: EXTRACTS IN TERMS OF THE PROVISIONS OF SECTION 85 OF THE PRISONS ACT, NO.8 OF 1959 AS AMENDED. In retrospect it was clear that 'they' were preparing their case. Was I going to plead ignorance? They could show that I was informed of the rules and of the punishment. Was I suffocated by not being able to communicate with my people? I had kindly been offered additional privileges. . . . Not long after I was called into the office and a big, bluff, red-eared major of the South African Police, and ex-sportsman of national renown, making it clear that he was not of the Security Branch, read out a series of very serious charges to me. It was to be terrorism all over again.

INSERT

*For the dream is saying to some extent that the flying
dreamer's native land is inaccessible to him.*

One comes such a long way before one dies. The alleys
you have to move through—the sky also has its passages which merge with a memory of blue—form the
intricate skeleton of a labyrinth. You enter, you dwell,
maybe you emerge. Flying with the birds signifies
that one will dwell with men of foreign nationalities
and with strangers. You who come out are free, and
yet there is the you which disappears into the twists
of mindless mind-seeking forever. Who comes forth
then? Is there really a you? Isn't there, in the final
instance, only an amorphous but all-encompassing investigator? You hover over the red ruins (which look
like a child's watered-down sandcastle from up here)
and you search for the you, in the same way that *it*
has always been waiting for you. The one is the lib-
erator of the self. I imagine an I.

   Sometimes you are cock-sure. You stride into the
barber shop and you flop down in the big leather chair
and you clap your hands (the low morning sun comes
glinting over the paving stones and the walls, deeper,
searching for shadows, to pale them in a bath of lu-
minosity) for the foam and the blade. Then someone
else walks in, flitting by its reflection, and executes
you with a single shot in the temple. Reverberating.
Creating corridors. And you sit there with foolish eyes
and mouth agape, sprawled as if flying, bathed in
blood, staring at the sprawled and gaping dead man
in the mirror.

   I write about South Africa—which is the quintessential No Man's Land. 'Owning' is usurpation. There will be much killing of the image. Reality is that the illusion will be executed. I write to no one, inventing an I who may mouth the words that I can neither swallow nor spew out – they are the stones of the labyrinth, with the mortar of silences. Too weak, too weak.

When you die a traitor you will be buried with a stone in the mouth. Like a tongue. Never trust a South African. It cannot be helped: in whichever direction you argue, you will always be faced by the outcome – the System is historically defined and conditioned, and the people come like words from the belly of the System. It cannot change by itself. It is structurally impossible for those who are bred from it to modify the System significantly from within. The *structure* must be shattered by violence. And violence will be blind because its eyes will be useless from the despair of having seen too much . . . of never having truly seen anything at all. . . . The land shall belong to no one. Not even to the deads.

What then? You must go on, even if you lose yourself along the way. I do not know whether what I aim for will be any better but I do know that this is unacceptable and that it will have to be destroyed to make it possible for the *other* – maybe better – to take its place. And I know I am lazy . . . my knees are weak . . . I genuflect so easily. . . . The temptation is to remain in the labyrinth which finally offers the security of the known. I have unceasingly to pull myself up by the bootstraps. My arms get tired from pretending to be wings.

It must be done: there can be no turning back; there is no self to turn back to. You must resist, you must become and remain aware, painfully—ignorance is the only sin—and work out the clues to the ethics of resistance which will not paralyse you. Beyond flying or dreaming or walking. You must move against the death-producing System which is a structure, knowing that your flight and your search is a *process* (the way all living structures are), becoming that which you are: a metamorphosis.

From meaning to mind. From maiming to meaning. King Minos of Crete, it is said, wanted a sign from the gods that his kingdom was limitless. He built an altar to Poseidon to pray for this. *If only I knew that I have no end.* Poseidon sent Minos a spotless white bull, without the stain or birthmark of either question or answer, commanding him to offer the bull to the gods. Doesn't it make sense? How else can you remain certain except by letting go of certainty? But Minos had a destiny: he cheated, preferring to slaughter a poorer doubt so as to deify the beautiful white proof (like an unwritten page) of his immortality. Poseidon took revenge by having Pasiphäe, Minos's wife and possession, fall in burning rear-end love with the bull. How was she to satisfy her love? At the king's court there was the man who had the mind which produced a knowledge of structures and of processes. Of prisons. Daedalus. He built for her a hollow wooden cow in which to hide (it was covered with real cowhide, since nothing is as illusory as the real) and which could be covered by the bull of whiteness when in rut. In this laborious way the Minotaur was born, black and ungodly—and needing young virgins to survive (was it avenging itself or its mother?). Minos was destroyed by the living sign of his limitlessness, but he had to accept it as his offspring: the bull, the son of Minos. On his orders Daedalus constructed, near Knossos, the labyrinth in which the half-god was to be hidden. The Minotaur is I.

The rest you know: how a half-mad Minos had Daedalus and his son, Icarus, put in chains; how Pasiphäe freed them and helped them to escape; how Daedalus, with his bees-wax mind, made wings for them both; how they managed to find the loops of dawn before the vengeful Minos and his fleet; how Icarus flew too close to the sun and plunged to earth in a plume of smoke and was buried on the island of Ikaria; how the grieving Daedalus (who could satisfy the lust of a woman wanting to destroy her man by sleeping with his bellowing soul, but could not bring sense to the mind of a man who wanted to die in the light) found refuge with King Kakalos on Sicily; how Minos searched for him high and low and tried to entice him to come out of hiding (be it in cow or labyrinth or foreign court) by appealing to his intellect (and the intellectual is always blinded by brilliance and by words), offering a reward to him who could pass a thread through the spiral conch; and of how Daedalus did it by tempting an ant, with a thread attached to its body, to find its way through a small hole in the labyrinth to the honey at the other end; and how eventually (out of gratitude for the reward which Daedalus graciously gave to his protector) King Kakalos had his two daughters take Minos to bathe, where they flayed him alive with boiling water . . .

And the Minotaur? Never mind. That is freedom. The I is out. It is outside the walls. For if it doesn't need walls, it is not a Minotaur. If it can be written about, it doesn't exist.

6

Up, Up and Away!

I was taken to the Pretoria Magistrate's Court and charged under the Terrorism Act, with a series of alternative charges under the Prisons Act. They threw the book at me. I was accused again of wanting to overthrow the government violently, of attempting to recruit people from prison and wanting to send them abroad to Russia for training in terrorism, of having tried to escape with the purpose of committing acts of terrorism in the country—notably that of destroying the tunnel in the Du Toit's Kloof pass between Worcester and Paarl, and blowing the Language Monument to hell. If I may open brackets here, Mr Investigator, so early in the proceedings, *that* is perhaps the one accusation to which I should privately have liked to plead guilty. The granite penis erected against the flank of the mountain above Paarl, that finger in the eye, is an abomination, and not only an insult to anybody's aesthetic feelings but also an incredibly obtuse and insensitive and arrogant insult to the non-Afrikaner people of South Africa. I close the brackets, for pity's sake. I was, furthermore, accused of having smuggled out writings and drawings. Down in the court cells I was approached, or accosted, by two gentlemen unknown to me. They introduced themselves as solicitors – Andrew Williamson and John Brand – and said they'd been appointed from abroad, by my wife, to defend me. I must admit, Mr Investigator, that my heart leapt with joy. Whether they were competent or not I could not yet know, but at least they weren't brought to me by the Security Police.

The case was remanded and referred for summary trial to the Supreme Court. I learned later that they had done everything possible to prevent my friends and family from knowing about the date and the place of the trial, thus making it difficult for the lawyers to contact me. . . . They were right. I was in such a bad state that I would have pleaded guilty to anything to get it over and done with. Upon being whisked away from the Magistrate's Courthouse I noticed on the steps my three loyal friends, the Musketeers (the publishers of Taurus) who came just to let me know that someone out there was still supporting me. From a distance they showed me the cover of a recently published selection of my poetry with the title of *Blomskryf*. Under such circumstances poetry seems a rather unrealistic and futile pastime. I doubt if poetry was going to save my neck; it might well have become the very noose.

There was not much to be joyful about. It seemed that they, the forces of law 'n' order, were going all out this time to finish me off. I found out at a later stage that bets were being laid by police and prison officials on whether I'd be getting the rope or not. The purpose of these completely far-fetched charges seemed clear: on the one hand to finish the job which had been started with the first trial and incidentally also to discredit me even more thoroughly than had been the case before, and as far as possible to implicate and to smear some close friends or associates. But this trial was going to be a different kettle of fish. They were going to have to do battle.

True to his word, Andrew Williamson very soon afterwards came to look me up in prison. With him he had a barrister, Ernesto Wentzel. Things looked black indeed. We studied the charge sheet carefully and I was asked by Ernie to recapitulate as thoroughly as I could all the events leading up to the present trial. Now, in retrospect, I know that Andrew Williamson, who is first of all a competent lawyer and who subsequently became a very loyal friend, and Ernie Wentzel, who had had enough experience trying to do the impossible for the politically accused, were most pessimistic about our chances. They also quickly discovered that I was not in a very healthy state of mind, so that they had to fight on three fronts – trying to build up a coherent defence, which in the end turned out to be devastating; trying, secondly, to help me pull myself together and find a means of psychological survival; and, thirdly, working through the court case and the preparations for it to have my conditions of detention ameliorated, and in general fighting the Prison Department and the Security Police directing the game from the shadows.

The State was not going to be cooperative; it was going to be difficult for the lawyers to prepare a proper defence. Andy and Ernie would arrive and I'd be allowed to see them in a room put aside for legal consultations. I would then go through my exhaustive recollection of the small imbecilities from which the accusations were fashioned. Ernie would roll his eyes to the ceiling and say, 'Dear God, you *know* that we are not really against your government. Tell that to the colonel, please man. I want this to go down on the tape *clearly*.' And his belly would erupt in gurgles. (As we say in prison: he's laughing like a whore who's just found a bag full of pricks.) We all knew that our consultations were registered by their ubiquitous microphones. Legal consultations are to be made available to a prisoner as soon as he's going through the processes of a court case, without the presence of any State official; the observers stand watching from behind a glass panelled door to make sure that documents do not get tucked into sleeve or trouser leg.

It was only later that I realized how worried Andrew and Ernie must have been about my condition. They joked and laughed (and they were good at hiding their concern about me), but they saw the implications clearly and they were utterly decided to fight this one as best as they knew how. It was going to be a clear political trial, no punches pulled. I must mention, Mr Investigator, that if I had any affection for you – which you must allow me to have after so many days and so many nights – I would wish for you after your death to end up in the same place as Ernie Wentzel. Because if it's heaven it will be made all the more agreeable in his presence, and if it is hell he would make even that 'possy' seem so funny that you will hardly notice your environment for the wheezing and the cackling.

They soon suggested that we should have a third

person for the defence. They explained that for this
type of case it would be advisable to have a senior
counsel take charge of the court proceedings. And
thus they brought along Johan Kriegler whom I now
met for the first time. He's not a big man, but ram-
rod straight; intensely nervous with a kind of cold but
very intelligent concentration, just barely holding his
passions in check; a broad forehead, blue eyes which
never waver, and then suddenly rather prominent
front teeth with a space for whistling between them
so that when he finally smiles it transforms his face
into that of a naughty kid. He chain-smokes and if you
watch you will see that his hands are trembling
slightly—a small indication maybe of the pressure under which he lives. You see, Mr Investigator, he is
that rarest of all Afrikaners: a completely honest man,
profoundly inspired by humane principles, and this
despite whatever political beliefs he may hold. It was
far more difficult for me to explain and to convince
Johan Kriegler of my innocence than it would be later
when I was actually confronted by the judge. His
questions were not only relevant to the actual events
but he also probed whatever motives he may have
sensed in my convictions. I assume that he must have
analysed as far as he could, perhaps in consultation
with the others, my character and my life and my
history. I won't know what his ultimate assessment
was, but I do know that from the moment he agreed
to defend me he never once went back on his ferocious
commitment to my cause. I could not have asked for
a better defender.

Even beyond the needs of their meticulous preparation, the legal team understood well the effects that
solitary confinement had had on me and so they in-

vented more reasons to come and see me regularly in prison. The fact that Williamson was in daily contact with Yolande helped still more. At first they arrived with briefcases stuffed not only with legal documents but also with all kinds of delicacies – homemade sandwiches, flasks full of coffee, sweets. Unfortunately the feast was rapidly stopped by the prison authorities. It would seem that fattening up the man who may be going to the gallows is not looked upon kindly by the powers that be. Sometimes they would come in on a Sunday and we would sit around the table and play Scrabble. The poor young warrant officer on duty one Sunday on the other side of the glass door was invited in to be a fourth for a game, and he promptly ended up winning. They also insisted on visiting the cell, the corridors and whichever area could be described as germane to the trial. Ernie, who had seen the inside of prison as a detainee, was particularly cutting in some of the remarks he made to the Head of the Prison accompanying them.

Towards the end of May 1977 the trial started. I was taken to court every day in a convoy, with handcuffs on and a warder (very often Arselow) in the back of the closed van with me. In the front there would be two armed warders and we would be preceded and followed by two cars carrying more warders in private clothes. I had my own private clothes back too – that was one pleasure. What an unfamiliar feeling to be wearing soft material, as unfamiliar and as sad as it was to be driven through the streets of the town. To see – through a small and dusty bulletproof window – life flowing through shops and office buildings; to see people with laughing faces and people carrying bags and people striding sternly. Court cells were as depressing as ever. The box in which I had to sit upstairs was an enormous one, obviously enlarged to accommodate the mass political trials that were going on during all those years. Once I was escorted from court to the prison at the same time as a lorryload of Black politicals were being driven back. Our van followed their lorry—a truck with its windows covered over with wire mesh. They must have been quite cramped, standing up during the trip. But all the way, right across the town, one hand stuck out through a hole in the mesh and a defiantly clenched fist was held out as a gesture and as a salute to the Black people quietly watching from the sidewalks. Remember this image, Mr Investigator: a Black captive, no personal future except perhaps death or long years on Robben Island, the arm is thin but the fist is resolute and it points forward—the struggle continues!

The State had built its case around Lucky the Pimp. I cannot for the life of me imagine what led them into this error; surely they must have known that the man was a liar and a megalomaniac. True, they did not expect me to want to defend myself, or else they were getting so sure of themselves that they thought they could get away with this *mise-en-scène*.

If I may sum up the events the way they became evident during the trial, I should say that at a fairly early stage after my first conviction it was decided to plant the Pimp, and perhaps a few other warders also, on me. Lucky the Pimp, having fairly regular contact with me, was to report immediately after every talk we had (or that he imagined we'd had, or which he'd invented) to his handler—a sad warrant officer in the Security Police, with thin shanks and striped socks and the run-down face of a travelling salesman—who was now coming to the end of his career. Together the two of them sat down at night and wrote up what I was supposed to have told the Pimp. The Pimp had been issued with a tape recorder (just like a real spy, man) but standing as he was, 10 to 15 feet above my head in an enormous reverberating concrete hollow, the tapes were entirely useless. Even sidling up to me in the yard with the machine taped to his breathing body did not much improve the quality of the sound. The Pimp was not satisfied by doing only what he was told – he showed some initiative of his own – but on the whole their idea was to get me to make contact, or to renew contact, with whomever I felt close to outside prison, and in so doing they were going to be able to trap a certain number of other supposedly subversive people. It had to be even more dramatic, so the Pimp was to come along with the idea of escaping. He was to claim that I had recruited him for Okhela, that I actually enrolled him during some mumbo-jumbo ceremony in my cell – all in all the type of junk one finds in very cheap spy thrillers. To explain how it came about that he 'switched sides', how he started informing the police, he invented a visit from some mysterious, raincoated, green-hatted fellow speaking with a thick Dutch accent. This super-agent knew exactly where to track him down; he came right into the prison compound, and said that the passports for the Pimp and myself were ready (he let the Pimp have a peek: they were green, with 'Botswana' printed on them) and that the route for our escape had been worked out. And – thus spake Lucky the Pimp – the man said that if he (the Pimp, that is), did not abide by the plans, 'we' would know where to find him (frowned eyebrows, gnashing teeth, 'Know what I mean?'). A threatening visit, your Honour. At this time Pimp caught such a *skrik* (fright) that he promptly lost all faith in me and my cause and he contritely remembered his devotion to State the Father, State the Prime Minister and State the organs of the State present everywhere, and he promptly reported to his superiors. To Big Brother. Yes, m'lord, he indeed saw that communism was coming to rape his mothers and to use the toilet bowls for wash basins. (Those are the distinguishing traits of a terrorist.)

He was exhibited in all his pristine innocence on the witness stand. In newspapers published during that time you will see photos of the Pimp showing off his pistol and his rifle and his determined sneer because, he said, his life was put in danger of death by my comrades, my fellow terrorists. Johan Kriegler settled his gown on his shoulders and in that quiet, penetrating, but absolutely merciless way of his, tore Lucky the Pimp to hums and to haws. I think the poor young man ended up being afraid to yes-sir or to no-sir when asked whether today's day was Monday or Saturday. To some questions he had no answer at all so that Kriegler would allow silence to do its own demolition before softly suggesting, 'But Mr Groenewald, all we want is a simple *yes* or *no*;' and Mr Groenewald, the Pimp, desperately scrutinizing the ceiling for help from above, knowing somewhere by now that he's utterly lost, whether he brays or whether he bleats.

At the outset the State team was confidently backed up by a number of self-satisfied security policemen and Brigadier Dupe of Prisons, but as the destruction job on Lucky the Pimp continued the State people drifted off with their tails between their legs to leave unfortunate Warrant Officer van Rensburg sitting there all exposed. The case for the State was led by the assistant Attorney-General of the Transvaal, a certain Mr Jacobz whom I referred to as 'Klip', meaning 'stone', because stone will never be diamond no matter how long and how often you rub it. The beak presiding was Mr Boshoff, acting Judge-President of the Transvaal Supreme Court. I came away with a fair respect for Judge Boshoff: his intelligent eyes behind very thick glasses didn't miss much and he obviously had at his disposal an incisive, legally trained mind. The State pulled a few other witnesses from the hat, more in an attempt to make good for the failure and collapse of the Pimp than anything else. A general in the Prison Department, called Bliksem, appeared on the stand to try to prove that I had actually worked on plans not only of escaping myself but also of helping at least one other White political prisoner, held in Local, to take the gap. For that purpose, Bliksem swore, I had obtained a map of Local Prison drawn by Marius Schoon. Johan Kriegler had no trouble at all in destroying this amateurish effort at smearing me. But the *boere* are tenacious and their communal imagination knows many twists and plots and figments. Bliksem was followed to the witness stand by Beau Brummel himself, he of the one green and the one brown eye (and both of them evil) who set about, in an entirely unsubstantiated way, to link me, through So-and-so now living in London, with certain acts of sabotage that had been committed in Natal roughly during the period covered by the charge sheet, but Johan Kriegler immediately questioned the admissibility and even the validity of such testimony and had the man removed.

At some point during the trial my lawyers demanded to be allowed to listen to the notorious tapes which the Pimp had made. Quite a nice outing it turned out to be. I had to be present. We were taken, under escort of course, to the buildings of the CSIR outside Pretoria. The Council for Scientific and Industrial Research is, theoretically at least, an independent research organization. In fact it operates as a think-tank for the Government and, more specifically, for the security forces. We were led to a sound laboratory and a nervous researcher started playing the tapes to us. Kriegler and Wentzel, alert and scrupulous as ever (and how tiring it must be to have to fight the system, within which you are obliged to operate, every inch of the way!), insisted on hearing the originals and not—as the red-faced official tried to explain—the 'cleared-up versions'. We listened to the originals and it was evident that the transcripts made must have been sucked from the common thumb of Humpty and Dumpty—Warrant Officer van Rensburg and Lucky the Pimp. What was more illuminating, though, was that we suddenly heard on these tapes, very bell-like, successively the voices of Jim Polley and of Yolande. Evidently the Pimp had been down to Durban where Polley was laid up in hospital after an operation (having had his pubic hair trimmed, he would say), and coming across as clear as daylight was the attempt made to get Polley involved in the thickening plot, the escape escapade. The tape of Yolande was obviously made with the intention of compromising her, to have her admit to passing material via Lucky to me. We weren't supposed to have heard this material and now they weren't going to be able to use it.

It was decided that I myself would take the stand.

The lawyers had used the trial as an excuse to oblige the authorities to allow me to read my own book, *'n Seisoen in die Paradys (A Season in Paradise)*, ostensibly because we would need it as evidence. (It was the first chance I had to read it after its publication, with a few cuts, the year before. The copy I was now given had been through the hands of some prison censor; in the margins, referring to heavily underlined passages, were comments like: *attack against the church*, or *subversive!*). Kriegler now guided me through parts of the book again, to establish the background to the events leading up to my return and my arrest and also to permit me to reiterate my political beliefs, or my moral ones, or my conception of ethics if you prefer. But taking the stand also meant that I was willing to be cross-examined and the Klip, sensing that the case was slipping through his fingers and finding himself more isolated day by day, threw in everything he had to try to break me down or, by default, to stain me. It became a marathon confrontation. During the breaks the court stenographer, a friendly lady, would come and ask me to help her spell the foreign names and terms which came up during testimony. ('Would you be so kind as to help us get your death sentence written correctly, Mr B.?') I remember, as I stepped on to the witness stand, looking back and seeing Andy sitting at the table of the lawyers and of how his face went white first and then a blotchy red. It gave me courage, Mr Investigator, to see how a man who a few short weeks before this had been an entire stranger could now be so close as to be physically sharing my ordeal. My legal representatives were not just paid mouthpieces – they were profoundly sincere and just and humane professionals who needed, and who need, to fight injustice in whatever shape they encounter it, for the sake of their own consciences. (Although I'm amused by the professional distortion of the lawyer which has him say to the person in the shit: *we* shall do such and so; *we* are innocent. . . . And when the crunch comes it is *you* who return to prison and *I* who go on to the next we!)

Klip tried every trick in the book. I don't think it worked at all except that it was very tiring and sometimes confusing. Kriegler had warned me not to be tempted in making grandiose statements but to stick strictly to simple answers, and Ernie had told me that the real reason for their act was their need to discredit me at all costs. True, when nothing else worked the prosecutor—in a *coup de théâtre*—had me read to the court the letter I had written at Huntingdon's behest to Withart, in which I had offered my collaboration. Johan Kriegler rose calmly and asked me whether it had ever been my intention to work with the police. I said no. Of course it had been a clumsy attempt at manoeuvring the *boere*. And that was that.

As during the first trial a foreign jurist attended the court proceedings as an observer. It was to be expected that there would be an inordinate amount of interest from the media, even from the South African Television. During the pause for lunch the prison van would go and fetch food for me from 'home', from the prison. This I would wolf down and then sit on the one chair in the middle of the cell under the glaring light, waiting for the circus to resume. The same aged, idiotic functionary was still in charge of the dungeons. The one I was in had no toilet. I had to hammer against the door to alert the shuffling old man to my needs. But when there were no warders present he was afraid to let me go to the toilet and I had to piss my anguish against the wall of my cell, like a dog. In the well of the courtroom I would daily see a few loyal die-hard friends, chafing perhaps under the impotence of not being able to help me in any way. There was present also an old man who warmed the cockles of my heart. I noticed him sitting near the journalists, not far from where my brother sat, looking intently at me, and I did not know who he was. He seemed like an old hobo, just come in off the street, thin, sickly, unkempt. I one day read the movements of his lips as he said to the person next to him, 'He does not recognize me.' And then I was told by Ernie Wentzel during the intermission that it was Dirk Opperman the poet, he who so many years before used to be my teacher at the University of Cape Town; that he had been very seriously ill rather recently, left for dead, but that he had returned to this problematical earthly paradise of No Man's Land after being in a coma for several months.

The two opposing sides entered their final pleas—the State asking for severe punishment and the defence adroitly dismantling the rickety structure that the Security Police and the prosecutor had had the effrontery to produce for the judge. They simultaneously brought the spotlight to bear on the conditions under which I had been kept for the foregoing two years. The teams had had enormous legal tomes carried into court. These with slips of paper marking passages were piled on their tables. *The law is.* The judge suspended proceedings and swept out. I was

escorted down and then brought back up again. The
court was crowded. In the doorways sat teenage typ-
ists who had forced their way in, munching their sandwiches and giving me bold looks. The judge was
deliberating, the judge has deliberated, the judge is
here! *Stand up in court!* Judge Boshoff looked through
his glasses and started reading a long, carefully balanced text. Lucky the Pimp sat, grinning sheepishly,
next to his girlfriend. As long as they talk about you,
you exist. Among the audience the armed warders
were scattered—Turkey looking like a stubborn red
spot trying to merge with a white background. During
this peroration I had to stand. Being talked to. Eyes
all over me and my clothes like a swimming of flies.
Silence in the head. Silence in the court! Life rum-
bling by in the streets outside. Sweet life. Yolande in
Paris (or London?) waiting for the outcome. People
eating somewhere. People in death's cells. Couples
mating. And so the judge found me not guilty of the
heinous crimes; he found me innocent on all the charges
barring the last alternative one—that of having smuggled out the letters and the drawings which had been
produced in court. (Which was just as well, Mr Investigator, since once having been evidenced it meant
that they were saved.)

Johan Kriegler hid his emotions by making a big
thing of taking off his gown, folding it, packing it away.
Ernesto Wentzel laughed until his face shone, took
off and polished his glasses and then laughed some
more. His unruly curls were neatly cut: he was off to
another political trial in Namibia. Sisyphus! Andy Williamson came and grasped my hand with a flushed
face.

Down in the court cells Kriegler embraced me and said, 'Now behave yourself like a good Afrikaner and a good Frenchman.' Some court officials actually came down to congratulate me and to wish me the best. So also did a few of the journalists who had been in court every day, particularly during the nearly two-week period of my cross-examination. As the witness box was next to their press table, they had tried—until stopped—to position newspapers on the table in such a way that I could read them. The judge sent down a messenger to ask what ought to be done with the R300 that had been used in evidence—the R300 which Lucky the Pimp had obtained from André Brink during a foray to Grahamstown when, directed by Brummel, an attempt was made to compromise the Professor. It was legally mine, the judge maintained. I asked the lawyers to have it returned to the donor.

(Thinking about the money brings back the farce of the meetings between Brink and the Pimp. I was told of how, when the Pimp went down to Grahamstown on the second occasion, the two of them got into Brink's car and drove to a secluded spot outside town, presumably the better to conspire. But Professor Brink had by now become suspicious: as they got out of the car the tape recorder that he had hidden away under his seat fell out with a clatter. Embarrassing moment, surely, particularly since the other recorder carried by the Pimp was still turning in its silences for tape-words. . . . And Kriegler's words about being French remind me now of how, during the trial, an official translator was summoned to render from French into Afrikaans one of my illegal letters to Yolande. How we argued! Like fishwives! This translator from the Security Police and I could not agree on the Afrikaans term for the French *con*. Here we were, in the middle of this court case with all its momentous implications, having an undignified semantic tiff. As so often before, Johan Kriegler had to suggest a solution. Why not, he said, render it as *doos* – which literally means 'box' in Afrikaans. A rather hermetic way of referring to the female part. . . .)

It was over. For the last time I walked out to the van with my bangles on. Back to prison. People going after their private concerns in the streets. No more private clothes now. No more stolen smiles exchanged with friends in the gallery. Back to four walls, a floor and a light bulb on high. A few days later I was suddenly told one morning to get my possessions together and, without knowing my destination, I was booked out of the Hills, put in a car with a Prison Department colonel and whisked down to Local Prison where the other White politicals were kept. There I had to go through all the procedures of being booked into prison again from scratch. My perfectly good Maximum Security clothes were taken away and I was issued with exactly the same outfit, but now belonging to Local. I was lectured and admonished and told that my hair was too long; then taken into the maze – so different from, and yet so similar to, that of the Hills. Finally I met my fellow political inmates. They were all already busy at their various tasks. The place looked OK. There was a big courtyard where they had planted a rose garden and where they even had a miniature tennis court. My first job was to walk around the courtyard stooped, picking up cigarette ends. Just *look* busy, one of the convicts advised me, but don't finish up the work. One should never liquidate work lest you be given some more.

In a workshop where he was engaged upon making furniture I was introduced to Moumbaris and immediately we started exchanging some words in French until stopped by the supervisor.

I was shown my cell, told about the rules specific to Local, promised (in a whisper) some illegal coffee by the prisoner acting as storeman and general handyman (the cells had hot water!), taken to the dining room, which came as a surprise because there were real red peppers and even some reproductions of paintings on the walls, and also well in evidence, a sound system donated, I was told, by Helen Suzman, which made it possible for the prisoners to listen to records of their choice from time to time. This was going to be much better! This was going to be just great! Back outside my hair was roughly clipped, short around the ears and the back, by an old shivering prisoner. I think it must have been Kitson. It was time for tea, which was taken outside. I met Goldberg and all the others,* and I could transmit to them the latest news (which I had picked up during my trial) about political cases. Then, even before lunchtime, I was summoned back to the front offices and without a word of explanation taken through the whole rigmarole in reverse: booked out, divested of my Local clothes, taken back to Maximum. In the space of half

*Arthur Goldberg—a White South African who is, with Nelson Mandela, a co-founder of *uMkhonto we Siswe*, and is serving a life sentence.

a day I was back exactly to where I started from. The deception was enormous.

To this day I don't know what caused this inexplicable forth-and-back. I can only imagine that the fact of my being able to communicate with another prisoner in a language they would not understand may have scared them, or else it was one more control experiment. Perhaps they were testing someone or something.

At last, a few weeks later, came the day for my transfer. I had not been told where to, no, nor when, but I was confident—after the publicity given to my conditions during the trial—that I would be transferred eventually. Thus, one morning, Arselow told me to get ready. Turkey got hold of some cardboard boxes because in the meantime, Mr Investigator, I had been given permission to study. Not that it helped any: although enrolled at the University of South Africa for a correspondence course, I was not going to be able to fulfil my tasks since it took them the best part of the year to let me obtain the books necessary for my studies. (In any event, a year later the permission to study was to be withdrawn from all political prisoners and it was only going to be reinstituted towards the end of my time. And then I could not benefit as I wanted to study Zulu, which was not allowed.)

I packed; I looked around my absolutely bare cell for the last time; I crawled in under the bunk and scratched my name in the wood underneath; and then, in the early afternoon, I was taken out for the final time through the front entrance, handcuffed, and put in the back of a van. It was 10 July 1977. I had been in Maximum Security for nearly two years and now I was off into the wild blue yonder, not knowing where-to, but anywhere was going to be an improvement on this. Not many of the people who were in Maximum Security when I arrived were still alive. They had been executed in the meantime. I was saved. Priapus, the god of gardens and birds and of thieves, no doubt wanted me to survive so as to be able to confess to you, my dear dead I.

I was not sorry to see the last of Pretoria. Indeed, I swore then – as I still swear today – that never will I freely set foot again in Pretoria. Let that bloated village of civil servants and barbarians be erased from the face of the earth. . . . The van was escorted by an unmarked car in which Brigadier Dupe himself took a seat. We left. These transfers are supposed to be discreet matters, sir. The warders accompanying you wear private clothes – in fact, they look very often as if they were going on a hunting expedition, with floppy hats, boots made for walking in the bush with, and very sophisticated firearms held at the ready. It was winter. The land was brown and grey. It was a dream to be driving along a highway with a slow darkening coming over the veld, seeing through the narrow slits of the slightly opened little back window of the van the headlights of private vehicles flooding the night. And then the moon. And realizing suddenly how bad my eyes had become over the years. Never stopping, Mr Investigator, moving at a fast pace. You have two or three blankets with you in the back. You have all your clothes on. They had given you a fair chunk of bread with maybe one or two hard-boiled eggs and some cold chicken. And you have two buckets in the back with you, which are now bobbing around, which you cannot secure – the one with water for you to drink, the other for your toilet needs. Your food has to last until you arrive at your destination, and as for your needs, these you might as well forget about since it is nearly impossible handcuffed, to do anything in that cramped space in which you cannot stand up.

We stopped at Leeukop Prison; we drove in beyond the inner walls and a number of shackled Black political prisoners were put into another van there. I could not see them but I could hear the chattering of the chains as they mounted the vehicle. Robben Island was their destiny. Misery and oblivion and fog and a salty wind. Sons of Africa. From there we left in a convoy. Somewhere during the night we stopped at Bloemfontein for fuel. A petrol pump attendant, grey with the cold, filled the tanks. Son of Africa. Men lying, quivering, wrapped in thin blankets, behind steel partitions. On into the night. Near Colesberg, I believe, we had a puncture and for the best part of an hour the van was immobilized on the side of the road. It started snowing. It does snow in the interior of the country in the winter. It was bitterly cold. On into the night. Driving through some of the towns you could see pink manikins in illuminated shop windows or sometimes other live little Black petrol-pump attendants, petrified by the cold, with Balaclava hoods nearly entirely covering their faces, staring at these prison conveyances. Could they know that there were people inside? They must know; they know everything; they are born with the wisdom of the oppressed. In the country, when you see convoys of people moving across the land to their doom, you *know* they are there. You cannot see them. And you on the inside, you know they are there on the outside, and you cannot communicate with them. Your heart thuds;

they shuffle their feet. They feed their eyes. We are all blind.

Light caught us somewhere in the Karoo. Maybe Beaufort West. The expanse of the land all around, Mr Investigator. The beauty of it, Mr Investigator. The glory, yes. It was building up in me. We were going South. I was going to see the mountains, sir, and I now saw the Karoo unfolding. I remembered how, when I was very small, we used at Christmas time to drive down to the seaside in an old lorry, and I recalled the excitement of the strange land. Sometimes we see things for what they are, stripped of all adjectives. I was singing anything that came into my head, Mr Investigator; it was pouring out of me, all the broken filth of Pretoria. I sang of rock and hill and bush and lizard and moon. I sang to my Lady One and to the ghosts of ancestors. I even sang for you. Of the breathtaking prehistoric beauty of the desert; and of the madness of conquerors and the humiliation of the oppressed. Up and up we went over the Hex River mountains, Matroosberg with its white cape of snow glistening in the sunlight, and far below in the valleys the green fertility, the silver snake of the river, the bare orchards with branches like children learning to write Chinese characters. It was home – a home that would never be home again, which I had become alienated from forever. But the alienation was not from the earth, which I still recognized, with which I still felt at peace.

We stopped in Worcester, just off the main street. I could hear people walking by; I could hear the laughter of labourers going to work. Some warder must have gone across the street to buy cool drinks or food. And on. On we went. Du Toit's Kloof, high up above Wellington, my old home town. Ah, it was too much.

We arrived, after driving through the outskirts of Cape Town, at some place that I'd never heard of nor even suspected the existence of: a big prison compound lying in the lee of the mountains where they run into the sea at Muizenberg. It was in the late afternoon of 11 July 1977. We drove right into the building. I was unlocked after twenty-four hours of being cramped and chilled. But I was happy. It wasn't so cold there, close to the sea. Arselow, who had been riding shotgun in the van, took me through some passages to an office and immediately I was struck by the different smells and by the hum and buzz of many voices. Obviously there was much less discipline here. The place was dirty. This was the Cape. I was shown, or rather taken, into the reception office which was well inside the building, and told to wait. Now at last my handcuffs were taken off. I could rub my limbs to get the circulation going. Behind the counter there was an old sergeant with a rather ridiculous moustache, hair cut short but parted, glasses, pretending very hard to be occupied. It was Pollsmoor – that was the name of the place – Pollsmoor, Cape Town.

An enormous plate of food was brought to me in this office. It had been prepared with quite a lot of oil. Such is Cape prison cooking – excessively so. Time buzzed like a fly. The sergeant, scared obviously to take any initiative, not knowing what to do with me, had me waiting. Other *boere* walked in and around me, looking me over curiously. All over there was a much more relaxed atmosphere. In the Cape things are not taken quite as seriously. Head Office is far away, in the north. An officer entered. The beginning of a belly like a soccer ball. And perfectly mad, bulging blue eyes.

'Ah, yes, so you are Breytenbach. Yes. Yes.'

INSERT

The year is nearly done. Already big dark-green pine trees are appearing in front of public edifices and on certain street corners, festooned with silver bunting. When I climb the stairs I can look, across the wall separating the courtyards, into rosy interiors. People wrapped in heavy coats and scarves move through the rooms; they pause in front of the windows, looking out for an instant upon the blind night; they have the slightly stooped shoulders of exiles from some totalitarian state. Memory.

I have travelled through many countries, I have visited many cities over the last months. I have carefully taken the thought of you with me on my journeys. I have seen the land sweeping by, white and virginal under a crisp layer of frost. (Wraiths of fog seeping from hollows.) I have seen the sun glancing off spires and domes and tall blocks of flats as the day became flatter and weaker. Often I have tried to establish for myself what it was – or is – about prison that is the most typical. That will sum it up. Tell me, sir, I then ask. People say, *how did you survive?* I say, *I did not survive.* People say, *but prison is a clear instance of opposition, of resistance.* I say, *resistance, if that is what you want to call survival, is made up of a million little compromises and humiliations, so subtle that the human eye cannot perceive them.* You know it, I know it. . . .

Prison, for me, is the absolute stripping away of all protective layers: sounds are raw, sights are harsh, smells are foul. The scars are there, like tattoos on the mind. You are reduced to the lowest common denominator – being alone (and scared and weak to the point of being suffocated by a self-disgust) whilst always surrounded by others. Don't trust. Never softness. The consecration of the worst in human nature. What do you gain? You lose all sense of importance, of hierarchy, of standards and of norms. Things are as they are. A dusty wall is as beautiful as a fresco painted by Brother Angel, a broken leaf has as much value as a bar of gold. Stars are ships emitting waves of sound. No more attachment. Death is clarity. Setbacks are experienced with a body-consciousness. Walking erect becomes the purpose of walking. Walking becomes a matter of moving hips and legs. What do you risk? To project yourself to the mountain. To make of the mountain a myth. To hear the voices in the earth and to lose yourself in memory of sky when the morning is fresh. When you have forgotten about the aches of night. To fly.

For years, right up to the end in the Shu Ch'un T'ang, I used to come awake at night with a shock, sitting bolt upright in my bed, and always I'd be looking to my right where I expected Hoang Lien to lie, or my brother Sebastiaan. The whole body is one mind, and how permanent are the imprints of memory on the mind! I last shared a room with my brother at the age of ten! Every night the mind would crawl back into the protective shell of remembered security; each morning would bring the stiffening taste of bitterness. . . . And when I came out, away from the

maze – here, so far from No Man's Land – I found myself running through the streets of winter at five o'clock
in the morning, tasting the tears of helpless despair.
I am not in exile. I am travelling. What is it I keep
on running away from?

I have looked at the possibility of suicide. Oh,
nothing spectacular, you know. But coldly, like a
professional for whom the essential sense is in the
breaks and in the silences, for whom there can be no
ethic beyond that of continuing to walk with awareness, of going beyond. There is no elsewhere. I have
thought about how it would be to die in one of those
monstrous, chromed Zurich toilets. Leaving traces of
blood on their shiny surfaces – how impure! Or vomiting at last, with black gloves on, in front of one of
Karl von Piloty's sublimely ridiculous paintings in
Munich's Neue Pinakothek. Smashing the dark glasses
when falling. Making death so small. . . .

But always, wherever I've been, however hard I
ran, whatever the temptations of oblivion, I've kept
up my intimate questioning of you, Investigator. I've
asked you to listen to the twittering of the birds in
trees becoming barer with the cooling of the year.
And I kept on trying to give you a free face. A name.
I have seen you as the Minotaur, which is the I, which
does not exist since it is a myth. . . . I see you now
as my dark mirror-brother. We need to talk, brother
I. I must tell you what it was like to be an albino in
a white land. We are forever united by an intimate
knowledge of the depravity man will stoop to. Son of
Africa. Azanians.

We must launch a dialogue. I must warn you that
the system by which we're trying to replace the pres-

ent one will grind us down, *me and you*, as inexorably. I must tell you that I cannot hold my criticism, my disaffection, in abeyance; that I cannot condone your (our) agreements and compromises—not even tactically. I love you too bitterly for that.

I hear you chuckling, you who are Black. . . .

7

I Was in Pollsmoor

Witnerf, the mad major, looked me over with his bulging blue eyes. I was in Pollsmoor. It was quite late in the afternoon when I was finally processed through the books and handed clothes which had the number 4 stencilled on every item – meaning that they belong to Pollsmoor Prison, White Section. I also now belonged to Pollsmoor. I was further given a sheet, and pillowslip, a towel, a tube of toothpaste, a toothbrush and soap, and takén up three floors through many corridors and locked grilles to the section for White male prisoners and into my new cell, which was enormous compared to what I had been used to. Joy of joys – in one corner of the cell there was a large washbasin with hot and cold water and a shower and a toilet bowl. A low wall separated this area from the rest of the cell. (In due time I would spend time at night behind that low wall, pretending to stare vaguely at the door and the corridor where the *boere* patrolled, my knees half-bent with an open – illegal – newspaper balanced upon them: they couldn't see it, but I was avidly feeding the mind with politics and sports and small ads!) There were two tall, narrow, barred windows in the one wall actually giving on to the outside. I had a bed, I had a small table, a chair to go with it, and several lockers built into the walls of the cell. I had in reality quite enough room for my few possessions as the cell I was in normally held up to sixteen prisoners when White and maybe as many as thirty or exceptionally even more when Black.

But back to the window, Mr Investigator: I could actually see one part of a mountain! True, only the beginning slope, but it was something, a landmark, life outside uncontaminated by prison existence, a limit to the void, to nothingness. I couldn't believe my eyes. It became dark and I imagined that with the dusk I could smell through the windows (which I could open or close myself) the faint aroma of magnolias or perhaps even gardenias. This was really the Cape then: memories came flooding back of that other night when I had met Paul somewhere in this same region and we'd gone walking through a sleepy suburb, smelling the intimate gardens and hearing the wind groaning in the oaks. Here from my cell I could surely, I thought, if I really tried hard enough, get a whiff of the sea. My sleep must have been filled with moonlight. This was paradise, Mr Investigator.

When I woke up seagulls were really flying over the prison, dropping their scissors-like squawks and screams in the concrete walled-in courtyards. Indeed, when I pulled the table close to the window and climbed on top of it I could just barely make out in the distance a thin but unruly blue ribbon. The sea. The limitless ocean. Looking at Antarctica.

Pollsmoor is situated in one of the most beautiful areas of No Man's Land—perhaps of the world. It lies nestled in the shadows of the same mountain chain which at one extremity is known as Table Mountain. Here in this part of the peninsula it finally runs into the ocean with the effect of creating a micro-climate. Wind there is enough of—the so-called 'Cape Doctor'. It became a constant companion during the months of the year—in fact it was a bench-mark by which the progress of the year could be measured. But that which particularly marked me and made me was the mountain: my companion, my guide, my reference point, my deity, my fire, my stultified flame, and finally—like a prehistoric receptacle—the mould of my mind, my eye, my very self.

The prison compound itself covers a large area which previously used to be several farms and a race track. It is confined partly by walls studded with watchtowers and partly by wire fences. These contain four separate prisons consisting of a large building called Maximum Security (which is where I now found myself), a series of single storey barracks-like constructions called Medium Prison, and two more modern constructions called the Female Prison and the Observation Station. A few years later the Female Prison would become Pollsmoor White Males and the women were to take over Observation. (When the day of moving came the White Males, each with his possessions slung in a bundle over his back, were herded on foot to the new home by warders with dogs and guns—all except me: I was taken there in a slow-mov-

ing closed conveyance. In the new place we found
minutely scrawled graffiti of the most outrageous obscenity.) There are furthermore the houses – with the
well-watered gardens – and the blocks of flats for the
warders and their families, the administrative buildings, the recreation halls and the club buildings for
the staff, their rugby fields and their swimming pools,
and quite extensive farmlands where vegetables are
grown.

Immediately beyond the boundaries of the prison
community and towards the mountain there were private farms, some with cows so that we could hear the
lowing of the cattle, and some with vineyards. On one
of the farms they must have had a donkey because for
a long period I used to listen every night for the lonely
braying of this animal. Somewhere not far off, towards
the sea, there were suburbs leading eventually to
Muizenberg, which is a popular seaside resort. Some
houses were built very close to the walls separating
us from the outside world. There were many trees
both on the terrain and beyond it, including palm
trees and a number of gigantic bluegums. An old prisoner later told me of how, in earlier years when only
Medium existed, they had to clear the grounds so as
to build the other jails from scratch, and how they
had to take out these big bluegums 'carrots an' all'.

I was now for the first time inserted in a prison
community. I saw other prisoners trotting by my two
little windows giving on to the passage, one on either
side of the door, and some of them actually stopped
and talked to me – although it was forbidden. I was
like a monkey that had been brought back to the jun-
gle, Mr Interviewer, hanging on to the bars, trying
to attract any passer-by's attention. Pollsmoor had (has)

a normal prison population of 4,000–4,500 people of
which maybe 200 at any given time would be White,
or rather whitish – since we were now in the Cape
where population groups merge into one another. (The
intake would rise spectacularly when the bulldozers
had been at their periodic dawn feast of shanties made
of cartons and jute and tin, and hundreds of squatters
would be swept off the Cape Flats and brought to
prison in lorries.) The staff – warders and various
tradesmen working either in the workshops or on the
fields – add up to about 300. Usually there'd be also
between twenty and twenty-six dogs with their dog
handlers. These (the Alsatians, not the *boere*) were
kept in fenced kennels situated just behind the building I was in. Whereas the dominant or prevalent sound
of Pretoria, particularly at night, was the constant who-
hooting and huffing of trains being shunted around
the station yard not far from Central, the Cape will
always be marked for me by the insistent growling
and yapping and barking of dogs at night. Whenever
the siren sounded the dogs would take up the echo
in a chorus of howling.

But one soon got used to that. We lived in a universe of sounds which became our allies – the sad night
birds, early every morning the wild geese raucously
on their way back from the marshes near the sea to
the mountain, the wind, the dogs, the guinea-fowl
living free among the cabbages and the radishes; and
the man-made sounds: the hissing as of an ocean liner
of the big boilers situated above the kitchens of each
of the buildings, the 'cat' – as the siren is known –
sometimes going off in the night to summon the staff
back to the prison buildings because there had been
an escape attempt or a murder or gang warfare in the

cells, the footsteps and the jingling of keys, the clinking of those who were chained and who moved under escort through the corridors, and the whimpers, the whispers and cries and curses of prisoner and of keeper.

To this I now had added the vision, a real vision even if impaired, of the blue sky and the sun and the tree tops bending, of pigeons coming to perch on the water towers, of first light paling (impaling and embalming) the morning star, and always – at the turn of a corridor, dimly observed, or, when you were out in the yard like an enormous voice standing over you – the mountain. The mountain with its richness of clothes as the seasons came and went.

The very next day Brigadier Dupe, who had escorted me from Pirax, came to fetch me in my cell and took me three floors down, plus one more, until we were actually below ground level, to a large artificially lit area which was the General Stores. This was where I was going to be employed for the rest of my stay in prison. Here I was to spend my daylight hours. The staff stood to attention as we entered.

Over the years some would be transferred to be replaced by others, but a core of two or three members never changed. There was Bles, with his shining bald pate, puffing away at his pipe; there was Pinocchio next to him, small and sinewy with a tooth missing (but a smile taking its place) and big ears and very rough hands scarred and stained by his passion for angling; there was Oom Flippie, grey-haired, drunk, pouchy eyes, a spare tyre bulging over his belt and a very smart moustache with long ends jauntily curling – these he would incessantly stroke and twist and he would profit from the movement to pick his nose at the same time. Others would come later: Wag-ter Basson with the long nose and the sad eyes; Cripple with his plastic container of thin white sandwiches (he never gave me any); Matthee who spoke with the slow enunciation of the Namaqualand people; Captain du Preez, blind but too vain to wear his glasses, never working, cursing the Department; Molemouth the smuggler who had had an open-heart operation; Duimpie who took a sadistic pleasure in hurting *bandiete*; Sergeant Japes, red-faced and huge, who had a full time personal *agterryer* (a tame prisoner acting as orderly) to carry his little suitcase with the coffee flask inside; Mad Mips who had a permanent erection and who was always on the go to fetch sandwiches (he always gave me some); Stargazer the half-wit who lacked three fingers on the one hand, who had been forbidden to work with prisoners because of his infantile but violent temper, who one day beat a prisoner to a pulp, butting him again and again with the head.

I was the only prisoner employed as clerk in the General Stores. I was to be told later that I was in fact the only prisoner in the Republic of South Africa officially working in an office, and that special permission for this had to be obtained from the Civil Service Commission. In reality a large part of the office work in all the prisons is done by convicts. During all my years there it sometimes did happen that other White prisoners worked in the Stores as teaboys or as cleaners, but the White *boere* preferred having Blacks there. It is a constant theme among them that they'd much rather deal with Blacks and Coloureds than the Whites who only give them trouble. Perhaps they feel less free to use violence with Whites. I can imagine, sir, that the relationship between White warders and White prisoners is far more ambiguous than the apparently simple master–slave hierarchy you will find between White and 'non-White'. At this level the *boer–bandiet* relationship is a violent one. *Boere* are always practising their proudly acquired karate blows on the *mugus*. When one is caught having stolen some food or a shirt, the warder would beat him up – it was easier, it was said, than having the man charged for theft because that necessitated writing out statements and appearing in a kangaroo court. Corporal punishment was in any event also officially part of the system – one could be sentenced to a maximum of six 'cuts' at a time, with a light or a heavy cane (depending on your age). You would then be stripped naked and strapped, spreadeagled to the 'mare', a three-legged easel-like structure, something from the Middle Ages, bolted to the floor of the central hall. A protective cloth would be tied over your kidneys, and the blows meted out, with great relish, in the presence of a medical orderly.

Over the years I got to know quite intimately some Black or Brown prisoners working in the General Stores. As they had far more freedom to move around than I had they would find ways and occasions to communicate with me, even though this was expressly forbidden.

In this way I met Voetjies, a man of all trades and all wisdom, and a master at manipulating *boer* and *bandiet*. He had already been in prison for twenty years, as a multiple murderer. He had actually been condemned to death and had spent time in the shadow of the gallows before being reprieved. He had escaped once, ten years ago, had committed some more crimes while cruising, had been recaptured and sentenced to more time. We called him Voetjies or Foots or Toes because he had cancer of the big toes and wore special shoes. Already bits of his toes had been amputated. This didn't stop him from running down his prey and knocking the unfortunate fellow senseless with fist and with forehead. (He was exceptionally strong and combative.) The cancer, he said, was provoked by stones falling on his sandaled feet when he was breaking boulders in the notorious prison of Barberton in the north. As these injuries were never treated properly, they eventually became malignant. He in fact ran the General Stores, and he was a walking information bank on prison lore and laws and myths and history. He had no hesitation in grassing on his fellow prisoners– he did so, judiciously, to retain the favours of his masters (whom he despised) and he betrayed me on several occasions. He was infinitely resourceful in obtaining the means for satisfying his three basic lusts: *dagga*, sex and power. And he was a dealer and a power broker.

I worked in a specially built glass-enclosed cage erected in the middle of this big storeroom so that the warders could keep an eye on me at all times. (No other staff member – not even an officer – coming to the Stores in the course of his work was allowed to talk to me. Towards the end the Brown warders weren't supposed to even enter the space where I worked. What did the higher-ups fear? Collusion? Contamination? I don't know.) In one wall there were the normal narrow windows giving on to a courtyard which at one end was closed off by two huge steel doors painted blue. These gates gave access to a street running down one side of the prison. Here the lorries delivering foodstuff or whatever to the prison had to enter. The windows in my part of the room were therefore painted white, so that I could not look out on the yard, and subsequently welded shut – I suppose to make it impossible for me to smuggle anything in or out to someone working in the yard.

When I needed to go to the toilet I had to obtain permission from the officer in charge in the stores and I would then be accompanied by a *boer*, who had to have the rank of sergeant at least, deeper into the prison itself, where a special toilet was made available to me. Since this toilet was in fact in the Black section, I was daily exposed to their conditions. Over the years I was plunged, despite the most careful measures taken by the authorities, into the complete prison universe, populated both by Black and by White. Always there were teams of Black or Brown prisoners on their knees in the passages, moving rhythmically and in unison forwards or backwards over the gleaming cement. Each had a floorbrush and pads made of old blankets under the knees. A *voorsinger* (or choir leader) would be standing up front, improvising a song, and the group would repeat the refrain or the key words, or sometimes just hiss or say *ja-ja* or make funny little sobbing noises, and at the same time sway their shoulders and shuffle their knees. And so the group would proceed or retreat as one brushing body. The leader's song – if you listened carefully – would often be a running commentary on the conditions or the daily events. (*The foodsafree. Ja-ja. The sleepsafree. Ja-ja. The fucksa-free. Free-ja. So why-ja moan. Moan-ja. Here comesaboss. Boss-ja. Sobigbigboss. Isbig-ja. So step aside. Ja-ja. Good morning basie. Ba-ja. Workashit. Sshit-ja.*) The activity is known as *gee pas*, to 'give the pace'.

Often warders with yelping dogs on leashes were

rounding up groups of convicts. There would be bedlam—screaming and cursing. When it came to meal times the long lines of poorly clad prisoners (nearly always barefoot and moving in crouched positions with their hands clasped before them because of the chill in these corridors, even in summer) would fetch their plates—on which the rations had been dumped pell-mell—on the trot. Run, grab food, run. Up by the kitchen the dixies would have been set out nearly an hour beforehand. On meat days small chunks of pork would be floating in the watery or oily sauce covering everything. A White *boer*, Sergeant Nogood by name, was often on duty there, guarding the rations. And as often I saw him methodically going from plate to plate, fishing out and eating the morsels of meat. (Not out of spite. Maybe he considered it his privilege, as a perk. Maybe he was just hungry, or greedy. Certainly he would consider that the authorities were just spoiling the 'dogs' by letting them have meat.)

The smell in those nether regions was indescribable. There were always far too many people. The single cells would house three men each—one on the bed, one under the bed, and one on the available floor space—and they would have to use the toilet bowl for washing purposes. Once, after a ritual murder when the victim had been laboriously decapitated with tiny penknives and his head exhibited on the window sill for the night (to grin at the passing warder who kept on telling him to go to sleep), it came to light that the cell which normally had room for perhaps twenty people had held forty-seven convicts—and not *one* was willing to testify to having seen the execution! There were never enough warders to allow people to have showers. Everyone was involved in some physical labour – often hard and dirty work, as when spans of Blacks were used to unload and carry in lorry loads of flour – and always on the double. Clean clothes were issued only on Sundays, for inspection. Blacks were given one small tube of toothpaste a month and three or four squares of toilet paper a day. People awaiting trial had it even worse – no change of clothing, since they kept and wore the clothes they were arrested in until sentencing, which may be a year or more in the coming. The sections had to be fumigated regularly to combat lice and other vermin. Groups of juveniles, from six or seven years of age to fourteen (a 'fourteen' is a short-timer, someone doing less than eighteen months, just there 'to dirty the dixies'), would be using the same facilities as the men and being raped in the showers. So there was the pervasive stench of unwashed bodies, old half-clean clothes, stale food – 'lightened' from time to time by whiffs of the tear gas used to control a cell when there had been a riot or a gang fight. Germothol, a disinfectant, was highly prized: diluted with water, it would be sprinkled parsimoniously in the cells just before inspection to make them smell 'clean'.

David was another one of the Coloured prisoners whom I met at work. But he was in for trouble. He was quite a few cuts above the average *skollie* (petty criminal, thug) – he had worked in the Municipal offices of Bellville as an accountant when caught and convicted to six years for fraud (he needed the money to send his daughter to university, he said). He wore glasses and good false teeth and was well-spoken, and because he was so obviously educated he was sent to work as a cleaner in the Stores. Trouble number one and break-in number one: he made the error of addressing a White warder as *meneer* (sir) and not as *baas* (master). 'A *meneer* is a *kaffir* preacher, you black arse; *I* am a *baas*!' was the lesson shouted at him. Then, within the space of three weeks, he was destroyed. By his fellows. With the *boere* assisting, laughing. You see, he thought he could be a *mister* (they said). First his glasses were broken – only one lens to start with, and a few days later the other one. Then he had to cough up his teeth, which disappeared. Simultaneously he was *slukked** when he tried to wangle a deal or two for some extra food or smokes. His formerly neat appearance soon became something of the past. He had tried so hard to keep his station, but the others took away his clothes and gave him patched ones in return. When sweeping out the office he would linger as long as he dared to near my workplace, and weep uncontrollably. His efforts at stealing some of the *boere's* coffee and sugar were clumsy. He was hungry. Then he was caught on his knees behind a stack of bags, praying myopically and toothlessly, but fervently, and Bles had Voetjies beat him up for shirking work. And the last I heard before he disappeared in the murky gang-controlled inner jails was that he had been sodomized, that it had been decided to make a woman of him. He stood on the carpet before the *boer's* table that morning, asking to be protected against his tormentors, saying that as a married man he did not want to go through that particular hell (already cringing, and saying *baas* three times in the same sentence), and the *boer*, annoyed at this freak who spoke so much better than *he* ever could,

* *Slukked* – from the Afrikaans *sluk*, to swallow, meaning to be taken in, to be cheated.

advised David to 'take a man – it will make you strong
and it's good for constipation too. Look, you should
have thought about this before becoming a prisoner.
And who the hell do you think you are anyway? A
mister?'

Upstairs, after the initial weeks of cautious observation, I was allowed to stand in line with the other
White prisoners when going to fetch my food or when
falling in for inspection in the outside courtyard. (On
the foodline the Brown cooks would wink, quickly give
a clenched-fist salute, and try to slip me an extra dab
of butter.) I was fetched for work early every morning
immediately after breakfast, brought back upstairs for
lunch, fetched again for the afternoon session and returned at night. We had to move through a large
number of locked gates each guarded by a warder
whose sole duty it was to man that point. After a while
I learned that whenever I was escorted through the
prison it had to be according to a pre-determined plan
upon which Smoel, the security officer, had indicated
with arrows the route to be followed. I had to be
accompanied by at least two *boere*. Before leaving the
Stores the security officer had to be informed by telephone that we were now setting off for my cell (in
the same building!), and due to arrive within so many
minutes.

My work was that of an ordinary pen-pusher – making inventories, entering on ledger cards the articles
we had in stock, booking out to various sections whatever they needed in terms of cleaning materials or
food or clothes and generally helping the storemen
do what they were supposed to be doing. The supervision never slacked off. In later years the Stores were

moved to another building in the compound; I would then be taken the 100 yards there in a closed van under escort of an armed warder, and a *boer* with dog had to be present when I got into or out of the vehicle in closed courtyards; the guardposts were also alerted so that they could train their guns on the passing van. Madness! But gradually my workload increased. I think there is a natural tendency for the bureaucrat to push off as much work as he can on to his lackey. In due time they lost control over what I was actually doing: I could have swindled the State out of millions by falsifying figures or making ghost entries. Regularly I was asked to rectify errors – shortages, surpluses, thefts – by cooking the books. Towards the end of my stay the Prison Department's activities were computerized and that went for our work in the Stores too. It was quite a challenge to learn how to prepare the material that would be fed into the computer system. I had to come to grips with codes. Since the work interested me – this visualizing of information, and the sense of being a small part of a bigger brain – I ended up being perhaps the only one in our Stores who understood to some extent what was going on. I'm sure there was serious resistance among the Stores staff to the very idea that I might be released, as they would then have to blindly grope their way through the work which they in their laziness had let me take care of.

A little while longer, Mr Investigator, and then my confession is done. Not that I'd have told you everything – there are stories of spies in the beginning and cowards at the end that I haven't even touched upon. And if I were to introduce you to all the people

I met in boop, and tell you their anecdotes, we'd be going on for ever. No, a short way more, and then I'll be out of it forever.

The prison community can be cut up in many different ways. The basic racist classification enforced in No Man's Land applies to prison also. First there were the 'Darkies'—that is how the Blacks are referred to. Most of them originated from the Eastern Cape and were therefore Xhosa-speaking, but many had been living in the Western Cape for several generations and they would thus speak Afrikaans also. Then you had the *Gamme*,* the Coloureds, mostly from the Cape area—and 'Coloured' could be anybody from white to black. Then there were the 'Whiteys', again from European pale to indigenously mixed brown skin.

However, if you want to understand anything about the prison universe—a world apart with its peculiar castes and culture and language, its own reality, in fact—then you have to know something about its constituent components. You will find that in the Cape particularly, prison life is run by gangs. The three major formations are the 'twenty-sixes', who specialize in money matters—they monopolize the network of smuggling, buying and selling; the 'twenty-sevens', who are the men of *igazi* (meaning blood), and that means that they are the professional killers, the executioners and nothing else; and the 'twenty-eights', who practise and idolize homosexuality as a way of life, the masters of sex, the procurers, the *maquereaux*—they who provide the rest of the prison popu-

Gam—Ham, the son of Noah, who the *boere* say, was cursed to have slave descendants because he had laughed at his father's drunkenness.

lation with *wyfietjies* (little women) whom they fabricate by rape and by corruption.

There's much rivalry (and murder) among the gangs and each has an internal structure and a division of tasks expressed in military terms and, ironically, also in legal ones; they have their 'judges', their 'prosecutors', their 'courts', their *tekeners* (draughtsmen, signers, writers) whose only job it is to sign the death orders; there are 'generals', 'colonels', 'captains' and 'soldiers'. Normally you only rise through the ranks by committing specified acts of violence: sticking a knife into a warder, for instance, is worth instant promotion to 'colonel', and the insignia will be tattooed on your shoulders. A gang general is indeed somebody with vast power, to be saluted when passed in the corridor.

The *kring* (the circle), governing council, will decide upon a death. Once its decision has been carried out, parts of the body of the victim may be eaten ritualistically. (Pause here, Mr Investigator, and consider how structuralized alienation has brought about a society of cannibals. These men eat human flesh as rats will devour each other – for similar reasons – and not because it has ever been 'traditional' anywhere. Don't try to shrug it off by saying 'they' are not like 'us'. Don't go and look for so-called Cultural so-called Differences . . . When you decide to release these confessions, Mr Investigator, you will have smoothly combed prison spokesmen denying *en bloc* the veracity of what I'm telling you. They will be sitting in smart offices, far away from the stinking death lying in the cells, and their civilized mouths will produce bureaucratic appeals to your 'understanding' – how frail is human nature! – by admitting to exceptions which have all been investigated, with the guilty ones punished. Will you be taken in? I'm telling you that what I'm describing is *typical* of that mirror which the South African penal universe holds up to the Apartheid society—and that it is *inevitable*.)

Of course, there are some people who do not belong to a gang. They are called *mumpatas*, meaning 'sheep'. Being a *mumpata* unfortunately does not safeguard you from being chosen as a victim. These gangs have links with outside ones operating in the Cape area, such as the Scorpions or the Mongrels, but their prison existence is far more organized and important than life on the streets. (The one is just a continuation of the other.) Originally they were born of the convicts' desire to stand together and fight for certain privileges: they still refer to themselves as *wetslaners* ('those who hit the laws' but also 'those who hit with the law, who constitute a law')—an indication of their original cause for existence. But this aspect of Prisoners United is now in abeyance.

I could relate to you many blood-curdling incidents of gang warfare, gang murder, gang anthropophagy, gang rape. It would have to be a confession of its own. Why do the authorities 'allow' these gangs to exist? Because it is finally of little importance to them if prisoners want to exterminate one another. At the heart of the South African prison system is the denial of the humanity of 'the other', and in that it is only a reflection of the larger South African cosmos; that is why those wielding power, they who believe themselves to be superior, are inevitably moral decadents; that is how and why they inhabit No Man's Land. Naturally there is some collaboration between the *boere* (White or Black) and the gangs since the gang leaders take over the disciplinary functions of the warders to a large extent.

Whites too belong to these gangs; you recognize them by the distinctive tattoos around the neck—a miniature gallows, a bow tie, a pair of dice (because they also 'walk with the number', i.e. belong to a number gang) or by the etched stars on the shoulders. There also you have ritual murders. White too would open up the belly of the victim, take out the heart, the liver, part of the innards—to eat them. We are talking of social climate, Mr Investigator. Of staunchness and of despair. Of 'laws'. It is grotesque. It is the dialectic, the revelation of the interaction of man with his environment pushed to its most awful and degrading consequences. I could tell you of people I saw who had their penises cut off at the roots; of the red stars I saw against the wall of a passage, rhythmically every few yards for more than a 100 yards, where a victim who had been knifed in the heart had run, spouting blood from the pierced pump—clinging to life until he had none left. I could tell you of a cell I saw with blood-encrusted walls, the spray from cut veins soaking a mattress, of the flies and the ants. I could tell you about people bludgeoned to death with the hammers used for crushing stones; about people left to die in epileptic fits, their medicine withheld from them; about people left absolutely naked in bare cells; about people being transported from court in a prison truck, everyone singing to cover the sounds of the execution of one suspected of having turned traitor, and again of how the head would be sliced off and come rolling out when the 'can' arrives at its destination and the doors are unlocked. I could describe to you how an informer is killed slowly, his stomach

cut open with small blades made from the flattened
filtertips of cigarettes, and his intestines taken out
while he is still alive—to be laid out in lengths all
around the cell—how such a man will beg for death.
The earth is grey.

The *boere* could tell you of how you have to be
careful, when shooting a *bandiet* attempting to escape,
to have the body fall *inside* the walls—*that* is allowed;
if it falls *outside*, you have to go through the bother
of an inquiry and maybe even face manslaughter
charges. And while you're at it, ask them to tell you
how excited some of them are when they can provoke
two prisoners to commit unnatural sex acts for them
to watch and comment upon.

To me the measure of the self-contained and ritualistic nature of prison mores is its self-destructive-
ness. Some convicts would do everything possible to
be condemned to death, and bathe in the glory of
being a 'rope', of going up, of becoming part of prison
mythology. Worse even, infinitely worse, is the way
in which the fellow-prisoner victim nearly always col-
laborates with his executioners. The killing often takes
place over several hours. So trapped is the prey, so
much a part of the rites, that he will often assist at
his slow death with open eyes, trying to muffle his
cries and his sobs. Acceptance! Home at last!

Apart from the ubiquitous major gangs there are
smaller ones too: the so-called 'Big Fives' for instance.
To be a Big Five in prison lingo is to be a pimp,
somebody who squeals on his mates, who reports to
the authorities—a stool pigeon in other words. This
function is recognized in prison life to the extent that
a small gang will be formed proudly calling itself the
Big Fives. In the North there's the Air Force, the

equivalent among Blacks of the White Springboks.
Each gang has its own emblems and its own way of
'picking up' – the signs made by the fingers of the
hands to communicate and to indicate what gang one
belongs to.

More permanently perhaps you will recognize in
the prison community certain categories of people.
You will see the *lanies*, the tough ones, the leaders,
those who cannot be broken down – more often than
not doing a very long sentence. You do not cross swords
with them. (I had the good fortune of being under
the protection of a *lanie* or two – to offset the spies
and the pimps circling around me.) There will be the
dealers, trading in drugs, money, groceries, books –
you name it, somebody will have part of that market
cornered. There are the bookies with whom you place
your bets. You can certainly play horses regularly –
you will find people running up incredible debts, losing or winning fortunes in prison, and of course sometimes losing their lives when they cannot pay their
debts. (Yitshak was reduced to being a baker – making
for sale or on command innumerable 'boop puddings'
from left-over bread and hoarded jam and peanut butter, in an effort to reduce his betting debts of, at one
time, 150 packets of cigarettes and nearly 70 packets
of tobacco.) You thus have *boop* millionaires, people
with a fortune in the prison context, obviously worth-
less outside. You will find the pimps. You will find
the 'hawks', also known as *ringkoppe* (meaning
'ringheads') – these are the male partners of the homosexual concubinages. They are the hunters. ('Ring-
head', quite apart from its obvious sexual visualization,
also refers to a member of the Zulus' council of elders
who wear rings around their heads.) You have the

laities, the little ones or the 'female' ones, the 'women' in a homosexual relationship; but it can also just mean the young ones or the small ones. In the same order of ideas and indicating the various 'types' you will find in the predominantly homosexual community, there are *poephol pilots* or *hol buddies* (*poephol* being 'arse-hole'); you have *moffies* and 'rabbits' and a more refined specialization in the 'grocery rabbits', the subservient and opportunist ones selling their graces for food.

There will be other categories, defined either by the social status or origin of the inmates – such as the *lallapype* ('pipe-sleepers', those who are so poor that they'd be sleeping under culverts outside), the *maplotties* (those who live on small free-holdings or plots around the big towns), the *vlamslukkers* or *bloutreinryers* ('flame-swallowers' or 'riders on the blue train' being those who are reduced to drinking methylated spirits, which is tinted blue in South Africa), or the most distinguishing feature of their condition in prison. In this way you have those called the 'chains', convicts who wear chains either because they have been condemned to death or because they have tried to escape or have been recaptured or because they are considered particularly dangerous – these chains are worn day and night so that you hear them turn over in their sleep with the click-click-click of iron links. You have the 'condemns', even in Cape Town where they will be kept for some time before being removed to Pretoria. There are those called the 'fives', indicating the Jewish prisoners (the name may have originated in Cockney slang); there are the social cases, the down-and-outers, the very old or the very poor who have no income and no means of raising any and often no family outside – the 'socials' will normally be the skivvies of the others, their servants doing the washing and the ironing, cleaning the cells and doing odd jobs for tobacco or for a few sweets every month. (Some of these ancient outcasts were on their last legs when they came in. It would be the final station before death. After two or three days they would go into fits of terror, a private hell, delirium tremens. They would see dogs skulking in corners and bloody children and toads raining from heaven. They'd be calling out the names of long-buried and forgotten relatives. Happy Botha arrived after having burnt down the White Horse Hotel in Long Street; he never remembered a thing about that. Percy Runner had to be stripped of his rags when he was admitted; I remember seeing his clothes in a bucket in the courtyard, and the lice floating on the water. He was released and found dead in the Public Gardens two mornings later.)

You have *roebane* (robbers) and *trassies* (transvestites, some very beautiful and provocative, exciting the fellows no end), and 'grubbies' (gluttons, those who go digging in the rubbish bins for throw-away food) and *howwe* (the lot taken to court) and 'hard labours' (sentenced inmates) and 'coats' who are *langanas* (long-timers) and GBHs (sentenced for assault with grievous bodily harm) and *jollers* (those who really lived it up outside) and *rokers* (pot smokers).

Skommel, a toothless youngster who worked as cleaner in the *boeres'* office in our section, had tattooed on his back (I give it to you, Mr Investigator, exactly the way it was written – look after it well):

A roker-boy came home one night
And found his house without a light

He struck a match to go to bed
When a sudden thought came to his head
He went into his daughter's room
And found her hanging from a beam
He took his knife, and cut her down
And on her breast, these words he found.

My love was for a roker-boy
Who smoked his *dagga* just for joy
So dig my grave and dig it deep
And plant some *dagga* at my feet
And on my breast a turtle dove
To show the world I died for love.

Now all young sheilas bear in mind*
A roker's love is hard to find.
If you find one good and true,
Never, ever, change it for a new.

(Skommel had worked in the outside world as a steward on the trains. Coffee, to be really good, had for him to taste like 'Railways coffee'. He told me a visually funny but very sad story. During the course of his duties he once inadvertently opened the door to a compartment to announce lunch or dinner. Inside he found only one occupant: a woman, not so young anymore, wearing a fur coat. She was on her back, her dress lifted high, having her small lapdog do something to her. At the sudden sight of him the poor lady got such a fright that she chucked the beast out the open window of the moving train!)

There are naturally also real women in prison,

*Sheilas—young girls in slang.

although we never saw them. They are called the 'flat ones', or 'scissors', or 'slits'.

In general we, the prisoners, were known in the Cape as *bandiete* or *mugus* or *skebengas* or *skollies*. The warders remained, as ever, *boere*.

In the Cape, however, I came across a new category: racist Whites refer to Coloured people as *Hottentotte* or *Hotnots*, which is a pejorative term; now for the first time I heard Coloured warders being talked about as *Hotnotboere*.

My own situation gradually improved in some ways, Mr Investigator, although there would also be sudden clamp-downs for reasons which I did not always understand. When three White politicals escaped from Local in Pretoria I returned to my cell to find more, and more complicated, padlocks securing my inner grille and my outer door and the gate to the courtyard where I was taken for exercise. But in fact the security set up never changed. I shall never be trusted, it doesn't matter how long I live, or where in the world I find myself. I know, Mr Confessor, that what I have to tell you will be read avidly by the Greys and all the other *boere*, and that they will find by hook or by crook or by cowboy the means to avenge themselves. In due time there will be 'revelations'.

But that is for later. That will be the postscript. For now I must underline that I was never considered a normal prisoner. Witnerf laughingly confirmed this to me. 'We know you,' he said, 'if you're given half the chance you'd be flying out the window.' Thus it happened that a special crew of *boere*, dressed in battle greens, would go at night and search my place of work from one wall to the other. Poor Bles, who was personally responsible for me, found himself in murky waters because I had been allowed to work with carbon paper. 'Can you not see,' Witnerf told him, 'how dangerous this may be? Don't you realize that he can multiply political pamphlets and stow them away in these parcels so that they get distributed all over South African prisons?' Tch, tch, how stupid of me never to have thought of that possibility myself. We did indeed handle many parcels containing the clothes of people who were continuously transferred from jail to jail across the country. In the same way the sheet of blotting paper on the table where I worked during the day was carefully removed every night and the wee doodles or jottings that I whiled my time away with were photocopied to be forwarded to the Security Police for analysis and study.

What a cumbersome industry just to look after one person! They had to keep a multitude of books to record my activities or their observations of same. A daily report had to be written by my supervisor at work and this had to be summarized in a weekly and then a monthly account. The same held for the section sergeant. Every morning I was given an impressive ledger to sign, in which whatever requests or complaints I might have had were noted, as also the ultimate reactions to these. The idea, I assume, was to keep their record with the International Red Cross straight. Then there were several other books which I was not supposed to be aware of, but which I did find out about through my 'agents' (if I may call them so): one in which the sergeant or warrant officer responsible had to note daily the fact that my cell had been searched—ceiling, walls, floor, bathroom, pipes, bed, cupboard—and that no holes were found, no gnawing, nothing hidden; or if anything hidden, what it was, where, etc. A book of et ceteras. These entries had to be signed and countersigned by superior officers. Next there was a book entitled 'Incidents: Security Prisoner'; again the poor bastard on duty had to jot down whatever I'd done or said in the course of the day or the night – anything out of the ordinary perhaps?, the people whom I might have talked to, what I talked about, and if nothing of the kind, that too had to be testified to. Did I have a request that necessitated a written report? Write it out in duplicate, please. Again these would be filed and commented upon by the security officer or the head of the prison.

Now, from all this material a weekly extract had to be made. I once saw (quite illegitimately) the instructions pertaining to these weekly extracts issued by the Officer Commanding. It was specified, for instance, that any untoward gesture ought to be noted. Has the prisoner given the Black Power salute at any time? I presume that these summaries were duplicated and forwarded to the concerned intelligence organizations.

After some time I obtained permission to play chess (the permission was soon to be cancelled), which I was very happy about until I learned from one of my partners that he had been sent specifically to try to get me to talk politics.

Enough, Mr Investigator, you know enough by now. I think that you have always realized far better than I do what this is all about. What I'm attempting to say is that my alienation as a subversive criminal is permanent; nothing can ever bridge the gap between the authorities of the Afrikaner tribe and myself. And I accept this and I would not be happy otherwise, because I do not consider myself to be an Afrikaner. To be an Afrikaner in the way *they* define it is to be a living insult to whatever better instincts we human beings may possess and struggle to maintain.

Nevertheless, given this background of utter and permanent distrust, prison life did become progressively more relaxed. It took some time but ultimately I was occasionally allowed to walk the yard with the others. Even if you managed only to exchange a few words spread over the whole day or over several days, these added up to a conversation. It is vital to be in contact with other human beings. More important, Mr Investigator—as Don Espejuelo explained to me—more important than the banality of physical relationships is the deeper need for showing tenderness or kindness to another human. Man is born with the capacity and the imperative need to care for others.

Over the years I'd made some very good friends. Some I knew only for a short period before they were released or transferred, others deceived me or became enemies, and all of them have since become robed in the fog of time (despite the fact—allow me to mix my metaphors—that I now regurgitate them in words); but it doesn't matter: they made it possible for me to talk and to laugh, to situate myself, to give little presents, to learn about the final loneliness of human fate.

In this way I became friends with Cone, who was doing time for fraud. I was to exercise all by myself over lunchtime but P. Cone soon joined me; since he was suffering from a heart condition the doctor prescribed extra exercise for him and the only available time for that was when I was in the yard. He was a leading cause for my being sent to the 'bomb'. I had been caught on two previous occasions with illicit newspapers in my possession (two catches out of twenty I considered not a bad average) and sentenced first to three meals, that is, deprived of food for a day and locked up in a small cell, and then to five days' 'bomb'. During the period when I knew Cone, Major Witnerf had taken away all our library facilities because one convict in his cussedness had torn up a book. Cone, being an orthodox Jew, had been permitted some religious works; I on my side had finally obtained the permission to be allowed some books on Zen. One day after discussing religion in the yard during our walk, I promised to lend him one of my books. This was found in his cell and we were both accused – he of having an article which he was not entitled to and me of trying to proselytize, that is, to subvert a fellow prisoner. Witnerf, who acted the presiding magistrate, let off Cone (because of his heart) with the suspension of some of his privileges; I was sentenced to ten days' isolation in the punishment cell, and to spare diet. (The kangaroo court imitated the real outside court in that sentences were cumulative. Smoel once judged three chaps for talking to one another on the food line; they appeared before him successively: the first got five days, the second ten, and the unlucky third accused a full fifteen. 'What?' Smoel said. 'Another one? This must stop somewhere!')

I mentioned before, Mr Investigator, that this food punishment is quite refined and worked out, reputedly, by dietary experts. Over ten days, for example, you will be on 'spare diet' for four days – meaning that you will be getting a small, carefully measured quantity of absolutely dry unsalted maize porridge without sugar or milk in the morning, one cup of unsalted soup made from some indistinct soup powder for lunch, and again the same porridge in the late afternoon. That is all. You may drink as much water as you wish. Then two days of half-rations – the normal food but rigorously only half the quantity; one day of 'full' and back again to 'spare'. Thus your starvation and your hunger will be dosed. You lose weight fast. The doctors collaborate by giving you a cursory glance-over before you go in, to declare you fit for punishment. You may only do thirty days at a time. If you've been sentenced to more you are allowed a break of ten days before recommencing. You're naturally also deprived of all smoking material, books and any company. You may receive neither letters nor visits during this period. I knew one incorrigible youngster, called Dampies, who spent 217 days of his eighteen months in prison in the hole.

During my third 'bomb' stretch – I had five 'internal discipline' convictions in all – the prison cook accompanying the 'bomb' *boer* to ladle out the crud actually tried to help me by slyly introducing some sugar *underneath* the porridge, and he added several minutely rolled smokes as well. In return he would, when the section was quiet, sneak up to one end of the barred corridor and over a distance of twenty yards hoarsely whisper his poems at me. I was to give my 'expert' appreciation. He was an Australian – his father actually a consular official in Cape Town. Alas, his sugar trafficking was discovered and he was promptly flung into the 'bomb' too, not far away from me. The poetry! The poetry!

I now started running and exercising regularly. In Pretoria I had continued doing *Zazen*, some yoga, and even *Tai-Chi* in the confined space at my disposal.

Now I grabbed any chance I could get hold of to jog round and round the inner courtyard. (I once worked out that, had I been going in a straight line, I would have been halfway up Africa by the time I was released.) The Red Cross arranged for me to be given shorts and had insisted to the authorities that I should have half an hour exercising a day. My feet became quite tough. I learned that one must discipline oneself very strictly if one wants to survive. There must be the basic physical commitment of trying to remain fit, of listening to your body, of taking care of it (as Buddha had said) the way you would look after a sick man, not allowing it to go to flab and to apathy as happens to so many people behind the walls. You must furthermore discipline yourself intellectually by stealing with ears and with eyes, attempting in all possible ways to feed the mind. And you have to impose a moral discipline upon yourself, sensing and avoiding the crude simplifications and dichotomies the authorities try to have you conform to. Always remember the simple truth that denying the humanity of the person facing you is a sure-fire way of diminishing yourself. Keep away from the slothful slotting of 'them' and 'us'. I'm not talking about moral rectitude – it is an exigence of awareness, a consciousness tool for survival.

In passing I shall only refer to a few of my fellow inmates; the others – too many to mention – the night folk, the people of midnight populating No Man's Land penal universe, you will have to read about in *Pi-K'uan*.

I should mention Jerry Fox, the Slovakian. In his dishonesty he was true to himself and without any illusions about the nature of man or the essential nature of being a prisoner. Could there be a difference? He had done time before in Czechoslovakia, for smuggling people across the border. He had really worked in a salt mine; he had known Novotny; and he was appalled by the lack of solidarity among South African prisoners. 'Never ever again trust an ex-prisoner,' he said in his atrocious English. 'The spring will be broken. To survive he would have had to compromise. The weakness remains.' In South Africa he was living by his wits – in fact, he was pushing his prison sentence under an assumed name. (The 'real' Jerry had died in the Namib desert.) Outside he preferred the company of Coloureds even though he did not quite understand their language or their customs – and he didn't trust them either. He was constantly smuggling – being in the metal workshop helped – and I shared in the spoils.

Through Jerry I met the Tampax Kid, a young Afrikaner who had studied theology at the University of Stellenbosch. That one was the archetypal Afrikaner crook: looking you straight in the eye, bravely suffering his predestined fate, attending all the religious services, and capable of stealing your underpants while you're having a shower. (Captain Sodom had finally forced me to hand in my private underpants, threadbare by then; I was provided with the voluminous Santa Marias which pass for underwear in boop.)

The Tampax Kid, alias Mighty Mouse, had a penchant for the knife in the back. One lunchtime he came to my cell with a message from one of the 'chains', van Niekerk (considered to be a high-security risk), who – so Tampax breathed – wanted to escape and take me with him on condition that I would arrange for passports to leave the country once we were outside.

I still believe it was a trap, carefully prepared by the little runt. When the thing became known, as it nearly immediately did, he wanted to be transferred to an easier prison because, he claimed, van Niekerk was going to beat him to death with his chains. Maybe he was also angling for some time off. Then arrived the day for him to be let loose and he came to my cell to swear undying fidelity with his hands on the Bible and tears in his eyes. Jerry Fox was there also, laughing derisively. I told the Mouse that little fable of Scorpion wanting to cross the swollen river and asking Frog to take him to the other side, and Frog being coy, saying that he's not dilly in the head, that Scorpion will sting him to death in midstream, of how Scorpion scoffed at this reticence declaring that he would do no such thing as it would assuredly entail his own water-death too, so please; and of how they then set off and how, halfway across, Scorpion did jab his sting into the docile flesh of the amphibian, who gurgled as they started going down to death. 'But why, why? Now you will also die!' And Scorpion answering 'Yeah, glub-glub, I know. But I can do no else. I'm glub-glub *made* this way.' I told this to the Tampax Kid, asking rhetorically how it could be any different since the Afrikaner is a product of the system which he has produced. No, he swore, he would never do anything to embarrass me.

Three days later Witnerf himself stormed with all his bullies into my cell and took everything apart; he even painstakingly probed my chess pieces with a needle. It was only afterwards that I learned that the Tampax Kid had gone to a national weekly newspaper with the story, splashed over the front page, of my being involved with van Niekerk, the bank robber, in

an escape attempt. I learned that he'd even been paid
for the story.

Often we had foreigners with us. Some were illegal
immigrants – the Japanese would be with the Whites,
the Chinese did their time with the Coloureds. We
had several Yugoslavs – they seemed to have monop-
olized a part of the underworld. There were quite a
few Portuguese, of course. Skippie – named thus because of a gloriously sinking three-master tattooed on
his chest – one of them, was always going on a hunger-
strike, being sent to the 'bomb' because of his hunger
strikes, and then going on another hunger strike because of the unfair punishment. Sometimes he came
in as a White, sometimes as a Coloured. Eventually
he was declared permanently mad and referred to
Valkenburg, the madhouse.

I met one Spaniard. He was called Jesus. Small of
stature he was, dignified and portly, and speaking a
consonantless French. He became a barber in prison.
And he played a mean, if dithering, game of chess.
To my chagrin, he had me fooled and off the board
in less than twenty moves. He was disgusted with
South Africa and was leaving as soon as he could, even
if it meant walking on the water.

There were Poles and an Austrian pastry chef and
fractious Germans. There were Greeks – nearly always
in for contraventions of the Foreign Exchange Act. In
one instance we even had an Iranian, condemned to
death (he had killed some Indians in a shoot-out over
drugs). In the middle of the night he would get up
with a clatter of chains echoing down the corridor to
start chanting his morning prayers to Allah.

Americans and Israelis never stayed very long –
theirs were the only two governments with the pre-

requisite influence to have their nationals repatriated
rapidly. In Big House up north – people who arrived
from there told me – there was Kozlov, the Soviet spy,
moving quite freely among the other prisoners. The
extreme rightist Italians were also kept there: I remember one transfer arriving in Pollsmoor with a (private) T-shirt bearing the legend: *Paracadutisti 'El
Alamein' Pantere Indomiti* under the drawing of a
snarling black leopard. The shirt was the fruit of some
swop with one of the Italians.

Several Britishers came and stayed. A few were
hitmen or specialized gangsters sent into South Africa
on a quick in-and-out mission, and then the out got
fouled up. One sympathetic Englishman I became
friendly with was Tuchverderber. Before being sentenced for a farcical currency offence he had been a
prosperous factory owner, but now his whole life was
ruined. As they were going to deport him from South
Africa upon completion of his sentence, he was obliged
to sell his baronial mansion and his Mercedes Benz
at ridiculously low prices. He still had money though,
and the influence which money brings, and this he
used judiciously to bribe the *boere* – amongst others
Major Sodom – to bring in all kinds of sweets and fruit.
From these I profited too, Mr Investigator. Yes, for
a while I even had peanut butter for my bread. (I was
then not yet allowed any purchases. Only A-Group
prisoners may do so. Prisoners normally attain A-Group
status after six or nine months of their sentence, 'politicals' only once they've done half their time – whatever the length of their sentence.)

The one Dutchman I got to know during my stay
was Keulder, a big man with a lot of hair down his
back. Keulder had quite a harem going. His weakness

was for strapping young Afrikaner boys. These he would corrupt with favours. Tony, one of the sad-eyed Greeks sharing a big cell with him, recounted that the love sessions could be quite embarrassing. He (Tony) told of how he'd wake up in the middle of the night (he slept badly – dreaming of his wife and of boats) and be forced to listen to Keulder and the favourite boyfriend of the moment making love under the blankets. (Remember that the other ten people were all lying there, side by side on the floor.) And, he said, they'd be making the sounds of people slurping up tinned food. There could be no love *in petto*.

In Pollsmoor I also met Galgenvogel, the Hungarian exile, a big nob in the South African drug trade. He was a cultivated man who had studied for the priesthood until the discovery of Kierkegaard had opened his mind to darkness and to bitterness. His fingers were black from smoking and he had the racking cough of a thinker. His chess wasn't bad (it was certainly better than his chest), but occasionally the veneer of cultivation would crack and the real Galgenvogel would emerge to launch himself in a veritable philippic against mankind or even to get involved in some bloody bout of fisticuffs with another miserable specimen (nearly always a German). He lost all his fights. He also lost the appeal against his conviction. Then he lost his wife (or mistress). He lost a few tobacco-stained teeth. He played bridge for tobacco, and lost. He was not really a winner.

And all the time escape attempts were going on. People tried to 'make a break' or to 'kick out'. Stinkfoot solemnly greeted some of us by hand while we were up on the walled-in roof where the library was, scaled the wall and tried to climb down the outside. We were four floors high. They found him sitting on a ledge like some ungainly bird with cold feet, brought him back to earth, chained him and posted him to Pirax. Afkop and Nel got away as far as a house in the neighbourhood where within half an hour they tried to 'scale' (steal) a car, making such a racket that they were immediately recaptured. They were brought back in chains and savagely hit and kicked by the *boere*. (The *boere* refer to this exercise of baton-whipping and stomping as a 'carry-on'.) Swart Piet Vangat, drunk as a lord, came to my cell window to preen and to bluster, 'See how we got your chums?' People tried to have themselves carted away to freedom with the rubbish bins or the bags of washing. The only successful breaks were from court, or when chaps were taken to hospital or to an outside specialist, or from the train during a transfer, or running away from the fields when working in the agricultural span. These would be mostly Coloureds.

One White was arrested upon his return from abroad, on a trumped up charge. A year went by and still his case wasn't heard. So he 'threw sick' (feigned a malady), was taken to Groote Schuur Hospital, and took the gap. He was caught within the hour. The prosecution dropped the original charges against him, admitting now that it had all along been a matter of mistaken identity, but for escaping from custody he was jailed for a further nine months.

One ancient 'blue-coat' got away nearly by accident. I met him after he'd been recaptured and brought to Pollsmoor. He told of how he was being transferred by train from somewhere to Sonnies (Zonderwater) and how the warders with him were having a profound philosophical conversation with a bottle and that bot-

tle's descendants. Arriving at Germiston station the
coat asked for and obtained permission to make a quick
phone call to his old wife. To give her some instructions about his pension. He got off. They'd given him
a few coins. He entered the telephone booth. And
was a long time in establishing the damn contact. The
South African telephone system is not quite what it
ought to be. The train hooted twice and slowly left
the platform. And Hurry Harry, as the old man was
known, all of a sudden found himself left in the lurch.
He went outside to the main road and decided to catch
up with his two guardian angels by hitching a lift. But,
he said, no cars wanted to pick him up. There was
very little traffic going the way he was heading, and
maybe he looked a bit too much like an old prisoner.
So he walked across the street and by and by found
somebody willing to take him, but oh dear, going to
hell and gone in the opposite direction. He was foot-
loose for many months – he had meanwhile started a
transport business – before they caught him again for
driving an overloaded lorry. During this outside time
(this walkabout) he had written a letter to the Prison
authorities to say he was just having a break, sir, and
would be back soon-soon, and that they shouldn't be
too angry with the two deep-thinking warders.

Some people broke out because they felt that not
enough attention was paid to their griefs. One fellow
was so upset at not being allowed to have an interview
with a senior officer that he escaped from Zonderwater
and made his way to Vermeulen Street in Pretoria,
to Prison Head Office, to complain to the Commissioner himself.

And quite a few times I found myself involved –
without knowing anything about it – in some far-fetched

escape scheme. Once I was taken down to the commanding officer's sanctum and, in the keenly head-bobbing presence of his senior staff, accused of being the moving mind behind a planned escapade which included my having prepared passports and having bought a boat lying offshore ready to take me and my fellow conspirators to the distant shores of freedom of Never Never Land ready immediately lets go go go!

I remember how all the prisoners were once gathered in the big yard to be told by an officer what the advantages offered were for pimping another prisoner. If you were instrumental in uncovering an escape attempt you could get a reward of up to R30 paid in on your name, plus/or a reduction of sentence not exceeding nine months. As Lofty, one of my fellow *langanas* pointed out loudly, this was an open incitement for the short-timers to try and shop us. It's just not fair, Lofty said.

In retrospect it all sounds quite funny. Even at the time Tuchverderber and I agreed that if we ever survived, we would one day, looking back, remember just the hilarious bits. In such a way does the human memory try to escape from itself. But it wasn't so pleasant then, I can assure you. I remember how I one day realized with a shock that my nerves were shot to bits.

A squad of *boere* with their excited dogs came charging in unexpectedly. It was a shake-down. We were all chased from our cells and up a long corridor with both ends blocked off. We were thereupon body-searched individually before being led back to the cells which were similarly cleaned from top to bottom. Apparently they were after the copy of a key that they believed someone had succeeded in making. I had in my pocket once more a folded strip of paper. What was scrawled on it? The beginning of an undying poem? A reminder to tell Mr Investigator one day of this incident, or of that one? Let it be. . . . I literally went to pieces at the thought of them finding it on me. The violent reaction – the loss of control – took me by the throat as if by surprise. I stood with my back against the wall, shivering. Without my knowing it they have succeeded in making of me an unpredictable risk.

White long-term prisoners used to be held in Victor Verster Prison near Paarl, but in 1980 that institution was closed down for them, and they were all brought over to Cape Town. That is how I got to know Shorty, an old wrinkled monkey of a man, and Dennis, his right arm, who looked like a wiser version of Claude Lévi-Strauss. Shorty had been in prison ever since the Second World War. In reality he had passed straight from the Army into prison. When given half a chance he would harangue us with a rousing speech steeped in the sentiments and expressions of his war years. He was the permanent secretary to the Sports Committee which was really just a cover for the prisoners' mafia – collecting donations supposedly for buying sport equipment or something extra for Christmas, but in fact fed into the smuggling circuit.

I also made a friend of the head cook, old Angel. He was a bald-headed man with one gammy leg, and lovely, rosy gums. He had some nasty stains on his arms and his face, which turned out to be cancerous. I can't remember what crimes he was doing time for (inadvertently selling stolen cars, I think), but the source of all his problems was alcoholism. He had been inside before for something to do with bankruptcy. Life was a fuck-up to be lived unobtrusively and looked at steadily through thick glasses. His teeth he lost to a policeman's baton. (Those rubber batons are called *donkiepiele*, 'donkey pricks'.) His leg was the result of a car smash in Namibia. He used to work on a boat. He once went to Argentina but returned after a week because he found the hotel room stuffy. He dreamt of telepathy and astral journeys and was so rigorously honest that he sometimes wrote only three lines to his mother – his only correspondent – because he had nothing to say. During one of his fits of delirium tremens he was introduced to a small gentleman living on his shoulder. This gentleman, seemingly, never left him again. Angel was shy about his appearance. When I teased him too cruelly about his vanity or his death-wishing commercial schemes, he would react in a diffident way by telling me that he himself didn't mind much but (softly) that the little fellow on his shoulder (who was of a grumpy disposition) didn't take too kindly to all this ribbing.

Every once in a while, on a Sunday, Angel would produce a magnificent set of flashy false teeth which he had bought from a fellow convict. These did not fit, they were too big, and when he wore them he could not eat – but he would don his best suit of prison greens or his starched white cook's outfit, polish his glasses, and suddenly present himself with these grinning dentures in the face. These altered his appearance and his enunciation so completely that even his eyes seemed to pop behind his glasses. Indeed, so different was he then that I pretended not to recognize him. On such days he was known as Professor Hans Smilinks.

Angel lived in a wonderful world of sweet sadness. He must have been one of the only people ever turned

away from a whorehouse in Lourenço Marques because his sexual appurtenance was found, after short-
arm inspection, to be too awe-inspiring. He used to
talk to the flies on his wall. He it was who introduced
me to Reti, the god of retribution, by whom all long-
timers swear. Somewhere up there in the lands of
clouds and of bliss is a living force who will for sure
wreak revenge on our enemies for all the miseries
they have subjected us to.

Perhaps, once in a blue moon, one got some earthly
recompense too. Angel was on occasion employed,
years before, as a prison cook during a big week-long
show in Pieter-Maritzburg where the Department also
had a stand. Cooking was hot work. He had already
bribed a *poisan* (a Black warder) to provide him with
a bottle of wine, but when the latter refused to organize the first bottle's mate, Angel decided to do
justice by himself. It was two o'clock and stifling. The
officer in charge had taken off his uniform and, stuffed
stiff, had lain down for a nap in the next room. So
Angel borrowed his uniform, plus a portable radio
belonging to a warder, and left for town. He was even
saluted on his way out! In town he sold the radio and
then ensconced himself in the coolness of the first bar
he came to. It was late that evening when he finished
the last of the money and – in an absolute stupor by
now – told the barman to please phone the Prison Department to come and fetch him.

There are many more angels, Mr Investigator. I
knew Jood, a fisherman by trade, who had spent perhaps twenty years of his life in prison. He was old
now, reduced to shuffling, and suffering from rheumatism. His time in the yard he would spend looking
for bees, which during certain seasons got blown over

the roof and were too weak to fly away again; these, if they were still alive, he would catch and have them sting him, because he believed bee stings to be a cure for his aches.

I knew Franz, the gentle killer with the background of a trained psychologist. During his trial he pleaded with the judge to give him the rope, but his pleas fell on deaf ears and he had to be satisfied with a twenty-year sentence. Already this had been increased because of an unsuccessful escape effort from Victor Verster Prison. Franz told me in a clinical fashion, what it was like to kill someone, to shoot him at point-blank range and to watch death come over his eyes like a cheesecloth. He had felt nothing, he said, but he knew that he had smashed something essential in himself. Towards the end of my time in prison Franz tried to commit suicide out of sheer desperation when his young lover was released. This young lover, Romeo, was going to stay on in the Cape Town area. To break the link between outside and inside the authorities now suddenly threatened to remove Franz to Pretoria where – so he said to me – he was sure that his soul would be killed, and he didn't want to become a vegetable. His family was also in Cape Town; he had some of his books with him; and he was under the care of Zorro, the visiting outside psychiatrist. So Franz one night slit his own veins at the wrists and in the armpits. Quite by accident he was saved before bleeding to death. Zorro insisted that he should not be left in Pollsmoor. The authorities agreed but they wanted their pound of flesh by punishing Franz for the unsuccessful suicide, sending him to the 'bomb' for thirty days. Then, at the end of that period, they lured him into an office under false pretences, jumped him from behind, overpowered him and handcuffed his hands behind his back, chucked a few possessions in a carton, and shanghaied him to Big House. Thou shalt go and kill thyself in another command.

I met Hottie, the champion grubby of the whole of Pollsmoor: thin as a rake, but with an insatiable appetite. Hottie was so deeply in debt buying food off others, gambling in an attempt to pull even, irrevocably sinking deeper in debt, that he too tried to make an end to his days when his creditors started putting pressure on him. But it was a half-hearted effort. He was not so sure of the eating facilities in the other world. (Maybe he knew too much about decomposition, having been an undertaker by trade outside.) He cut his wrists and then tried to rouse his neighbour in the next cell. The neighbour, Trevor Universe, a fanatic body builder who treasured his sleep to increase his strength, snarled at Hottie to shut up and die but for God's sake to let him sleep in peace. Hottie found himself in the 'bomb' where he made matters worse first by writing a 'stink letter' (of outrage) to the Head of the Prison, because of which he was then charged and convicted, thereupon by going on a hunger strike in protest, whereupon he was charged anew—and then he got so frustrated that he attacked the first *boer* he could find with a sharpened spoon. It happened to be a pathetic warrant officer known as Chicken Breast.

Hottie was not to be in circulation again before Christmas. It was a pity that, because with a syndicate of accomplices I had started grooming another birdie, known as Skew-Eyes, who naturally had an unnatural appetite, with the aim of organizing an end-of-the-year eating championship in which the first prize would

have been a huge pot of porridge. We were banking
on our candidate with his nearly divine ugliness putting the other camp's – Hottie – off his stroke.

There was a high percentage of killers among the
long-timers who came over from Victor Verster. In
general they were the ones with whom I got along
best; they were normally quiet and reserved, and at
least not as totally dishonest as the robbers, the fraud
artists, and even the rapists. A special connection with
whom I shared some of the monthly delicacies (his
boyfriend made nice puddings) and who joined me in
my daily exercises in the yard, was Moineau. He had
been the leader of the unsuccessful break-out from
Victor Verster in which Franz too had been involved,
and in the process he was shot through the cheek with
the bullet lodging in his nose. The *boere* left him lying
in his blood for an hour before they carted him off to
hospital. Moineau was one of the *lanies* of our prison,
an exceptionally gifted sportsman and a strong fighter.
It was his dream to leave prison before he was too
old, and to become a sports instructor or trainer. His
problem was his ambivalent sexual urges, or the problems of self-acceptance and adaptation caused by those.
(His victim had been an unfortunate drunken ped-
erast.) Despair was darkening his mind. Already he
had had his once fine body covered by tattoos, and
regretted it (with slogans one sees so often in jail, like
Death Before Dishonour and *I broke my mother's
heart to please my friends*). Probably he will kill again
and end his days in the darkness of prison, or throw
his life away in a desperate run for freedom.

I got to know Alf, a sixty-year-old bull of a Portuguese. He was doing the coat for theft and had
already been inside for nearly ten years, but he kept

his body in excellent shape. He didn't smoke, didn't drink coffee, didn't smuggle, had no boyfriends, never asked for any favours, and maintained the principle of never talking to any warder in any circumstances — even when they addressed him — and further refusing to compromise or to collaborate in any way with their social workers or their parole boards or their chaplains or their shrinks. Repeatedly he was punished for refusing to see these parasites. I think they were quite afraid of him.

Quite often one came across ex-policemen or ex-warders in prison. (We also had with us, briefly — because their sentence was a sham — some of the mercenaries involved in the débâcle of the attempted Seychelles *coup d'état*. And towards the end the first convicted religious objectors to military duty started coming in.) One of the ex-coppers was a certain Onslof, formerly a detective-sergeant on the drug squad. His crime was stealing state evidence and bringing it back into circulation by selling it. He tried very hard to become acceptable to his ex-victims, and he was not really such a bad fellow. His speciality for earning some credit in prison was to embellish the penises of the inmates. From the plastic handle of a toothbrush or from perspex he would fashion little pearls. With a blade he would then make a small incision in the loose skin around the organ of the client to insert a 'pleasure bead'. Left alone the slit would close up in due time (theoretically that is, because some of the wounds sometimes did fester), and the bead would stay there forever. Some people, as he himself, had as many as nine of these mobile knobbles situated around their penises. It was, so he told the credulous folk, an unfailing way of giving excessive pleasure to one's sexual partner. Hottie had disagreed vociferously. He had been quite upset at the idea; according to him it was calculated to hurt the receiver and ultimately to provoke cancer.

Another of my friends was Mac who was at that time already pushing two coats for an accumulation of minor crimes and several escapes. In fact, I became involved with him in another ludicrous effort. We arranged (paying two packets of snout) for him to be knocked over the head by a fellow prisoner. The idea was to have him transported to outside hospital from where he was to run for it and ultimately come and arrange for me to do the same. So he was discovered lying with a messy scalp on his cell floor, ostensibly in a coma. They took him to Groote Schuur Hospital where the doctors tried to revive him. They directed light beams into his pupils and were baffled by the fact that the eyes contracted normally, but when they pulled out some of his chest hairs with a tweezer he never budged. Unfortunately for Mac and for me, he had been shackled to the hospital bed and when he saw that they were going to keep him tied down, be it until he died, he opened his eyes and ended the game.*

I must admit that I had been mixed up in some

*At the time of confessing this (December 1983), Mac—who had broken out on several previous occasions, by absconding from the dentist or diving, handcuffed, through a train window—was on the loose again. This time he escaped in the company of an ex-policeman. Mac is a gentle, humorous bloke, not given to violence, but the newspapers (and the police informing them) are creating an atmosphere of terror which would provoke and justify the shooting to death of the escapees if ever they are cornered. As far as I know he is still free. . . .

other improbable schemes. Barns, upon release, promised that he was going to return one misty night and get on to the roof of the prison (I just had to have something white fluttering from my window) to force apart the bars with a jack. We had agreed on a code; I never heard from him again. Jerry, once free, was going to arrange for me to obtain enough soporific to put out the *boere* in the General Stores at the time when he proposed coming by, with someone else in a delivery van using the pretext of bringing foodstuff to the prison. Blackie, also due to go, said that he had worked out a way of returning with a Coloured accomplice, both of them disguised as prison officials, to kidnap me at the moment when I was transported from the prison to my place of work. Needless to point out that none of these flights ever got off the ground.

Eventually I also got to know another terrorist, a man of the extreme right called Van der Westhuizen. He had been arrested with a real fanatic, Beelders, and convicted of taking potshots at a political leader of the Progressive Federal Party, of disrupting their political meetings violently, and of destroying property of government opponents. After being sentenced to five years and seven years respectively they had been brought to Pollsmoor prison. Immediately after their arrival I was warned by some of my 'spies' that they were threatening to *katang* me, meaning to wipe me out. We were never in the same section. Not many months later an intermediary—another one of those ex-warders now a prisoner working in the kitchen— came on their behalf to the door of my cell with the suggestion that we should escape together. They would provide the means of getting out, I was to procure travelling papers and undertake to make them ac-

ceptable to the overseas world. Of course I turned
down this silly idea. Surely they would have slit my
throat within half an hour of us being outside the
prison walls. Or was this just another attempt by the
authorities to bait me?

One Saturday afternoon a second emissary, also a
kitchen boy, a German doing nine months (unfairly,
he protested) for having shot and killed a Zulu on his
farm, came with the same proposal—and warned me
to watch out. Well, the German must have been looking for a reduction of sentence because the very next
Monday I was suddenly brought back from the General Stores and taken into an office to be confronted
by Swart Piet Vangat and his officers accusing me of
having wanted to escape with the other two terrorists.
The matter, Vangat intoned pompously, had been
brought to the attention of the Minister himself. He,
Vangat, had just come from the Buildings of Parliament. He had, he said—pointing with a fat index finger
at his black briefcase—he had *documents*!

The German pimp was promptly released. Beelders and Van der Westhuizen were transferred to Pretoria the same day; they were obviously not going to
be bothered in any other way. But of course the authorities were going to try to make out a case against
me. Nails Van Byleveld came, supposedly to investigate the matter. Nothing came of it.

A year passed and Van der Westhuizen was brought
back to Pollsmoor, this time to be put in the same
section as I was. Yes, Mr Investigator, I even got to
sympathize with him. After all, we were now objectively in the same situation. He told me that he had
broken all links with Beelders. Beelders, he said, was
an out-and-out Nazi with serious identity problems,

first because he had difficulty with his homosexuality, and secondly because he was not sure of being a White. It was rumoured that he – a White supremacist – was in fact Coloured! Van der Westhuizen related to me how the two of them, with others of their extreme-right organization, had been directed by the Security Police as heavies or as thugs to go and terrorize suspected opponents to the government of No Man's Land. They would be summoned, he said, to an outlying police station (such as the one at Blaauwberg Strand), often by Van Byleveld who was their handler, and given instructions to go and burn out the motorcar or put fire to the house of so-and-so at such-and-such an address. The alarm would be given, the fire brigade and the police would be called for, but miraculously they would always arrive too late or go to the wrong place.

Van der Westhuizen also told me that Beelders had confessed to him that he'd been the one who assassinated Rick Turner, shooting him to death before his wife and daughter through the window of his own sitting room. He had relayed this confession to the police, Van der Westhuizen said, and a laborious inquiry had been launched.*

It is all coming back in bits and pieces, Mr Investigator. I am vomiting words, I have the sour taste, I'm trying to hold on to the thread. These things sur-

---

*Other well-informed sources claim however that Rick Turner was killed accidentally by an English mercenary who was hired by the then BOSS to give Turner a fright. . . . Maybe Van der Westhuizen was trying to do Beelders in, maybe Beelders was indulging in fantasy, or maybe Van der Westhuizen was. As for the inquiry – I'm sure it was never intended to be completed.

face from somewhere intimate, and yet I do not know them. If I were to know my own nature well I should be knowing universal nature. I discovered gardens. I was living in a cemetery for horses. I went screaming down passages of darkness. I was going ever deeper into the labyrinth. See here, I hold it in my hands. I have the black gloves. And silences. Salient incidents remain like shards in the mind. I dare not remove them from fear of provoking a bleeding that can never again be stopped. (This is a confession, not a saga.) I don't know if I have a mind. I dare not look into it — it is so sore. I'm tired of talking to you. I lie down on the floor for a rest and to look at the roof window full of daylight and the invisible stars beyond, it brings back memories, and I get up to continue confessing. I sing into the microphone. A coldness has come over the world. A brittleness too. This morning I was up in the dark to watch the windows nearly imperceptibly growing blue: and the morning star glittering above the buildings. Memories are made of this. Look how dark it still is when you rise at 5.30 in the morning, or a little earlier when you want to cross your legs and kneel facing the wall inhaling and exhaling the flow of emptiness. Even earlier when you stood on your head in the darkness and Warrant Officer Donkey, on night shift, came by and asked you all manner of silly questions through the barred window. 'You must finish your shit now, Breytenbach,' he said. 'It is not worth it. You have caused enough shit.'

See how dark it still is when you are let out into the yard to line up for work. See the matrix of stars. Know that they will not fade but that your eyes will soon be saturated and blinded by light. Smell the new day, the waking mountain. Hear the wind of daybreak.

See, when they come in the van to fetch you to work, the spotlights washing the façades of the prisons – and look, outside Medium in that alley between two high wire fences the hundreds of prisoners squatting there in the glare with their hands on their heads, to be counted before going off in a shuffle-trot to their tasks.

I shall continue. I shall remember Nyoka, the vain young warder (who claimed to be a Catholic) making it his ambition to humiliate me, turning over everything in my cell, taking my so carefully collected half jug of jam and spreading it out on the floor to walk in it and to wipe his shoes on the blankets he's ripped from the bed. He had his hang-ups, Nyoka. The homosexuals fascinated him the way a bee is bemused by flowers. He would summon one of them to the office and have him describe minutely the ways of sodomy. Often it would be Marlene who had to give the story of the ring and its variations. 'She' was in exactly because of repeated more or less public acts of sodomy outside, and often said that for 'her' to be in prison is rather like locking up an alcoholic in a bar. Poor Nyoka – vanity fair! – so carefully combing his hair, his face pale from the repressed tension.

It was due to him that many of the moffies ended up working in the kitchen. One of the chosen ones was called Gatiep. A nasty job. He used to sell food to the hungry by having them commit fellatio with him – to satisfy his desire for having someone kneeling before him. Days. Nights. More nights. A darkness and people moaning in their sleep. Warrant Officer Donkey at my window. 'What are you doing at this hour? No man, Breytenbach, you must leave your shit be now. You must come right!'

I shall remember Sergeant Prins who had to look

after me during exercise periods. For him I felt true affection. He was another one of life's eternal losers. All he ever really aspired to was to be on a farm of his own, among his horses and his sheep, and here he was whittling his life away in prison. He confided more of his private life to me than he'd ever do to anybody else. A simple man looking for understanding. Still, if he had been ordered – after knowing me for five years – to take me out, stand me against the wall and shoot me, he would have done so. With tears running down his cheeks. But he would have done so.

And there was the death of Paine. He had come in suffering from thrombosis; his legs were of a nasty blue colour with the varicose veins standing out in ridges on them. In the winter it would still be bearable because the medical stockings he had to wear were covered by long pants. Came the summer however, and we all had to dress in shorts. He was very upset; he asked consistently for permission to be allowed to keep on wearing his longs, to hide the ungainly stockings, but this was refused. The friction between him and the *boere* built up. Early mornings, immediately after breakfast, the medicine trolley would come round and those needing medication would line up. Paine was always in the queue, of necessity. He just had to be given his daily pills. One *boer* particularly, Muller by surname, would go for Paine; every morning while he was waiting in line he would pester him, taunt him, accuse him of being a shirker, mock his legs, do everything possible to make the man's life a misery. One morning Paine exploded and chucked his dixie of hot porridge at Muller's face. Muller dragged him off to the office, a few other warders hurriedly arrived, and Paine was obviously given a very bad hiding. Paine was then taken to the 'bomb' section without any of us seeing him and we learnt later—from someone who happened to be doing a 'bomb' stretch at that time—that Paine had knocked several times on his cell wall during the following night, that he had also called out for help. The next morning he was found dead. Verdict: heart attack.

Attack of the heart, Mr Investigator. Listen. I must tell you this too. Listen. Early on during the month of April 1978, Witnerf one night entered my cell to tell me that my mother, Ounoof, had died.

She had been to visit me on several occasions since my arrival in Pollsmoor Prison. The year before it even happened once, on my birthday, that I was called into Witnerf's office to find Hoang Lien and my mother and my father there. For one brief minute I was allowed to embrace them. As she put her hands around my shoulders, my mother said, 'Klong, I thought I'd never touch you again.' And her lips quivered. The last time I saw her was perhaps two weeks before the fatal heart failure. Johan Kriegler and John Brand had come down from Johannesburg to discuss some legal matters with me, and my parents—hearing that the lawyers would be there that day—drove into the city from Onrus, where they then lived, to see them; hoping also that they might be allowed to see me. Their request was denied. (You should have thought about the security of the State before bringing such children into the world, old woman. . . .) But as I was taken from the consultation room down the mirror-smooth passage where the offices are, back to my cell, I passed in front of an open door and glimpsed my elderly parents sitting there in the small waiting room. They were looking at the wall opposite them. She was holding a handbag, he was holding a hat. When did they become so grey? They did not see me and I was not allowed to stop.

Now Witnerf came in. It must have been seven o'clock. For the first time I saw him dressed in civilian clothes – a rather garish and outdated, blocked jacket, and some vulgar private shoes. I think the shoes were two-toned, black and white. He had just been riding a motorcycle, he said. The wind, wow! His son also wanted to have one when he grew up. ('Boys will be boys, you know.') Then he invited me to sit down next to him on the bed, and he announced the death to me. He must subsequently have given me a heart-lifting talk. I don't remember anything of it. He asked me whether I wanted something to make me sleep and I said no. He might have touched my hand. He left and I found myself in this big cell, in a kind of neon loneliness.

It was all abstract. In my mind my mother had been dead for years. I would never *experience* her death. I knew that she had died but I would never *know* that she's dead.

The warders were probably instructed to keep me under observation, or maybe they were just curious to see how I would react. For whatever reason two of them remained outside my windows, staring in at me. I had nowhere to go, Mr Investigator. I could not stay on the toilet forever. There was not a single nook, no hiding place, no nothing. There was nothing.

I turned my back and hunkered down in one corner of the cell with my arms around my knees to cry in privacy.

During that period the lights were never switched

off in Pollsmoor's cells. You slept and you woke at two o'clock or four o'clock, not knowing what time it was. I often tied a rag around my eyes in an attempt to get some darkness. Now, with the cloth, I was at least oblivious behind my eyelids. I could talk to my mother.

Swart Piet Vangat himself passed by the next day to look at me through the window. I had not been taken out for work. It was quiet in my cell; I was doing slow *Tai-Chi* movements. Death is just a continuation, a walking on to the other land, a slightly modified rhythm, a deeper space. Vangat called me out and took me down to where the Commissioner, General Du Preez, sat in an office. I was told that my family had requested permission for me to attend the funeral, but that this had been turned down. Later that same afternoon I was taken downstairs again and was now informed that I would indeed be allowed to go to the funeral, but, as Du Preez said, it would be under the strict escort of senior officers; and he added that as my eldest brother Jan would be present at the grave too they had no qualms: if ever I tried to escape, he said, I shall have the shit shot out of me. (I'm trying to translate verbally the crude words he used.)

My family was allowed to come and visit me the next day. My father was withdrawn, silent, looking at me with an immense sadness. My sister was there with him. The following morning it was the turn of two of my brothers, Jan and Cloete, and—as could perhaps be expected—I was shown into an office to meet them without any supervision. Later that afternoon I was told that the decision to have me attend the funeral had been reversed again. It was over and done with. My mother was put into the earth in the cemetery overlooking the village of Hermanus and the sea.

I don't know whether she died happy or unhappy. Does it make any difference? I only remember that she had had a marvellous life, that she had listened to the music of that life, and that towards the end it had been made sombre by an unnecessary anguish. She was like a bird nevertheless, always optimistic.

Around me life was continuing. People mutilating themselves. People finding the most impossible means of drugging themselves. At one stage someone working in the fields came across some *malpitte*, the seeds of an indigenous weed (*Datura stromonium*). These he brought back and they were eaten by a few inmates. A characteristic of *malpitte* (madness pips) is that they cause the mind to hallucinate. For more than a week those who had partaken of the pips were indeed mad. One of them had his eyesight impaired permanently.

Vangat left Cape Town and was replaced by Brigadier-General Charles de Fortier. He was another type of person altogether—straight, honest, humane. My father still came to visit me every month and then just sat there, silently. He could not go on living all by himself in the house at Onrus; he wasn't even eating properly or regularly anymore. So he moved over the mountain to a boarding house in the Strand. Then he became ill. It was decided that he should go to live with my sister in Grahamstown. He came to say goodbye, holding his hat in his hand the way the old people do on formal occasions. De Fortier had the gate separating us unlocked so that I could embrace him. I have very seldom seen my father cry.

He left and soon after arriving in Grahamstown he had a stroke. He has been partly paralysed ever since.

Sometime during 1980 I was suddenly granted permission to start listening, in the Stores where I worked, to taped news and taped music. With the snorting and the shouting going on all around me the conditions were atrocious, but at least if I bent my ears close enough to the tape recorder I could hear a voice giving me the censored news of a few days previously. Connection, Mr Investigator. Somebody just like me talking into a little machine, confessing, confessing. Illegally of course I had managed to stay abreast of the news events to a certain degree. What was earth-shattering, what was fantastic, what was like an electric shock shaking my carcass – was the music. I shall never forget the first time I switched on the machine: there was silence, then a hissing noise, and then the opening bars of Bach's Brandenburg Concerto going right through my head. You will never hear anything like it, Mr Investigator. *Nobody* has ever been music the way I was then. Perhaps my body itself will never again be just an extension of the vibration of sounds.

The *boere* unfortunately also understood the value that music could have in such a context and spitefully they would take pains to ruin the cassettes either by taping the music at the wrong speed or, after my repeated requests for classical music, sending me hymns lustily sung on a Sunday evening somewhere in the church. I was told by one of the officers to whom I complained that it was much worse on Robben Island. There the politicals once had to endure the same record being repeated for weeks.

Communication with the outside world remained difficult and limited: to the end the powers that be tried to keep it secret that I was actually in Pollsmoor.

Some people did manage to receive permission to come and see me. Dirk Opperman, the poet, arrived one day. Despite his weak condition he had himself brought from a hundred miles away. He assured me that I was still alive as a poet, that there was interest for my work among the students, and said that it would be fatal for me to break entirely with the Afrikaners. Soon after he was also to suffer a paralysing stroke.

On two occasions I'd written letters to Opperman (after obtaining permission) to thank him for a volume of poems he'd sent me. These never reached him. They were just stolen by either the Prisons or the Greyshits. But I threatened to lay a charge of theft when they held back one of Yolande's life-giving monthly letters. So Smoel brazenly turned up on a Sunday afternoon with it, claiming that he'd had to go himself to the Post Office where he'd found it on the floor! (The prison censor's dated stamp was carefully snipped off!)

Smoel left for the Island. Saayman took his place, a huge pig of a man, subservient to his superiors, bullying—violently at times—the prisoners, but above all lazy and incompetent. He was also just a liar. His conception of censorship was to 'lose' the incoming letters, or to hold back mine and then to have me rewrite them to his specifications. I wrote to Yolande once lyrically praising the talents of some chocolatiers —Bernachon in Lyons, Corné de la Toison d'Or in Belgium, etc. (it was getting on for Christmas, my mind was sweet with absences) and when she wrote back asking how I knew about these things I answered admitting that I'd always been an initiate of the Secret Order of Chocolate Lovers but that I could never tell her this as it was supposed to be a secret. So Saayman launched an inquiry; he wanted to know exactly what 'politics' was hidden in these codes. . . .

Frederick van Zyl Slabbert came to see me. Although he is the leader of the official Opposition I don't think it was that easy for him to arrange for the visit. (They tried to discourage him by telling him that his visit will have to be in the place of a family one.) He listened attentively to whatever I had on the heart. Only afterwards was I to realize how particularly kind he'd been to Yolande, making it possible for her to pursue her efforts to have me liberated. He is a discreet, efficient man, always following up on the initiatives that had been started.

Thanks partly to him I was now also allowed to receive the visits of a man of letters. Professor Kharon from the Afrikaans department of a university in a neighbouring town was allowed access to my manuscripts, and afterwards we could discuss these. For the first time since nearly seven years I now talked literature to an enthusiast. For me it meant that these writings were resuscitated from the dead. Kharon is an intelligent man, with wide-ranging and sensitive literary interests. The exciting experience was that I could talk about really important matters to someone who would disagree absolutely with what I'd done with my life and with the notions which had inspired me. Despite these differences, although I was a *bandiet* (and would remain one in my mind) and he a man moving in the vicinity of the powerful, sniffing the heady scent that I would find nauseating, I could sense a true affection developing between us.

More time passed. I built time itself into my system by running, by *Zazen* and by *Tai-Chi*, by escaping through the walls and walking up the mountain to smell spring with its first warmth being wafted down from the trees growing on the slopes. I knew that attempts were being made in the outside world to have me released, that even in the inner chamber of the ruling circles there were dissident opinions, but I did not believe in any of it. I also learned that Mandela had been moved from Robben Island to Pollsmoor together with Sisulu and one or two other political prisoners doing life sentences. A special cell had to be built for them on the roof of Maximum Security. And since some of the expert builders were White prisoners, acquaintances of mine . . . I knew that area well anyway; when we were still housed in Maximum it used to serve as our library.

Working in the Stores I was involved in equipping Mandela and his comrades with clothes and furniture, and I did so with tremendous glee, I can assure you. The *boere* so obviously hated having to find proper clothes and yet they had no choice because everybody was scared of the repercussions if Mandela complained to the Red Cross. ('Just give me a pickaxe handle and leave me alone with the bastard,' Bles growled. 'He thinks he's too big to stink? He's just a *kaffir* like the rest of them. All he needs is one good bashing and there will be no more of this *mister* business. It is the only language a *kaffir* knows and appreciates!') Brigadier de Fortier had the Stores on the jump. He insisted – as always – that things be done correctly and promptly. The storemen tried to frustrate his directives by passing the buck to the *boere* on the Island who were supposed to have sent clothes along with the prisoners. The Department was obliged to let the prisoners have the privileges they were expressly entitled to. But *never* would they be accorded a minute or a word or a potato beyond the precise allowances and instructions.

It is not clear yet why Mandela and the five others were transferred to the mainland. I know that the Prison Department intends eventually to close down Robben Island – it has become too expensive to keep it up, to continue transporting water and food there. (The island's own water is brackish, unfit for humans.) Perhaps the authorities want to move the leaders to even more secure (and dehumanized) institutions: there was talk of a new prison being built for that purpose near Kimberley and the maximum security sections of Leeukop and Pretoria Local have also been reconceived and rebuilt. The real intention however was probably to cut Mandela off from his own – to stop the Island being, as it had become, the 'Mandela University'.

Christmas would come and go. It was always the most nakedly horrible time of the year. But there were compensations. We would be allowed to buy, with our own money, 1 lb of fruit, cake and sweets each. For these orders we would prepare weeks in advance. One had to be astute; in conjunction with one's friends one would spread the orders to obtain as large a variety as possible. We'd also willingly give up our sugar rations and our milk rations for the weeks preceding the day so as to make it possible for the cooks to prepare something special. And always there would be that one extra letter allowed in and out.

How could I be with my people? I put myself in a letter. . . . One year, towards the end of my stay there, the letter that I'd sent out to Madame Bubi never arrived at its destination. It was the only present I could give her – how else was I to try to make a grey European festive season somewhat less sad? The letter naturally had to contain 500 words only. Not one more. (The letters handled by Saayman would reach me with a pencilled – '25 words too many'.) I had counted my words carefully, I always count my words carefully Mr Investigator, I have an angel with a drawn sword before my mouth (albeit a drunken one), but without a word ever being said it was just gobbled up by the administration. Maybe it is still lying in a file somewhere; perhaps even now some security expert is trying to work out the coded message. Will he see the light? Will he find the key which will make it possible for White, Christian South Africa to turn back and at last remake History? Will the dark doings of the communist mind be laid bare for all to see? Will the hardworking secret hero finally get his well-deserved promotion? Don't stop now! Please read on. . . .

If you may only write 500 words you have to make a draft. I found that draft again, Mr Investigator, tucked away among the drafts of monthly grocery orders. It was there with the odds and the ends that I managed to leave prison with. Please permit me to reconstitute it here.

Now it is again nearly Christmas. Would you be so kind as to pass along the belated missive to her ladyship? Please allow me to bring my humble present at last:

Once upon a time long ago in 198- there was a bandit with only one heart who lived in Nosemansland. Where he planted words for a living, hoping finally to make some grow sense whose odour may please the masters who are most particular in such smatters. It was very dry in Nosemansland. It was dry during the day and even drier at night and when it rained the rain was

*dry, but the masters sniffed and snoofed and said,
'Nosesmell is better than smell which may not be very
noce.' So that the bandit with only one heart was (100)
really risking the unnecessary in doing what didn't
have to be done. But that is not the point. The point
is that he had a dream which kept on getting longer
(because it was a longing dream) about One Lady who
lived far far away in another world called Pararis.
Lady One was an u'bbi. The amu'bbi (ecoli u'bbiti),
as everyone knows, have nam-nam knees and small
noces although they may make quite a noise when they
feel like it. This Lady One was very beautiful—not
just for an u'bbi but altogether urbi and orbi—even
though somewhat ecleccentric. (200) She used to wear
a veteran fur coat and bicycle shoes of different
colours—also other clothes when these fitted; and as
an alibi for buying sold rags and riches and plastic-
palms in a blue swimmingpool. She also had a mother,
Munch, and many many friends (not for sale). And
she collected rings and cameras to take pictures of
friends wearing rings with not for sale either but for
steal exclusivement.*

*So the one-hearted bandit (named Huan) went with
a plea to the masters. He bore with him some words
which he intended to break open hoping the (300)
scents would sway them in the absence of sense. Bulb-
nose referred him to Snout and Snout to Gallowsnoose
and Gallowsnoose to Mose and Mose to Snovel. Snovel
snorted, 'I can make no decision because Beak only
decideth and he cannot because actuhelly's smother-
wise occupied committing udder heartpatients to the
infinimity of asylums so I must make the nositions for
him. What exaggectly is't you whish to probosce?'*

'Please sir (Huan sad with 'eart in 'and), Isumever

*wish to memograte to Pariris for this heart's very sore
from longing for Lady One. Had I but-two it wouldn't
mutter but this-one beats (400) terribly from missing.
It goes miss-a-moomph miss-a-boo-by. Listen. Please.'*

*'What matter of nosesense is this?' (snarled Snovel).
'Knose alone knows I expiacted all kinds of batty scense
but not those! Your wordshaveworms, my friend! You
want to go to anozzle world? That den of thieves,
anarchists and mad plumbers?'*

*'But please, sir, there b-also goldenlight and plane-
trees and treeplanes (whether moony or not) and clouds
and houseplants. And this heart aches because it belongs to the dream which belongs to Lady One who
belongs in the dream. The ache is of the heart, not of
the dream, and for fivehundred worlds* it aches because she etc., and since she etc., I don't want to split
her personality (though she's a twin) and therefore
must etc. Where the heart goes I go etcetera.'*

*'Fine phrases, but juiceless' (Snovel sneered). 'What
for this wordthsickness? My noes are my noes. Go
back to your dream. Don't come noise around here.
And whatta-whatta-whatta-whatta.'*

*So time became past tense. With the passing of
time more time passed away untillit was the dead-
timetimes (but not quickly enough even if it's known
that the longer the time the quicker it goes . . . like
a dream). (512)*

*Eventually Huan could take nomore, afraid that
the heart may come to belong to the ache. It was then*

---

*Mr Investigator, when I got so far did I throw all caution to the
wind to continue, and was the letter then sunk by its specific
weight? In fact I'm redoing the draft here: I know that I did cut
back the lost letter to 500 words, and to incomprehensibility? (50)

*the season of kindnose, blessé to the world and pearce
to mankind. (Also when people spoke funny—like
falseteethsticking to chewing gums.) So he applicated
to Bulbous who scent him to Snoot who scent him to
Galloresneeze who scent him to Mouse who inscent
him to Snivel.*

*'Sir,' (he pedaled) 'since I know it is against your
primciples to let me go—although I'm rerabbitated—
and you cannot howmever (532) much you may want
to because only Beak can do that and nosesing can
move Him (nor tide nor time) as He believes that any
move must surely crumble Nosemanslund into heart-
space and the danger of beauty, and it being now
Crossmast and I having no sother present to present
to Milady except this one heart belonging to her and
wishing to reunight her with sa-id somesing to pull
up her nose at so that it may grow and become like
unto ours' (this he advanced so that Snivel may take
nosice) 'and I muzzle delay but hurry! hurry! time's
runnin just like wordels from a broken throat—please,
may I not thenetc.?' (563)*

*'Well,' (sighed Snivel) 'allwright, howsomever, wrub
it up in no smore than 500 whatta-chatta.'*

*Which, Lady One, is why you receive today one
battered habitat of ventricles and tubes (the ache and
the sadness I'll keep as echoes)—with ardour I hope
not malodorous or malheureuse.*

INSERT

sempre più oltre

How does one survive? I did not survive. This is important to point out. True, there is a sum of attributes

which can be called by name. 'Come out, Breyten Breytenbach!' you may want to call; and from the gloom, wrapped in words as if in cheesecloth, Bangai Bird will emerge. (He has the smell of writing on him; he is utterly deconstructed to stuttering utterances.)

It is important that you consciously (I'd be apt to say 'personally') assist at the putting down of the I. That is if you wish to parry destruction, to unsurvive. (As if 'survival' were going to inquire after your wishes!) The I not only as a concept of (para)physicality, as a screen of illusions, as a hole-ness—but in its most mundane manifestations.

You are the way; the walking and the walk, not the walker. The I which blocks the view must disappear by 'deconception' for a sense of movement to be actualized—a feeling of metamorphosis. And if you are furthermore a weaver of shrouds—well, then you can be the spaceman.

Does it sound too clever to be true? One mustn't be like those who always simplify 'reality' by attempting to understand it. One must live it; one should flow with the rhythm. You develop an awareness of the living structure—of that which is constantly *doing* itself: the patterns, the dialectic, the breaking points, the *limits* which are only the outer edges of pages and pages of silence, the relationships, and then where you lose all comprehension as the earth tilts away from you. Such is the structure of understanding.

But it is important to know that you are nothing. And to search without ever stopping, be you awake or withdrawn into the wakefulness of sleep, for the hairline cracks, for the gaps and the unexpected moments of deep breathing, for that space which is created by alleys and by walls.

Power is a totalitarian concept. To realize that you are marginal is of itself a way of making distance your own, of becoming as permanent as an ice block going downstream, of disregarding coercion. It is to come upon an interstice of freedom.

Once you have moved into the territory of the enemy and beyond the hindrance of oppositions, once you have been totally isolated and undone—then you will find the most permanent comfort in humble things: the ants and the flies you always tried like a madman to kill from some hang-up about sanity, the blotched tattoo on a back which someone has erased by redesigning along the same lines with Steradent, that fluff of wool in the corner, a cloud, a tin, the hoarse cry of panic slicing through the night, the boot on concrete, the smell of the septic well, the mountain, the mirror—like reminders of the limitlessness these things have a terrible one-by-one beauty.

Prepare yourself for the interstices of freedom. It requires a discipline, a directing of the sum of attributes. The better prepared you are, the more chance you will have of finding them. Knowledge becomes intuition. You will experience the mountain because you will *be* it. When you walk, walk! When you sit, sit! And there will be nothing that can take hold of you.

8

This is How it Happened

This is how it happened: during the month of May 1981 it was made public by the spokesman of the Minister of Justice (and other fancies) who in turn acted as the mouth of the government (which exist only as delegates of the State), that a certain number of prisoners would benefit from an amnesty to celebrate the twentieth anniversary of the glorious Republic of South Africa. Violent robbers, murderers and specifically political prisoners were excluded from this measure of mercy. Sir, I was shown my name on page one of a national newspaper the morning amnesty was announced: there it was said that it had been decided, for love and kindness, to set so many free, but among those *not* getting any time off only my name was singled out.

However, about a year later, in May 1982, the government piloted through Parliament an amendment to, I assume, the Prisons Act, which henceforth

413

would entitle the Minister of Justice, by way of the Commissioner of Prisons, to accord a remission of sentence and/or parole to political pariahs. *Any* prisoner in South Africa, whatever his sentence, could now be released at the discretion of the Minister acting on behalf of the Cabinet of Ministers and basing his decisions on the advice of the Prison Department and other interested or concerned organizations such as the Security Police and the Department of National Security. A board of advisers to the Minister was created, consisting of a few academics and senior civil servants, to review the case of each political prisoner individually. Like all the other politicals, I was read the copy of a declaration of the Minister in Parliament, spelling all the above out in answer to a question from the Opposition, and it was stressed that the rulers had decided upon this in their own wisdom and not on your bloody life because of any pressure exerted from wherever, and especially that any political exploitation of the intended relaxation would jeopardize it immediately, if not sooner. Shorty, knowing more about these matters than any *boer* ever would, came to inform me that Head Office in Pretoria had 'pulled' (demanded) my file. He winked, showed a rotten tooth and assured me that it was in the bag—when *they* pull a file it's a sure sign that some little luck is in the offing. 'Just watch it!'

So what? I didn't believe any of it. I could not afford to. I had more immediate concerns. It was all just another sick joke, I thought.

Later that year a certain number of Black political prisoners were indeed released before their time was up, but those benefiting from these measures did not include any of the better-known national resistance leaders. Still, this apparent loosening up of the political repression pertaining to prisoners inspired some people to renew their efforts to have me liberated. Newspapers started speculating. One or two Afrikaans papers even asked in editorials that the government should reconsider my situation.

Over the years people never stopped showing their support for me, approaching the authorities with petitions and pleas on my behalf. About some of these *démarches* I learned only after I was let out. I have in my possession now, for instance, the copy of a letter my father received from the then Prime Minister, Big Chief Vorster himself. It would seem that my father had written to his holiness about my case quite early on during my purgatory. Vorster had answered saying that he did not feel free to be of any assistance to my father and advising him to be consoled by the fact that he had another son, Jan, an Afrikaner hero. He went on to illustrate his point by referring to the precedent of General Christian de Wet who was a Boer hero, and his brother, also a general, called Piet de Wet, who after two years of fighting had gone over to the British. Yes, Vorster said, unfortunately we know from history that within the same family we can have a hero and a traitor.

The successive Ministers of Justice and of Police had either refused to receive any delegation wanting to plead my cause or else they had given them the cold shoulder and the runaround. Jimmy Krüger, 'that ridiculous little man' responsible for the forces of repression at the time of my sentencing, was downright uncouth to any such instance approaching him. Never as long as he is alive, he swore. And he often added that he'd love to see all dissident writers behind bars. Le Grange, he of the low forehead, the large hands and the mean wit, was hardly an improvement on his predecessor. Yolande has told me of how she once, unassisted by anybody, fought for me with two ministers at the same time – Schlebusch and Le Grange. Schlebusch was obviously the more humane of the two, but he was over-shadowed into (perhaps an embarrassed) silence by the hard and intransigent Le Grange. Now there was a new broom at the ministry called Coetsee. From what I heard of him, and according to the estimation of professional minister-watchers, Coetsee at least had (and has) the laudable intention of ameliorating the conditions of political prisoners and maybe of speeding up the release of some among us. (But oh! where will he find the strength to do it?)

You must understand, Mr Investigator, that this 'humanization' arrived at a time when the Whites felt more sure of their own powers (truly draconian) than ever before. One can see that they thought it to their advantage to try to improve their image with the outside world. It furthermore must have become obvious to the more sophisticated among them that releasing a few mangy politicals was not going to bring the Republic crashing down around their ears.

The political considerations were clear. But just as clear was the fanatical opposition to any let-up emanating from the sadly misnamed intelligence community and the Security Police. The decision to let me go must have been in the making for at least a year; until the very last moment strenuous efforts were made by people like Huntingdon and Brummel to stop it from happening. Yes, they were exerting pressure on their own boss, they would even try to blackmail him in their bitter commitment to keeping me cooped up. What do you do when your own dogs make it difficult for you to pretend to be the master? I tell you, Mr Investigator, there is real fear among the politicians of the monster they have created.

The actual decision to let me go must have been the result of an accumulation of approaches made to the authorities and of careful opinions expressed either publicly or in private by influential groups of individuals. The French government, by way of Monsieur Plaisant, their envoy to Pretoria, continued asking their South African homologues to release me; PEN International as also PEN groups in various European countries and America asked for the same thing; writers both abroad and in South Africa would at various occasions signal their concern. Allow me to point out here that Amnesty International had nothing to do with my release or the conditions of my imprisonment. Friends and colleagues in Holland and in Paris had formed committees to support me; when they approached AI for help they were turned down because I 'did not conform to their definition of someone incarcerated for his beliefs and opinions'. In a similar way the French MRAP (*Mouvement contre le racisme, l'anti-sémitisme et pour la paix*) dropped me like a hot potato – evidently at the behest of the South African Communist Party or their local comrades. You must know that behind the façade of the noble struggle for human rights there are sad marionettes for whom it is an ideological game. AIDA, a recently formed international group of concerned artists, did try to help in their own way.

There were, I've since learned, more far-fetched efforts – involving senior politicians of at least two European countries and some African ones in behind-the-scene manoeuvres – to arrange for an exchange of prisoners from which I could have benefited. Still along the same lines of cloak-and-dagger footwork, a colleague of mine, originally from the United States, told me of a rather funny incident. His uncle by marriage is a senior CIA official. In desperation my colleague, who had had no contact with this family member, finally wrote a letter asking him whether 'they' couldn't do something to obtain my freedom. Apparently this uncle (or this godfather) responded by saying that 'they' would look into the matter. He thereupon confirmed some time later that they did indeed look into same and that he would let the young whippersnapper know if their looking encountered anything worth looking in or into. Who looks shall see, through keyhole or by spy satellite. My colleague heard nothing more until the morning after my release when he had a mysterious phone call from Washington and the voice of this unknown uncle asking whether he'd seen the news: 'And are you satisfied now?'

No, Mr Investigator, I do not believe for one hilarious instant that my liberation could be ascribed to the intervention of the CIA. It is much more likely that an opportunistic attempt was made by this official to take some credit for something that he or 'they' had nothing to do with (rather in the way that certain barren journalists invented the story that I might have been released in exchange for the French providing South Africa with another nuclear plant!). What *is* true, though, is that there certainly were influential members of the ruling Nationalist Party in South Africa itself who discreetly tried to point out, in inner circles, the possible benefits of such a step.

The last bit of the puzzle I wish to show to you is that I had agreed with Yolande that legal proceedings should be initiated by the lawyers who represented me – but on their own behalf – in order to make public the fact that certain promises had been made to them in return for my pleading guilty and my foregoing a political trial in 1975. Pieter Henning was the moving force now. We were nearing the end of 1982. Hoang Lien was in South Africa on a biannual visit; her visa was about to expire and she was due to return to Paris on 5 December. Ten days before that I learned from her that I was about to be visited by Johan Kriegler and John Brand, to finalize our strategy for the intended proceedings. Brigadier de Fortier then came to see me and told me to ask my wife to have the visit cancelled. He suggested that my case was now under active reconsideration by the powers of heaven and earth and that any legal proceedings or visits even from my lawyers could only adversely affect any pending decision. My gut reaction was not to take any heed of his advice, knowing that the Prison Department would shamelessly walk the extra mile, would use any imaginable excuse and argument, however dishonest, to prevent any embarrassment to themselves. After all, my birthday – which would have been a fine occasion for them to make a gesture – had come and gone with Yolande already in the country (especially with that hope in heart, I subsequently heard), and nothing had happened. Yes, 25 November came and went: nothing more happened. I was now entering the eighth year of my sentence.

Then came 1 December. I'd gone out to work as normal. It was a Wednesday. Madame la Générale was to come to say goodbye on the Thursday before returning to Paris.

That morning, it must have been about half past eight, Thick Saayman the security officer, suddenly pitched up at the Stores and said he was taking me back to the prison to appear before the Board. Appearing before the Board is a six-monthly ritual: a committee consisting of the head of the prison, the psychiatrist, the officials responsible for you at work and in the section, sit to review your conduct and your position and your dashed hopes. They very evidently had no mandate materially to modify the sentences of politicals, but we all went through the motions anyway. Smiling. I had just recently seen the Board and couldn't understand how come I was to pass before them again so soon. Saayman had me get into his car, for once without any escort, and off we went. He drove right by the prison and continued on down the road. Looking at me he said, 'I bet you must be asking yourself where we are going now.' And I said, 'Yes, I am, but it's no use asking you because you will not tell me.' He said, 'Right you are.'

Right I was, Mr Investigator; it could have been my execution or the circus – listen, whatever was due to happen would be 'normal'.

He took me to a house I didn't know, asked me to enter it, and there was Brigadier de Fortier in civilian clothes. The two of them talked about the weather and the price of eggs. After that de Fortier invited me into his bedroom and asked me to try on one of his safari suits. I did as I was asked. It fitted rather well, even if I say so myself. He also handed me a pair of shoes, but the socks we could do nothing about. I kept on my prison ones. My own outfit I left lying on his bed. Cinderella was ready for the ball; the detainee was ready for another interrogation session, or a further trial, or to be put on show for a foreign newsman. De Fortier asked Saayman, 'How does he look?' Saayman said, 'He looks all right, Brigadier.'

His wife arrived, offered us some coffee. Their little dog came to sniff suspiciously at my legs. (What – a *bandiet* in the *baas*'s house!) Then de Fortier announced that it was time for us to leave. Saayman was no longer there. We got into the brigadier-general's car and left the compound in the direction of Cape Town. Not a word, Mr Investigator – no, don't say a word.

De Fortier, by nature a kind-hearted man, said, 'Look, I'm sorry but I'm not allowed to tell you anything. Just stay calm.'

We glided along the highway to the heart of the city. He was talking to me. My mind was divided between mumbling yes-sirs and oh-officers, and the etched experience of drinking in the passing sights. It was so long since I'd lost all notion of movement in a motor car. I saw seventy-eight trees draped in a finery of flowers, eighteen women in aprons in their backyards, hundreds of people wearing civvies, vehicles and a mountain. As we rose and came across the neck above Groote Schuur Hospital, descending now along De Waal Drive into Cape Town itself, the brigadier slowed down to allow me to feast my eyes on the magnificence of Table Bay spread out at our feet.

In the City we drew up before an imposing hotel whose existence I'd formerly ignored and got out. De Fortier said we were perhaps a bit early and that we should just stand there. I was invisible. No, not a word, Mr Investigator. Then he glanced at his watch and said maybe we had better start going in all the same. We entered the lobby of the hotel. I walked on his right. I did not open doors. People passed by us without taking any notice. He exchanged a few words with the receptionist behind the counter, who directed him to a lift.

We flew to the eleventh floor. On that floor there were only two doors leading off a small foyer. He now knocked on the one which had a little name plate identifying it as 'Concordia'. A man with a belly and a waistcoat opened the door. It was the Commissioner of Prisons in his own body. He had obviously spent the night there: the bed was unmade. He smiled, said, 'It's good to see you're on time,' and led us to the second door, on which was written 'Felicia'. (These must be bed nests for the recently or bogusly wed.) The same ritual, the deferential knock and the cough. The door was opened and the Man himself, much shorter than I expected him to be, invited us to step into his parlour. His bed was newly made. I think he was there only for that meeting.

No, don't ask, Mr Investigator. I have undertaken not to tell you. That is why I call him the Man. We sat down and the Man inquired whether we would like coffee or tea, or something stronger perhaps? He rang for room service. They discussed the price of eggs and the weather. As if this was the most usual midmorning male tea party. An elderly Black gentleman in a white jacket (who sees without looking and without observing) brought in a tray of cups and teapots and instant coffee and hot water, and left. This went on for a long time. I could not hear the traffic in the streets below.

Then the Man turned an inquisitive eye on me and started putting what we shall now call hypothetical questions. What, he asked, what would be my itinerary if ever I were to be released from prison? Did I intend to stay on in the country? What was my attitude to the authorities going to be? Clearly, he had to master some arguments which he would afterwards have to present to his colleagues. The meeting, I sensed, was to be hush-hush. I wondered from whom he was hiding (the Security Police, perchance?). The third clear, though unspoken, message was their fear that my possible release could mobilize anti-government forces. It was evident that if they were to release me, they would want to give the outside world the impression that there were no strings attached. No, Mr Investigator. Although there must have been some message that they tried to convey to me. Basically I think it boiled down to: if we release you, it would only be if we were sure that you would not rally the dissidents (students and intellec-chals) around you; that you would not embarrass the government by insisting on staying in the country with your wife. . . . All of the foregoing was presented in a carefully wrapped package of political blah-blah: the possibility of change in the country, the need to strengthen the forces of reform, the resistance to reform from certain quarters, the difficult passage to be franchised by those in power at the moment because if you want to beat a dog any stick will do and how easy it is to upset the apple cart.

My answer was simply that I would want to get away as far from this country as possible and to rejoin my wife in Paris to continue my writing and my painting, that I had a life to catch up with, that I could not

expect it of my wife and myself to stay in South Africa
even if things were 'normal', as we'd always be 'in the
eyes', that I'd like to be allowed to return to it from
time to time because my father was aged and infirm
and my heart beat for him, and oh but your land is
beautiful, that I think I know what could be waiting
for me abroad, the pitfalls, the tunnel vision of exile,
the temptations of simplification, that much moral outrage covers political string-pulling and twisted patronizing, or ethical ineptitude, that man uses man,
that I could only tell what I know, that I will be
solicited by many who don't care a damn really about
South Africa, the land of hope and of tragedy, that I
could not say that I have been physically tortured,
no, because it is not true. No, I did not make a speech.
I did plead for other prisoners. I did say that any man
after five years in prison is no longer a man. The Man
was shocked at my prison language.

I did not believe for one moment, Mr Investigator,
that anything could come from this interview – however extraordinary and off-beat it might have been. I
had had too much experience of their penchant for
fun and games, of their cruelty; and in any case, I had
long since become far too conditioned by prison life
to expect it really, fundamentally, to change. But I
was and I am too well-trained a prisoner to leave
without trying to score. So I profited from this once-
in-a-lifetime chance to ask the Man if I couldn't please
have a 'contact visit' with my wife the next day, that
is, the day of her departure – a visit without interven-
ing glass panels and talk boxes, breathing the same
air (in the attentive presence of a *boer*)? Can heaven
be any better? Will my heart not burst with joy? He

promised to look into the matter and let me have an answer soon enough.

It was time to go. There was nothing to be had there. I left with de Fortier. We drove back along the road we came in on. Again he slowed down to let me have a last look at the sea; he even invited me to turn down the window to get the smell of the salty wind. He warned me against the danger of building up false hopes based on the interview we'd just had. Sea-mews wheeled over the car. He told me to stay cool. He made me understand that he personally would be relieved if something positive came out of all this. There were brilliant green trees against the lower mountain. He understood, he said. If they were to ask him, he'd say.

Back at his house I went through the same procedures in reverse—taking his clothes off, thanking him for their use, no smell of mine in there, putting my own back on, feeling much more familiar, feeling all me-ish, and Saayman came to pick me up and took me back to prison. I was not to talk to anybody about what had happened. My concern was now whether the cooks had kept my food or, as so often happened, whether some fink had stolen it or sold it to a grubby. This was where life was at.

I returned to work in the afternoon. Nobody noticed any difference. There was no difference. Afternoon. Evening. In the evening I wrote a letter to Yolande. It was never mailed. Here it is now. This is how it happened.

Private Bag X4
7965 Retreat

1st December, 1982

I thought of writing to you tonight – even though I'll be seeing you tomorrow for the last time this trip, before you return to a wintry Paris. I wanted to hand it in tomorrow early, before seeing you, so that it may wing away and get to you there in the cold not too long after your arrival. Something white to go with the ice on the windowsill.

But tonight there's madness. I feel that the mind, with its turmoil of emotions, is speared. A restlessness penned down. Forgive then the meandering sentences, the broken thoughts. Often I wondered: what would happen once the day of release were at hand; not afterwards, not from there *on*, but immediately before. One must come to a point, *faire le point aussi*. One must take stock surely, of the years spent in this situation. What will the essential be at that moment? What shall I take with me? And will I remain clear?

I don't know whether that moment has arrived. Despite what happened today I cannot permit myself to hope. It would be too horrible (for you and for me and for us) if nothing came of it. Like climbing down from the stake, half consumed by the fire. Now I don't know whether your visit tomorrow is to be the last of this series – or the first of a never-ending kind, with liberation a stretch of the fingertips away. We shall soon know.

Despite what occurred today. I cannot tell you about it in full. I dare not. I love you. The day was big and blue and burnt. How incredibly beautiful the surroundings of the city! With what majesty the mountain folds its contours, tumbles its growths along the lower slopes. It accompanies one into town, it is a moving presence. And then, in the city, once the car stopped, I felt in my head and my chest that peculiar smell of sea and harbour, and other street odours too. I love you. People were passing by on the pavements, crossing arteries and squares – women with slim backs and freshly moving limbs, men lingering in front of shop windows – and all blissfully unaware of the fire crumpling me. But enough of that for now. I believe I know how an extra-terrestrial must feel if he were to land here.

On the edge of the night. Late last night the moon was slow and full – all bone and silk. I pulled and pushed until it was framed in the long thin space of one of my windows open upon the dark. How sweet and how serene and how overpowering. I had to press my palms together and bow. A premonition bird-swift then, a prayer nearly, a praising. It was indeed the Buddha's belly. And later this afternoon – upon returning from the city, the dream not yet dislocated, something of leaves going up in ecstasy – I couldn't stop running round and round the inner yard; I had to perspire, I wanted tiredness to unflutter the birds; and when they called us in ('time, gentlemen!') the sun was still aloft, silver, incandescent, fierce, alone, pure: I felt obliged to stretch and open my eyes to it so that I came into the dark interior with a blind whiteness deep-eyed as temporary memory. Tonight (I think) it's overcast. No moon in any event. I'm not looking for it.

When all is shrivelled, what remains? I love you. It's a stupid expression – inadequate, cheapened a million times, endlessly in all possible ways.

The courtly tradition of the knights of yore. Illusion. But what else can I say? I must embody it in its most ordinary and shallow and common form. When what I want to say is that I'll never come to the end of you. Your natural *pudeur* wants to make you tell me to cease. How dare I *étaller* thus what is intimate to us? Let the world know because it will never know!

All these years you came closer to me, ever more precious. And I know you less now than I ever did. You are so strong it is a mystery to me. You are so terribly fragile. And yet you fought, more tenacious than a tiger. You are timeless: from how far you've come! Lives and lives away, the flower opening endlessly. But you are so young. You are too beautiful. Sometimes I'm jealous that others may see the sadness and the lilt of your beauty. Then again I *want* to show it to the whole world. Were you or I to die tonight our togetherness will surely continue, just as it has forever been. (Agreed – you don't have to remind me – I abused it, but we were different people ten years ago and we shall continue changing. Growing closer.) How else must I say it then?

It is late now. From the small insects flying in through the open window it would seem that rain is not too far off. To perish all mangled and crushed. The prison is quiet. Or as quiet as it ever gets. A cough now and then, a sigh too loud. Outside is alive with sounds. Dogs. Nightbirds. A car very far away. Other clean mountain-noises perhaps. All these years you came and you supported me. You gave me of your strength and I survived. I died and you were there waiting. I was in my grave and you wrote to me. Perhaps tomorrow; perhaps from then on it won't be too long anymore. The terror must fade. The husk of alienation and hurt will be shucked.

One day we shall be free. We shall walk down a beach and we shall enter the water. We shall sit at a table. The sun will be in your eyes. Your hair will fall, black and straight, over the half of your face. One day. Maybe soon. Will you turn my salad, please? We shall bicker and argue and sulk even, and we shall be happy. Maybe not too far off in the future?

Thank you, young lady. You know it. Understand — I had to write, for you are the star I carry with me from here. You are my memory. You are there, coming, going, ever present. Here I am with you.

Goodnight, my sweetness, my secret love

Then came 2 December. It wasn't raining. Radiant sun outside. Hot. The head of the prison was called Reindeer. He was in the dining hall that breakfast. Was I to go out to work, or should I stay in, I asked him. 'Yes. Why not?' But I was expecting a visit, I said. 'Well, we shall see.' And I happened to have seen the brigadier the day before — the major wouldn't by any chance know whether my request for a contact visit had been granted? 'No, we shall see.'

I was fetched for work. Everything was 'normal'. No, Mr Investigator, neither earthquake nor volcanic eruption, no fire-fingers running along the black mountain. Weather even, chance of wind rising towards midday, temperatures in the eighties, no storm warnings: early summer in No Man's Land. People were being shunted off to court. Somewhere someone was trying to nick his best friend's tobacco. Somewhere a bird hanging on to the bars to steal a look outside. Old men squinted at the sun.

About an hour after arriving at the Stores the phone rang and de Fortier instructed the *boere* not to let me return to the prison until he had been to see me. Ninety-three minutes later he turned up, accompanied by Professor Kharon. They took me into an empty office, the brigadier put his hat on a table, and the same questions pertaining to a hypothetical eventuality were put to me. I gave the same reassuring and finally non-committal answers. (See previous pages.) The two of them left, ostensibly to make contact with 'Pretoria' (by telex?), and I was told to wait.

I continued working. The twelve o'clock siren howled, echoed by the dogs. It became time to go in for lunch and nothing happened. The *boere* were cursing because two of them now had to stay on duty to guard me. I was cursing because I was missing my lunch. It meant two irregular lunches in a row, maybe even a no-lunch. Things were going too far.

More or less at one o'clock the two messengers returned. Again they summoned me to one of the empty offices, but there they found Bles eating words from the telephone. Hand signals were made, and as he feigned incomprehension his line was summarily cut and he was sent out.

De Fortier then turned to me, took off his cap and said, '*As from this moment you are free unconditionally.*'

Two things happened, Mr Investigator: my ears immediately went dead – I could hear nothing but the distant silence – maybe the blood had risen to my head;

and a thought slashed my mind: *fuck it, there goes my Christmas order!*

Then I thought: *free*. Then I thought: *what a joke*. Then I thought: *if I don't say anything, it may come true*. I was at the window. A white cloud pursued its quest for silence above the mountain.

I looked at de Fortier and to my astonishment saw tears in his eyes. I said, 'What time is it, please?' He said, 'It is now fifteen minutes past one.' Kharon stood behind him, not knowing what to do with his hands or his paleness.

Thereafter things were speeded up as in an old movie, Mr Investigator. God had spoken to the Prime Minister who had spoken to his Minister of Justice who'd spoken to his Commissioner of Prisons who'd spoken to the Officer Commanding Pollsmoor Prison Command who now summoned and spoke to the head of the Male White Prison, saying, 'Look, this man must be transferred to Pretoria immediately. Nobody is to know about it. How long do you need to get everything ready? Whom do you have that you can trust absolutely? How many members do you need to get him through the books? I give you exactly three-quarters of an hour.' And Major Reindeer, white as a sheet, jumped to attention and with three stretched fingers to the peak of his cap bravely swore, 'Three-quarters of an hour, sir! One sergeant, sir! Trotter Truter, sir! I think. Sir!' (It had been specified that the Department was keeping my release a secret. At least for a few days. The staff was to be given the impression that I was being shanghaied to Pirax. From there, God the State alone knew what might happen. One or two of the *boere* gave me funny, penetrating looks. Did they guess? But they were afraid to take-taste the thoughtword 'free' on the tongue lest it become a curse blighting their careers till doomsday.) We needed cardboard boxes for my possessions (study books). And so the head of the prison spoke to the sergeant in charge of the packing facilities at the Stores who took me out into the backyard where he spoke to the Prisoner in Charge of Cardboard Boxes, Rags and other Cleaning Material. God's divine intervention nearly trickled away in the sands of reality right there when the lowly *mugu* turned away his head to spit, rubbed the spittle into the earth with a toecap, grinned, and reported, 'Sorry, *baas*, we ain't got no boxes.'

I was escorted back to prison. On foot! I walked in the front door! Kharon rapidly lent me the R50 needed to pay the outstanding fine Judge Boshoff had imposed during the second trial. Despite Reindeer's brave undertaking, all the sergeants present in reception had to get stuck into the books in the gigantic task of processing me through them. I was given my manuscripts. Counted. Sign here. These I clasped under my arm. No way was I going to leave them. In the cell my locker was cleaned out rapidly and, as will always happen in that type of institution and situation, my fellow prisoners, those who just happened to be around, the halt and the lame and the permanently 'off work' and the *slimmetjies* who knew every trick and feint, such as Shorty, immediately sensed that something was up and as rapidly they were there to score, to profit from whatever largesse there might be. 'You won't be taking that flask, will you now?' Or, 'How's about leaving us some snout, I say?' Dougy came along with Shorty to help carry the books. Commiseration. Solidarity. 'So they're moving you? Trust the bastards – always up to something evil!'

I shall waste no more time now, Mr Investigator. I looked round my cell in which I left most of my bric-à-brac, none of it of any importance. All that mattered was the manuscripts under my arm. If I could not take them with me I was going to refuse to leave the premises. Don Espejuelo came and crossed my palm with his, and with his lopsided smile said, 'Just remember – *un fascista es una nada, hombre.*'

I was taken to the administrative offices, smuggled in a back door there, given an outsize apricot-coloured suit and some private shoes provided by the Stores (all long-timers having to face the free world get clothes and money), and bundled into a car driven by Professor Kharon.

Kharon took me to the house where Yolande was staying with friends. She had by then been informed by a spokesman of the Department not to come to the prison that day but to wait at the house for a phone call. She knew no more than that. Not a word. The house is situated in a suburb called Newlands. At first we got lost, and when the professor eventually found it he went to see if there were any other people present before allowing me to enter. There I was, left all by myself in unfamiliar, borrowed clothes in a car on a suburban street. The thought, Mr Investigator, crossed my mind to get out there and then and make a run for it, uphill downhill, to freedom! To find a hole in the ground. I could escape! But the forces of custom held me back. Who knows what unseen *boere* were lurking behind the trees? I did, however, work up the initiative to step out of the car and stretch my legs on the sidewalk. The door in the wall surrounding the house opened and Yolande emerged. She saw me, stopped in her tracks, and asked, 'What are *you* doing *here*?' (Well, that of course was a long story.)

We were immediately taken by Professor Kharon to his house, where we were to discuss means of leaving Cape Town. From the time we arrived there I was absent to the world. Even before that. I remember only flashes of what happened. I saw the mountain bowing low. I heard the sea cheering. We entered the house of the professor as if in a dream and I asked him if we could open the windows. (For weeks wherever I went I felt the need to open large all doors and windows.) I recollect being embarrassed, afraid nearly of the tumult of objects in the building; of being scared that I might bump my head against the unfamiliar ceilings; of instinctively lifting my feet very high. Outside the one window there grew a loquat tree, its branches darkening the roof. Yellow fruit were ripening on those branches. Small fires grow up to be big conflagrations. With the evening meal we drank a local wine, Fleur du Cap. Did I taste it? I don't know. Did I taste anything? At odd moments, yes.

The plan, their plan, became evident. I was to stay on in Cape Town, or in South Africa at least, for a decent period to create the impression in the public mind (the public mind being a creation of the media) that I was entirely free, and Yolande meanwhile was to return to France, where I would eventually join her. But she would have no part of that. Nothing at all. No, not a word. Kharon, a man of traditional and conservative Afrikaner stock, did not expect this opposition; he especially did not take kindly to it coming from a small, non-Afrikaner woman. 'Understandings' were being questioned here. Commitments to higher-ups. The poor man – after the tension of the previous days, and his own emotional investment, he must have felt thwarted. So he raised his voice the way patriarchs and prophets do. But when he raised his voice she told him that she would not be spoken to in such a fashion (had I been with it, I could have told the unfortunate man so before, heh-heh) and that he was to contact the minister and tell him that we were leaving together that Sunday. It was up to them to make the necessary arrangements. She would not wait another day. His argument that she had waited for more than seven years and surely a few days extra would make no difference was rejected with the answer that it is exactly because it has been seven and a half years that she would not wait a minute more.

(Her fears and those of some friends too, never expressed publicly, were that I would be, upon release, a walking target for some White fanatics, be they manipulated by the security hounds or not.)

From time to time Kharon went into the next room to phone, leaving us alone to discuss these matters and options of momentous import and then she would shake me to try to convince me that I too could now make decisions and stand up and participate. Alas, all to no avail, Mr Investigator. For too long have I been in no condition or position to decide for myself about anything pertaining to my life.

Many phone calls were made. (The next days would be strung together by phone calls.) The lady imposed her will. (My inclination, informed by a deeply imprinted fatalism and fear and superstition would probably have been – don't letsh rock ze boath.) We returned that same evening to the house of Yolande's friends where we spent the night and went through a hilarious version of the old-fashioned bedroom farce. I did not yet exist officially. I was still in prison. Nobody was to know. We had to keep up appearances. The girl working in the house, who got to know Yolande quite well, was not to find a man in her bedroom the next morning. She knew that Yolande's husband was where so many Brown husbands habitually went, and what a shame and a shock it would have been to find the lady comforting herself with another presence. If, on the other hand, she recognized Yolande's husband—well, that would have meant having an escapee on their hands! And then? So I had to tiptoe about, and kept being shooed away.

Morning came. The glory, sir, of sitting in a big garden under a huge tree and the even huger sun. Birds fluttering. Blue dome. Soft morning sounds. I borrowed the host's clothes. Wrote a note or two to particular friends whom I couldn't see from fear of compromising them. A girlfriend of the lady's came to say goodbye to her and I had to run upstairs and hide in the room of the son of the house. A boy's kingdom. Model aeroplanes. Stones. Scientific experiments. Books. Comics.

It had been agreed that I'd be allowed to go and say goodbye to my father in his hospital in Grahamstown (it was the one favour I insisted upon) but Hoang Lien was not permitted to travel in the country with me. She was to fly to Johannesburg and wait for me there.

It was now Friday, the 3rd. This is how it happened. We separated. A police captain came to Kharon's house, walked in, bared a shiny set of dentures in what he must have wanted to have pass for a friendly smile, clicked his heels, bowed, presented a hand and immediately pointed out that he's not from the Security Branch. We drove into Cape Town. All by myself I had to go into a pharmacy to have photos taken for a passport. I had been given money to pay for these, and dropped most of it on the pavement in my clumsiness at handling such unfamiliar things. My fingers could not yet read coins. A Brown vendor on the corner was singing the praises of his fruit and immediately incorporated a friendly warning to me in his sing-song. No need to throw it away, he sang.

We had lunch at Kharon's and that same afternoon we left Cape Town in his son's Alfa Romeo. This was the start of the death journey. I was a mummy sitting there looking at the horrendously beautiful country rushing at us. The road going along the south-east coast crosses the mountains enclosing False Bay; from up there I looked back on the Cape smoking in the distance, Stellenbosch a little deeper inland, Somerset-West and the Strand strung along the ocean. I was seeing everything for the first time. I was seeing everything for the last time.

The road branches away to the interior before you reach the hills around Hermanus. There my mother lay in her grave, close to the come-and-go movement of the waves, her hands folded, looking with an eternity eye at the blue haze. She would have laughed with joy until the tears came to her cheeks. She was living for this day too.

Kharon talked and talked. We stopped to buy dried fruit. In Swellendam we stopped to fill up with petrol. Every time we stopped he would go off to make a phone call. Our progress had to be followed hour by hour. I wandered around, waiting for him. Through a window giving onto the street I saw an old man still employed at making harnesses for horses, working with awl and gut. Poplar trees and green canyons. My parents' people traditionally lived in this region. No one left. Not a word, no. Must be cemeteries for horses up there.

We drove by Heidelberg and then Riversdale where Oubaas had had a farm when I was small. We stopped in the town. I had spent part of my school years in Riversdale. We went into a bar for a quick drink and were accosted by a drunken client draped over the counter. He insisted that we should either drink with him or else fight him right now on the sawdust in that corner. Friday night blues. He lisped, tried to stop the ss-es from dribbling over his chin, and informed us that he was a warrant-officer in the Prisons Service. I didn't know whether to laugh or to run, Mr Investigator. He would not recognize me, I knew, because he would never expect to see me there (one only recognizes that which you expect to recognize), but if he did, surely he would pull out his pistol and shoot both my knees off immediately.

On and on we drove. In the town of George, electoral seat of the Prime Minister himself, we dined. We asked our way to the nearest eating place from two brazen teenage tarts. Maybe young country whores. Dark place. Bad food. Bad service. Bad wine. Kharon went to phone. A moon flowered above the horizon. The full one of a few nights ago. A lifetime. How come I'm still up at this hour? The night sergeant has long since switched off the lights. Wonder what people are doing—Moineau, Piet, Oldface, Dougie, Pimples, Stinkfoot, Pa, Skommel, Nefesj, Jakes, Ampie, Ghana, Goodbye Charlie. . . . Sea somewhere on our right.

Moon must have eaten butter. Yellow orb. Warrior, its body rubbed smooth and shiny with butter, rotting, but as cheeky as ever. In dark glass bowls and scales starfruit are put out, kind with kind. Come judgement day and the mango will be separated from the pear and from the fig. Blood yellow. The land, primordial, ancient, unchanging, shifting by. In the distant hills must be the blown away graves of captains and of shepherds. Stars sucking up a thin light. Men leading men must have shouted at the sun here. Land singing nakedness.

We spent the night in a hotel at the top end of the main street of Humansdorp. If you were drunk, you could wend your way from hotel to hotel down the hill to its foot, where the sea was a distant rumble and slosh. Tired now. Kharon went to make a call. Also went to ask(?) something at the blue-lamped police station. (I believe he had a special dispensation from the minister to drive as fast as he wanted to.) We shared a room. I still had on my jail underpants. (I walked by waters of unrest, in unfamiliar hotel rooms I lay me down.)

Then it was 4 December. Up and away early. It's the early worm that catches the bird. We left for Port Elizabeth. Imperceptibly the land changed. The moon was blue and the country singing a lonely barrenness. We crossed dry riverbeds. Along here the land is so poor that it will eventually be ceded to the Blacks. We passed by the intriguing nameplates delimiting the emptiness. *Gamtoos* (an ancient Khoi word); *Mondplaas* ('Mouth Place' or 'Mouth Farm'); *Voorstekop* ('First Head' or 'First Hill' perhaps) belonging to a farmer called Emile van Papendorp.

From Port Elizabeth I called my sister in

Grahamstown – just like that, out of the blue, I too could use the telephone! – to warn her that I was on my way. In the booth reading the instructions on how to telephone, in both languages. (Quiet! Quiet now, my heart!) And ssshh. And to ask her to have our father brought to her house for the meeting. I could not show my face in public. I was not released yet. No, not a word.

Then we waited in front of a bottle store for nine o'clock, for official opening time. In fact, we walked in just before nine but the Indian owner lifted admonishing eyes to the clock on the wall. In South Africa we all respect the law. *The law is.* I wanted to take at least one bottle of good wine to celebrate with my father the return of a lost son from the land of swines, to pour a small libation for the gods. It was already hot, man! In Port Elizabeth there are crumbling houses. Some have Chinese characters traced on the façades. I saw a centre for martial arts. Years ago, in the dim past when I was involved in the activities of Atlas and Okhela, we had a code name for South Africa/No Man's Land/Azania: we referred to it as 'Elizabeth'. Do you want to hear more, Investigator? (You old voyeur, you.) Stay with me. Stay with me till the end.

On the pavement before the shop a Black Father Christmas sat steaming already in the early morning heat. He had on a red woollen suit. Hot, man! He had pulled down below his chin the white cotton-beard attached by an elastic band around his ears. I could not help but go up to him to touch my own white-tipped one, and say: 'Ah, but I have a *real* one.' At which he responded by: 'Ja, good morning, *baas*', and promptly put his own back in place again.

We arrived in Grahamstown. We looked for and found Rachel's house. Kharon diplomatically went off to phone from somewhere in town, leaving me time, that first time, that time which cannot be wrought in words, leaving me time to enter and to see my father. He was sitting in the living room wrapped in a blanket and his eyes were very alive and black and fully aware. His paralysed hand was hidden under the blanket. With the other one, the left one, he grasped me. There was still strength left in that arm. But I could see the praying-mantis thinness of the limbs, the stillness, the low flame quivering now over the ashes. His mouth was soft. And he wept unashamedly. He tried to talk to me. He mumbled pain and happiness. My sister explained that he had not been able to pronounce any word at all up till then, but now he spoke my name and even a few more syllables. He said, '*Klaar!*' (It is *finished* now, it is *past*.) And then he clicked his tongue in frustration at not being able to continue. His eyes never left my face. His eyes are there forever. I live with my face lifted to his eyes. Every once in a while he would say, '*Magtag.*' (It means 'damn'; it could also mean 'powerful'.)

Rachel had asked André Brink, to help bring Oubaas to her house (asking a male nurse might have raised suspicion). And he had deduced quite correctly that I was coming.* He now walked in and announced that

* Quite by chance a newspaper which had asked for my release six months earlier chose this day to contact the Prison Department, to follow up on their request, to ask if any decision had been made. The Prisons spokesman went into stasis – when in doubt bury thy head – and requested the reporter to call back later. The newsman, suspicions now thoroughly roused, called Brink to ask whether he, perhaps via the family, had picked up a scent somewhere.

it had been arranged that we should all have lunch at his place. There was a slip-up there. I had only three hours left to see my father. I was selfish. But I could understand that my sister was overtaken by the events. Kharon walked in too, and the two professors—they are not quite bosom-friends—circled one another with bristling neck hairs. And so we all went up the hill to fetch a pail of water, to Brink's baronial mock-Moorish mansion overlooking the domain of Grahamstown. Yes, Mr Investigator. Now, for the first time in my life, and surely the last time too, I had the privilege of carrying the old one in my arms from the car up to the house. This big sunburnt man with the dark hair striding across the fields of my mind—how light he had become! How small had he shrunk!

We lunched and we swam in the lord's swimming pool. My sister cut up my father's meat into edible pieces. My father was ill at ease. He was ashamed at being out in his pyjamas. When one has lost so much one doesn't want others to see. He had no choice. The wine was good. The food was good too. The two professors circled one another warily. It was time to fly. It is always the time to go. Time, gentlemen. Not a word. We left. No, not a word.

Kharon drove me back to Port Elizabeth from where I was to catch the connecting flight to Johannesburg. I had a final request: to take just one dip in the sea. We stopped off at a beach outside the city. Kharon had an extra bathing costume in his car. Look, that's me running into the waves there. Look, it is a green wave with white foam, and there's another and another. See how the years are of no consequence. See how carefree (because over the edge, nonexistent) that me is when touching and smelling the ocean, how integrated in time. Look at the little stones in the sand. Now I am human. That is what the garden is all about: the stone which is not there. That is why a poem is about words.

I found that we were inadvertently swimming in a part of the ocean reserved for Blacks only; emerging from the waves I was surrounded by small Black children who saw nothing wrong with this Whitey being in the water with them. Ignorant little bastards – haven't they learned about Apartheid yet? I was still damp in my clothes when we arrived at the airport.

There I had a tug-of-war with the security personnel, who wanted to take away my briefcase of manuscripts. *They* were looking for bombs and *I* was hanging on to the fragmentary scenario of my identities. The lone and rather ridiculously exposed controller/observer sitting behind his newspaper in the middle of the departure hall looked on from a distance. I said goodbye to the good Professor Kharon, who was utterly exhausted by then and who probably still had to go and make a phone call. I left. The plane banked over the glistening land, rose until it became small, and flew through the vast halls of arms of cloud castles to Johannesburg.

At the foot of the passageway I was approached by a modishly dressed young fellow with longish hair. The pistol in his waistband was making an obnoxious bulge. The slightly older obligatory partner was hanging back in the crowd there, his glance flitting from face to face. The youngster introduced himself as being from the Prison Department, delegated as a measure of courtesy to render any assistance I might need. Will you hide your mirth, Investigator? Don't be a fool! Sure, I know – I'd just spent more than seven years in the inner chambers of the Other World, I was raised by hand you may say—and never could a prison-*boer* be that suave, never would he be allowed to wear his hair that long. But that didn't matter. We shall play hide-and-seek till the skies cave in.

He escorted me through the little-known byways of Jan Smuts Airport with Partner dutifully bringing up the rear. If I had had any Gauloises I would've offered him one, for old times' sake, but I had given up smoking too. I told him about the queries from the newspaper to Brink. He frowned.

He led me out to where a middle-aged gentleman was waiting in an unmarked car parked unobtrusively some distance away from the exit. I was introduced to Major Somename, also from the Prison Department, yes. But when his young subordinate related to him the story of the bungled stall leading to awakened interest from the press, he exploded, saying, 'The Prison Department never told *us* anything about this!' He took me to the house where Yolande was waiting. (These secret cars cruise so nicely!) As we arrived he remarked upon a vehicle parked nearby. 'Funny, that wasn't there just now. . . .'

We went in. He met Yolande and her friend, the gentle and shy Ukwezi. He sniffed around a bit—you can't teach the tricks of an old dog—and then left us alone.

Time was of no more importance. Everything was dying, everything reborn. What was left of the previous night's moon now swam like a shimmering dolphin in the pool. I joined it. We fried meat outside. Tang of smoke in eyes. A festive tablecloth. The food was good, the wine was better. It was deep and red.

I started to taste things. No, no word. Here the heart is getting thin.

The telephone rang and Major Somename asked if he could come by. He just happened still to be working. An old horse, you know, what? He sniffed around some more. No, he wouldn't eat anything, thank you. Well, just one glass then, if you insist. Never do it on duty, you know. He needed a photo for my application for a French visa (which was going to be granted that night). And wondered whether I minded very much just signing this statement. It was a typed page saying that I'd been released and that I was leaving the country of my own free will. That I held no grudges against the South African government. Give — I'll sign. Give more! I'll sign anything. I signed.

He also said that the Prison Department was now going to confirm that I'd been freed, but they would say that we had gone on the Saturday night flight. He left. We laughed. The phone rang again: an excited journalist informed Ukwezi that I was out of prison and that we were already winging our way to Europe. We laughed some more. Then we slept. The moon stood guard above the dark pool and the trees and the house. Here the heart is getting thin.

Then it was Sunday, 5 December. This is how it happened. Yolande packed the bags. Ukwezi in the background, smiling. Unexpectedly John Brand turned up for breakfast. (But it seems that Yolande had called him.) Stupefaction. What a beautiful day. The doorbell went. Major Somename. He was to take us to the airport. Gave me a passport with a valid visa inside. They were actually going to facilitate our going!

Little traffic on the road to Jan Smuts. Major Somename talking about the weather, and had we noticed how expensive eggs had become? Ukwezi and John Brand following in another car. Airport. Someone from the French embassy to take charge of us. Major Somename solemnly saying goodbye now. Must be off, he says. Huntingdon had said, years ago, smiling sarcastically, that he'd still be taking me to the airport one day. Maybe he was there. Maybe I just didn't see him. I didn't look. *Chef d'escale* of UTA there. Very friendly. No trouble weigh-in, check-in. Ukwezi with Sunday papers. Announcing my release. Must be something in that. John Brand very tense. Monsieur Plaisant the ambassador, with book. I sign. I have to scratch through. I cannot spell simple words.

This is the true story of what happened. Embrace Ukwezi. Embrace John Brand. Now the heart is going thin. Monsieur Plaisant's wife is suspicious because he left the residence so early on a mysterious mission. In the distance, trying to merge with the background, Major Somename. Looking away embarrassed when I wave to him. Through customs. No one looking for Galaska. *Chef d'escale* UTA downstairs opening bottle champagne. Other employees coming by murmuring encouragement, good show. Everybody already in the aeroplane. Go up steps. Beautiful summer's morning. Now the heart.

Take-off. High in air above land. More champagne offered discreetly. Compliments of personnel. Africa underneath, slipping away, my love. Confusion when food tray arrives: can't remember how to use knife, fork, in what order dishes. Use spoon only, so long. So long. Not a word, no. Africa going. Yolande, Lady One Hoang Lien's hand in mine. Then she flakes out.

To sleep the sleep of the very, very tired. I plug in the earphones. Handel: *Concerto pour orgue en Fa Majeur; 'Le coucou et le rossignol.'* We are to arrive at Roissy–Charles de Gaulle at 21.40. It will be raining. It is done. . . .

Pretoria/Pollsmoor/Palermo/Paris, 29 December 1983

Notes

1

A Note on the True Confessions
of an Albino Terrorist

Die woord is 'n engte. The word is a narrow; a slip of
land between two dark oceans; a tongue. The word is
also a confinement. Yet it is the only way that I know,
the only space. I realize now that the preceding document is in itself for me an interstice of freedom.

I had to write it. I had to purge myself, and this
I had to do before memory itself becomes obscured
by the distortion of time. If I say 'purge' it may imply
that there are events—that I myself have done
things—which are improper, which I ought to be
ashamed of. It is true: I am not a hero; I am not even
a revolutionary. In retrospect I should have done this
or that—with support, in a slightly different context,
if I were better prepared, if I were less naïve, I would
have done so maybe. It does not matter now. I don't
believe in trying to change the past, except to the
extent that a forever changing future continually throws
another light on that past. Mutation continues. What

will I do next time . . . ? But I tried also not to paint
myself prettier than I am.

Even without the aspect of personal appraisal (is
it provoked by pride?) there is the filth – the degradation of human relationships imposed on one within
the interrogator–detainee or warder–prisoner context – that one has to get rid of if one wants to go on
living. As for myself – I feel that there are areas that
will never be alive in me again, but I had to di-
gest and transform that period of alienation before I
could turn my back and go on to what is unfolding.
Life is good. Survival is also a choice. It is important
to walk on.

I had to write it. That is, I dictated it. The document itself took shape from the obsessive urge I
experienced during the first weeks and months of my
release to talk talk talk, to tell my story and all the
other stories. It must have been rather horrible for
him or her who happened to be victim to my vomiting.
So I was advised to talk it into a tape. This procedure
defined the inner structure and tone of the book. Inevitably it then also became the story of doing a book.
More – it had to become the reflection of a search for
what really happened, and for the identity of the nar-
rator. It is by walking that you learn to walk. It is by
being, which invokes questioning, that you discover
being.

My wife typed the tapes. I used her transcripts as
'rough copy'. These I would blacken, add to, delete
from, change about – and she would retype a clean
version for me to go over again if needed. Therefore
I was in the first instance, in all intimacy, talking to
her; telling her all which I'd had to hold back over
the years. Without her it could not have been done.

My account of what happened is neither objective nor complete. I consciously left out much that I knew about, or now know about; all the outside moves and happenings. Others will have to complete the story if they feel called upon to do so. I don't think there is any total objectivity ever. There must be however, I believe and I try, a constant attempt at remaining fully aware under all circumstances, which again means that there are choices to be made and responsibility to be taken for the awareness and for the choices. I have attempted as closely as possible to describe only that which I experienced or saw. Some of it will be considered hearsay by a court of law. But a prisoner is not a scholar. We are all subject to the fantasies of our world which is – consciously – being deprived of the checks and balances of an open environment. Yet I tried always to remain clear and to penetrate to a feeling for truth in what I heard and learnt from others. (When you are forced to live forever on the *qui-vive* you develop an instinctive appreciation, a gut evaluation, of those you meet.)

There may well be mistakes in the text – minor ones of names and dates. Some that may look like mistakes I have put in on purpose: those concerned will understand. And some 'errors' may still provoke revealing reactions.

In some instances I have used the real names of the people involved, mainly because it would have served no purpose to camouflage them. In many other cases I have modified or replaced the names – but behind every name there's a real person, and you may rest assured that the people concerned will recognize themselves. In one case only did I split one person by making two 'personages' of him. It was a natural thing to do. And I have not 'invented' or transposed any event. It will be clear to the reader that I often emit opinions or allow myself judgements. These are my own.

It was not my intention to take revenge on a system or on certain people – at least, I don't think it was. We are too closely linked for that. In the same way that the ideology of Apartheid is only an aberration – a stillness – of what is potentially present in all of mankind, the butchers and the interrogators are not monsters but people like you and me. That is what makes them so horrible and so pitiful. And that is exactly why we must continue condemning and combating their acts. I believe that the torturer is as depraved by his acts as the one who is tortured. We will be fools and mere objects of history if we go looking for the causes of depravity in 'human nature' only. We make society and society makes us, all of us. But there are certain fabrics once torn that cannot be mended again; certain transgressions that can never be condoned.

It was my intention to produce a political text – if it turned out to be more 'literary' than expected it can only be because I couldn't help it. It is the lability of the job, it is the seductiveness and the *life* of the word. But the two approaches are not all that far apart.

When you are interested in prison accounts as a genre you will soon see that prisons are pretty much the same the world over. It is rather the peculiar relationship of power-repression which seems immutable, wherever you may hide. And when you scratch a little bit you will see that our century is stained by large scale and institutionalized acts and even policies of brutality in growing areas of the world. The tolerance is less; totalitarianism is on the increase. Never before has it become so all-important for all of us—especially for the most 'ordinary' citizen—to struggle with all the inventiveness at our disposal against the dehumanization of man. The least all of us can do—the marginal ones, the outcasts, the displaced persons, the immigrant workers, citizens of our various countries—is unite to expose *all* the intelligence services and the spy organs and the security or political police and the secret societies of the world. Pipe dream! So much for universality. Still, if what I had to describe is of any documentary value it can only be because I tried, as a White African who has had the privilege to enter into a world known only too well by the majority of South Africans, to paint as *fully* as *possible* my view of *that* society as it exists *now*.

I want to dedicate this book not to Mr Investigator, but to the multitude of detainees and tortured ones and prisoners in the land of my birth, and not only to the 'politicals' but also to the 'common criminals'; and with a kind thought to some of the poor bastards who lead their twisted lives defiling mankind by extorting and oppressing and punishing and ruling in the name of 'security'.

2

A Note on the Relationship between Detainee and Interrogator

The detainee and the interrogator both know that there is, obscurely, a measure of ritual involved in their relationship, a ritual as old as the history of human intercourse. Perhaps because in a specific kind of power set-up people will go through the moves in very similar ways. There are predictable reactions to objective conditions. The needs and the gestures and the effects of the relationship seem to be permanent: There is the struggle for domination – to have the other do what you want him to do (for the relationship seems to be permanent: there is the struggle for job); there is the effort to destroy – because the opposing forces are irreconcilable, or because there is the pathological human curiosity for killing, for altering permanently, or just 'to see', or because the dismantlement has revealed *vis-à-vis*, a brother-I, a mirror-image or only a miserable human-conditioned pile of flesh and faeces which is unbearable and needs to be done away with;

there is thus already the tendency to identify with the other (and the roles can be inverted) and the blind desire to force a solution to and a resolution of the irreducible contradictions – precisely because you cannot accept the (self)-image revealed to you, nor the knowledge that never the twain shall meet.

And yet this twilight zone of jerking or being jerked according to the specifications of preordained roles, this macabre dance, this fatal game (because there are certainly elements of a game present) should not obscure the fact that the situation and the steps and the rules are always personalized and localized and in no way can the players be exonerated from their responsibilities. Knowing that human congress has always been sullied by this destructive and self-destructive *face-à-face* does not take away from the horror of it.

It must be repeated that the phenomenon is not indigenous to certain countries or cultures or political systems only. Africa knows it, you will encounter it in Chile and Vietnam and Italy and Russia and in Northern Ireland: wherever there are political dissidents and 'terrorists'. The process – employed in the name of 'security' – which involves the mutual destruction of human dignity, seems to be an integral part of most police and specialized agency methods. The really powerful reject these gutter ethics with their lips only: compromises and corruption have led to *de facto* condonation. It is as if they wish to say, 'what right have *you* to appeal for purity when *we* have been obliged to dirty our hands! Life is not a rose!' It would seem furthermore that there is no religion or structure of public mores strong enough to eradicate, or even to contain, the custom. Its virulence has nothing to do with backwardness and with ignorance; more advanced technologies have merely brought a greater sophistication to the methods employed.

The interrogator will be someone who looks and behaves as if *normal*. He will lead an unremarkable family life. If he is a doctor or a psychologist he will probably also have a mundane practice to look after. He will be Mister Everyman. These people are not monsters: they have no reason to feel ill at ease in society; on the contrary, they know that they are tolerated and accepted by the powerful. They may even fondly believe that they are implicitly supported by the so-called silent majority. They will at most consider theirs to be 'a necessary if dirty job'. They have to *simulate* their normality obviously. What happens in bare rooms where all time has been twisted is not just dirty work – it is the heart-rending flowering of evil which will profoundly modify all the actors.

This much you, the detainee, will *know* in advance: that the interrogator disposes of a panoply of powers, which include the 'right' and the willingness to kill you (it is signalled clearly: not for nothing have well over seventy South African people over the last decade been done to death in cells by the security forces); the 'right' and the desire to maim you, because you must be destroyed; the 'right' to manipulate and to circumscribe your environment – physical or moral – in terms of food, space, isolation from and contact with the world, family pressure, privileges offered or withdrawn; the 'right' to mould time because he regulates it, he plays with it, he has an unlimited amount at his disposal. The interrogator's power is absolute and having the detainee know it is his most efficacious weapon, but ultimately it rots him utterly.

The prisoner will inevitably end up confessing. There can be no doubt about that. His only leeway can be to hold out, desperately, for time. He may have to decide *when* to safely let go, about how long he can hold out, how many false confessions he can make before cracking, how to remain *conscious* (if not sane) in the coils of his inventions and his lies and his hallucinations. He will be raped. His problem is to realize it, to handle it, and to know that it is the humanity he shares with the aggressor that is being raped. He must also realize that the damage done is permanent.

The self-disgust of the prisoner comes from the alienation he has been brought to. That in which he participated (because the mortification lies in that he is forced to participate in his own undoing) will play havoc with his conception of himself and it will forever modulate his contact with other people. He will have the leftover knowledge that he has been used as a tool, that he was coldly and expertly manipulated, that he was confronted with his own weakness. Worse, far worse, that he ended up looking upon his tormentor as a confessor, as a friend even. This development is so profoundly unnatural that it makes him sick of himself.

The two of you, violator and victim (collaborator! violin!), are linked forever perhaps, by the obscenity of what has been revealed to you, by the sad knowledge of what people are capable of. We are all guilty.

The deception flowing from this realization is destructive to the extent that one is a prisoner of one's own illusions about human conduct. To reduce a person to a weakness of babbling, to confuse him in private and to parade his humiliation publicly, constitute a sickening spectacle which affects the whole society. It is an abasement which cannot be undone again. Humans are fragile. It is not difficult to bring out the worst in man. Respect and dignity are also matters of make-believe. We need to maintain the illusions if we intend to cohabit in a civilized way.

The horror is that this morbid relationship makes no sense, it can finally have no purpose beyond that of being a catharsis for the interrogator. You can never destroy the image because you cannot efface consciousness.

With the struggle for some freedom intensifying as it is bound to, there is not the slightest chance that those in power politically will want to lay down guidelines to guarantee the dignity of the detainee and the interrogator and thus to sanitize public life. It is not sure that they could call off their dogs even if they wanted to. And they don't want to. It is therefore incumbent upon all of us who are concerned to provoke a public exposition and debate of the issues, and to arrive at a code of conduct to be adhered to when faced by the police and the secret agents. It will be another way of strengthening the political and class consciousness we still lack. A mistake which is often made by our South African militants is to assume that we are cleverer than the police, that we can outmanoeuvre the 'hairybacks' and the 'rock spiders', that we don't need to report fully on *any* and *all* contacts we may have had with the masters. Our weakness has always been (apart from the infiltrators among us) the arrogance which makes us blind to the fanatic commitment and the determination and the intelligence of the minority in power and of their executants.

3

A Note on South African Prisons

Any society – so Winston Churchill declared on occasion – can be measured by its attitude to its prisoners.

At the risk of emitting a series of platitudes and pious wishes I'd still like to make the following simple remarks.

Prisons only serve to create prisoners. If society views prisoners as its outcasts, its anti-social elements, then they will indeed become and remain that. Penal reform, the treatment of prisoners – these are not the problems of specialists but of concern to everybody. The solution to crime is one of social consciousness to be solved by the whole of society.

In South Africa the prime motivation when dealing with those found guilty in terms of laws promulgated often for the protection of sectional or class or ethnic interests, is the notion of punishment. It moves from the premise that you can educate or rehabilitate a person by punishing him. You don't. You may break him: you strengthen the reasons that brought him to the predicament he is in. A fellow prisoner, Kenny van Niekerk, once said, 'Whereas no man should break the law, the law must not break man either.'

There are obviously people who are, knowingly and willingly or not, dangerous to society. No judge should be allowed to decide about their fate all by himself. And when such a person is removed from the company of his fellows there is no reason why he cannot be kept in a humane fashion in decent surroundings. The individual life, as an expression of the whole of which we are all part, must be inviolate. When the State executes someone (murders him in a reflex of barbaric revenge) it is a destruction of freedom; it is a negation of the dignity of man, any man; it is also an admission of its own incapacity to improve the social environment.

Who are the people ending up in South African prisons? From my observation the first remark must be that many of them ought never to have been there at all. (To show you how repressive the South African legal system is: from a population of not yet 30 million there are on a daily average more than 110,000 people in the gaols without counting the detainees, those awaiting trial, those in reformatory institutions, those who have been 'endorsed out' or dumped in distant rural camps, those in work colonies.) The laws governing Apartheid—the pass-laws for instance—based on purely racial criteria, account for a large percentage of prisoners. (They are however not regarded as 'politicals'.) There are many who must be described as socially feeble—the old bums, the vagrants, the weak-minded. There are many for whom the basic problem is alcoholism. But all seem to suffer to a certain degree from social disfunction and maladaptation, or from an immature or impaired sense of reality. The attitudes of irresponsibility and selfishness, the need for affection—these may well be the end results of an insufficient preparation for adult life, or weak or broken or hostile family ties. The individual functions badly and aggressively with reference to his social unit, but the 'fault' is not necessarily his or his only, and the way to a solution must in any event be found by all involved.

What is that world like? It is one of repression and of baseness where the lowest instincts prevail; it is a world of humiliation and whore's values; it is a world where the harshest forms and expressions of racism are institutionalized; it is a world with its own culture—language, customs, laws, myths, structures; it is a world of promiscuity, of closeness in fetid cells, of living in the clothes and the beds of others, of greyness, of losing all sense and appreciation of beauty until only sentimentality is left; and it is also a world of fancy where you will encounter the generosity of make-believe—people extending to one another the courtesy of accepting their lives as invented—and never any trust or confidence. It is the incarnation of split perceptions.

South African prisons are overcrowded. There are people who for petty crimes end up doing long sentences with hardly a comma or a semi-colon from time to time. They exist only in terms of the prison world—outside that they would be nobodies. Cheek by jowl with them you find the youngsters coming in for the first time. The effects of isolation from everyday life, of marginalization, are intensified. It is not that prisoners are particularly antisocial, but that they are obliged to constitute a social grouping of their own, another society because of the prevailing inclination of the larger community to hide its problems behind walls, because of the separateness of prison life, the distillation and the concentration of the weaker elements. The confused ones, those who feel rejected by the 'normal' world, are confirmed in their alternative way of life. The weak become weaker. No wonder then that recidivism should be so rampant.

It is said that we inherited our archaic legal notions from the British. Certainly our administrative practices, and to some extent the ideology informing these, are a legacy from our colonialist past. (The local contribution can be seen as a cruel Calvinist and racist twist to these notions.) It is unrealistic to even dream of doing away with the stays of incarceration corseting the South African nation. But it is all-important to keep on pleading for the realization that solutions can only be found along the way of communal responsibility, once we move away from the atavistic attitudes of punishment and of revenge, once we move away from the alienating concept of leaving prison matters in the hands of the penologists and the criminologists, once we move away from the totalitarian stance that the State (or the Party) will judge and decide and regulate.

At the moment incarceration still means breaking the fragile ties the prisoner may have had with his family and with society at large. Everything must be done to reinsert the prisoner, to help him readapt to the outside community. Those having the care of prisoners should go out of their way to *multiply* and to *diversify* the contacts with the outside world, in an atmosphere of mutual respect. Training programmes should be pushed much further and should involve outside experts. Why can prisoners not go through the regular apprenticeship periods outside, under supervision (as would be normal) of craftsmen and tradesmen and trade unionists? Everything must be done to involve 'outside' agencies and concerns in the attempt to find a collective solution to the problems of 'crime'—without necessarily making everyone a warder. The prisoner needs to know that he is doing something useful, with initiative and responsibility. He must be paid a decent wage for the work he will be doing and he must be given the normal (but so important) right to put that money at the disposal of his outside dependants.

Inside you will often hear the reflection that only a prisoner can rehabilitate himself. Well-meaning psychologists, sociologists or social workers cannot do so. The key, to my mind, is not obedience and acceptance, but a critical awareness and social responsibility. Everything ought to be done to help awaken, strengthen and reward initiative, responsibility and maturity. There is no reason finally why inmates cannot run their own affairs and their own institutions. The prisoner needs to feel that he has a grip on his own fate. A nefarious side effect of living in a totalitarian structure is that you become lazy, apathetic, content with the commonplace. A conscious effort must be made to go against the grain. Why not allow outside teachers to come and direct classes in prison? Why not allow publishing houses to donate their works to prison libraries? Involve them! Why not permit prisoners to take care of one another – to share whatever expertise they may have – through discussion groups and classes? Why not allow them to establish a trade union, involving also ex-prisoners outside? It could be named SAPU: South African Prisoners Union, later to be abbreviated to APU only!

4

A Note about Torture in South African Cells and Interrogation Rooms

By now it is sadly no longer necessary to prove that torture is practised by South Africa's police and security agents. There have been too many deaths they could not camouflage, or did not want to hide. Regularly, during security or political trials, there will be 'a trial within the trial', usually held *in camera*, when the presiding judge or magistrate has to consider allegations of torture raised by the accused. Enough affidavits have been made and testified to by those who survived. Ever more often too there are examples of the police authorities settling out of court the claims of criminal law detainees who had been assaulted or tortured by their agents. (The police are unhappy with such procedures: money the State has to pay out in this way will then be recuperated by deduction from their salaries.)

The methods employed (they have been described repeatedly) will be anything from sheer brutality and bestiality – hitting with fists and batons and anything that will concuss but not burst the skin, kicking, stomping, burning with cigarettes, pushing down stairs or out of windows – to the more 'refined' ones employed elsewhere in the world, too – strangulation by putting a wet sack or a plastic bag over the subject's head, holding the subject's head under water until he drowns or loses consciousness (the 'submarine'), beating the subject while he is being twirled hanging hand-cuffed from a stick in the fold of his elbows or his knees (the 'aeroplane ride'), beating the soles of his feet with batons and with canes, applying repeated electric shocks by electrodes attached to the subject's extremities or his sexual parts or his nipples ('telephoning' or 'playing radio') – to the more patient and slower forms – depriving him of sleep and/or other physical relief, having him stand in a certain posture for hours on end, having him squat on his haunches or sit with legs outstretched for days and nights. To this must be added the various forms of mental coercion – isolation, calculated confusion, false confessions, etc. Even more horrifying are reports filtering down from 'the border' (Namibia, Angola, and other neighbouring countries subject to incursions from the South African Defence Force) of Military Intelligence interrogators, aided by medics, using drugs or in some cases the withholding of painkillers from the wounded, to 'break' their captives.

A few remarks need to be made:

(1) Brutality, police assault, torture – these methods are much more widely and freely used than we ever thought. Time and again I have met prisoners who were beaten, shocked, half-smothered, half-

drowned – sometimes in a nearly off-hand fashion, sometimes because the police wanted specific information quickly. According to my informants this is standard procedure with the Murder and Robbery Squads, particularly those of Brixton in Johannesburg and Woodstock and Athlone in the Cape. Some of these prisoners could show the physical marks and scars on their bodies. Many of them seem fatalistically to accept this as 'a risk of the job'. To give you an example of the casual horror: F., an ex-sergeant in the South African Police, now a prisoner, told me of how he assisted one Sunday afternoon at the torturing of a Black detainee. Not because they wanted information from him, but because the men on duty were bored, because they wanted some amusement, maybe also because the *kaffir* had to be kept in his place. They had the prisoner undress completely; they then emptied his cell of everything except a blanket; the cell was hosed down, the blanket soaked in water too. The naked prisoner was then locked in the wet cell and the blanket, through the bars of the door, connected to an electric current. The fun was to see the man trying to climb up the electrified walls.

(2) There is nothing – no ethics, no moral or religious code – restraining the political or criminal police in their absolute power to do with and to the detainees what they want. These attitudes and actions are tolerated in the never-contested climate of racism where to be a Black or Brown or Indian prisoner in the hands of a White (or subordinate Black or Brown or Indian) policeman means quite simply that your humanity is reduced to exploit-

able weakness. These attitudes and actions are exacerbated by a siege mentality having to oppose a 'total response' to what they paint (and at least some of the painters must know that the picture is false) as a 'total onslaught' against South Africa. They furthermore justify these actions in terms of a crusade against communism, Marxism, nihilism, atheism, permissiveness, liberalism, immorality and pornography. The higher-ups in fact cover up for this policy by their feigned ignorance. The only impediment the torturers do have – and they are unhappy about that – is the bother of red tape in the case of death. F. explained to me that it is better not to be in an office where someone is put to death: it means having to write out statements in triplicate, and probably answering questions. A waste of time.

(3) Revealing the assaults and the torturing has not inhibited those involved. Public inquests cause some discomfort. The actors may be photographed with their short hair, their dark glasses and their tight smiles. They may be transferred to another area. (That is the risk you run when you're stupid enough to be caught at it.) They continue their careers; are often promoted. (Not so in the Prison Department – in Pollsmoor I knew an officer whose promotion had been held back, or so he believed, because he had been involved in the killing of a prisoner.) Magistrates do not allocate blame to the torturers when they preside over an inquest. How could they? Whom should they believe? Dead men don't talk, and survivors – being 'terrorists' – are *ipso facto* 'unreliable witnesses'. Magistrates normally conclude that death must be ascribed to this or to

that accident for which nobody can reasonably be held responsible. No outcry has yet succeeded in inflecting the basic thrust of the repressive interrogation system – which is to maintain a calculated atmosphere of terror.

(4) Not only are these acts not disavowed in practice – the 'anti-terrorist strategists' *want* their opponents to know that, when captured, they will be brutalized. The clearly signalled intention is itself part of the strategy. They believe that it is a simple matter of 'them or us', and, cynically, that the ends justify the means. They also believe that foreign rulers and investors, despite hypocritical sounds of disapproval of necessity made from time to time, do in reality understand their politics.

(5) Torture is spreading in South Africa. Security forces in the supposedly independent Bantustans have been taught well by their masters. The same methods are now part of the arsenal of police and army units in the Transkei and particularly the Ciskei – and are used there with enthusiastic abandon.

(6) The only forces which could oblige the South African torturers to scale down their actions to within 'defendable limits' would be the 'sympathetic' foreign powers: the United States, Britain, West Germany, Canada perhaps, France maybe. No pressure in that direction could reasonably be expected from South Africa's allies – Taiwan, Israel, some Latin American countries.

5

A Position on the Struggle for the *Taal* (being Afrikaans)

Afrikaans is a Creole language. (For this contention I'll be eaten alive by Afrikaans linguists and historians.) It evolved in very much the same way or conditions that other Creole languages came about (such as the French spoken in the West Indies or in the Indian ocean area, or as pidgin English), and for similar reasons.

The Afrikaner establishment's historians and academicians, the lords of culture and of tribal identity, pretend that Afrikaans is the youngest in the family of Germanic languages. They need to say this because they must accentuate the European heritage and predominance with all its implications of cultural-imperialist 'superiority' not yet disavowed. But to be African is to be a bastard. The heart of Africa is metamorphosis.

True, Afrikaans (which is just the Afrikaans word for 'African'!) developed largely from the seventeenth

century's seafarers' Dutch and other dialects spoken
in the Low Lands. The language, however, was born
in the mouths of those – imported slaves, local
populations – who had command of no European tongue
and who needed to communicate in a *lingua franca*
among themselves; who had to be able also to understand the Master. Not for nothing was it referred
to as 'kitchen Dutch' for so long.

In its structural simplifications it was influenced
by the language spoken by the Malays; in its vocab-
ulary by those of Khoi-khoi and Blacks.* One can trace
to some extent the proliferation of diminutives, the
shifts in sound and in meaning, the repetitions – so
typical of Creole evolution.

In its present sociological context and political impact Afrikaans bears the stigma of being identified
with the policeman, the warder, the judge and the
White politician. Afrikaans is the language of oppression and of humiliation, of the *boer*. Official Afrikaans
is the tool of the racist. That is why the majority of
South Africans mock and nearly instinctively reject
the *Taal*. But this is not entirely true. Afrikaans is not
even now the exclusive property of the Whites – already it is spoken by more so-called Coloureds, and
in one form or another by a larger number of Blacks,
than there are Whites in the country. Attempts are
made continually to 'regularize' Afrikaans, to purify it
from foreign contamination and to teach it in its academic form, and already the language which is spoken in township and prison and in the army, on fishing-
boats and in the factories, has escaped entirely from

*Khoi-khoi literally means 'people of the people', the way the 'Hot-
tentots', so named by European colonists, referred to themselves.

the control of the Afrikaners. In that shape it is a virile medium, ever being renewed, which so far finds but little reflection in the writing.

To be an Afrikaner is a political definition. It is a blight and a provocation to humanity. Afrikaans, however, is a means of communication intimately interacting with the specific characteristics of South African life and history, and enriching the land in a dialectic of mutual shaping.

Does a language, of itself, have only one political meaning? Surely not. It is true that the Nazis used the German language to impose their ideology. But Goethe and Heine wrote in German too. So did Brecht. A language is what you want to make of it. Insofar as it reflects conventions prevalent among the people using it, it obviously will be associated with the dominant cultural precepts and pretences of those people. Their attitudes may infect the language itself. I believe there are still traces to be found in modern German of the Nazis' attempt to 'Germanize' the language. And it is revealing to see how Solzhenitsyn is trying to 'cleanse' Russian of words of foreign or tainted origin. In Afrikaans too, words still currently used have been accorded a definitely derogatory racist content. But it is possible also to express alternative concepts in the language.

To me it is of little importance whether the language dies of shame or is preserved and strengthened by its potentially revolutionary impact. Of course it will be a loss if it were to die: a language is a living organism, not just a reflection of life, but also a precursor and a crucible thereof.

But I most certainly do not agree with the need to wage a struggle for the survival or the imposition of Afrikaans. Those who do so are, to my mind, objectively strengthening the ideology of the White rulers. They justify their power monopoly (and the accompanying oppression of others) in terms of their so separate and so specific cultural identity, which can first of all be indicated only by Afrikaans.

Similarly I have felt for some time now that the attention paid to the contestation of Afrikanerdom, within limits of loyalty and fealty, by the so-named *Sestigers* (writers of the 1960s), the self aggrandizement and the bloated self-importance of these authors, have helped entrench the reactionary forces in the country. This happened first of all because the debate around and by the *Sestigers* obscured the far more important political issues of the time (suppression of Black parties, impoverishment of the majority, militarization and 'securization' of the country, the start of aggressive military foreign policy), including the wiping out of a decade of Black writing which was of greater significance for the future than the 'existentialist' deviations of the youngish Afrikaners; and secondly because the charade was foisted upon the world that *Sestiger* dissidence (as for that matter White dissident writing at present) could influence the political future, could effectively alter the set-up, could expose the real implications, could translate *the* South African reality – so much so that it was not seen that the *enfants terribles* were endowing the Afrikaner establishment with a greater suppleness to resist real transformation, and simultaneously serving as lightning conductors to close the eyes and the minds of people to the true death (and hope) moving deep down through the land. The tragedy is that with the pretensions of being 'open' we closed more doors, erected new walls, blinded more eyes. It could be argued that it wasn't done consciously. I'm not so sure. Besides, ignorance is no excuse. And neither is arrogance. (White writers — of the 'liberal kind' — are in reality just getting a personal kick out of flaunting some tribal taboos.)

During the early part of 1976 I wrote the following poem. It is not prophetic — but it shows that even in isolation behind prison walls one sensed to a degree the atmosphere that was to lead to the Soweto uprising. It was smuggled out at the time and later published in an English translation done by Denis Hirson. The following is a new translation.

THE STRUGGLE FOR THE TAAL
CLEAN AS THE CONSCIENCE OF A GUN
MIROSLAV HOLUB

We are old.
Our language is a grey reservist of a hundred years
   and more
with fingers stiff around the triggers —
and who will be able to sing as we sang
when we are no longer there?
As we did when alive we will spurn the earth
and the miracles of the flesh which grows
throbbing and flowing like words —
It is you who will serve as bodies for our thoughts
and live to commemorate our death,
you will conjure up tunes from the flutes of our
   bones . . .

From the structure of our conscience
from the stores of our charity

we had black constructions built for you, you
   bastards—
schools, clinics, post offices, police stations—
and now the plumes of black smoke blow
throbbing and flowing like a heart.

But you have not really understood.
You have yet to master the Taal.
We will make you repeat the ABC after us,
we will teach you the ropes
and rigours of our Christian National Education . . .

You will learn to obey,
to obey and be humble.
And you will learn to use the Taal,
with humility you will use it
for it is we who have the sunken mouths
poisoned with the throbbing and flowing of the
   heart.

You are the salt of the earth—
with what will we be able to spice our dying
if you are not there?
You will turn the earth bitter and brackish, glinting
with the sound of our lips . . .

For we are Christ's executioners.
We are on the walls around the locations
gun in one hand
and machine gun in the other:
we, the missionaries of Civilization.

We bring you the grammar of violence
and the syntax of destruction—

from the tradition of our firearms
you will hear the verbs of retribution
stuttering.

Look, we are giving you new mouths for free –
red ears with which to hear red eyes with which to
    see all
pulsing, red mouths
so you can spout the secrets of our fear:
where each lead-nosed word flies
a speech organ will be torn open . . .

And you will please learn to use the Taal,
with humility use it, abuse it . . .
because we are down already, the death rattle
throbbing and flowing
on our lips . . .

We ourselves are old . . . .

6

A Note for Azania

The temptation, when writing about No Man's Land/
Azania, is to pour forth visions of apocalypse. Or to
give way to the temptation of trying to be a prophet.
Or both.

At the end of the book is a reproduction of the
Okhela–Manifesto as we proposed it in 1975. Much
water has run into the sea since then. Also some mud
and blood. The Apartheid state is for all practical in-
tents and purposes stronger now than it was then. The
authorities have dismembered the country further,
creating the Frankenstein structures as excrescences
and expressions of their policies which will profoundly
affect the reality of a new Azania beyond liberation.
One can say of those in power that they are not only
actively ensuring their own doom (in an orgy of self-
fulfilling repression) but that they are also sowing
enough dragon teeth to make the ultimate reconsti-
tution of a viable state most problematical, if not

impossible. In this, as also in their aggressive desta-bilization of the other regimes in southern Africa, they are enemies of the future, foes of humanity. Is it be-cause they cannot help themselves, like the scorpion stinging to death the frog? Or are they in all con-sciousness destroying the future of all the South Af-ricans?

The Manifesto's analysis of the possible role to be played by Whites in the struggle for liberation is prob-ably still fairly valid. But it must be remembered that we proposed that line of action with specific people and conditions in mind, and that it flowed from certain experiences and chances we then had. All that is past now. In a sense the political struggle is at present even more polarized along ethnic lines; in another for the first time in years we assist the attempt to find communal and non-racial forms of political expression, as with the recent creation of the Union of Democratic Forces.

The shifting sands of time have created new pat-terns. I remain as convinced as ever that majority rule will eventually come about and that South Africa has the potential – human first of all – of becoming a great country in accordance with its natural beauty and its richness in history and strategic resources. I am sure also that the contribution of its experience to mankind, distilled in the struggle, will be of enormous value. But I fear that the price to be paid – in the cruel game directed and enforced by those now in power – will be exorbitant; the suffering will rip the country asun-der and create generations of blindness, bitterness and hate. Are we not heading for an ungovernable Le-banon-type situation where killing will be the only form of communication?

The African National Congress – or some organization still called the ANC for I am now projecting my mind into the distant future – will eventually rule the country. What's left of it. Judging from its practices in exile, inside the organization and towards other South African political groupings, its alliances and its ideological examples and commitments – it is conceivable that the present totalitarian State will be replaced by one which may be totalitarian in a different way, and intolerant of alternative revolutionary schools of thought, more hegemonic but minus the racism. As things stand now the External Mission, in the grip of the dogmatists, will be stronger than the ANC inside the country, and probably they will shut them out in an ensuing power struggle. This is my personal view.

And yet there is no other way. How can we advance unless we destroy racism? I don't believe that enough Whites of the ruling caste can be influenced to become humane and thus obviate a dragged out civil war. They are captives of the system they still create and maintain. Racism and corruption have alienated them too profoundly. (And their White critics are just dogs yapping behind the hill.) They are conditioned by the ignorance and the fear they generate. Their power monopoly must be destroyed if we want to have even the smallest hope for change. I don't believe the Western powers are really intent upon using their leverage to prevent a war (they are even now allowing the South African rulers to wage war in Angola) despite an increasing awareness of the complexities and the interdependence of North–South relationships – and the extent to which a South African conflict will bedevil these relations. The short-term interests of the Western powers are too profitable for that. (War and unrest are lucrative too.) And I don't believe there's any chance of the ANC transforming itself into a free democratic organization. (It is 'free' and 'democratic' now in the double-speak, Orwellian sense.) It is the victim of its friends, its history, and the conditions imposed on it by the struggle for freedom in an arena controlled by a cruel and criminally irresponsible adversary.

So what do you do as an individual, as a writer perhaps? The implications of the unfolding drama are too momentous for you to afford the luxury of 'tactics'. Holding back, hiding your game, is a form of paternalism and disdain for your fellow South Africans. You have to try by all means to see justly and clearly. You have to speak your mind directly. Fight your own fear: 'they' handicap you by the fear they instil in you. Guilt and all wishy-washy or breast-beating sentimentalism engendered by guilt – these are out. Leave that to the judges and the preachers. Don't be a preacher or a judge. You are an African. Assume that fully. Solutions must be found *within* the country, *with* the people, *all* the people. Nobody is clean. No heaven exists. Combat dogmatism. Try to force a dialogue, try to keep it open, along lines of honest recognition of differences in background and forms of struggle. Self-knowledge is not self-abasement or self-rejection. Don't be manoeuvred into defeatism. Strive for the growing realization, through heritage and through struggle, of one South African cultural identity composed of an incredibly rich variety of sources and expressions. Promote tolerance. Don't expect it of yourself or of others to be a hero. Don't judge people. But remember that to transform is to fight laziness, your own first of all. Be patient and realize that there will *never* be a perfect society *anywhere*. Move on. If you are a writer, watch out for the words—they are traitors! Be pliant and weak when you have to. Cry if you must. Try not to go to prison; it's never worth it. Survive, so as to continue to struggle. Try to see it as a continuous *process*, not a rigid goal or structure. Realize that ruptures can be flashes of comprehension. Do yourself a selfish favour: if you want to remain whole, recognize the humanity of your enemy. But recognize also that there are irreconcilable interests. Don't make a fool of yourself by killing him. No cause can justify the destruction of life.

After all, we are all blood brothers and sisters.

Thirteen poems

from the outset*

from the outset of the poem we are once more
as at all times before
at the end of all time

look
here I come on my way
out of a savage wasted region
taking what there is for creed
I come to blow on life's coal-ash
I come with my gallows gladness
and a knapsack full of words for the day
when the mouth is dumb as dust
a sheath of swords reddening to rust
to feel for the fish and the worm
squirming in the earth
pyramids full of the roots of words
verses mirrors of soil and steel
from a black and bitter land
where the word is voicefruit and tonguefood

with swordwater and bulletjuice in my veins
riding a mount

*Note: All the poems in this section have been translated from
Afrikaans by Denis Hirson.

my body has no need
of me now
soul in hand
sighs leaving the anus

the spirit moves me
not to meditation but reflection
not to vision but recognition
the veil stripped
and I come out of a black and savage land
or can I really be here?

for to come or to go
both mean staying the same

plagiarism

a man made himself a poem
for his birthday the sixteenth of the ninth—
o, not a fancy affair with room and rhyme
and rhythm and iambs and stuff, or a soundless
    rustling
or a bone to pick or other poetic knicknacks—
not under such meagre circumstances as at
present, mountain-sucking-eyes, steady hours,
    tree-with-stars,
wife and sea gone—almost
all elements sadly lacking;
still, there were certainly odds and sods around—
he scraped and scrounged, aped what he found
and tried to turn the leftovers
into something with his breath—
even in the desert the tongue has its shade:
first then the man himself, hump on his shoulders—
old humpskull, bumptious baboon,
(but ruin already alive in his seed—that's part of
    Death's art)
and then the fine hairs on his hands, and the fly
(rechristened Stalin) since it really is a cloud
in the be-all of a cell, and some further words
    thrown in for free—
the sixteenth of the ninth brought him

to sinews and blessings, ten against one, pins and
    puns—
and running out he had to bring his pants
into the poem—the short khaki ones
worn away by so many, stitched up with purple
    cotton
here at the waisted parts like an appendix scar
the stigma partly grown into the skin, and the
    spoon
with 'maximum' stamped (chewed?) into the handle
    wrought
of unblemished steel, to help get him to the end of
    the line
('I am defiled! defiled!') (with a dying flourish he
    spooned out the thought)
and then there was the ant dragging its body-one-
    leg-broken
which strayed in from who-knows-where,
and like punctuation when sense is absent
                                the memory-of-love

having used up everything to hand
he wrapped it circumspectly in fresh paper
meaning to write it out neatly later that evening
but when around nightfall he unfolded the present
the damned paper had already gobbled up the
    poem;
and the man gripped his hump and humphed a
    groan:
'my poem, my poem—now what will I have to show
    for my
birthday the sixteenth of the ninth!'

(*from the Otherplace*)

snow falls thick

Snow falls thick flaked in my sleep
and white the coast and white
the forbidding sea—a dismal walk
through scourmarks, rustle and crunch, strokes
   slanting down.

Of grey cement
the deserted towns.
Of grey cement the streets and trees
hung with droplets
like small microphones
that catch the grey and make it loud.

Our neighbours are in the waterpipes'
   splashing
the hairy windowpanes, eyelashes
over the wet of the iris. Into
the white eye of your laid out body
I will descend. Your teeth are tiny snowmen.
I will diminish in the lens.

There are sentries
with black tongues—tongues
like the festering moon—and silver

machineguns
in the neck between the torn sea
and the bottomless snowfields of the interior:
a border post—

there is life

there are christs spiked against trees
prophets in the wilderness seized with fits
worshippers whose eyes bud under the sun
buddhas on one side conversing with figs

there is life greening in the clouds
and dolphins that shred through waves
the seagull's swerving gutlean shriek
the scragginess barefoot against the mountainflanks

behind magnifying air the crater's firespeech
slopes of snow like silences shifting
when heaven cracks open hairline wide
and out come black legends the swallow the dove

there are bones that bind the earth
and delight that breaks through transience
I might be a blunderer a crazy daydream
I will still grow rich on day's bright beam

the scales flamed throughout the night
I too might once have been a prisoner

but here the heart's pulsing contract is made
clear: a hundred years from now we will all be
   naked

do you still remember

do you still remember when we were dogs
how we used to trot
on sore little paws
through all the tunnels and sluices of the city
streets of flapping yellow sheets
across cobblestones mud banks loose planks
and leafy avenues
canals which even the rats never knew
do you remember how low down we kept to the
    ground
and how exhausted we grew
with flabby bloodlimp rags for tongues
and how we panted hard uphill
right through hedges glass walls shafts of concrete
past the fearsome knots of streets and spurting
    traffic lights
fundaments cellars cesspools and sewers where the
    self-slaughtered
still kicked in the breeze
with day and night but a dulling of the eye—
then we arrived at old Master R's quarters
where we could eat and smoke and drink
vodka for me and *tchai* for you
and sugary cookies for us both

and our knowledge of the city
no one else could know
that it was in reality
a rhythmic intertwining flow

do you still remember when we were dogs
you and I, best beloved?

your letter is delightful . . '.

your letter is delightful, larger and lighter
than thoughts of a flower when the dream
is the earth of a garden,
                              as your letter opens
there is an unfolding of sky, of word from the
    outside
of ample spaces,

I slept in green pastures
I lay on the ridge of the valley of the shadow of
    death
during the last watch of the night
listening to the condemned
being led down corridors underground,
                              how they sing,

their breaths in their mouths
like residents
about to quit a burning city, how they sing
their breaths like shackles,
                              how they sing,
they who will jolt from obscurity to the light
they who will be posted to no destination,
terror fills me at the desecration

the table before me, in the presence of my
    enemies,
is bare; I have ash on my head,
my cup is empty,

I fled to your letter, to read
that the small orange tree is a mass of white
    blossoms
opening with the sun,
I could smell it on the balcony,
                            I can smell you
more delicious, lighter than thoughts of a flower
in this dismal night,

I will be suspended by the sky of your words,
allow me to live in your letter
all the days of my life

envoi,
your letter is delightful, stretching out lighter
than thoughts of a flower when the dream
is the earth of a garden,
                        as your letter opens
there is an unfolding of sky, of word from the
    outside
of memory,

he will remember . . .

he will remember—
mornings before daybreak, the city dressed in grey
and the distant droning sprung from no visible
    source—
cantering hooves? an ants' nest, a flood—
restful warm back in bed,
the steaming bowl of tea and slither of bread
and then, rain flicking against an ice-cold glass face
on the pushbike through the misty canyons of the
    city
past trees that swell and drip and glitter with
    wetness
all the way to the *dojo*, (only later does the sun
    bark like a dog
            in a courtyard)
the cool black folds of breath,
the inward tumbling stillness,
            and now, from deep in the belly—
Maka Hanya Haramita Shingyo:

he will remember—
the rough work-clothes of cronies drinking in the
    bistro,

the greeting, clickety-click of words against each
  other
and knives, and the red blush on the white napkin
  of light
through the glass of wine, the beefsteak, green
  salad,
soft meeting with the eyes of friends
and now, to work!
the smell of fresh canvas and turpentine

he will remember—
flames glowing in the dark dreamed eyes
of the woman curled before the fire in the hearth,
journeys measured out in days by the twisting of
  mountains
so white the eyes feel naked, and down
between ricefields through goldspeckled Sienna
  evenings
he will remember how the woman goes looking for
  shells
where the blue sea brims
at the rim of the desert where the wind
blows soundlessly, and is peeled black

he will remember—
the wild moon like a glowing hand
from the ocean turning silver palm trees
to nothing but small feathered tongues while the
  shadows
well up of their own free will, blotch,
bear forests, and quack

he will remember
how for one measureless second

the sun flutters like a blood-streaked bird in his
   fingers
and then soars up like a wall reaching higher
than any rampart or prison's narrow now:

ghja tei, ghja tei, hara-so ghja tei,
bô-ji so wa-ká:

Hanya Shingyoooo . . .

metaspecks

when I climbed onto the chair
to wipe the southeast wind's gold dust
from the high windowledge
I saw in the sliced space behind the tungsten bars
that passes for an opening
two swallows hanging playfully in the dusk air
caught and released by turn in the dying earth's
   brightness
like leafboats from the endless blue heavenly
   bluegum tree
free, free, free
as they careened and heckled between fire and
   dream;
and there is life in the metabolism between eye and
   flight
around the spinning smoke-bound bow
my ladyfriend, my sister, my wife—
each hour since the making of the earliest sign
has been a rite of giving and taking—

in the middle of the night

in the middle of the night
the voices of those
to be hanged within days
rise up already sounding thin
with the terror of stiff ropes—
we each bear like shadow
                    thrown over our thoughts
the noose, or a cancer, or shattering glass
(and yet: grim the consciousness
that men's lives must be intentionally measured out
and emptied—or left brimming till the last?
like gulps from a glass)
                    what difference does it make
if you kick the bucket like a *bandiet* shot into space
or wearing silver socks, a cigar stuck between your
    chops
on a border or in the ice-box-ocean
sounding like old reeds on the air
or in a gloomy room somewhere—
while alive we all bear the great divide
and shadow inside us
                    the knowledge

and all at once (in the middle of the night)
a remembered image breaks through the white
   wall:
a rider on his horse stilled for an instant
in the rain that spatters silver
as he fords a river
one gloved hand flung up in nonchalant salute
standard Western cavalry outfit
(but a smile like a trout
              displayed under glass)
what Matinee Buffalo Bill is this out of the blue
caught in which of memories' webs
(in front of a TV set and a fire while rain lacquers
   the tiles)
now (why?) dragged up
branded strangely to be shaken
onto the retina of the imagination
(while rain drips like dead blossoms
onto the roof)

and so too this unexpected shameless joy
that I can think of you despite it all
you stay close to me
in the immense coupling and death of consciousness
          o my wife

(while gulp by gulp shadowvoices are drained
in the middle of the night)

when my mother was

when my mother was dying
I had to wade and flay through the seething current
to reach her where they had laid her out
on her bedstead in the yard: shimmering yellow
the sun stroked the arcadian scene
playing on the halfcircle of faces of old
deceased uncles and forefathers who sat
sucking peacefully at pipes to blow out carols of
    smoke,

strong and healthy she was under the white sheet
her eyes full of light and rounder without glasses
her plump arms moving with clarity
to bless and deliver the last messages
(only some tired grey hairs had already come loose):
visions of how everything would turn out fine and
    that she
was at rest now with *inter alia* Matthew and Mark
    left and
right the two old-timers indeed stood,

and she also kept on calling me by the name
and did not recognize me

but I had to get back before the authorities
suspected my escape in the current's
whirling rush I began to sink
and further down teeth chattering washed between
   banks
(finally engulfed?)
somewhere beyond farmlands where mudspattered
grain elevators slash heavenwards where haystacks
rot and turnips are swallowed up by the earth,

as they strained at their leashes I heard the stinking
dogs their throats clogged with cries of excitement

release

I arrive on this first day already glistening bright
among angel choirs: far and wide the feathered folk
   sing psalms
and my face smells marvellous and my hands
are embalmed – did I not store the leftover oil away
for years with precisely this meeting in mind?
I will lie very still holding in my glee
so as not to bump the earth on this last lap of the
   journey

dance the dust up my beloved – why the dullness in
   your eye?
let friends pick sprays of laurel leaves
and twine them into garlands of green victory
and don't anyone mourn or the coffin will shake
because I am yours now cleansed of all disgrace
yours where dolphins wheel soft as wind in the
   palms
yours turned entirely free in the gardens of the
   night

the return

in rue Monsieur-le-Prince
coming down the same side as the Luxembourg
   gardens
on the left, where the twigs are set on fire by the
   evening sun
as it nests in the trees
the same side as the Odéon theatre
a honeycomb of freedom
as long ago now as May sixty-eight,

in rue Monsieur-le-Prince
is the restaurant where we will meet
at precisely nine o'clock
you will recognize me, I'll be wearing a beard once
   again
even if it is of cheap silver
and the Algerian boss-cum-cook
with the moustache nesting in his red cheeks
will come and put his arms full of bees around my
   shoulders
saying
alors, mon frére – ça fait bien longtemps . . .

should we order *couscous mouton* for two?
I can already taste the small snow-yellow grains

and the bit of butter—
and a bottle of pitch dark Sidi Brahim
smacking of the sun and the sea?
and then what would you say to a *thé à la menthe*
in the flower-decked glasses all scalding wet?

listen to that same wind calling
through the old old Paris streets

you're the one I love and I'm feeling so good!

'to live is to burn'

Andrei Voznesensky

entirely luminous and still: to live is to be
  consumed
like this summer day's delight; to renew now
and always praise for the earth's onward rolling,
  supple foliage
of the brushwood, waterslopes, tongues of stone,
  birds' charmed
                        heart-notes spun
to light chain linking stillness to stillness; how
  entirely lush
the mountain, sun-caked, naked – only one plume
  flourishes
white already, where wind will soon swell fine pipe
  sounds
and streamers; and in their cycle's fullness, the
  seasons turn
                        around
heaving old worm-like wrinkles from the womb –
  see, we each
drive what passes, upright as the mantis, hands
  bleaching
at the reins of death's wagon. prayer by prayer our
  way meshes

and marks us, cool skeleton cupped in the daywear
  of flesh

burn, burn with me, love – to hell with decay
to live is to live, and while alive to die anyway!

Okhela – Manifesto

OKHELA-MANIFESTO
Draft proposal submitted to militants for comment
and/or amendment*

Paris, June 1975

I.   *The Nature of the South African Struggle:*
     – struggle for national liberation and socialism against
     settler colonialism, capitalism and imperialism – the
     question of race and class – prevailing conditions or
     needs for theory based on revolutionary practice –
     contradictions in South African society – call for the
     destruction of the Apartheid state –

II. *Traditions of Struggle and the African National Con-
     gress of South Africa:*
     – formation and development – alliances – armed re-
     sistance and the *uMkhonte we Siswe* – international
     solidarity and the *External Mission* –

*I took this document with me to South Africa in July 1975, with
the intention of discussing it with our contacts there. It was found
by the Security Police and used in evidence during the first trial
in November 1975.

III. *Present Perspectives and Demands Facing the Liberation Movement:*
– Black militance, the SASO and BPC – Black workers' organizations – problems of rallying to a concerted programme for national liberation –

IV. *Problems of Identification with the Liberation Struggle:*
– Black militancy and White activists – forms of struggle as determined by social and economic differences existing objectively inside South Africa –

V. *Role of White Militants:*
– conditions, possibilities and limitations springing from a scientific class analysis – national and international contacts –

VI. *Commitment to the Liberation of Women*

VII. *Creation of OKHELA:*
– international solidarity and lessons in internationalism – conception of needs of developing struggle – legitimacy derived from the *African National Congress* –

VIII. *Demands on Organization and Structures of OKHELA:*
– national liberation as first stage – internationalist and anti-imperialist outlook – clandestinity and security –

IX. *Our Aims:*
[Fourteen aims, a–n, listed in full below]

UNITY THROUGH STRUGGLE
POWER TO THE PEOPLE

I. *The Nature of the South African Struggle:*

The struggle for liberation in South Africa is a complex one – complex because of the history of the country and the diverse origins of its people; complex because of the nature of the forces involved in the struggle and those whom we combat; complex because of the international, political and geographical position of South Africa.

The nature of the struggle can be read on many levels: it is the struggle of the Black majority against the White minority for national liberation; it is the struggle of an indigenous people against settler colonialism and as such is part of Africa's continuing attempts to free itself from the results of colonialism; it is the struggle for socialism against a *strongly entrenched capitalist state* supported by world imperialism – and therefore it is a struggle with internationalist dimensions; it is finally a class struggle with the class divisions overlying the racial dimensions to a large extent. This struggle expresses itself politically, economically and also culturally since it touches upon national, racial, group and class identities.

These apparently divergent but interlocking aspects of the struggle make it essential to understand the role that each group, be it of race or of class, is called upon to play, and to define the grounds upon which each group can engage the combat. We, the South Africans, must still forge a comprehensive understanding of the reality of our conditions and a theory which will encompass the aims and the need for freedom for all the people – but this theory must be developed in the struggle itself; it will grow from our praxis and in turn define the latter.

As for the conditions under which the struggle is being waged, they are those of extreme repression, exile and a partial dislocation of the forces for liberation and transformation. On the other hand though, the conditions are also those of a growing awareness and a more perceptive application of our own power,

and the increasingly strong international solidarity with
our cause.

We, the South Africans, have a rich history of
resistance from which to draw our lessons and our
inspiration. It is important for us to understand these
experiences, to draw the correct conclusions, to apply
the lessons learnt and to take the initiative for a change.

The profound contradictions within the South African society must explode; the interests of oppressed
and oppressors can never be harmonized; the super
exploitation of the urban and rural proletariat has become insupportable; the alienation of the Blacks and
the accompanying dehumanization of the Whites can
no longer be accepted; the Apartheid state must be
destroyed.

II.   *Traditions of Struggle and the African National Congress of South Africa:*

At this point in our history we believe that the short
term goal of our struggle is the liberation of the territory of South Africa and the seizing of power by the
Liberation Movement representing the people of South
Africa. To this we are committed as South African
patriots. For us the tradition and the existence of
resistance are embodied in the African National Congress and the various political and labour organizations allied to this movement.

The ANC was formed in 1912 in an attempt to
give national expression to the claims of the oppressed
and exploited and disinherited people of South Africa,
to oppose and counteract the doctrines of racism upon
which the newly established South African state was
based. The ANC rapidly developed into a mass movement with a democratically elected and representative national leadership putting forward the demands

of the African people for equality and dignity in a reasonable and responsible manner.

Despite the fact that the ANC could claim to represent the majority of South Africans, Britain consecrated the colonial conquests of the settlers and in accordance with her own imperialist interests handed over power to the local White minority. Imbued by the ideals of non-violence, the ANC led the resistance to this state which denies the birthright of the people.

From very early on also, the ANC in alliance with the SACP and the trade union organizations gave expression to the interests of the working class.

When the all-White Nationalist Party came to power in 1948 it laid the blueprints for the rationalization of exploitation and for the ultimate dismemberment of the country. The national presence of the ANC reached a high point during the 1950s with the existence of the Alliance of Congresses grouping organizations representing all the different ethnic groups and the South African Congress of Trade Unions (SACTU). Reflecting the developing demands and the working class consciousness of the people, the Congresses mobilized nationally through successive stay-at-home campaigns and national strikes.

The growing strength of the Congresses as mass protest organizations and the unsuccessful attempts of the illegitimate State's authority to break the spirit of struggle – at the abortive 'treason trial' – culminated in the banning of the ANC, the disbanding of some other organizations and the brutal repression and hounding of the freedom militants.

uMkhonte we Siswe–the military wing of the ANC–came into being in the early sixties. The *External Mission* of the ANC had already been established and sent abroad where international solidarity work was started through its creation of national Anti-

Apartheid Movements in several countries. These developments showed:

a. the need for a visible part of the leadership to be seen continuing the struggle and to represent the South African people abroad; and

b. the need for the ANC to transform itself from a mass protest movement into an organization capable of carrying on the struggle in all its forms – and particularly the armed struggle and underground work; and

c. the broadening of the struggle against Apartheid by isolating the illegal regime internationally and at the same time broadening the international support base for the ongoing struggle at home.

The ANC was called upon not only to survive under difficult circumstances but also to start transforming itself structurally to face up to the new situation; to maintain, carry forward and strengthen traditions of resistance. This is an ever continuing process.

III. *Present Perspectives and Demands Facing the Liberation Movement:*

Exile, imprisonment, bannings, the need to reorganize the structures – all of these brought about a temporary dislocation of the work of the Liberation Movement inside the country itself.

During the sixties and the early seventies – filling the relative vacuum – a new generation grew into the struggle, propounding the ideas of Black militancy. The forms the struggle took were defined on the one hand by the restrictions imposed by the authorities and on the other hand by the need to assert or reassert the Black identity both culturally and politically.

At first the forums of self-assertion and self-reliance were the campuses, cultural and religious bodies. Black students broke away from the NUSAS and formed SASO; UCM and the BPC came into being. Early during the seventies the focal point of the struggle moved into the field of labour. The Black working class became aware of its growing power. The impressive series of strikes spreading to all sectors of the economy, organized and controlled by the workers, led to the formation of new trade unions and the revitalization of others. The students and the workers – two vital sectors of the population – were and are defining their means of struggling.

If these means of resistance and mobilization were seen to be less decisive than expected it is:

a. because of the repressive machinery of the state;
b. the lack of political cohesiveness among the various organizations with the accompanying danger that the trade unions for instance, will become ensnared in a purely 'economic' approach;
c. the imperfect coordination of the struggle inside and outside; and particularly
d. the fact that all struggle must be built around a drive by the Liberation Movement to wrest political control and central power from the minority.

IV. *Problems of Identification with the Liberation Struggle:*

The rise of Black militancy and the creation of autonomous Black organizations forced White activists to reassess their position and role not only in racial terms but also in that of class. The hitherto paternalistic approach of the Whites became exposed and was rejected. It became evident that the Whites themselves are in need of liberation but that national liberation will have to be fought for under the leadership of the Black movements. It became obvious that the function of the Whites is not to confuse themselves with organizations expressing Black consciousness and aspirations, but rather that they should turn to how best to assist the struggle of the majority for national liberation.

It became progressively clear that unity among revolutionary groups, whose forms of struggle are defined by the economic and social differences existing objectively in the country, can only be achieved in the struggle as a concerted programme under the leadership of the Black liberation movement.

The first step in this direction was the way in which White students turned their attention and efforts towards helping Black trade unions establish themselves. A second step is the way in which some sectors—areas of church and of culture—are, as Whites and in terms of their professional and moral interests, starting to organize against the reactionary power of the State. A third step will be the participation of White organizations in all forms of revolutionary struggle as led by the ANC.

V. *Role of White Militants:*

We believe that a clear conception and application of the role that Whites can play demands a thorough definition of our conditions, possibilities and restrictions springing from a scientific class analysis. We believe that the first priority of a revolutionary is to find what she or he can do taking into account the history of his or her people, the objective conditions which define his or her class, the effectiveness she or he must strive for and the national and international contexts within which the struggle is unfolding.

VI. *Commitment to the Liberation of Women:*

We furthermore recognize the political, economic, educational, legal, sexual and commercial exploitation of women in law, practice and attitude as being a tool to perpetuate the capitalist system and maintain the status quo.

We believe that the total liberation of women, as defined by women themselves, is a fundamental necessity for the victory of the revolution.

VII. *Creation of OKHELA:*

Over the years many White individuals have joined the struggle for liberation in one form or another. One foyer of activity became the international solidarity work of the *External Mission* of the ANC which, since it meant working with and among progressive forces in other countries, in turn strengthened the awareness of the anti-imperialist nature of our struggle.

Flowing from all the above developments and in terms of a clearer understanding and conception of the needs that the developing struggle indicates, and based on the experiences of a few comrades, it was decided to create an organization of White South African militants called OKHELA. This organization is called upon to play a specific role within the National Liberation Front being constituted.

We derive our legitimacy from the African National Congress who requested us to form this organization.*

---

*This is not true. In fact the office-bearers of the ANC, with whom we were in contact, could not and did not encourage us in the name of the ANC.

VIII. *Demands on Organization and Structures of OKHELA:*

The conditions under which the struggle is fought make it imperative for us to be clandestine so as to be effective. The needs of clandestinity, security and effectiveness define the structures and the functioning of our organization.

Our immediate objective is to participate in the national liberation of South Africa which in itself is lifting the first barrier barring the road to the revolutionary transformation of South African society.

We are present and active both inside and outside the country; our outlook is internationalist. We are profoundly aware of the anti-imperialist and anti-capitalist nature of our struggle.

IX. *Our Aims:*

a. To provide *'invisible support'* – materially and politically – to the Liberation Movement.
b. To develop the tradition and means which will enable us to fulfil our special role, to build our organization to be both flexible and resilient, an organization which can take the initiative for action and 'create the facts on the ground'.
c. To acquire all the necessary techniques and experiences for underground struggle – logistical support, information, communication, etc; to accumulate these experiences, transform and adapt them to our needs; and to transmit them by having the necessary training facilities.
d. To be a political and practical 'training ground' for White militants.
e. To assist the Liberation Movement develop its methods and forces so that a strong liberation front can be established grouping an alliance of all the forces for change, be they representative of ethnic groupings or political formations.

f. To consciously and ideologically develop the ideological grounds upon which we as White South Africans can become fully participant in the revolutionary struggle; to build a base on these grounds.

g. To work with and to coordinate progressive forces abroad supporting our cause.

h. In doing so to bring about a more progressive political commitment to our struggle and to channel the manifestations of this support into the country.

i. To develop the means of gathering political and economic intelligence without which we will be blind; to develop the most effective ways of using this information.

j. To develop the means of protecting our organization from the enemy and of assuming responsibility for our own safety and security.

k. To develop all the possibilities for support to militants in distress.

l. To develop all possibilities for defensive and offensive direct action.

m. To continuously evolve programmes – in terms of our objectives and strategy – which can advance the struggle, and the structures needed to accommodate these programmes.

n. In all of these ways we contribute towards the treasured ideals of the South African Liberation Struggle.

UNITY THROUGH STRUGGLE!!

STRUGGLE FOR POWER!!

ALL POWER TO THE PEOPLE!!

Index

Catalog

If you are interested in a list of fine Paperback
books, covering a wide range of subjects
and interests, send your name and address,
requesting your free catalog, to:

McGraw-Hill Paperbacks
1221 Avenue of Americas
New York, N.Y. 10020